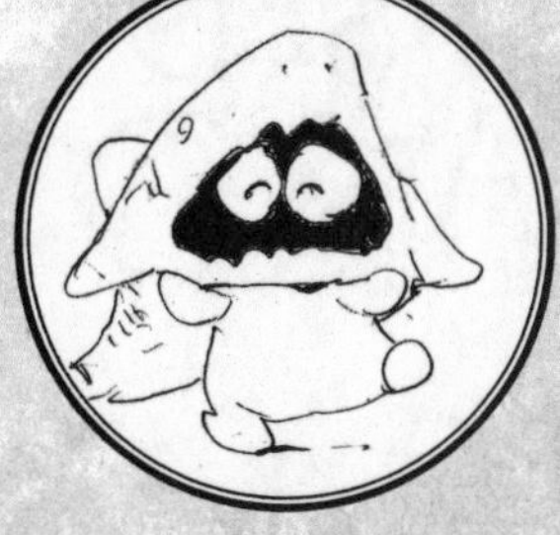

POSUKA DEMIZU

I hope you enjoy volume 20.

Thank you for staying with us through the four years of serialization.

The anime, movie and some short stories are still coming, so please continue to look forward to the never-ending Neverland!

Lastly, to Shirai Sensei! I'm very grateful that I was able to accomplish this huge project with you!

If I were alone, I don't think I would be here. It's been a miraculous four years.

I will keep working hard for just a bit longer to create more content.

Well then, everyone, let's meet again somewhere!

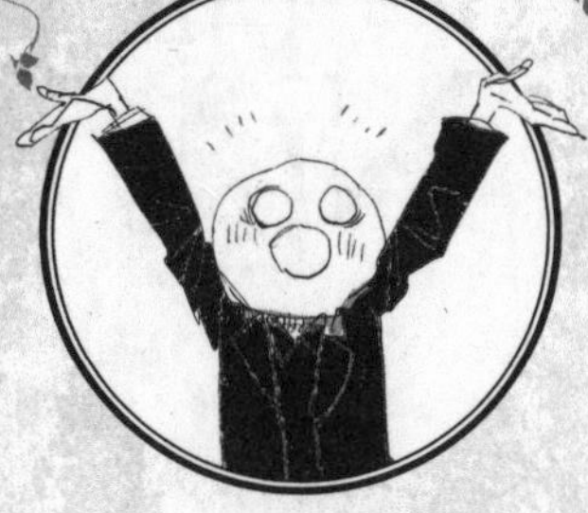

KAIU SHIRAI

Writer Shirai's personal highlights for *The Promised Neverland* fanatics, part 13!

1) It's not just the *special omurice*, there is also the *secret salted konbu*!

2) The name of the girl on page 170, in panels 5 and 6, is Lucy. (Demizu Sensei named her in chapter 105.)

3) It turns out that Gillian has been cutting everyone's hair since they've been in the shelter (and Nat too!).

The Promised Neverland and I are both here thanks to the miracle of meeting Demizu Sensei.

This is the final volume for the main story.

Please enjoy!

Posuka Demizu debuted as a manga artist with the 2013 *CoroCoro* series *Oreca Monster Bouken Retsuden*. A collection of illustrations, *The Art of Posuka Demizu*, was released in 2016 by PIE International.

Kaiu Shirai debuted in 2015 with *Ashley Gate no Yukue* on the *Shonen Jump+* website. Shirai first worked with Posuka Demizu on the two-shot *Poppy no Negai*, which was released in February 2016.

THE PROMISED NEVERLAND

VOLUME 20
SHONEN JUMP Manga Edition

STORY BY KAIU SHIRAI
ART BY POSUKA DEMIZU

Translation/Satsuki Yamashita
Touch-Up Art & Lettering/Mark McMurray
Design/Julian [JR] Robinson
Editor/Alexis Kirsch

YAKUSOKU NO NEVERLAND © 2016 by Kaiu Shirai, Posuka Demizu
All rights reserved.
First published in Japan in 2016 by SHUEISHA Inc., Tokyo.
English translation rights arranged by SHUEISHA Inc.

The stories, characters and incidents mentioned in this publication are entirely fictional.

Printed in the U.S.A.

Published by VIZ Media, LLC
P.O. Box 77010
San Francisco, CA 94107

10 9 8 7 6 5 4 3 2
First printing, July 2021
Second printing, July 2021

PARENTAL ADVISORY
THE PROMISED NEVERLAND is rated T+ and is recommended for ages 16 and up. This volume contains fantasy violence and adult themes.

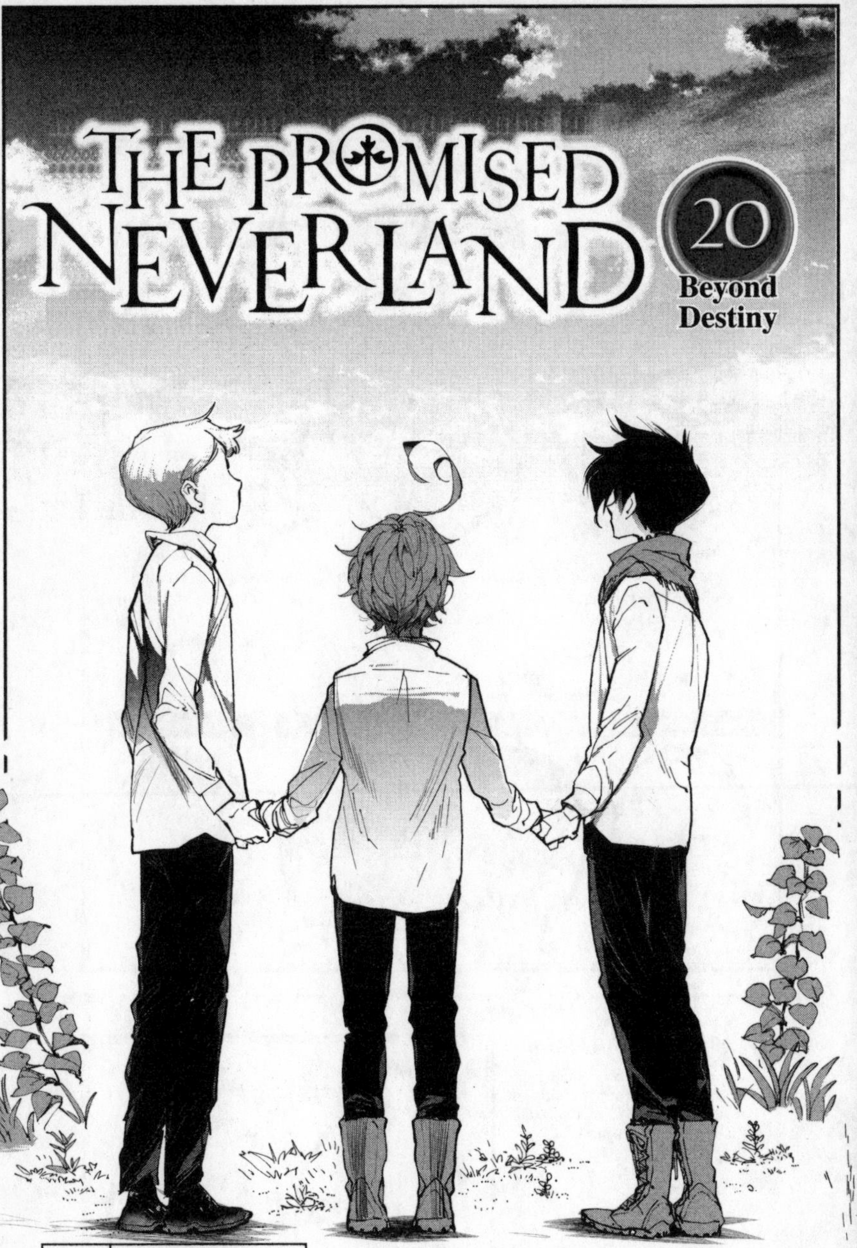
THE PROMISED NEVERLAND
20
Beyond Destiny

STORY	KAIU SHIRAI
ART	POSUKA DEMIZU

The Children of Grace Field House

They aim to free all of the children who are trapped in Grace Field House within the next two months.

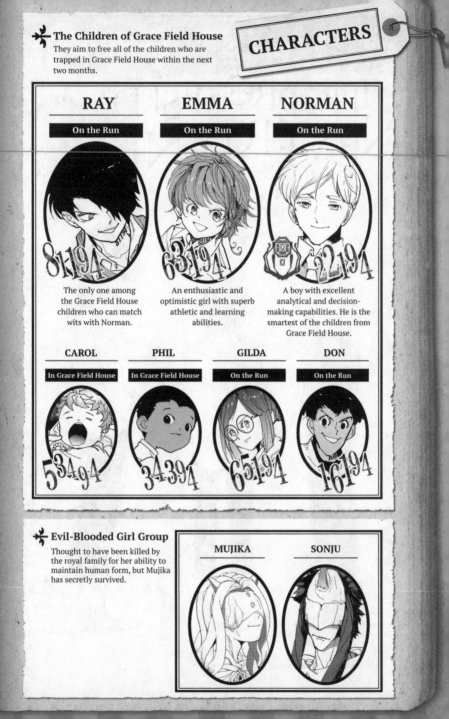

RAY

On the Run

The only one among the Grace Field House children who can match wits with Norman.

EMMA

On the Run

An enthusiastic and optimistic girl with superb athletic and learning abilities.

NORMAN

On the Run

A boy with excellent analytical and decision-making capabilities. He is the smartest of the children from Grace Field House.

CAROL

In Grace Field House

PHIL

In Grace Field House

GILDA

On the Run

DON

On the Run

Evil-Blooded Girl Group

Thought to have been killed by the royal family for her ability to maintain human form, but Mujika has secretly survived.

MUJIKA

SONJU

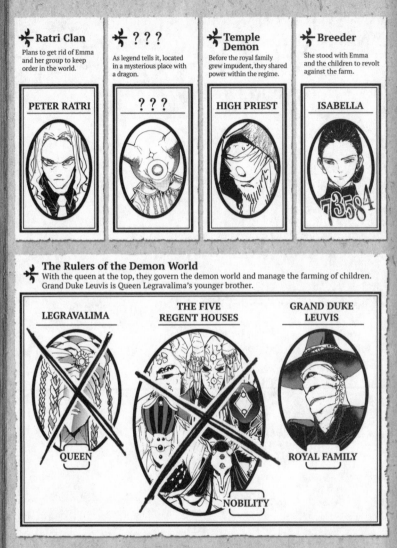

Ratri Clan

Plans to get rid of Emma and her group to keep order in the world.

PETER RATRI

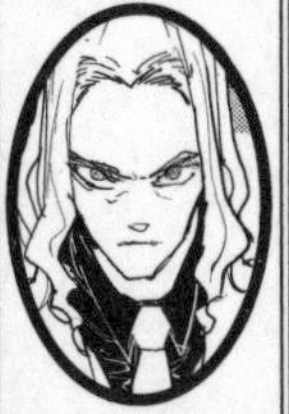

? ? ?

As legend tells it, located in a mysterious place with a dragon.

? ? ?

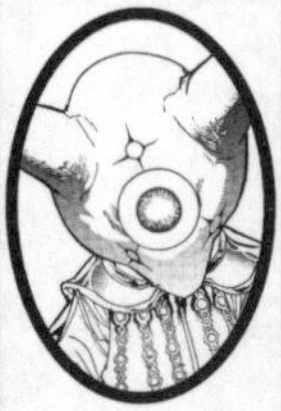

Temple Demon

Before the royal family grew impudent, they shared power within the regime.

HIGH PRIEST

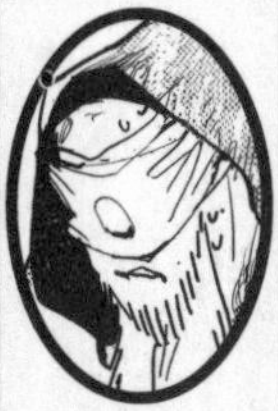

Breeder

She stood with Emma and the children to revolt against the farm.

ISABELLA

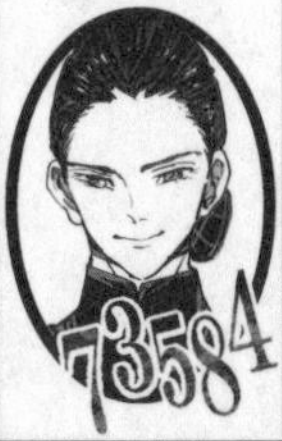
73584

The Rulers of the Demon World

With the queen at the top, they govern the demon world and manage the farming of children. Grand Duke Leuvis is Queen Legravalima's younger brother.

LEGRAVALIMA

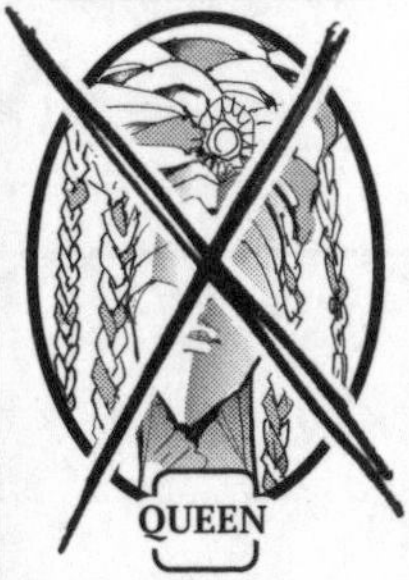

QUEEN

THE FIVE REGENT HOUSES

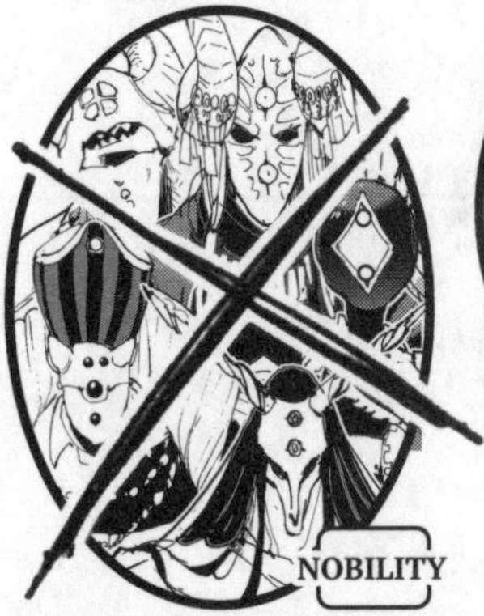

NOBILITY

GRAND DUKE LEUVIS

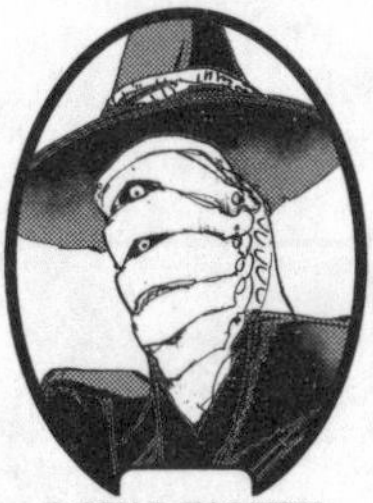

ROYAL FAMILY

The Story So Far

Emma is living happily at Grace Field House with her foster siblings. One day, she realizes that they are being bred as food for demons and escapes with a group of other children. After meeting new friends and gaining further information, she decides to free all of the children raised in the farms. To replace the promise made 1,000 years ago that changed the shape of the world, she manages to create a new promise. The Ratri clan abducts her friends and family, however, and Emma returns to Grace Field House to save them. She makes her way through security to face Peter Ratri in a final confrontation.

THE PROMISED NEVERLAND 20
Beyond Destiny

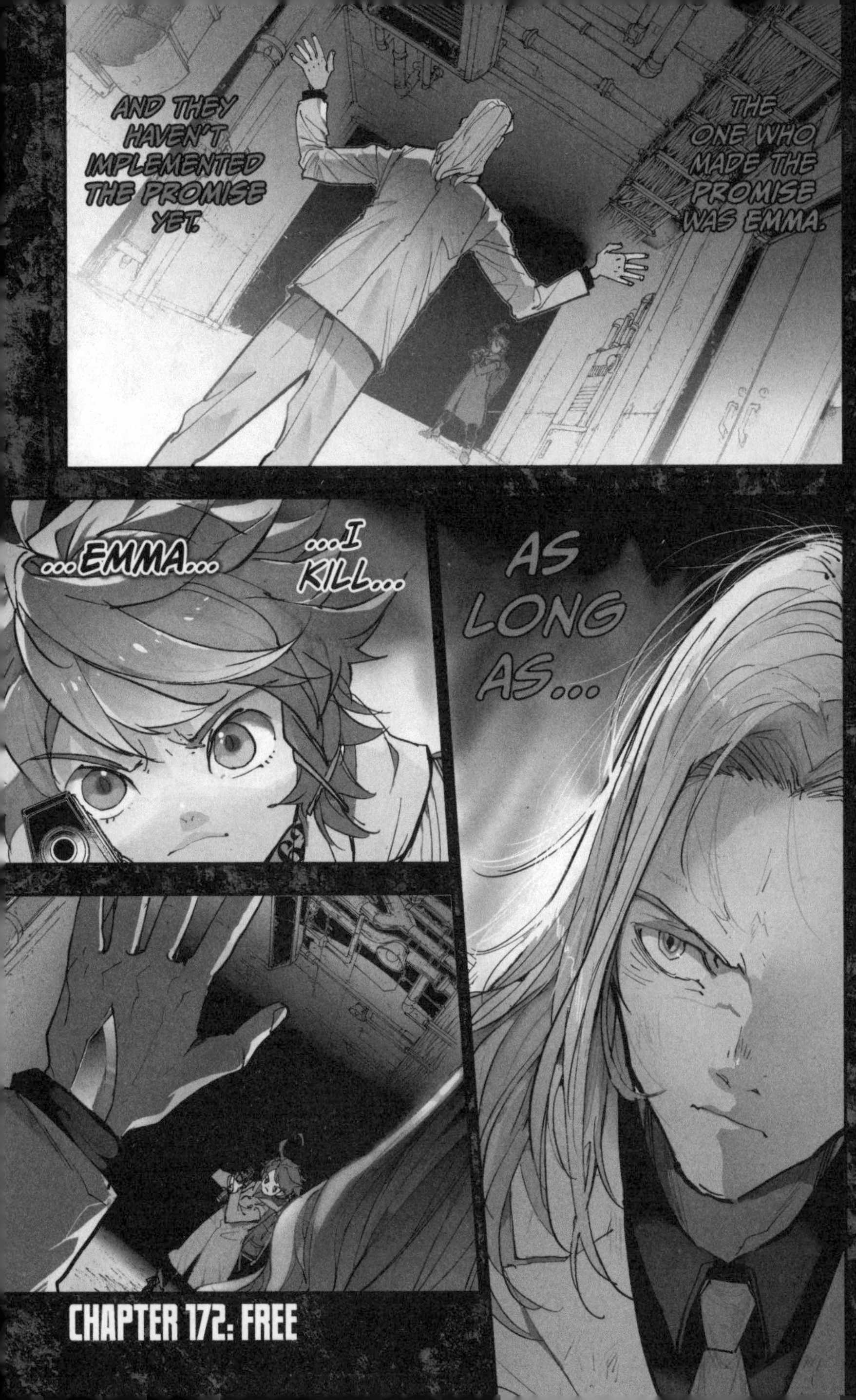
THE ONE WHO MADE THE PROMISE WAS EMMA.
AND THEY HAVEN'T IMPLEMENTED THE PROMISE YET.
AS LONG AS...
...I KILL...
...EMMA...
CHAPTER 172: FREE

CHAPTER 172: FREE

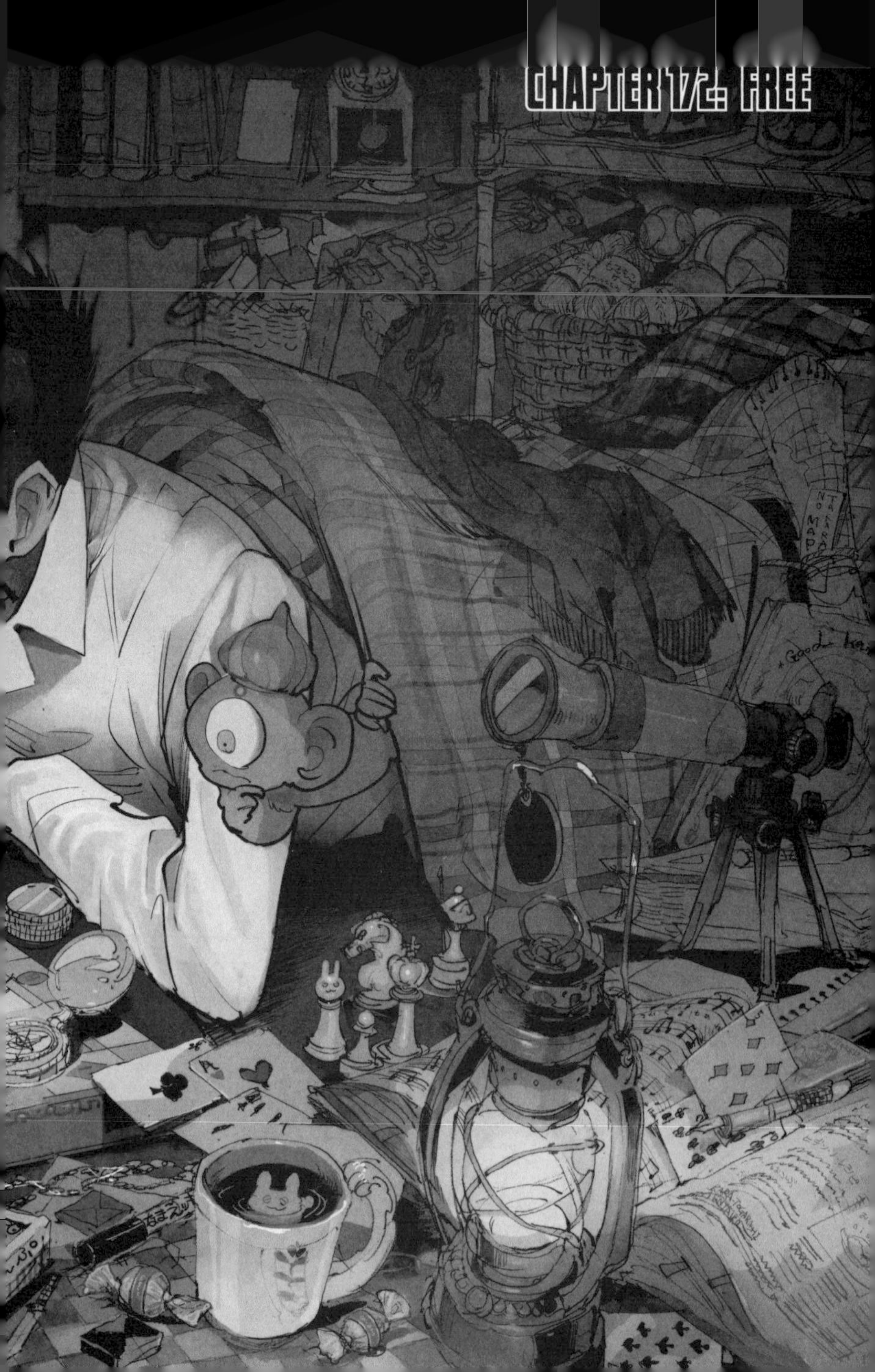

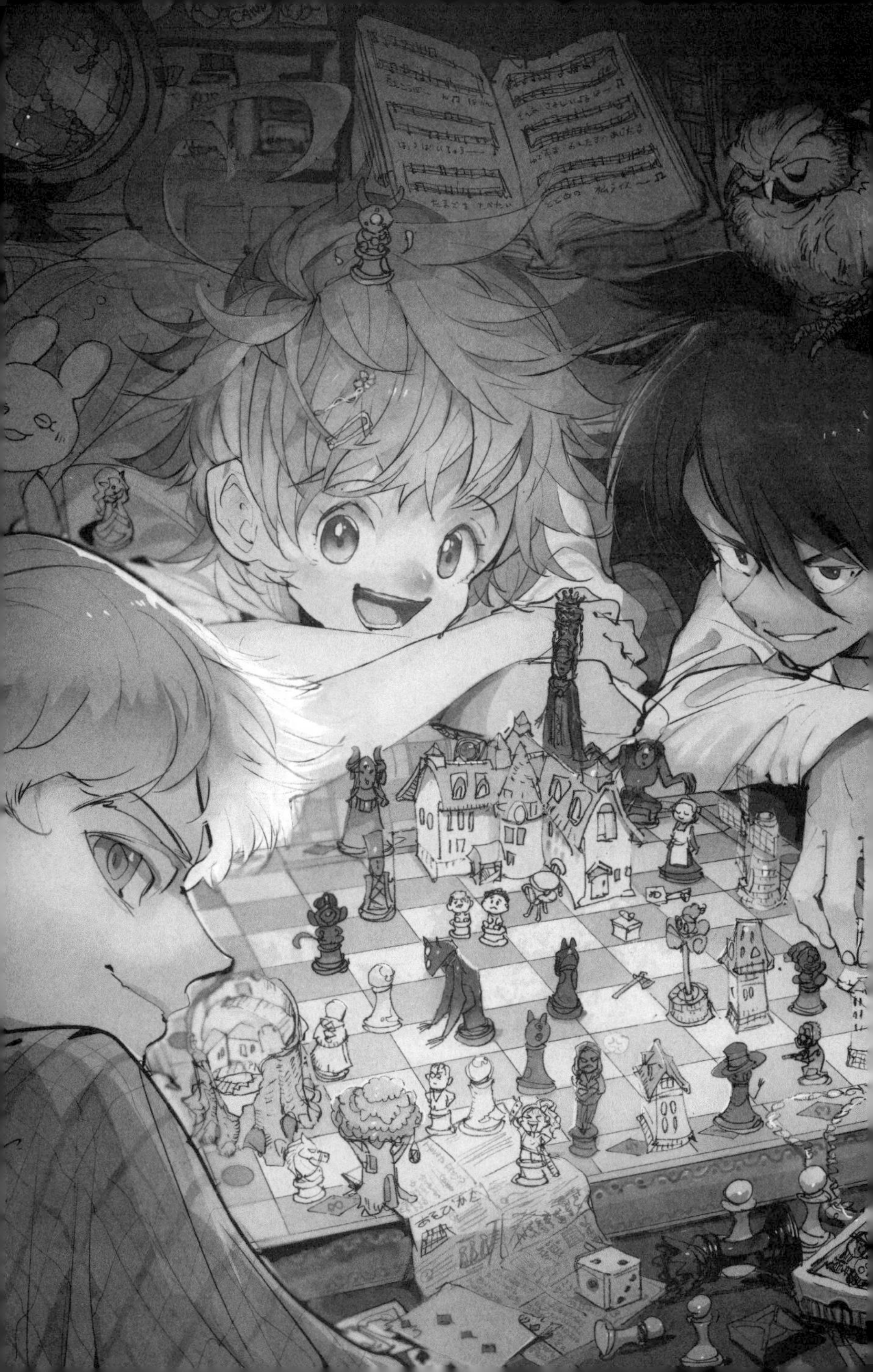

FINAL EPISODE!! HOW TO DRAW MOM, ISABELLA!

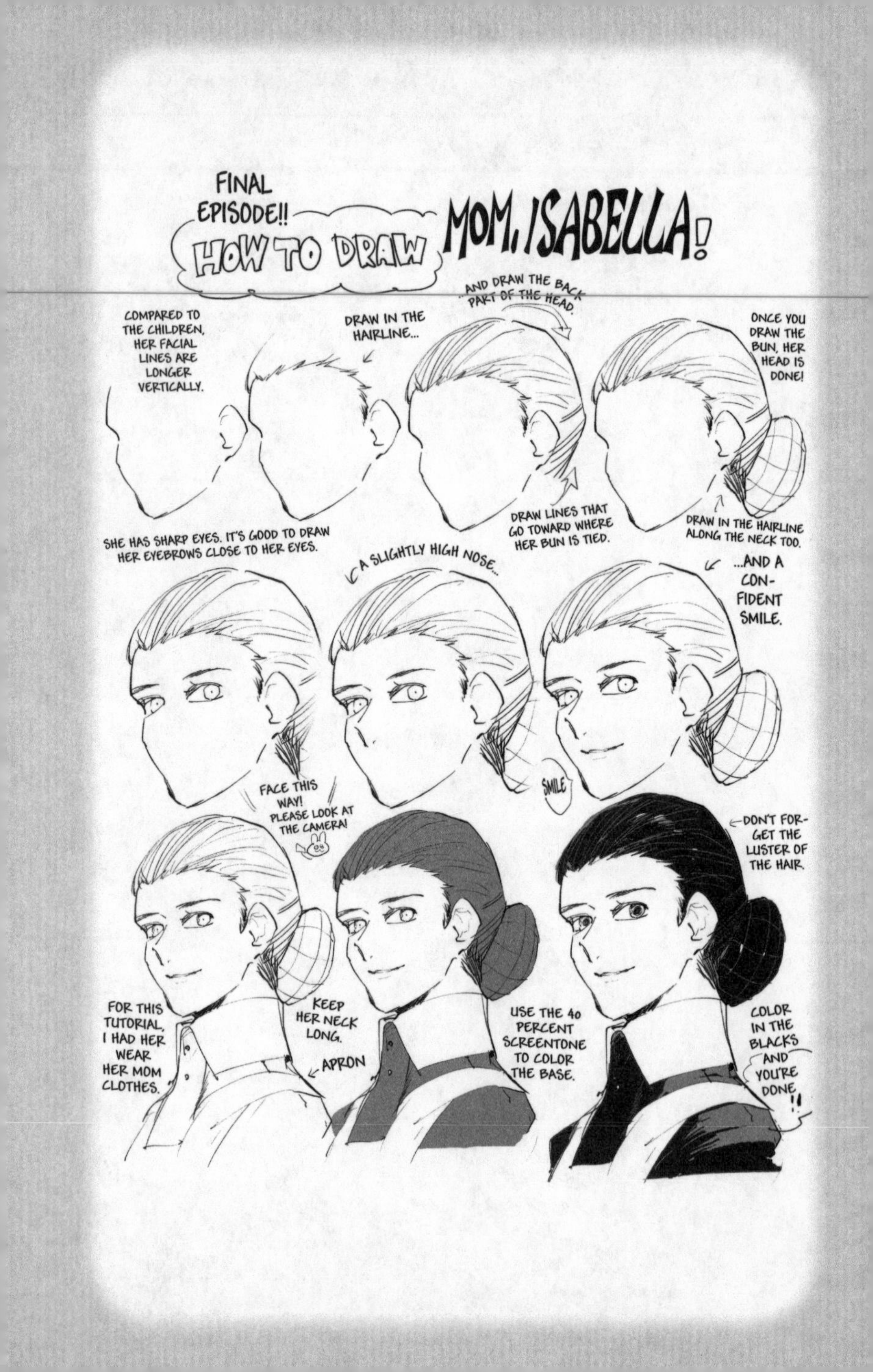

COMPARED TO THE CHILDREN, HER FACIAL LINES ARE LONGER VERTICALLY.
DRAW IN THE HAIRLINE...
...AND DRAW THE BACK PART OF THE HEAD.
DRAW LINES THAT GO TOWARD WHERE HER BUN IS TIED.
ONCE YOU DRAW THE BUN, HER HEAD IS DONE!
DRAW IN THE HAIRLINE ALONG THE NECK TOO.
SHE HAS SHARP EYES. IT'S GOOD TO DRAW HER EYEBROWS CLOSE TO HER EYES.
A SLIGHTLY HIGH NOSE...
...AND A CON-FIDENT SMILE.
SMILE
FACE THIS WAY! PLEASE LOOK AT THE CAMERA!
FOR THIS TUTORIAL, I HAD HER WEAR HER MOM CLOTHES.
KEEP HER NECK LONG.
APRON
USE THE 40 PERCENT SCREENTONE TO COLOR THE BASE.
DON'T FOR-GET THE LUSTER OF THE HAIR.
COLOR IN THE BLACKS AND YOU'RE DONE!!

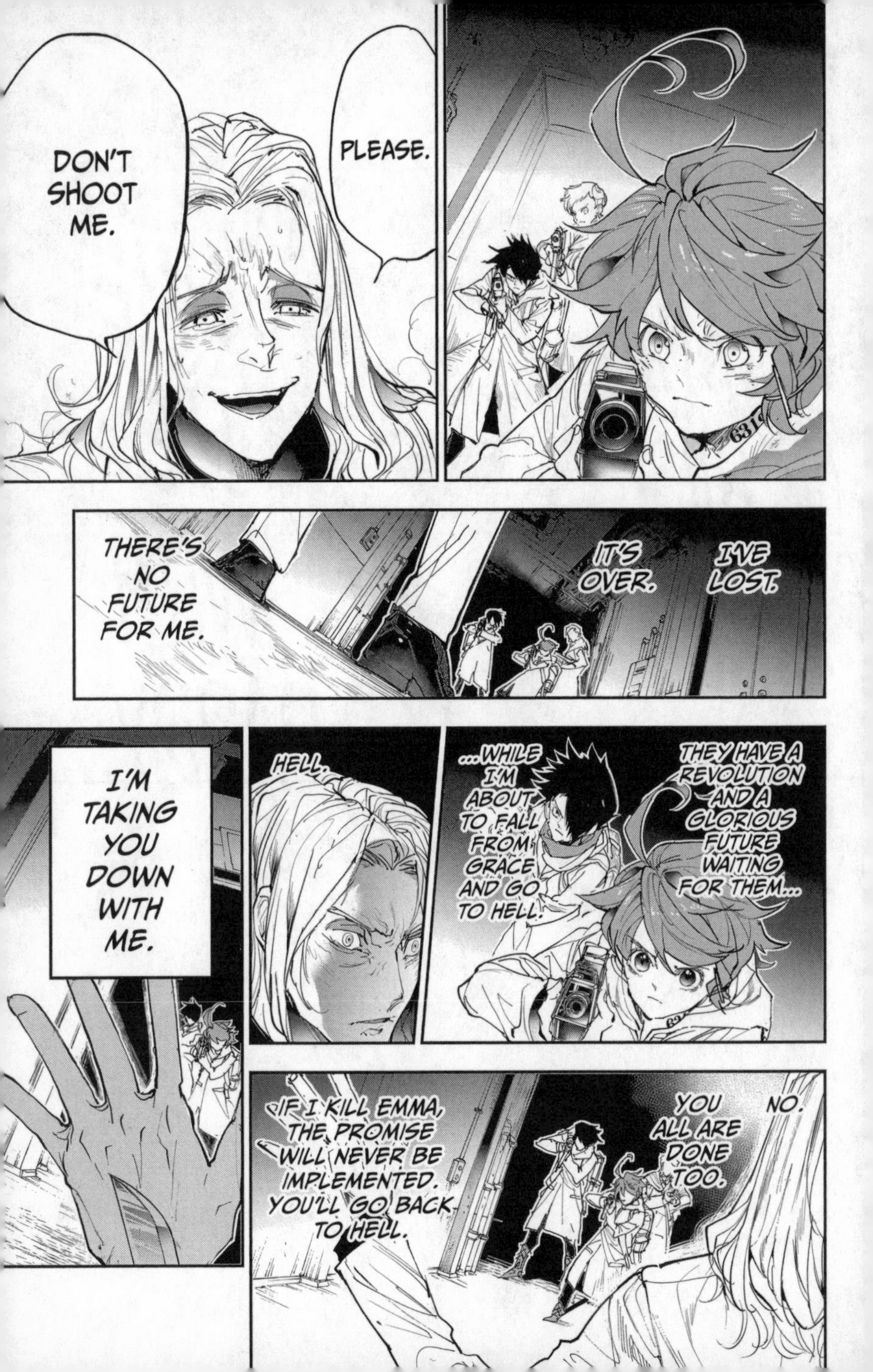
PLEASE.
DON'T SHOOT ME.
I'VE LOST.
IT'S OVER.
THERE'S NO FUTURE FOR ME.
THEY HAVE A REVOLUTION AND A GLORIOUS FUTURE WAITING FOR THEM...
...WHILE I'M ABOUT TO FALL FROM GRACE AND GO TO HELL.
HELL.
NO.
YOU ALL ARE DONE TOO.
IF I KILL EMMA, THE PROMISE WILL NEVER BE IMPLEMENTED. YOU'LL GO BACK TO HELL.
I'M TAKING YOU DOWN WITH ME.

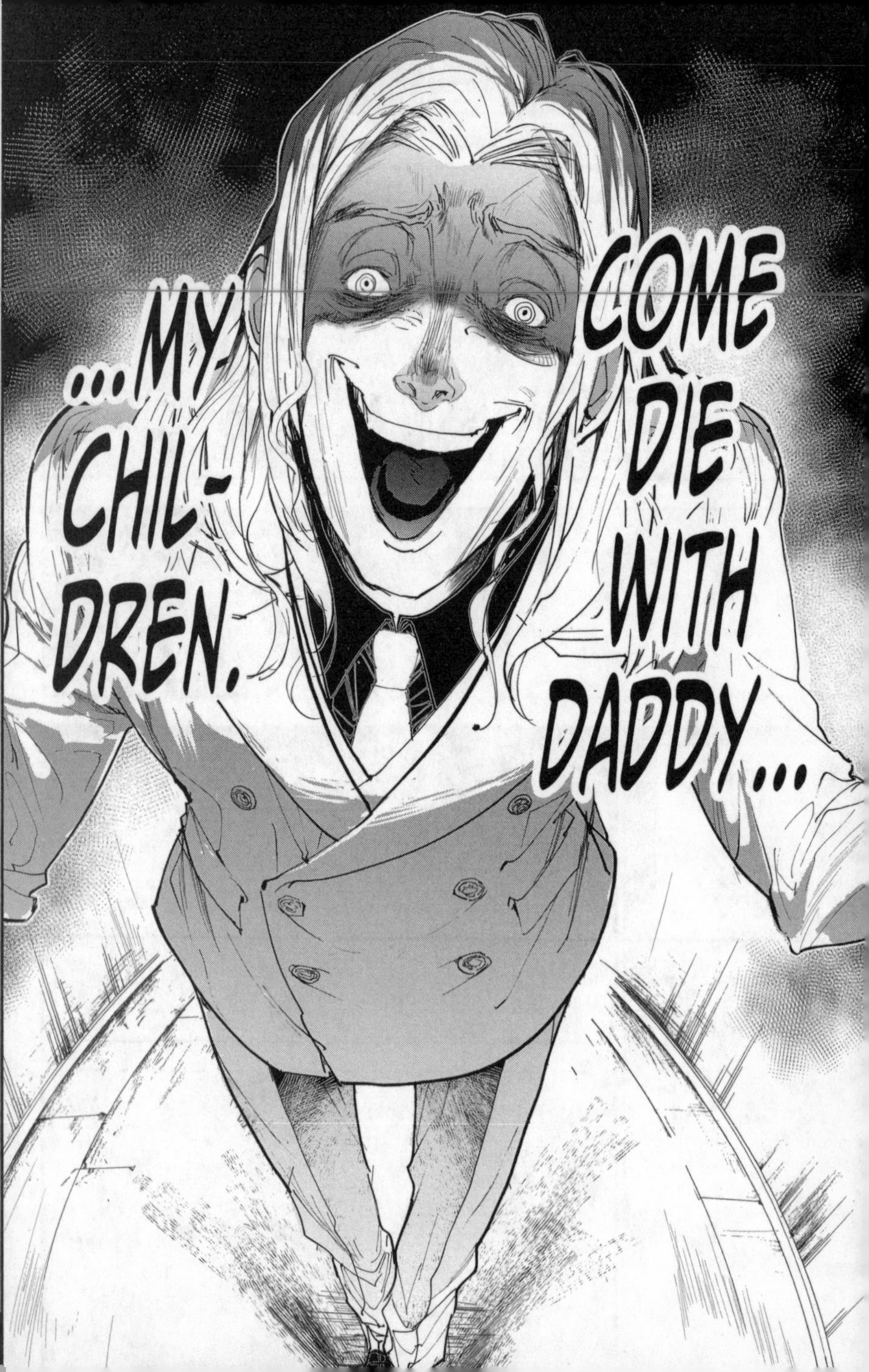
COME DIE WITH DADDY...
...MY CHIL-DREN.

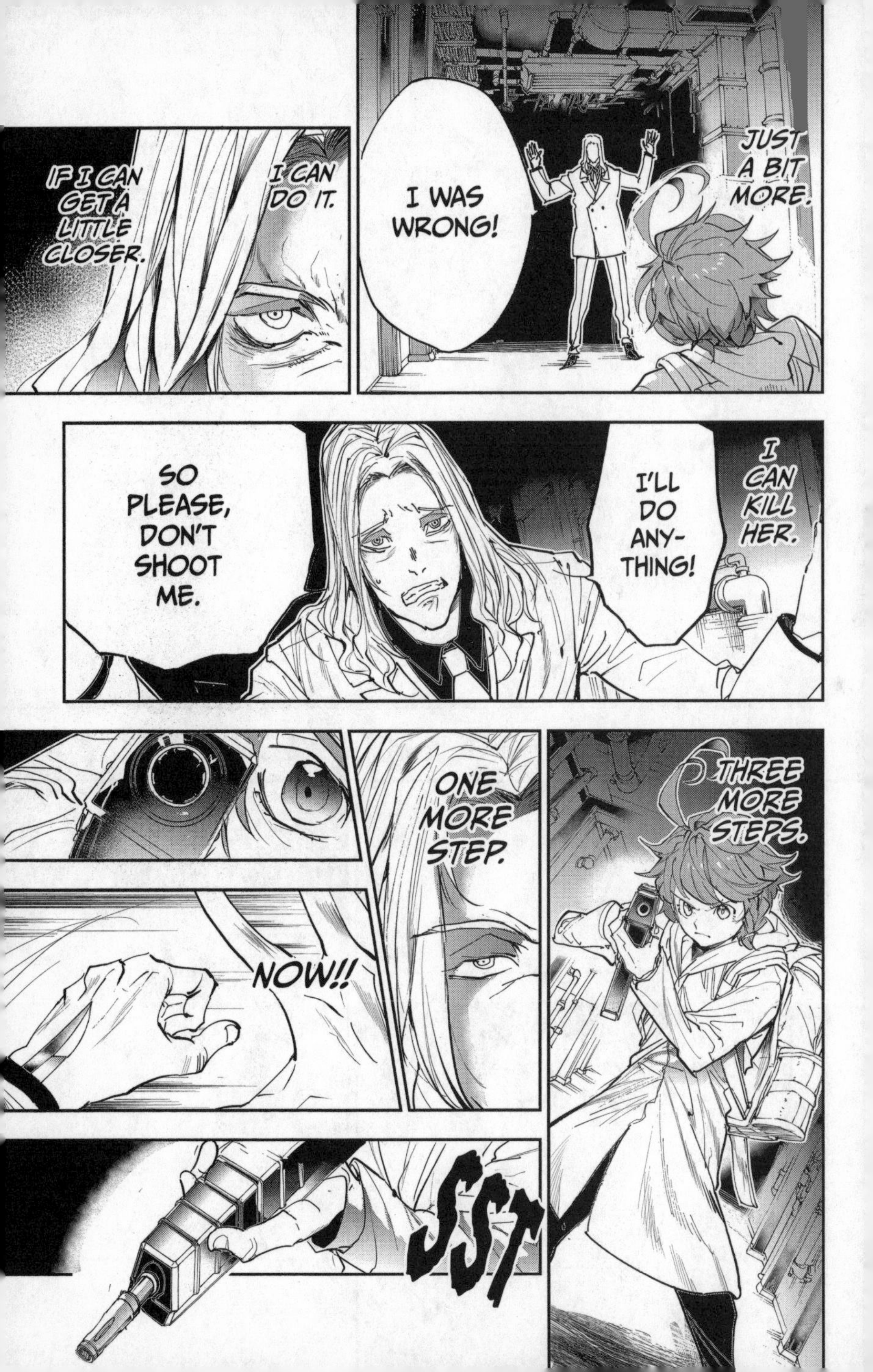
JUST A BIT MORE.
I WAS WRONG!
I CAN DO IT.
IF I CAN GET A LITTLE CLOSER.
I CAN KILL HER.
I'LL DO ANY-THING!
SO PLEASE, DON'T SHOOT ME.
THREE MORE STEPS.
ONE MORE STEP.
NOW!!
SST

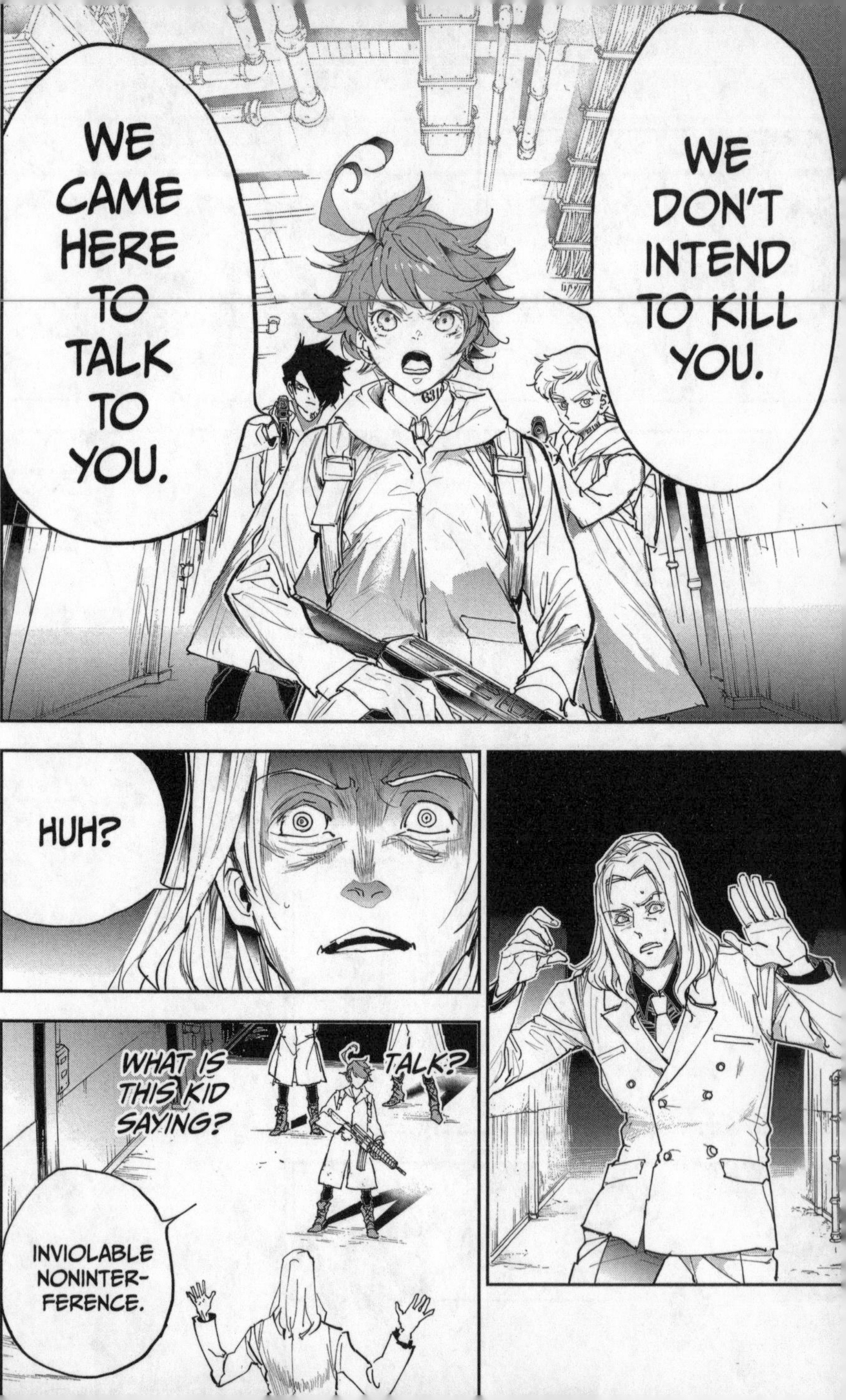
WE DON'T INTEND TO KILL YOU.
WE CAME HERE TO TALK TO YOU.
HUH?
TALK?
WHAT IS THIS KID SAYING?
INVIOLABLE NONINTER-FERENCE.

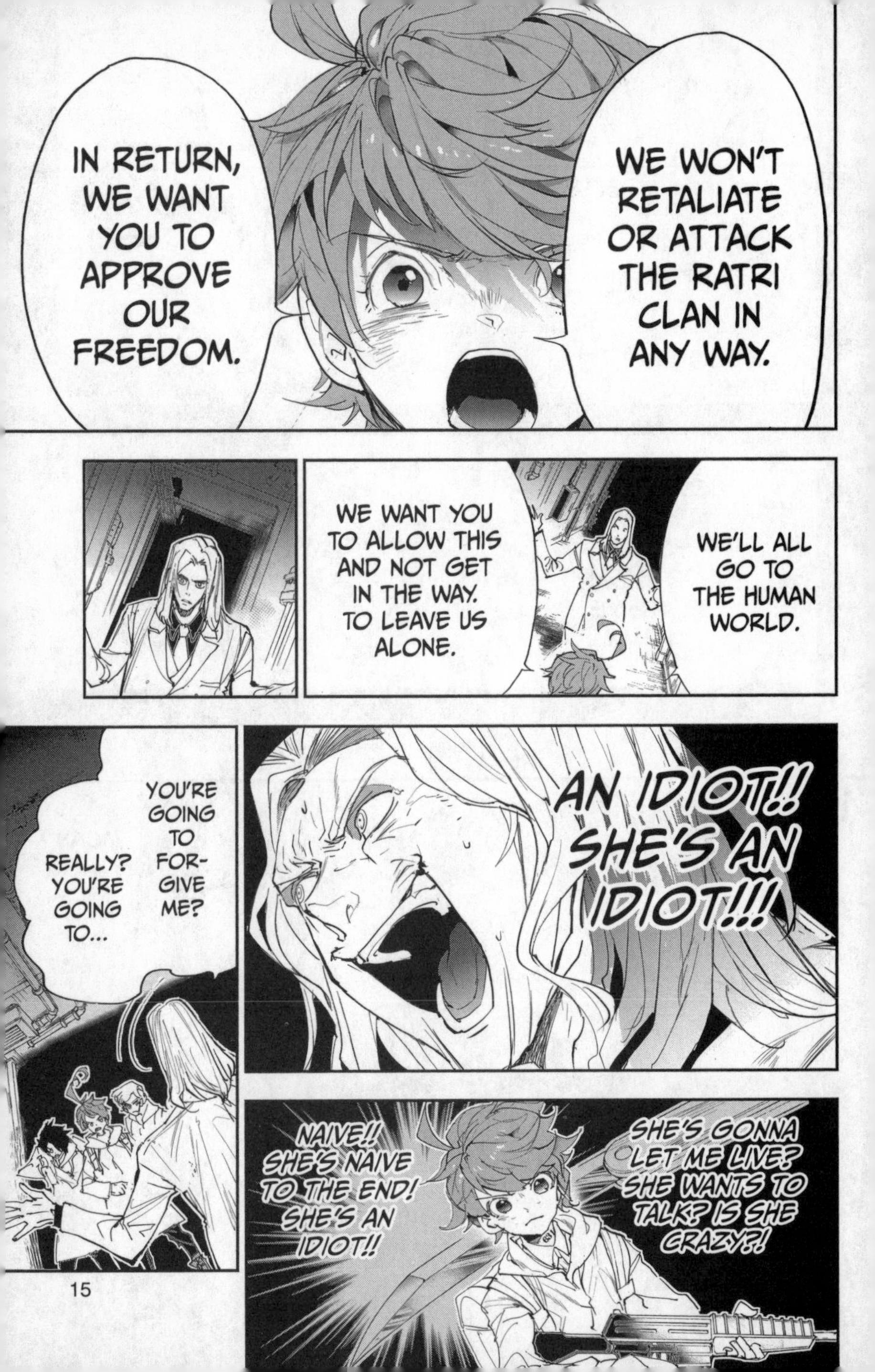
WE WON'T RETALIATE OR ATTACK THE RATRI CLAN IN ANY WAY.
IN RETURN, WE WANT YOU TO APPROVE OUR FREEDOM.
WE'LL ALL GO TO THE HUMAN WORLD.
WE WANT YOU TO ALLOW THIS AND NOT GET IN THE WAY. TO LEAVE US ALONE.
AN IDIOT!! SHE'S AN IDIOT!!!
SHE'S GONNA LET ME LIVE? SHE WANTS TO TALK? IS SHE CRAZY?!
NAIVE!! SHE'S NAIVE TO THE END! SHE'S AN IDIOT!!
YOU'RE GOING TO FOR-GIVE ME?
REALLY? YOU'RE GOING TO...

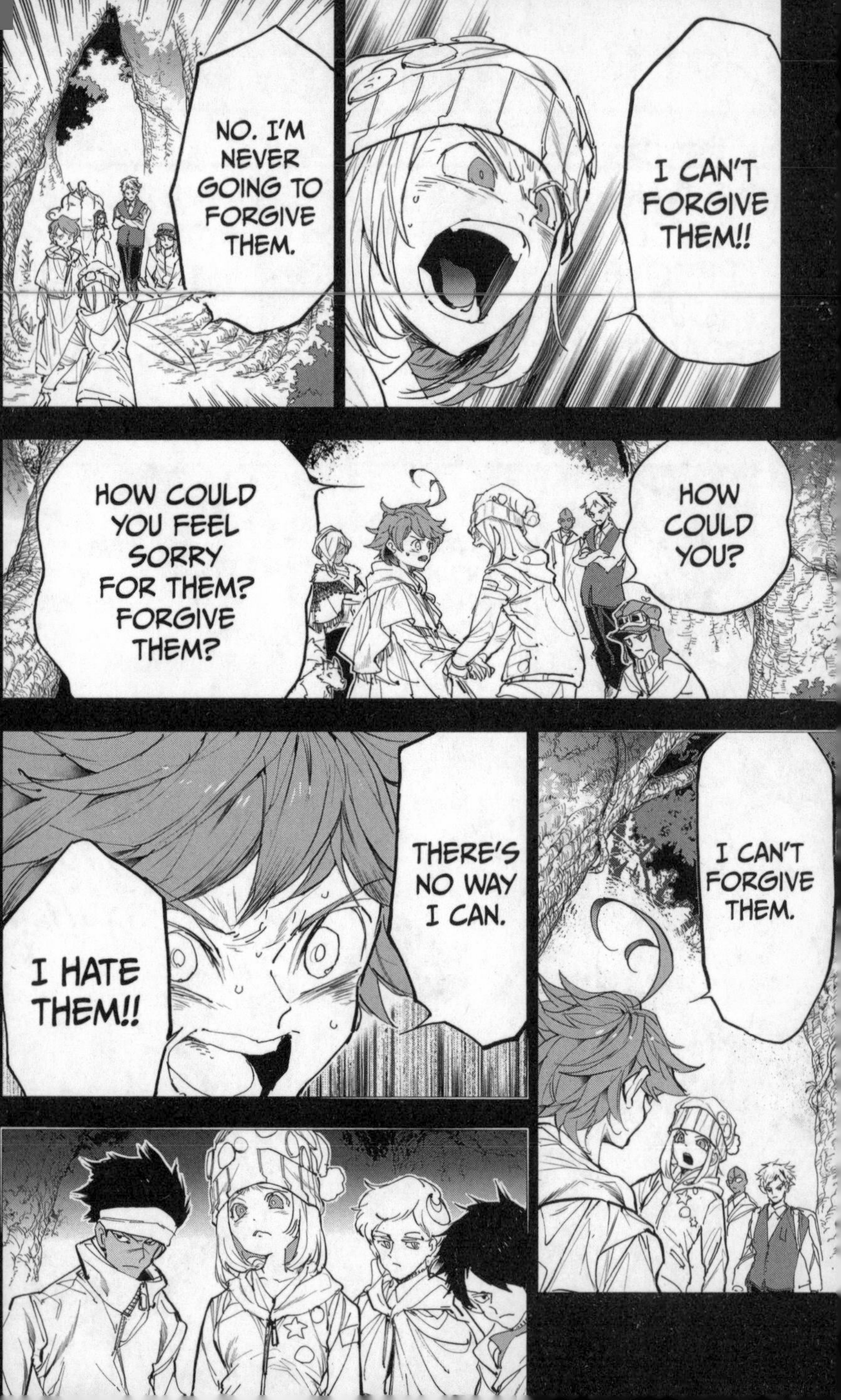
I CAN'T FORGIVE THEM!!
NO. I'M NEVER GOING TO FORGIVE THEM.
HOW COULD YOU?
HOW COULD YOU FEEL SORRY FOR THEM? FORGIVE THEM?
I CAN'T FORGIVE THEM.
THERE'S NO WAY I CAN.
I HATE THEM!!

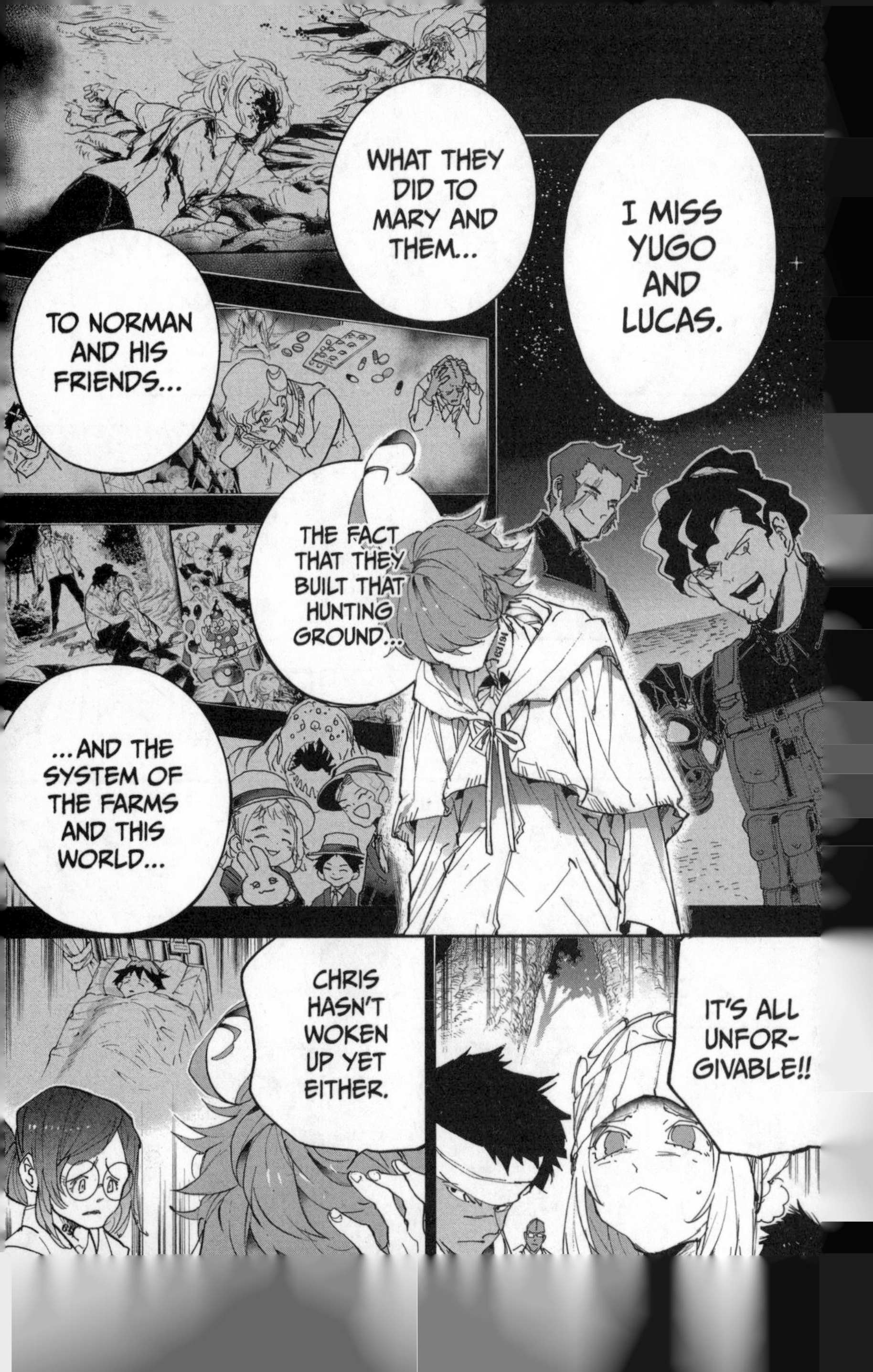
I MISS YUGO AND LUCAS.
WHAT THEY DID TO MARY AND THEM...
TO NORMAN AND HIS FRIENDS...
THE FACT THAT THEY BUILT THAT HUNTING GROUND...
...AND THE SYSTEM OF THE FARMS AND THIS WORLD...
IT'S ALL UNFOR-GIVABLE!!
CHRIS HASN'T WOKEN UP YET EITHER.

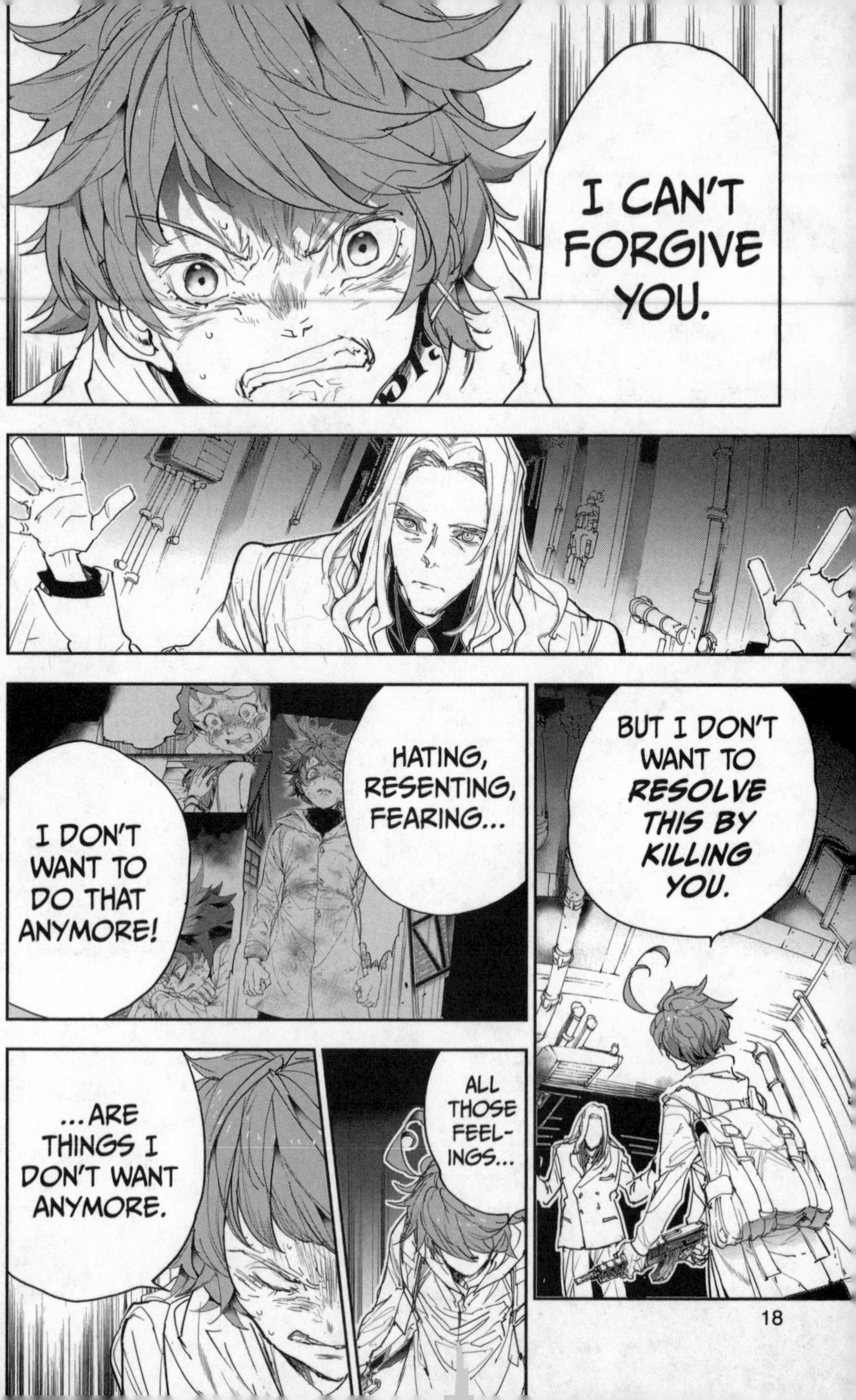
I CAN'T FORGIVE YOU.
BUT I DON'T WANT TO *RESOLVE THIS BY KILLING YOU.*
HATING, RESENTING, FEARING...
I DON'T WANT TO DO THAT ANYMORE!
ALL THOSE FEEL-INGS...
...ARE THINGS I DON'T WANT ANYMORE.

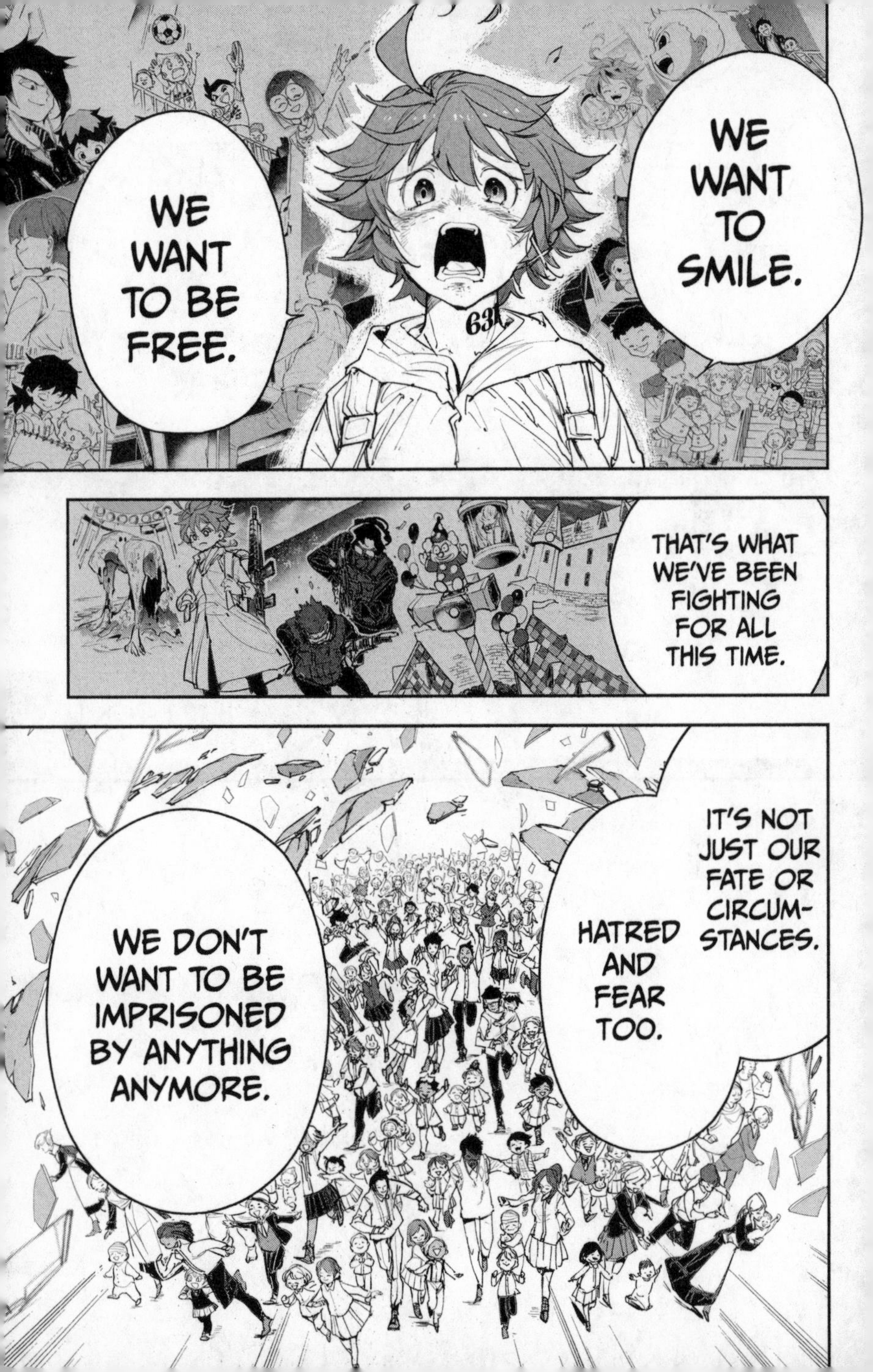
WE WANT TO SMILE.
WE WANT TO BE FREE.
THAT'S WHAT WE'VE BEEN FIGHTING FOR ALL THIS TIME.
IT'S NOT JUST OUR FATE OR CIRCUM-STANCES.
HATRED AND FEAR TOO.
WE DON'T WANT TO BE IMPRISONED BY ANYTHING ANYMORE.

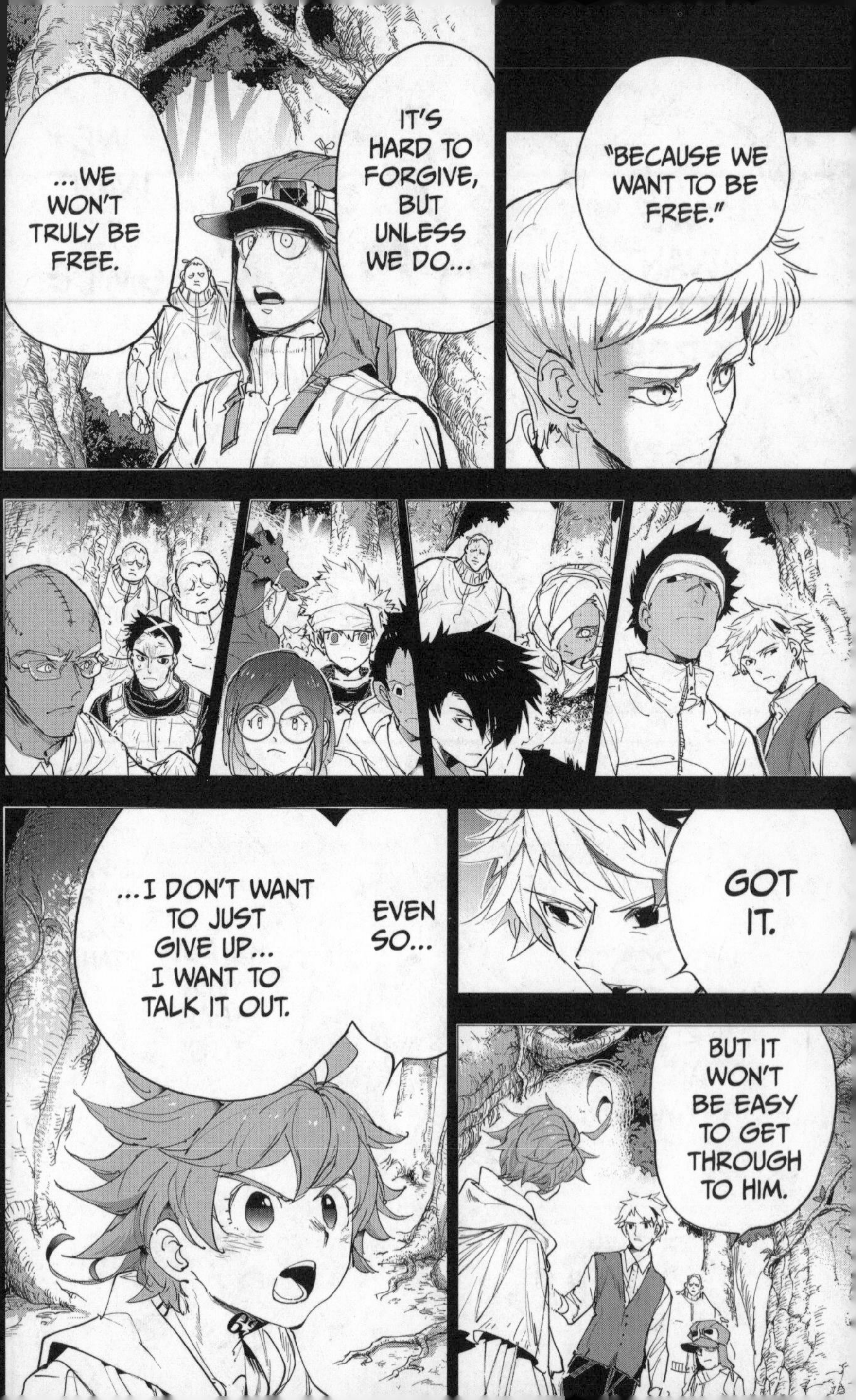
"BECAUSE WE WANT TO BE FREE."
IT'S HARD TO FORGIVE, BUT UNLESS WE DO...
...WE WON'T TRULY BE FREE.
GOT IT.
BUT IT WON'T BE EASY TO GET THROUGH TO HIM.
EVEN SO...
...I DON'T WANT TO JUST GIVE UP... I WANT TO TALK IT OUT.

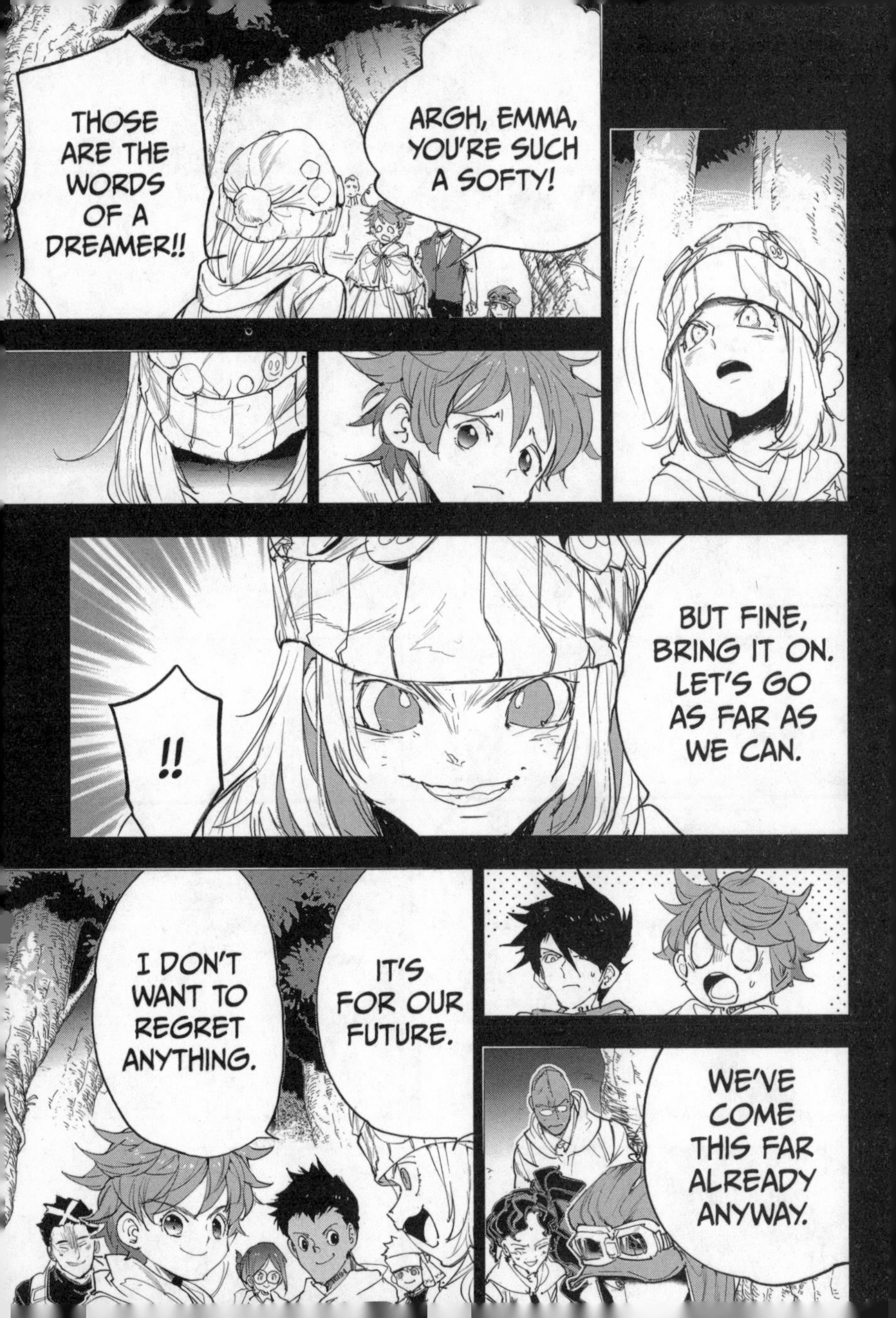
ARGH, EMMA, YOU'RE SUCH A SOFTY!
THOSE ARE THE WORDS OF A DREAMER!!
BUT FINE, BRING IT ON. LET'S GO AS FAR AS WE CAN.
!!
WE'VE COME THIS FAR ALREADY ANYWAY.
IT'S FOR OUR FUTURE.
I DON'T WANT TO REGRET ANYTHING.

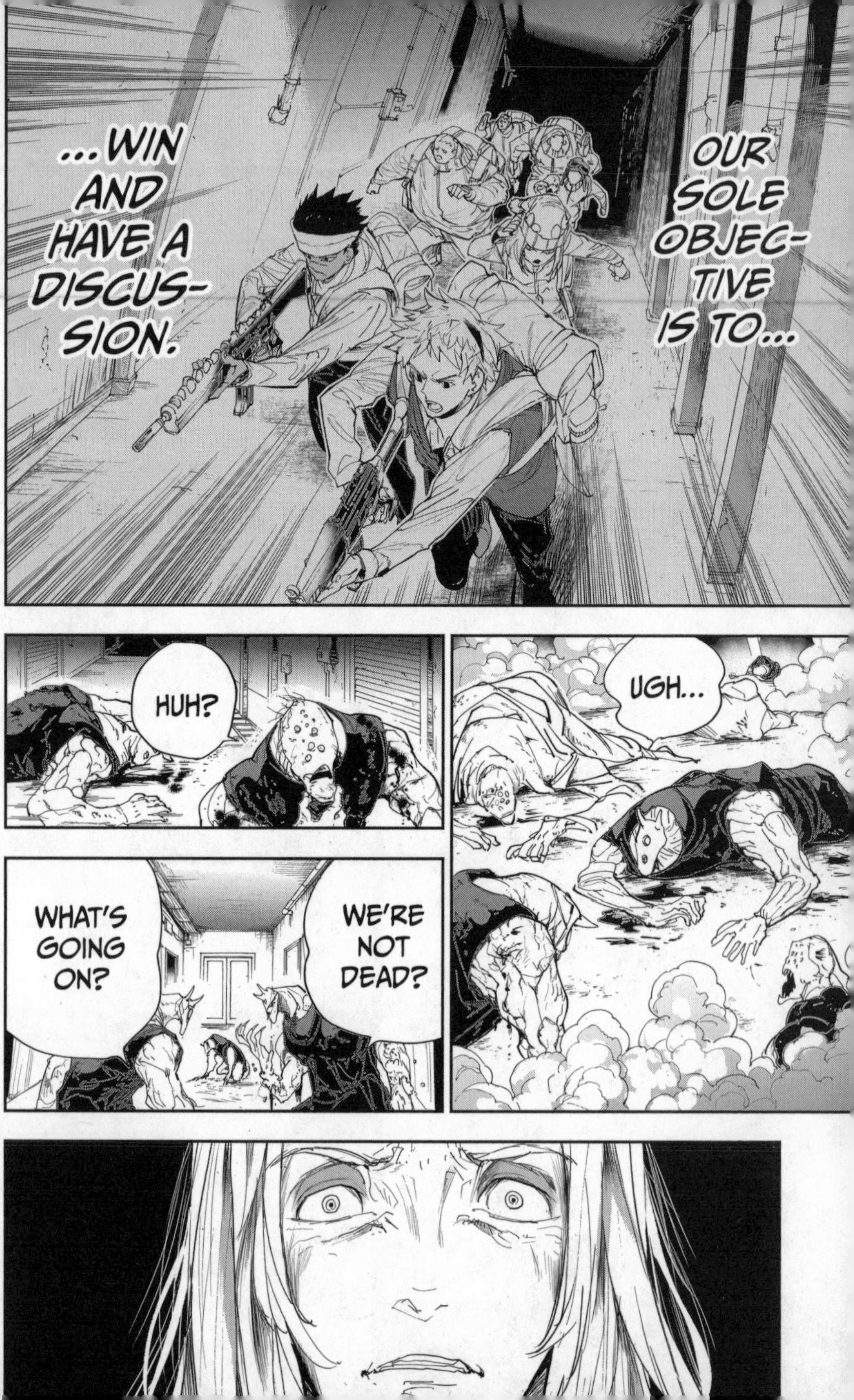
OUR SOLE OBJEC-TIVE IS TO...
...WIN AND HAVE A DISCUS-SION.
UGH...
HUH?
WE'RE NOT DEAD?
WHAT'S GOING ON?

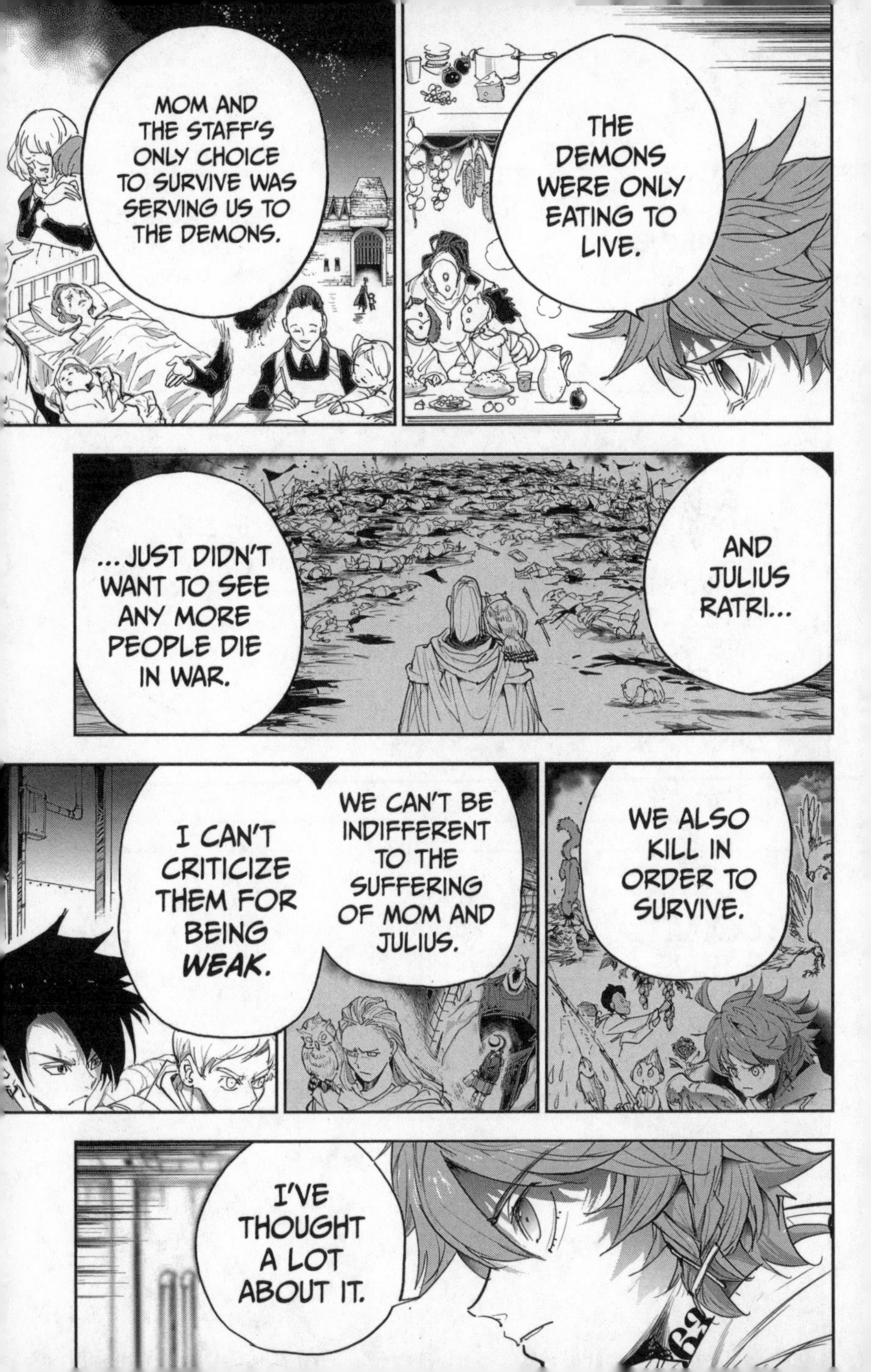
THE DEMONS WERE ONLY EATING TO LIVE.
MOM AND THE STAFF'S ONLY CHOICE TO SURVIVE WAS SERVING US TO THE DEMONS.
AND JULIUS RATRI...
...JUST DIDN'T WANT TO SEE ANY MORE PEOPLE DIE IN WAR.
WE ALSO KILL IN ORDER TO SURVIVE.
WE CAN'T BE INDIFFERENT TO THE SUFFERING OF MOM AND JULIUS.
I CAN'T CRITICIZE THEM FOR BEING *WEAK.*
I'VE THOUGHT A LOT ABOUT IT.

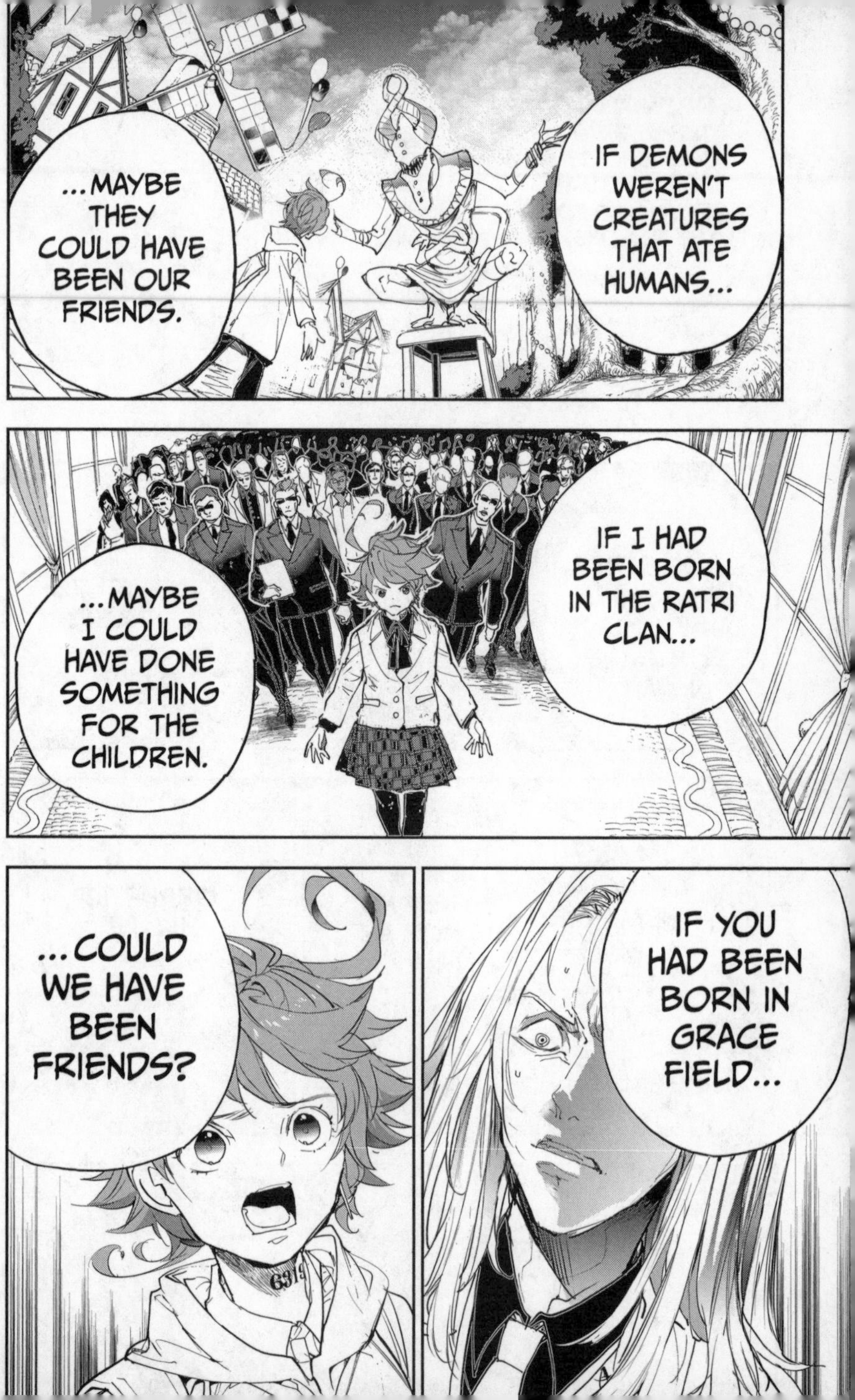
IF DEMONS WEREN'T CREATURES THAT ATE HUMANS...
...MAYBE THEY COULD HAVE BEEN OUR FRIENDS.
IF I HAD BEEN BORN IN THE RATRI CLAN...
...MAYBE I COULD HAVE DONE SOMETHING FOR THE CHILDREN.
IF YOU HAD BEEN BORN IN GRACE FIELD...
...COULD WE HAVE BEEN FRIENDS?

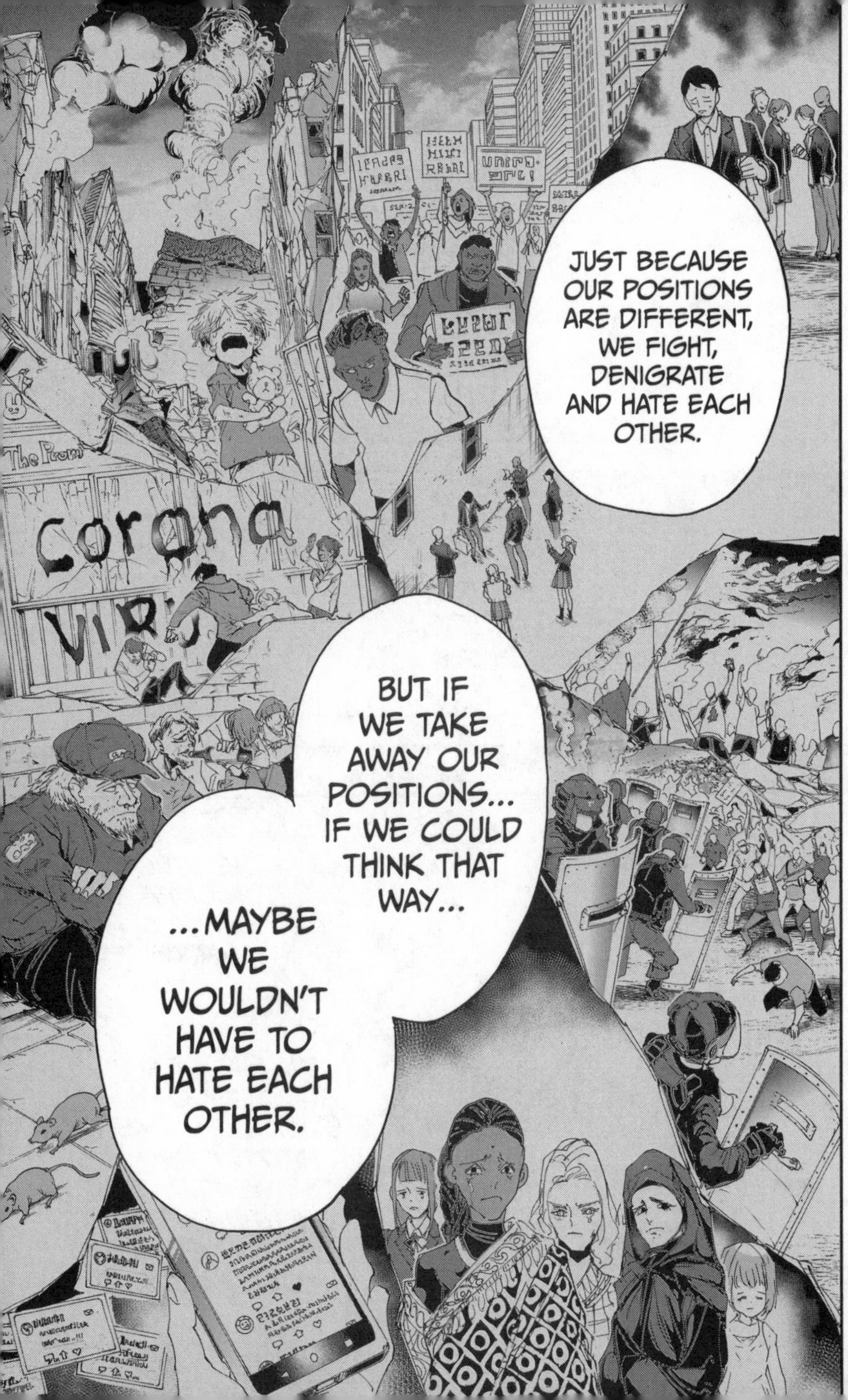
JUST BECAUSE OUR POSITIONS ARE DIFFERENT, WE FIGHT, DENIGRATE AND HATE EACH OTHER.
Corona
BUT IF WE TAKE AWAY OUR POSITIONS... IF WE COULD THINK THAT WAY...
...MAYBE WE WOULDN'T HAVE TO HATE EACH OTHER.

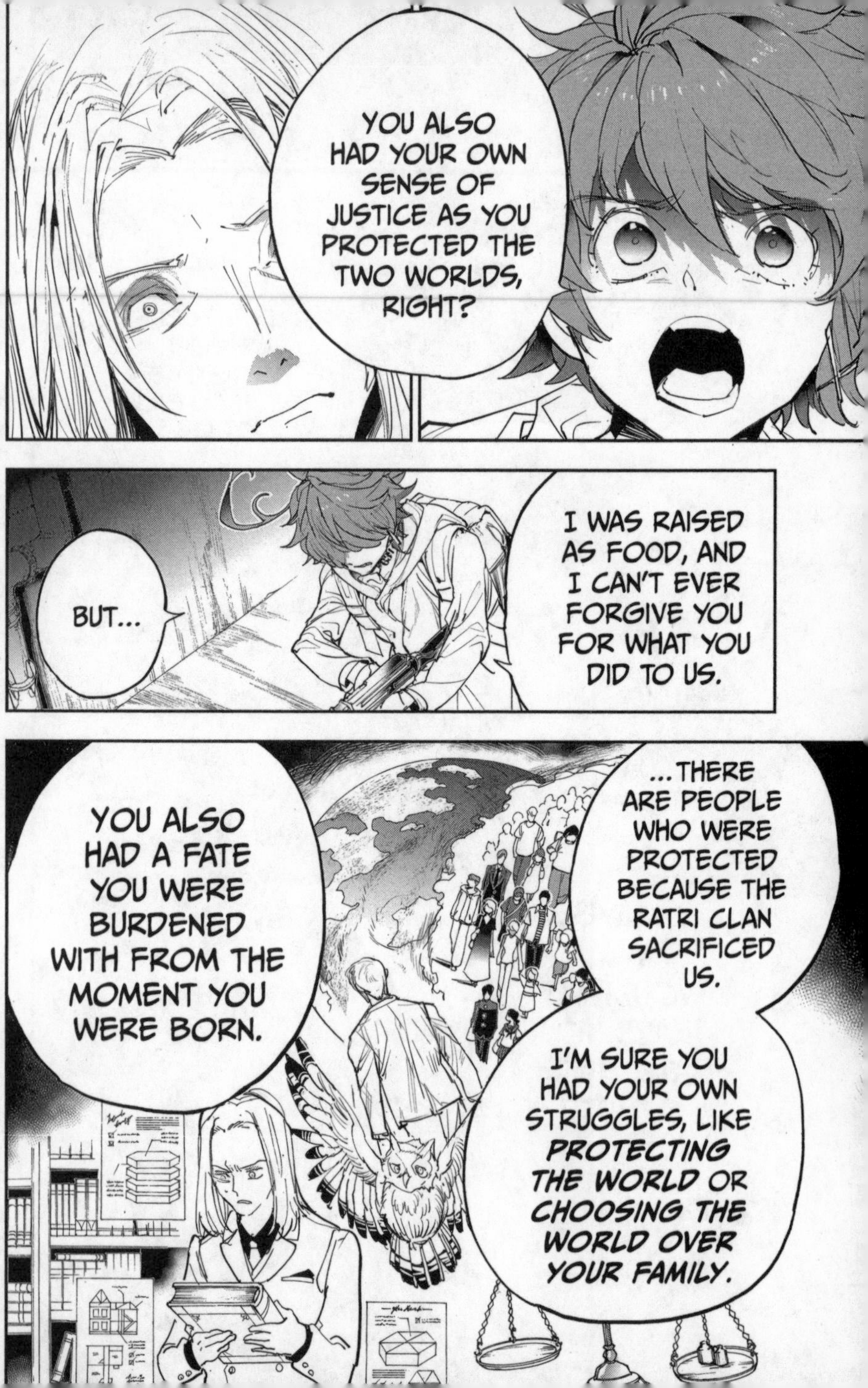
YOU ALSO HAD YOUR OWN SENSE OF JUSTICE AS YOU PROTECTED THE TWO WORLDS, RIGHT?
I WAS RAISED AS FOOD, AND I CAN'T EVER FORGIVE YOU FOR WHAT YOU DID TO US.
BUT...
...THERE ARE PEOPLE WHO WERE PROTECTED BECAUSE THE RATRI CLAN SACRIFICED US.
YOU ALSO HAD A FATE YOU WERE BURDENED WITH FROM THE MOMENT YOU WERE BORN.
I'M SURE YOU HAD YOUR OWN STRUGGLES, LIKE *PROTECTING THE WORLD* OR *CHOOSING THE WORLD OVER YOUR FAMILY*.

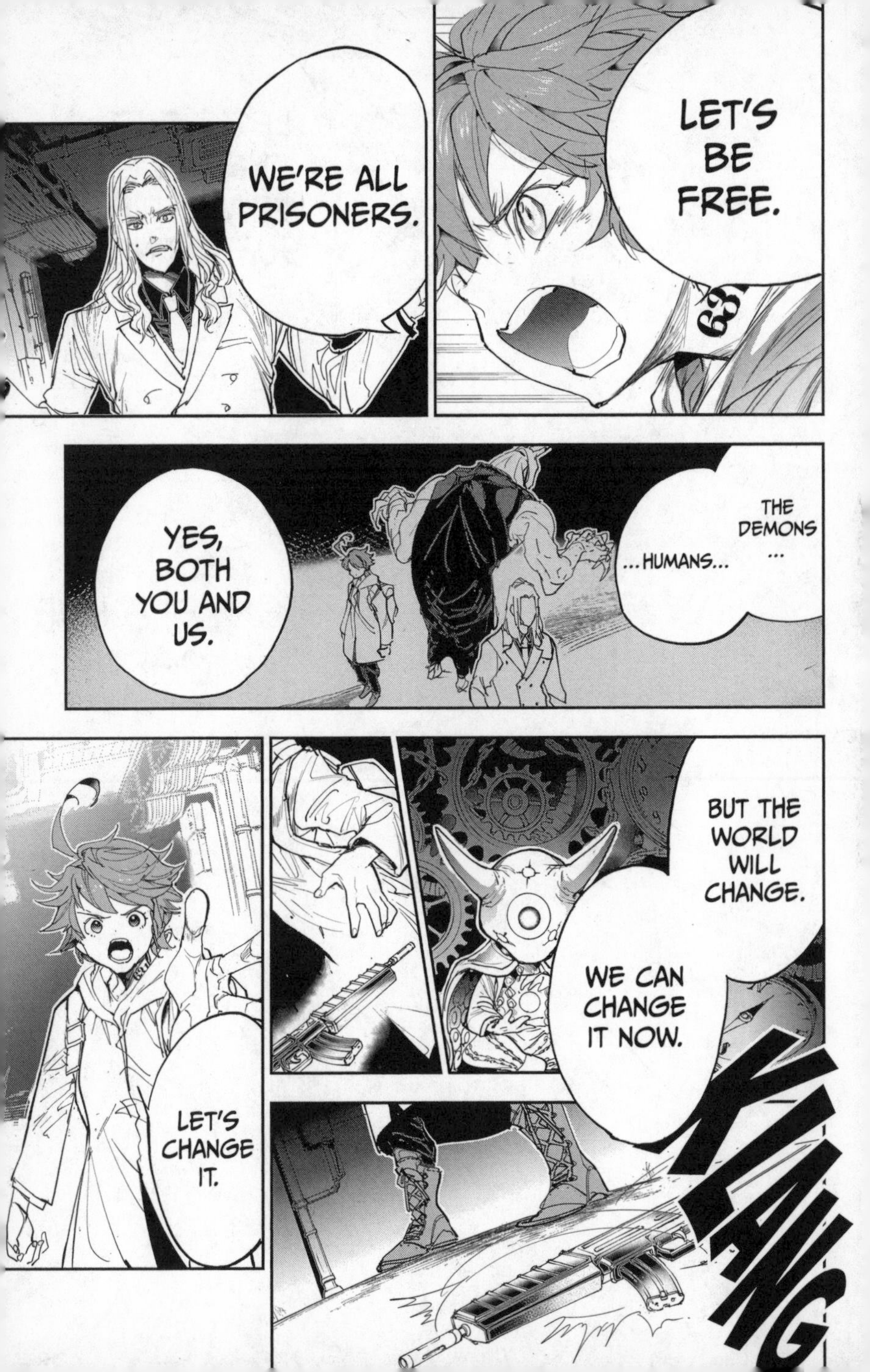
LET'S BE FREE.
WE'RE ALL PRISONERS.
THE DEMONS ...
...HUMANS...
YES, BOTH YOU AND US.
BUT THE WORLD WILL CHANGE.
WE CAN CHANGE IT NOW.
KAANG
LET'S CHANGE IT.

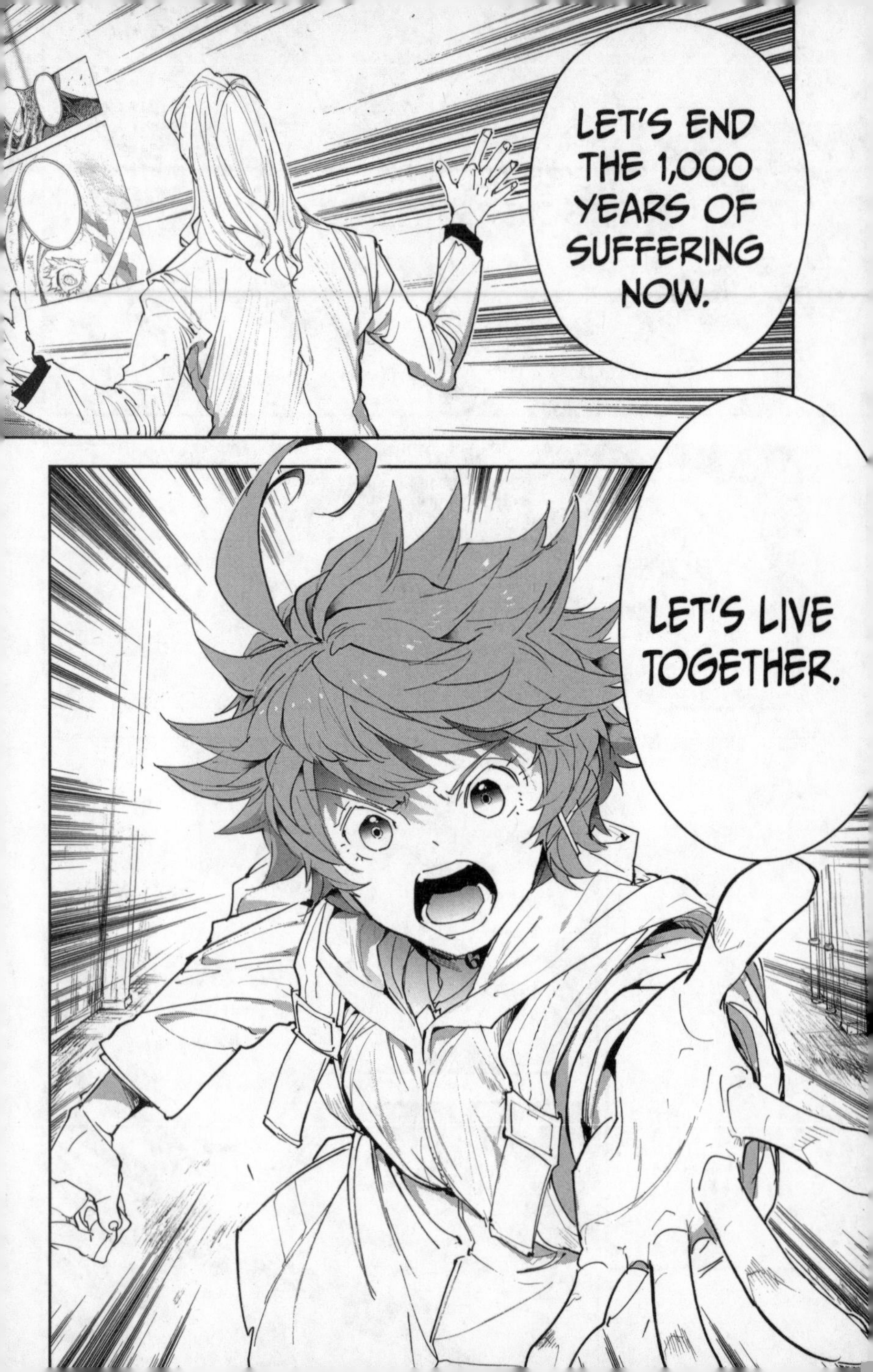
LET'S END THE 1,000 YEARS OF SUFFERING NOW.
LET'S LIVE TOGETHER.

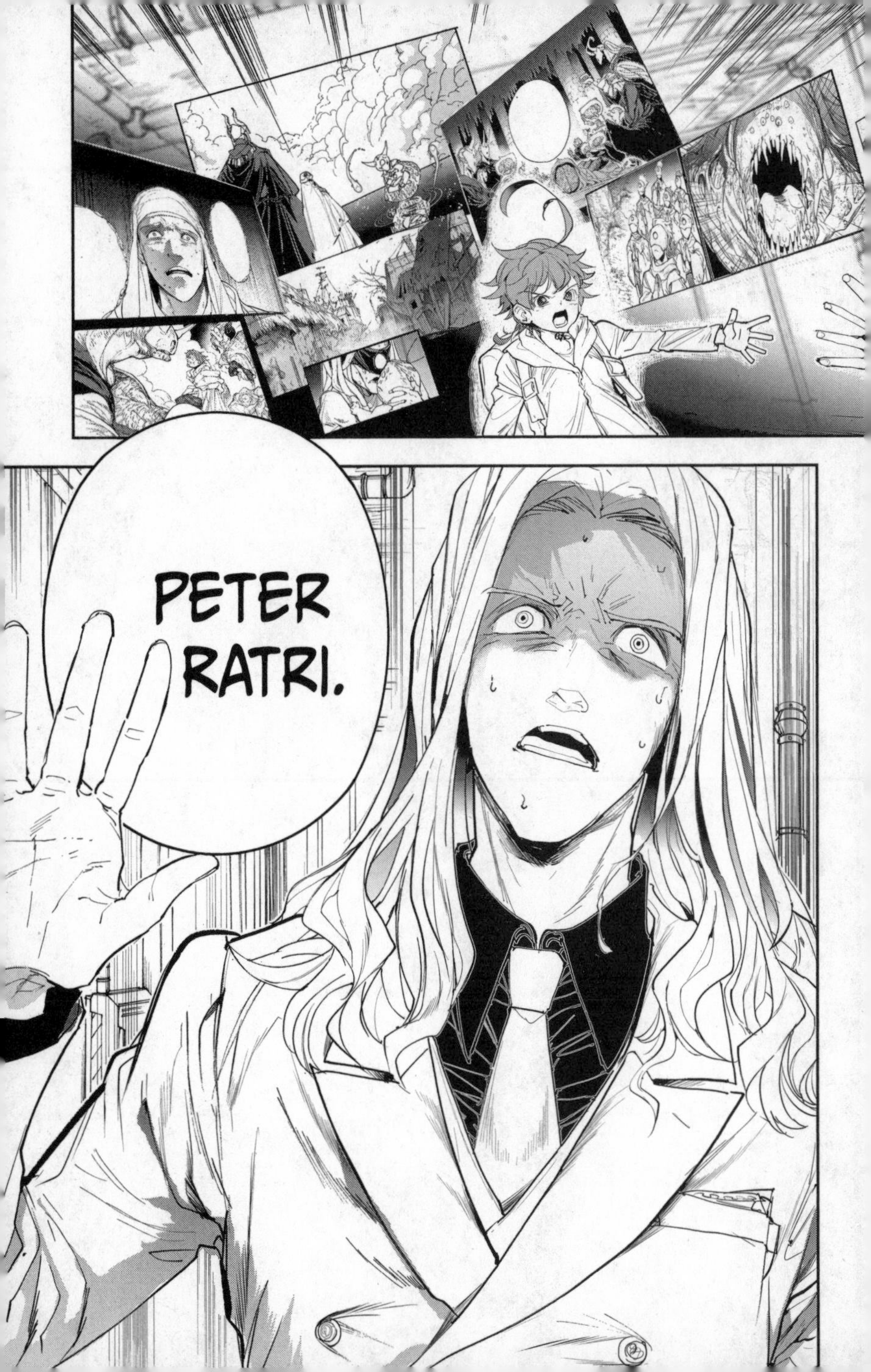
PETER RATRI.

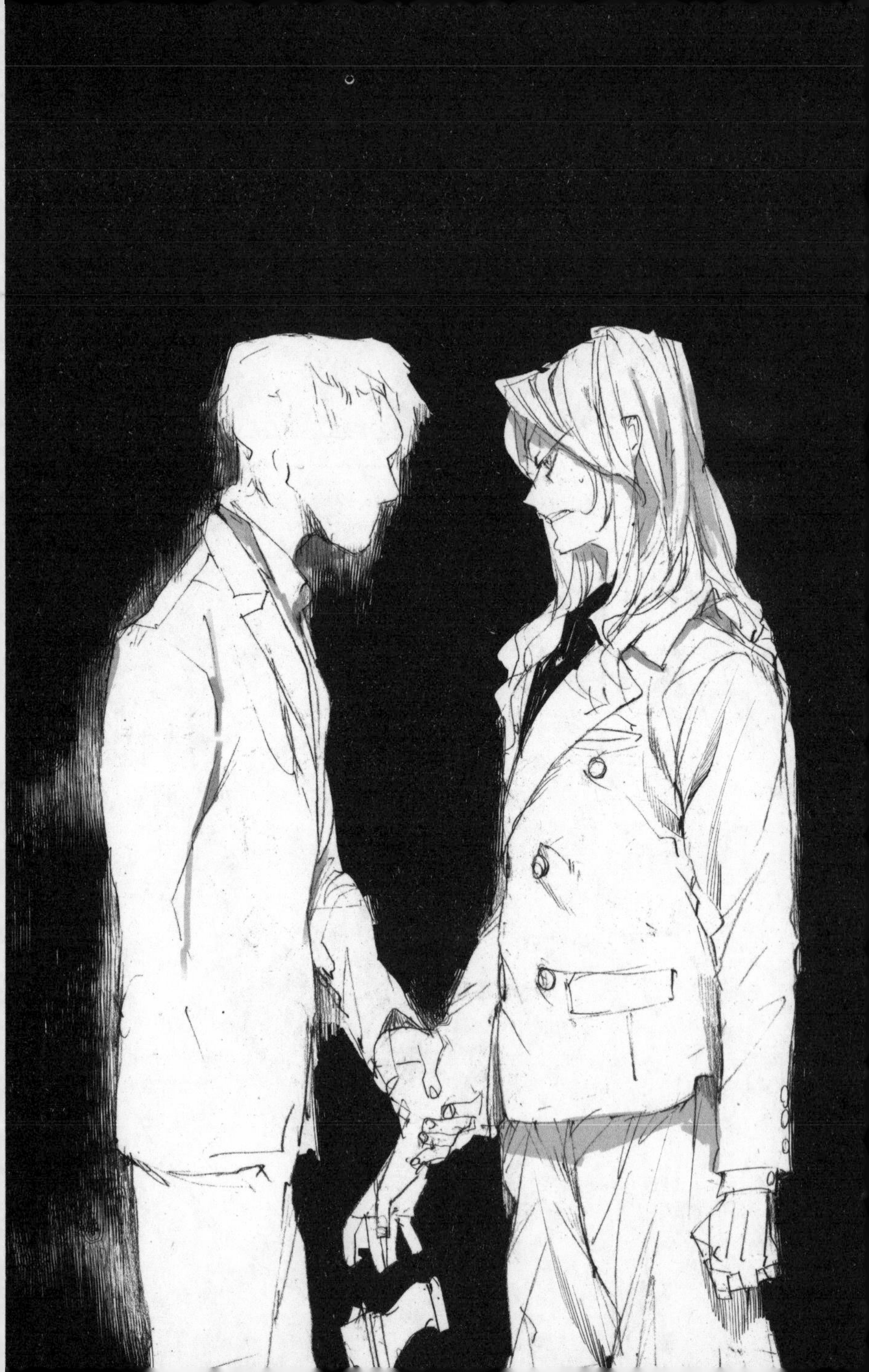

CHAPTER 173: PRISONERS

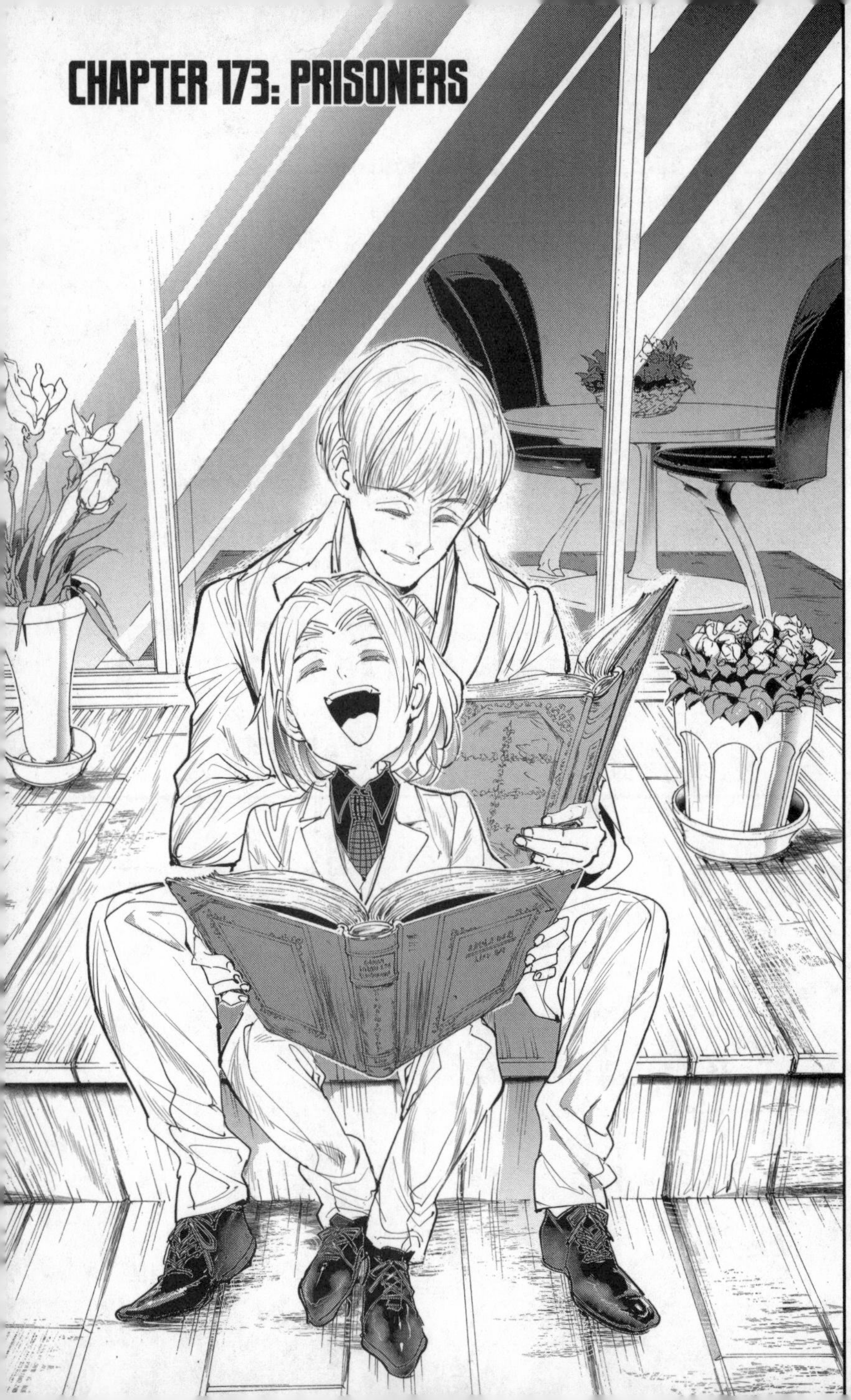

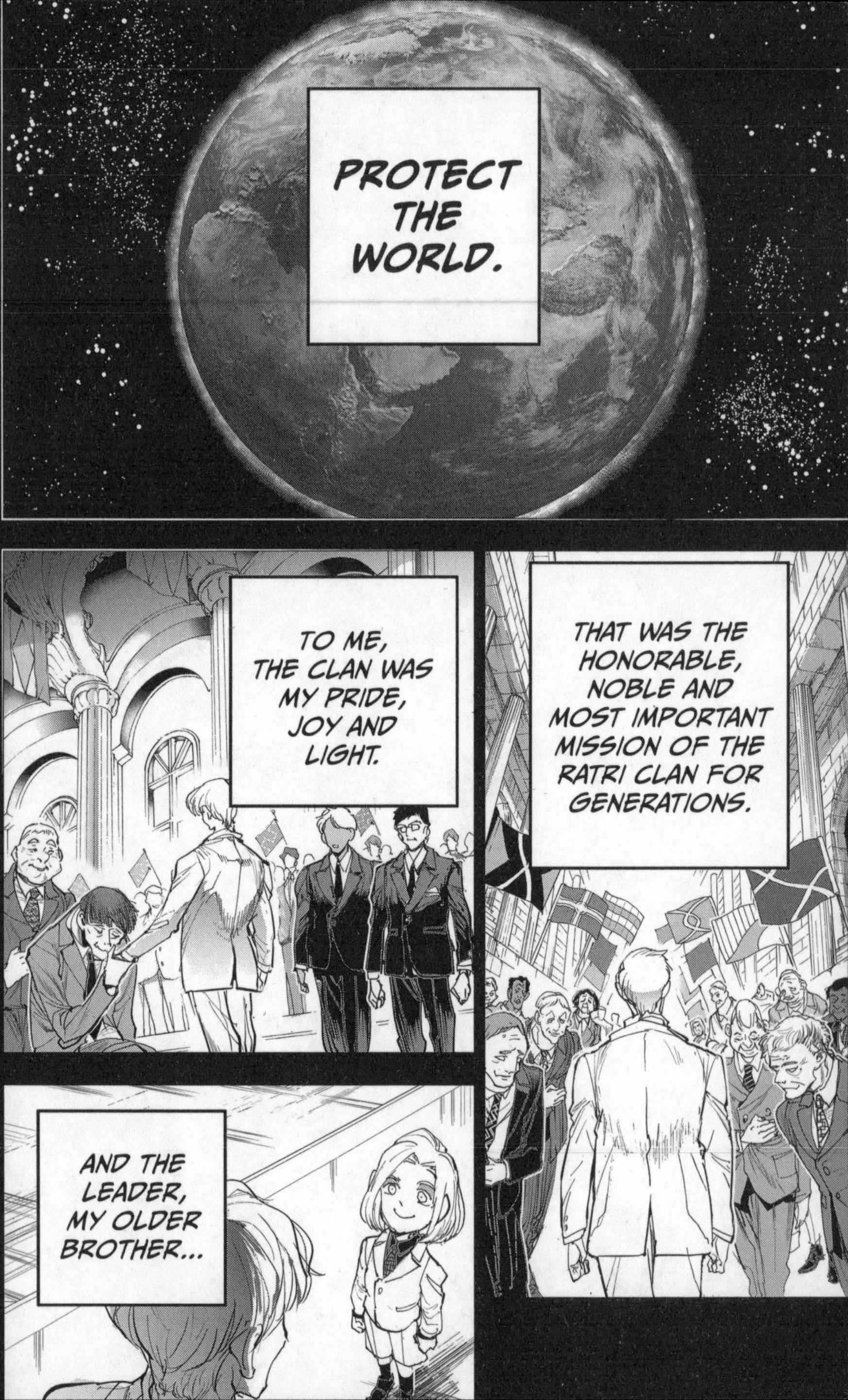
PROTECT THE WORLD.
THAT WAS THE HONORABLE, NOBLE AND MOST IMPORTANT MISSION OF THE RATRI CLAN FOR GENERATIONS.
TO ME, THE CLAN WAS MY PRIDE, JOY AND LIGHT.
AND THE LEADER, MY OLDER BROTHER...

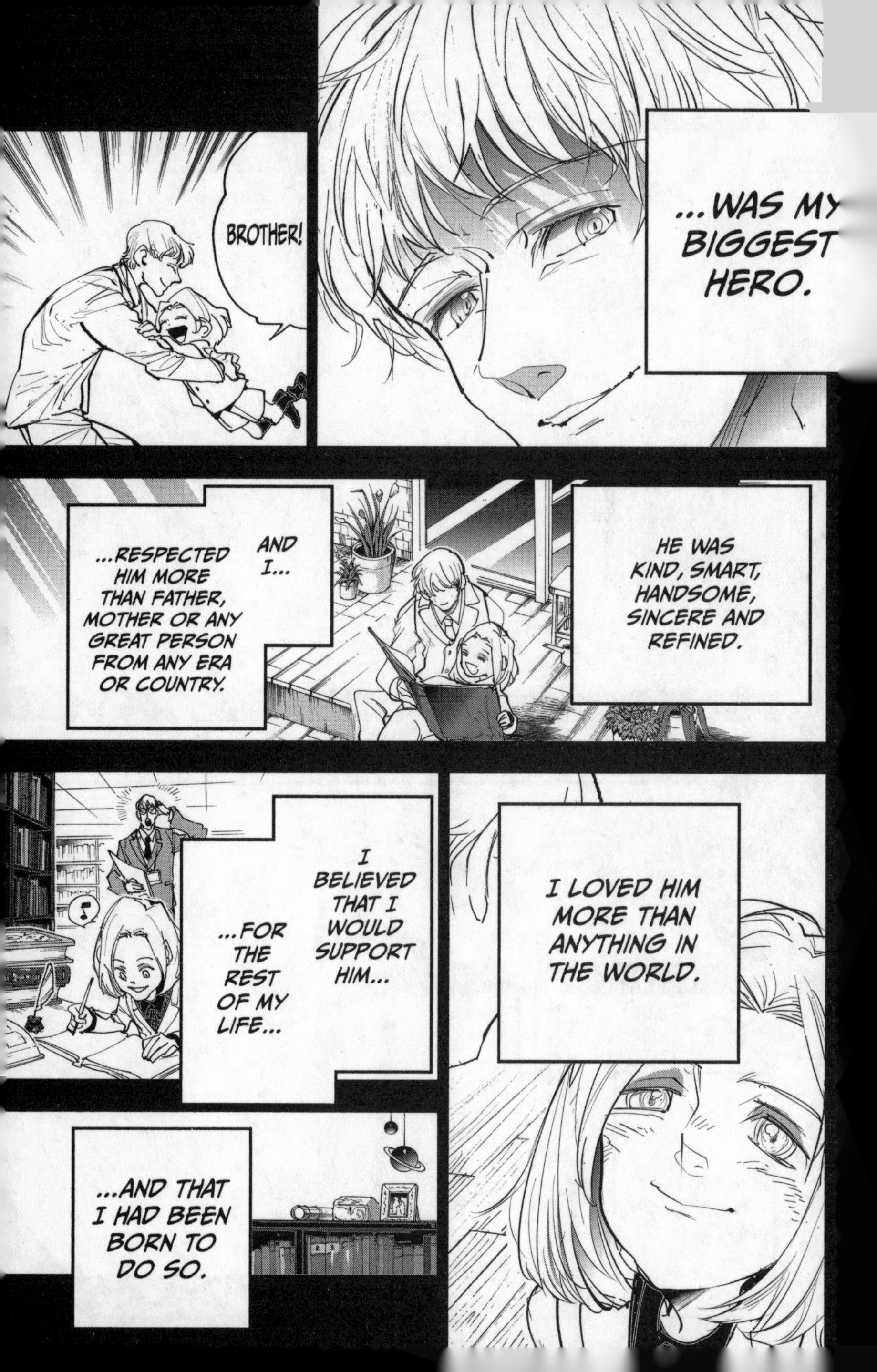
...WAS MY BIGGEST HERO.
BROTHER!
HE WAS KIND, SMART, HANDSOME, SINCERE AND REFINED.
AND I...
...RESPECTED HIM MORE THAN FATHER, MOTHER OR ANY GREAT PERSON FROM ANY ERA OR COUNTRY.
I LOVED HIM MORE THAN ANYTHING IN THE WORLD.
I BELIEVED THAT I WOULD SUPPORT HIM...
...FOR THE REST OF MY LIFE...
...AND THAT I HAD BEEN BORN TO DO SO.

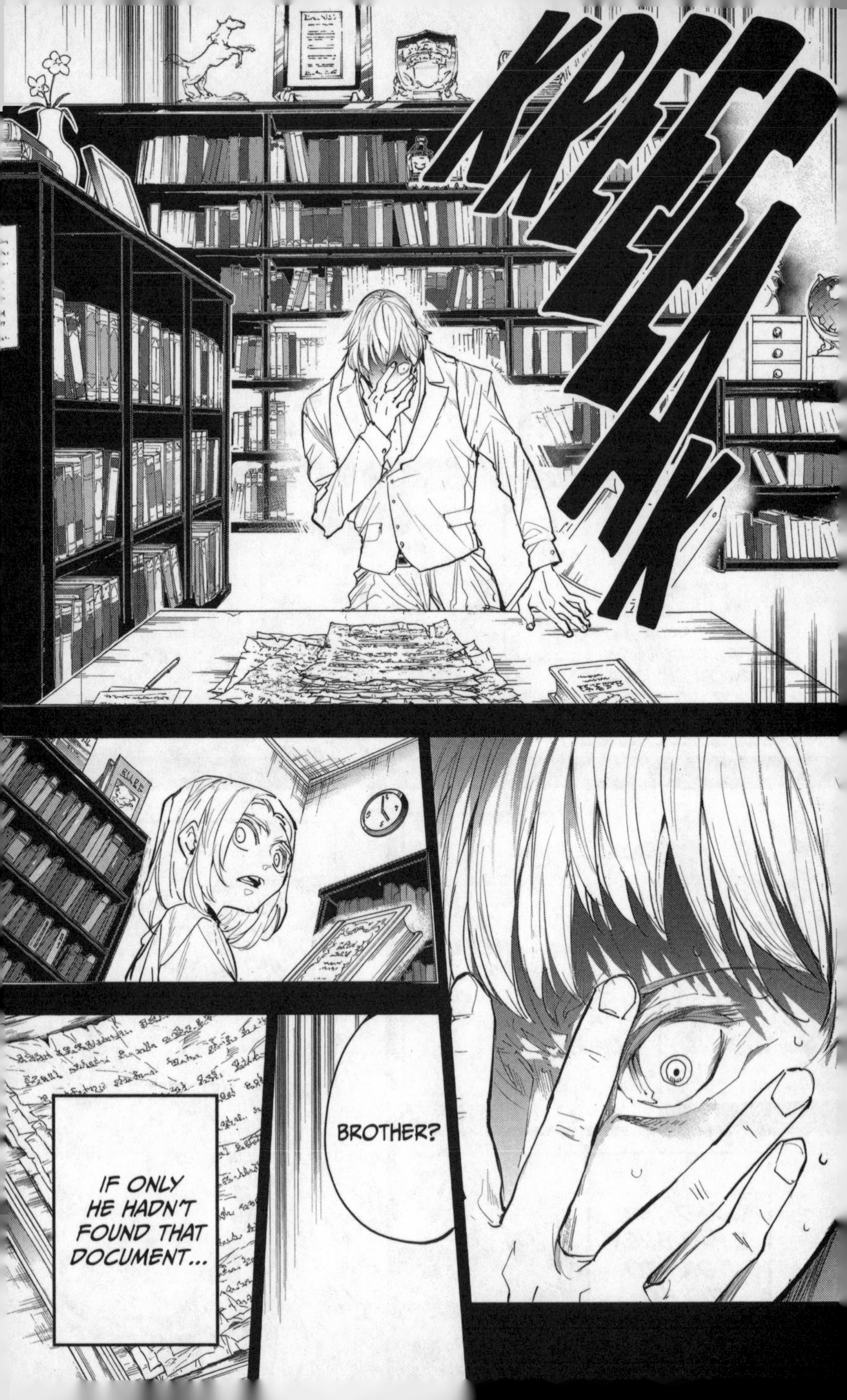
KREEEAAK
BROTHER?
IF ONLY HE HADN'T FOUND THAT DOCUMENT...

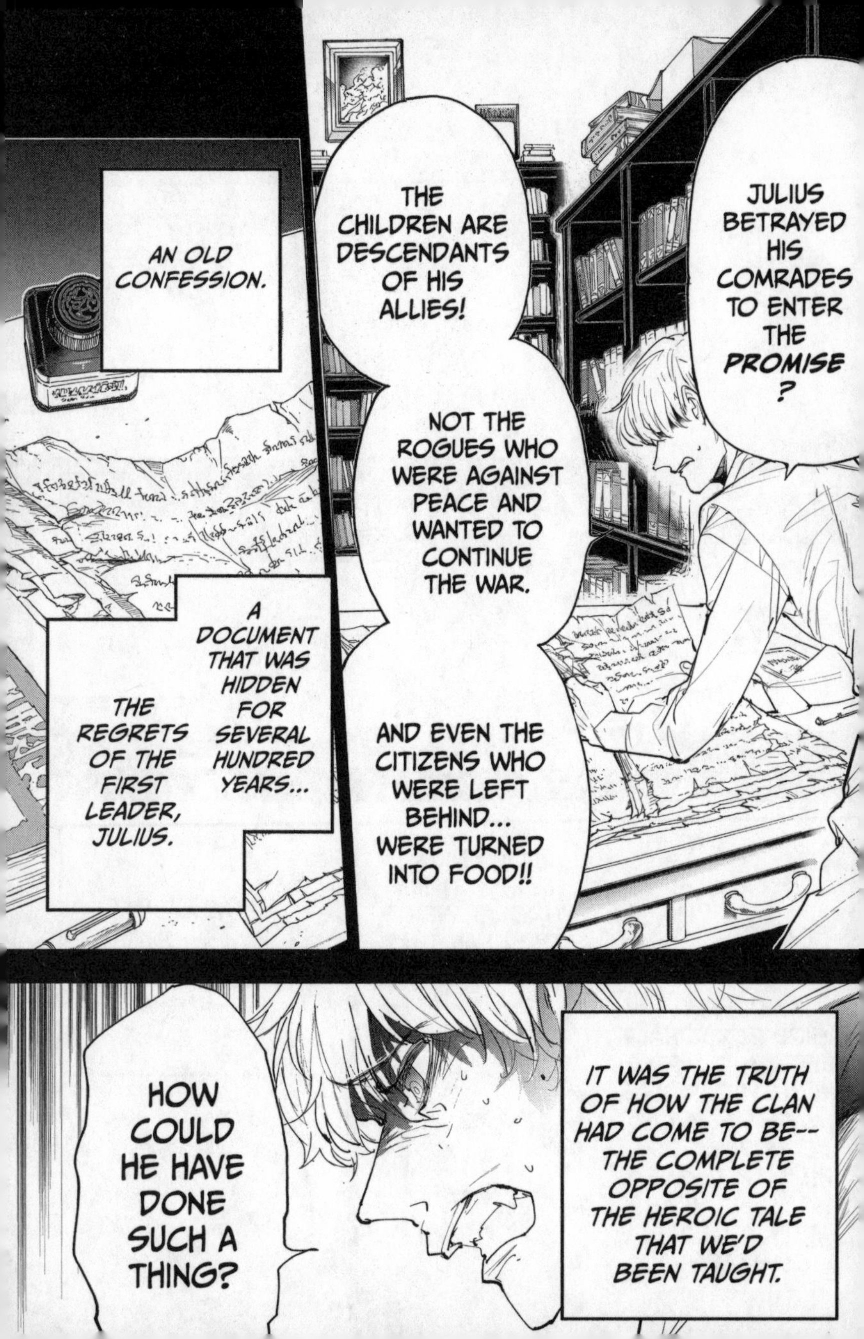
JULIUS BETRAYED HIS COMRADES TO ENTER THE *PROMISE*?
THE CHILDREN ARE DESCENDANTS OF HIS ALLIES!
NOT THE ROGUES WHO WERE AGAINST PEACE AND WANTED TO CONTINUE THE WAR.
AND EVEN THE CITIZENS WHO WERE LEFT BEHIND... WERE TURNED INTO FOOD!!
AN OLD CONFESSION.
A DOCUMENT THAT WAS HIDDEN FOR SEVERAL HUNDRED YEARS...
THE REGRETS OF THE FIRST LEADER, JULIUS.
IT WAS THE TRUTH OF HOW THE CLAN HAD COME TO BE-- THE COMPLETE OPPOSITE OF THE HEROIC TALE THAT WE'D BEEN TAUGHT.
HOW COULD HE HAVE DONE SUCH A THING?

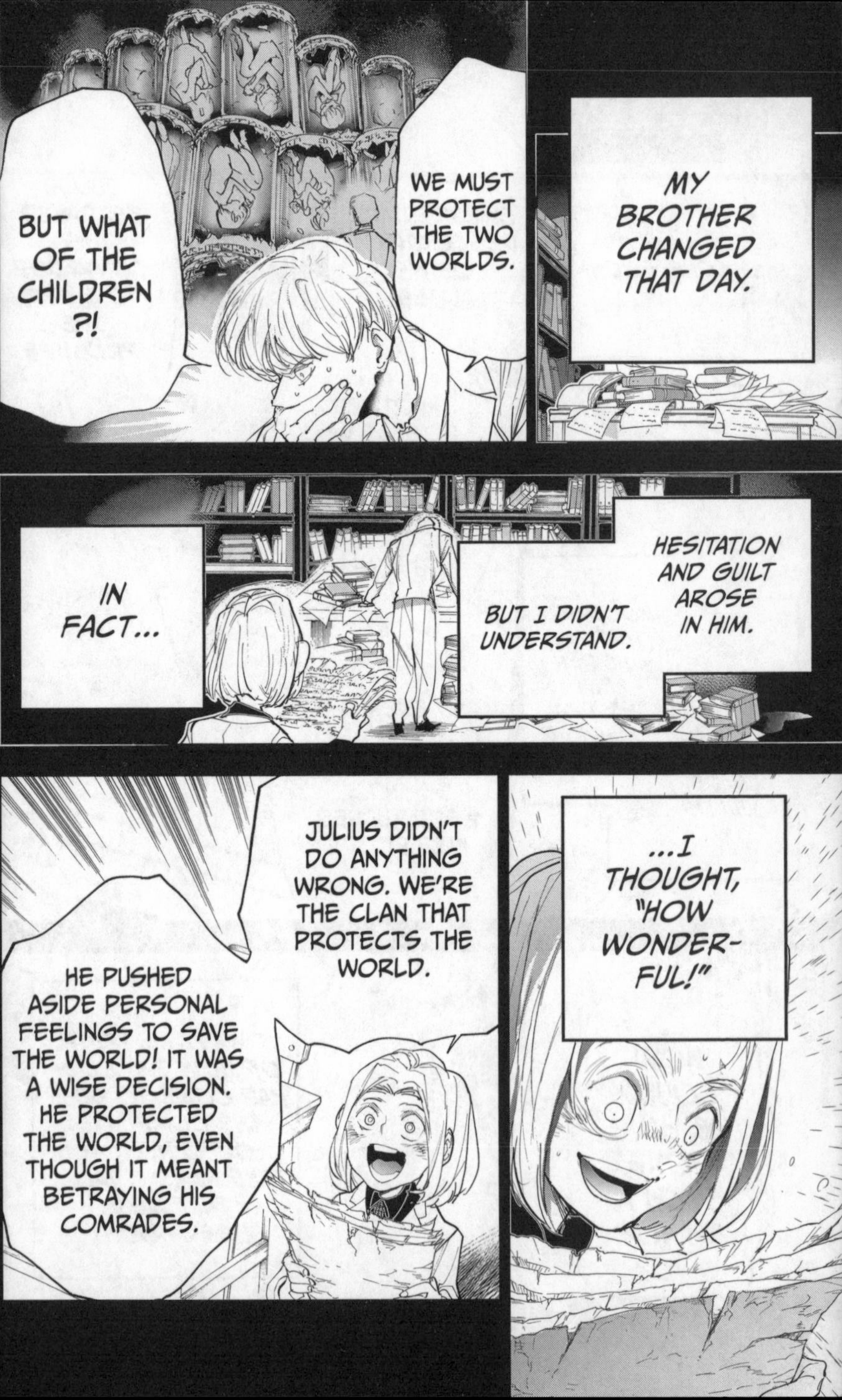
MY BROTHER CHANGED THAT DAY.
WE MUST PROTECT THE TWO WORLDS.
BUT WHAT OF THE CHILDREN ?!
HESITATION AND GUILT AROSE IN HIM.
BUT I DIDN'T UNDERSTAND.
IN FACT...
...I THOUGHT, "HOW WONDER-FUL!"
JULIUS DIDN'T DO ANYTHING WRONG. WE'RE THE CLAN THAT PROTECTS THE WORLD.
HE PUSHED ASIDE PERSONAL FEELINGS TO SAVE THE WORLD! IT WAS A WISE DECISION. HE PROTECTED THE WORLD, EVEN THOUGH IT MEANT BETRAYING HIS COMRADES.

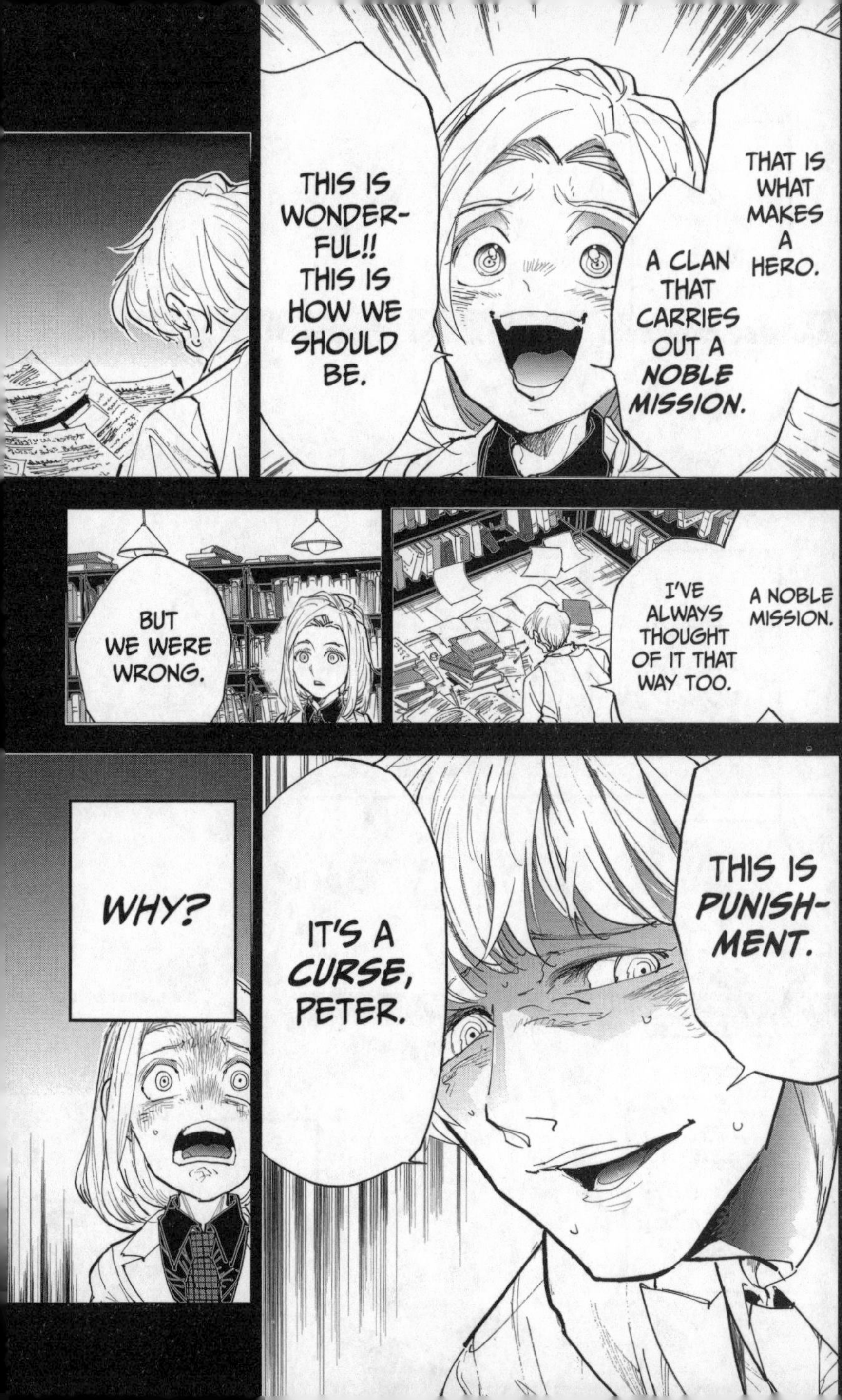
A CLAN THAT CARRIES OUT A *NOBLE MISSION.*
THAT IS WHAT MAKES A HERO.
THIS IS WONDERFUL!! THIS IS HOW WE SHOULD BE.
I'VE ALWAYS THOUGHT OF IT THAT WAY TOO.
A NOBLE MISSION.
BUT WE WERE WRONG.
THIS IS *PUNISHMENT.*
IT'S A *CURSE,* PETER.
WHY?

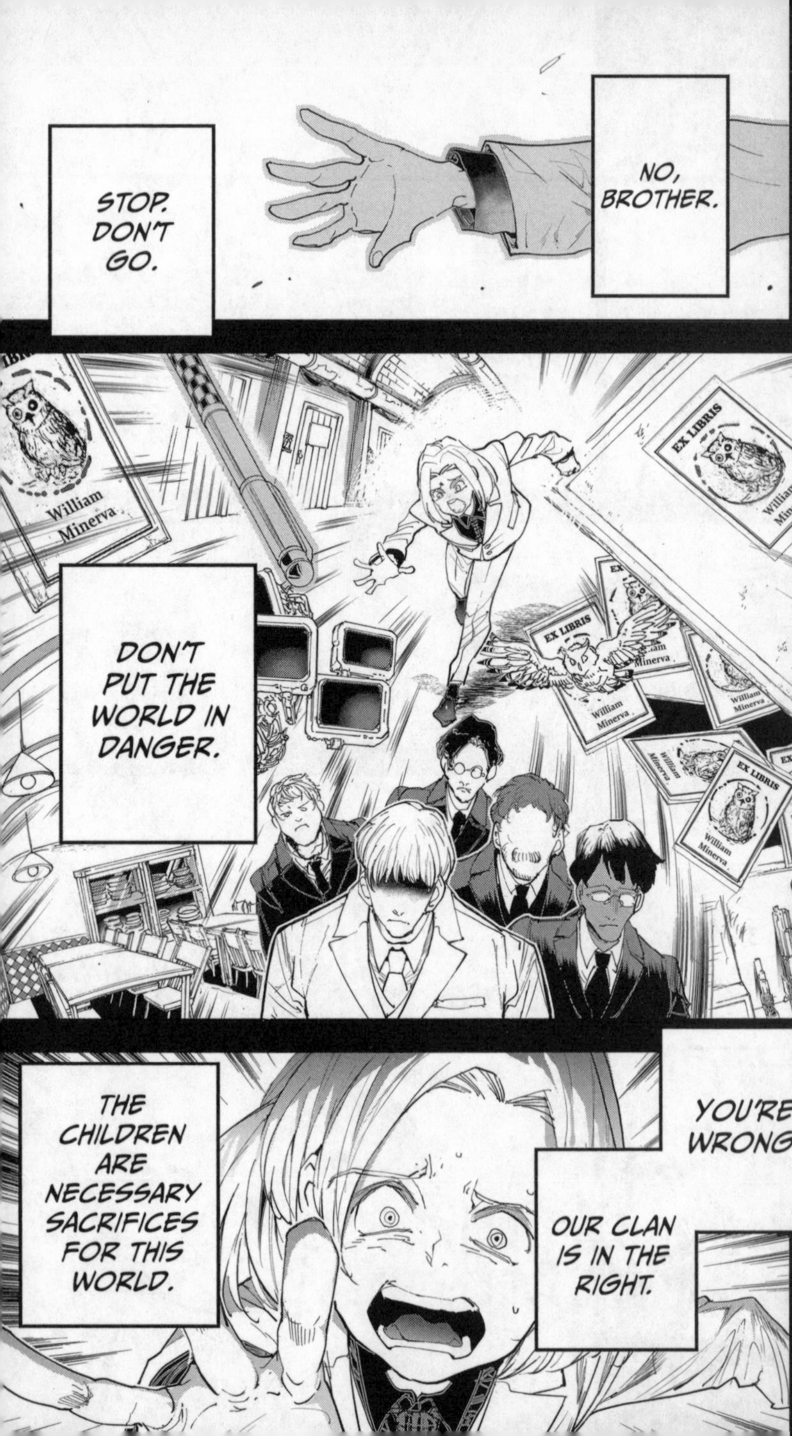
NO, BROTHER.
STOP. DON'T GO.
EX LIBRIS
William Minerva
DON'T PUT THE WORLD IN DANGER.
YOU'RE WRONG.
OUR CLAN IS IN THE RIGHT.
THE CHILDREN ARE NECESSARY SACRIFICES FOR THIS WORLD.

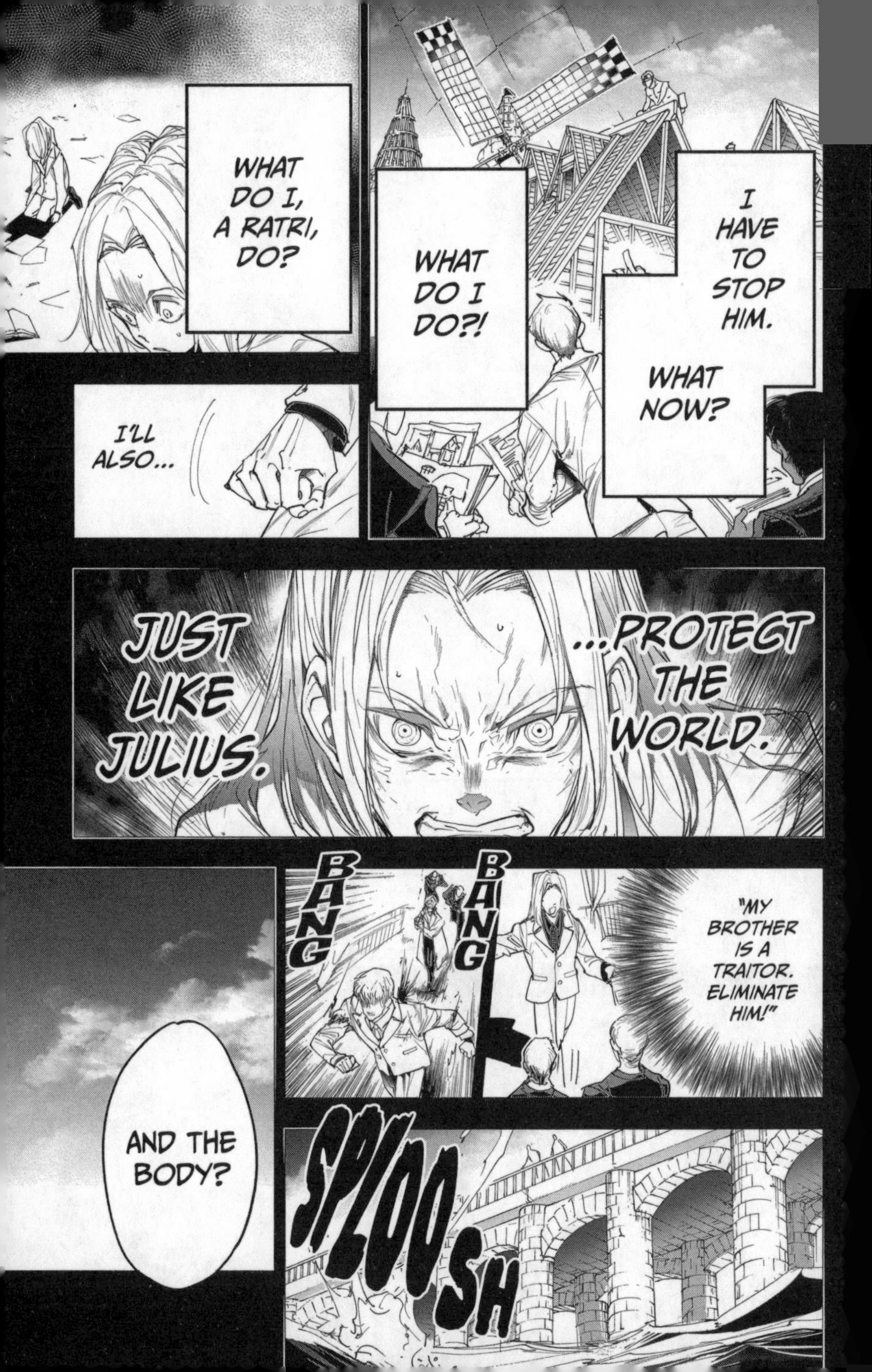
I HAVE TO STOP HIM.
WHAT NOW?
WHAT DO I DO?!
WHAT DO I, A RATRI, DO?
I'LL ALSO...
...PROTECT THE WORLD.
JUST LIKE JULIUS.
BANG
BANG
"MY BROTHER IS A TRAITOR. ELIMINATE HIM!"
SPLOOSH
AND THE BODY?

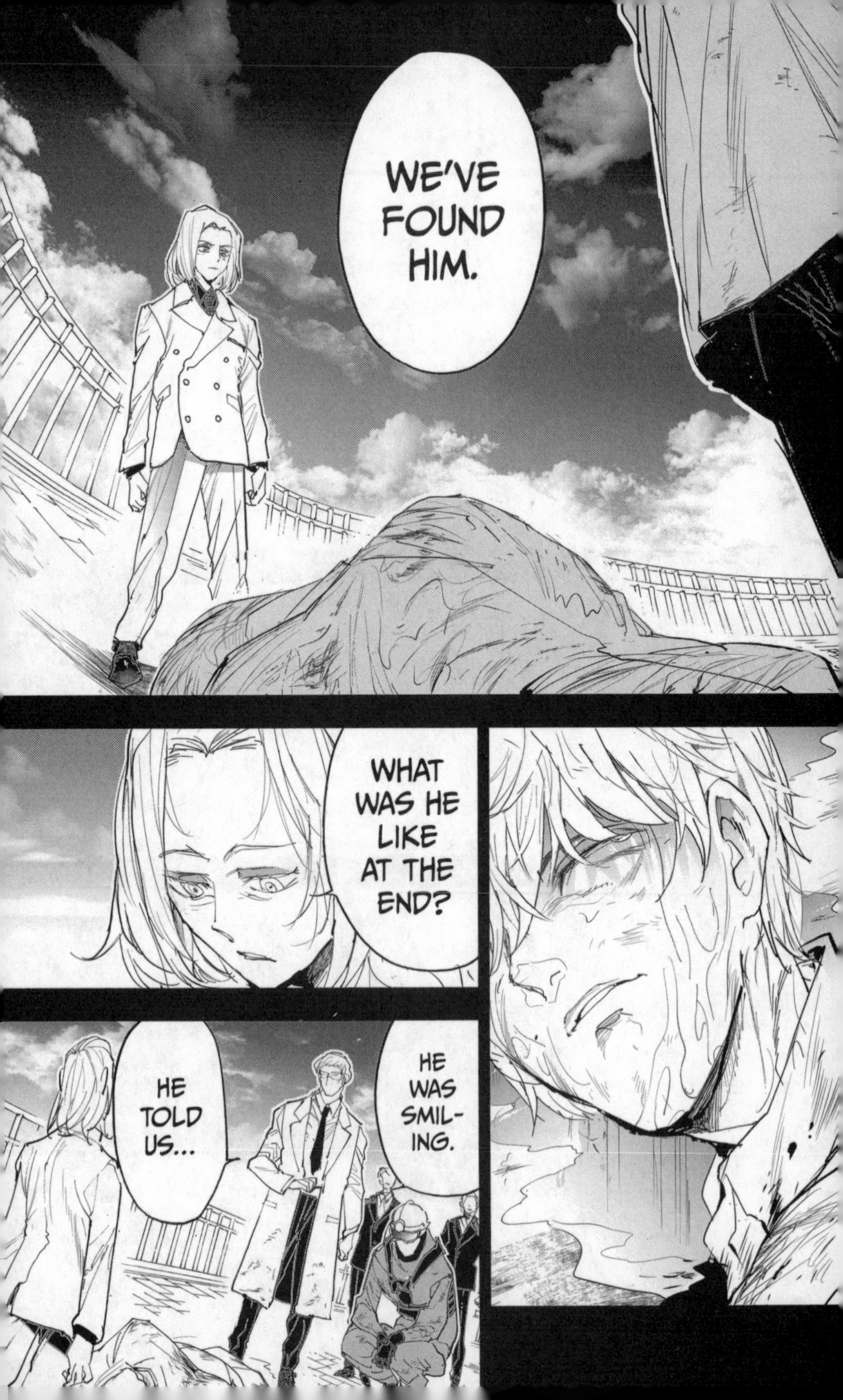
WE'VE FOUND HIM.
WHAT WAS HE LIKE AT THE END?
HE WAS SMIL-ING.
HE TOLD US...

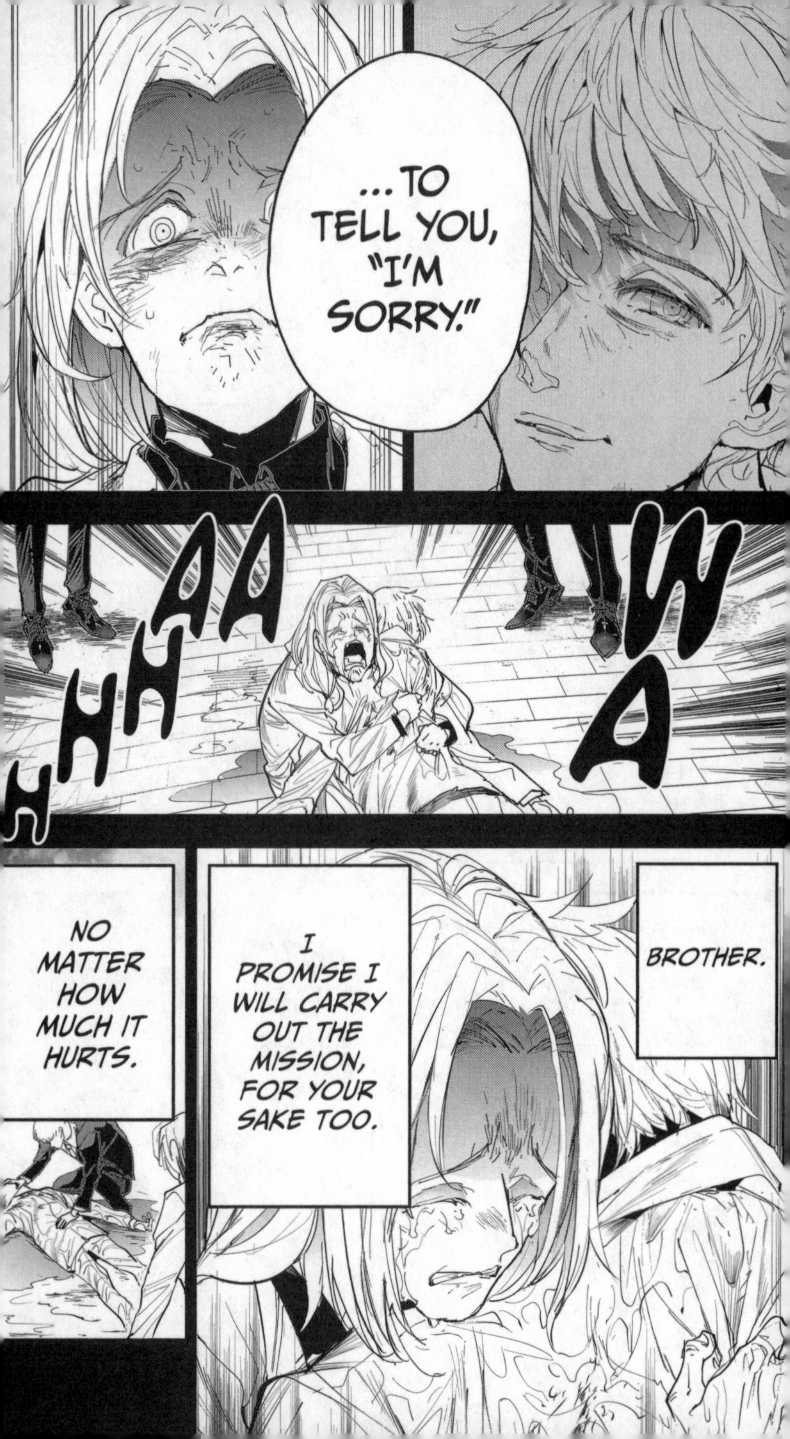
...TO TELL YOU, "I'M SORRY."
WAAAHHHH
BROTHER.
I PROMISE I WILL CARRY OUT THE MISSION, FOR YOUR SAKE TOO.
NO MATTER HOW MUCH IT HURTS.

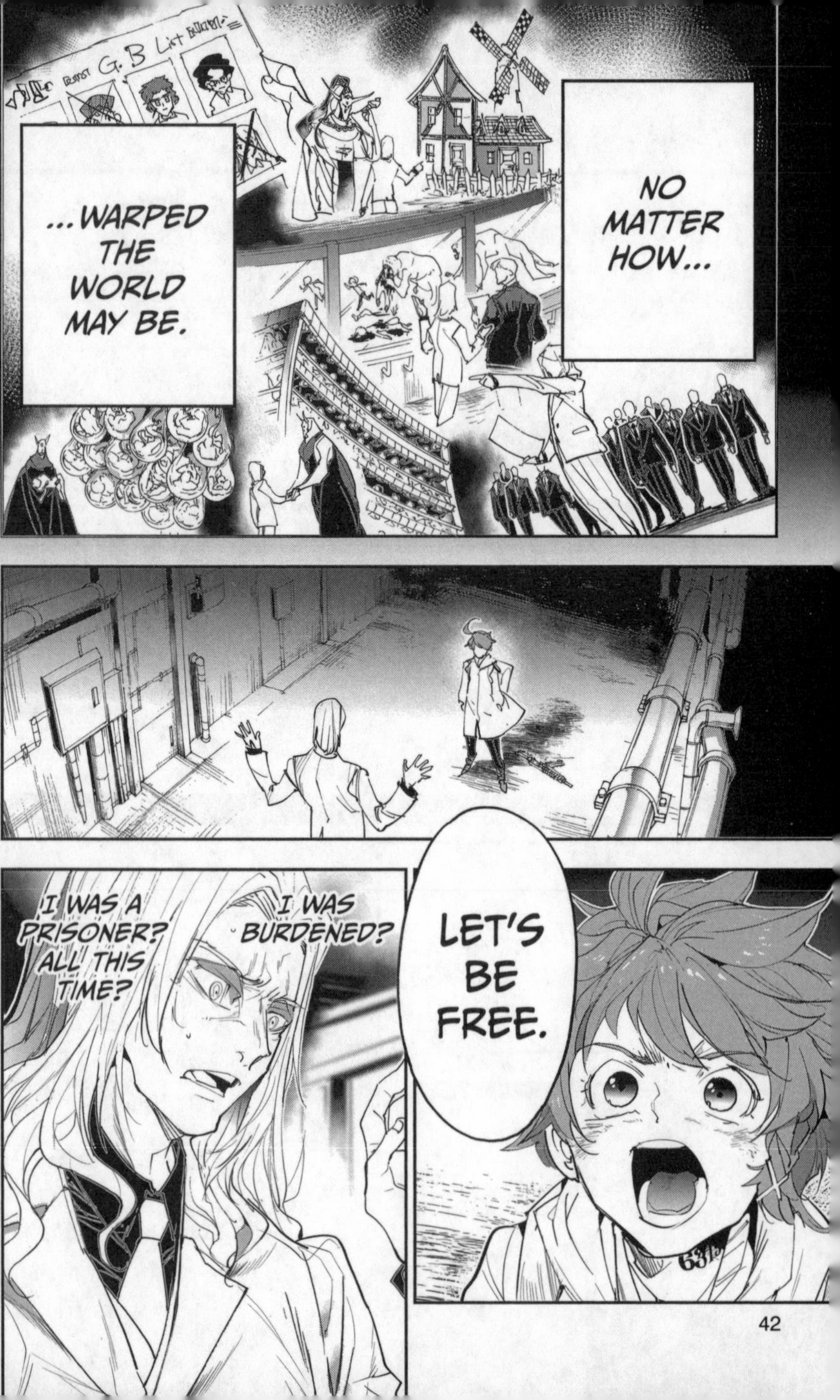
NO MATTER HOW...
...WARPED THE WORLD MAY BE.
LET'S BE FREE.
I WAS BURDENED?
I WAS A PRISONER? ALL THIS TIME?

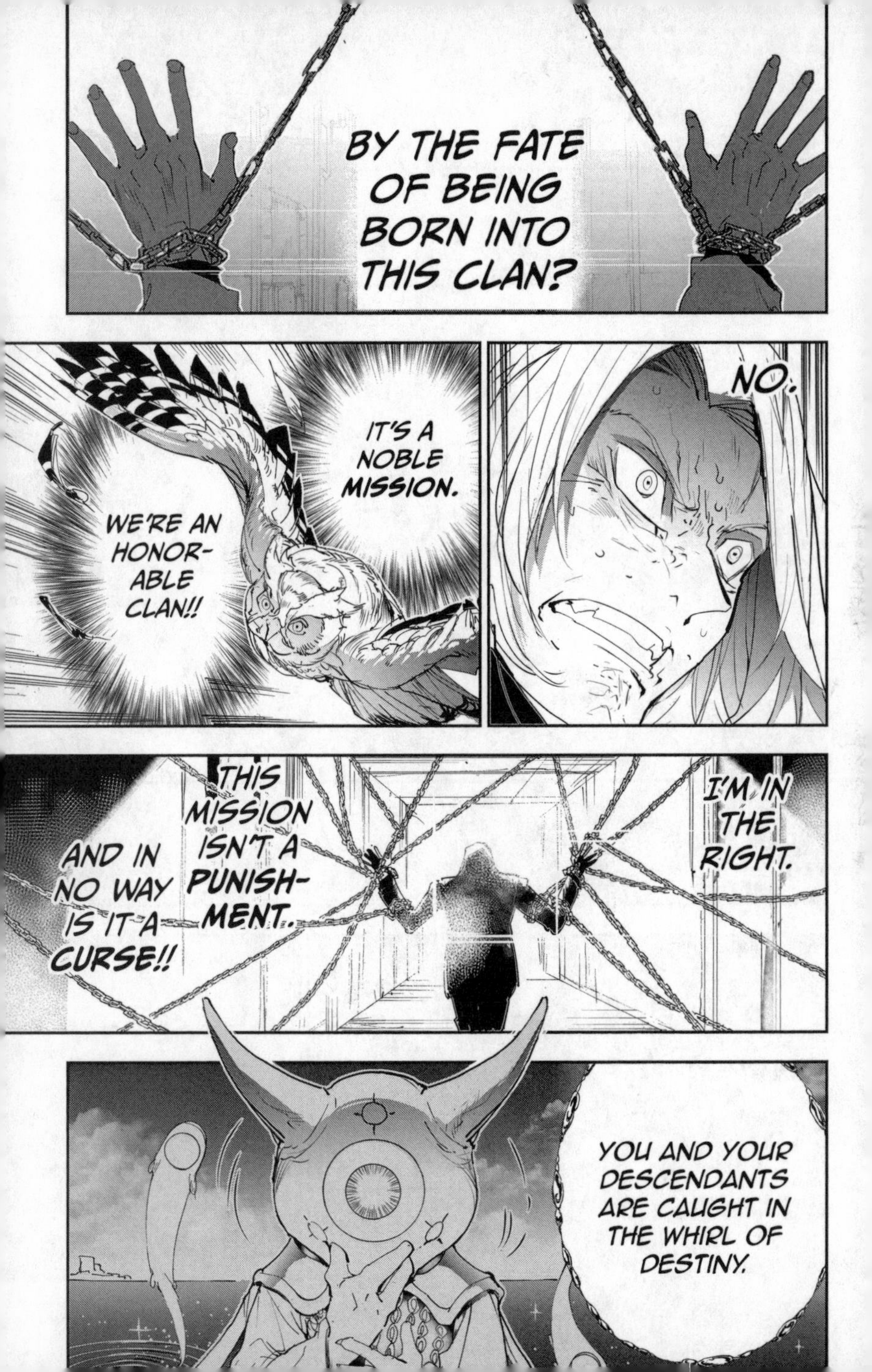
BY THE FATE OF BEING BORN INTO THIS CLAN?
NO.
IT'S A NOBLE MISSION.
WE'RE AN HONOR-ABLE CLAN!!
I'M IN THE RIGHT.
THIS MISSION ISN'T A PUNISH-MENT.
AND IN NO WAY IS IT A CURSE!!
YOU AND YOUR DESCENDANTS ARE CAUGHT IN THE WHIRL OF DESTINY.

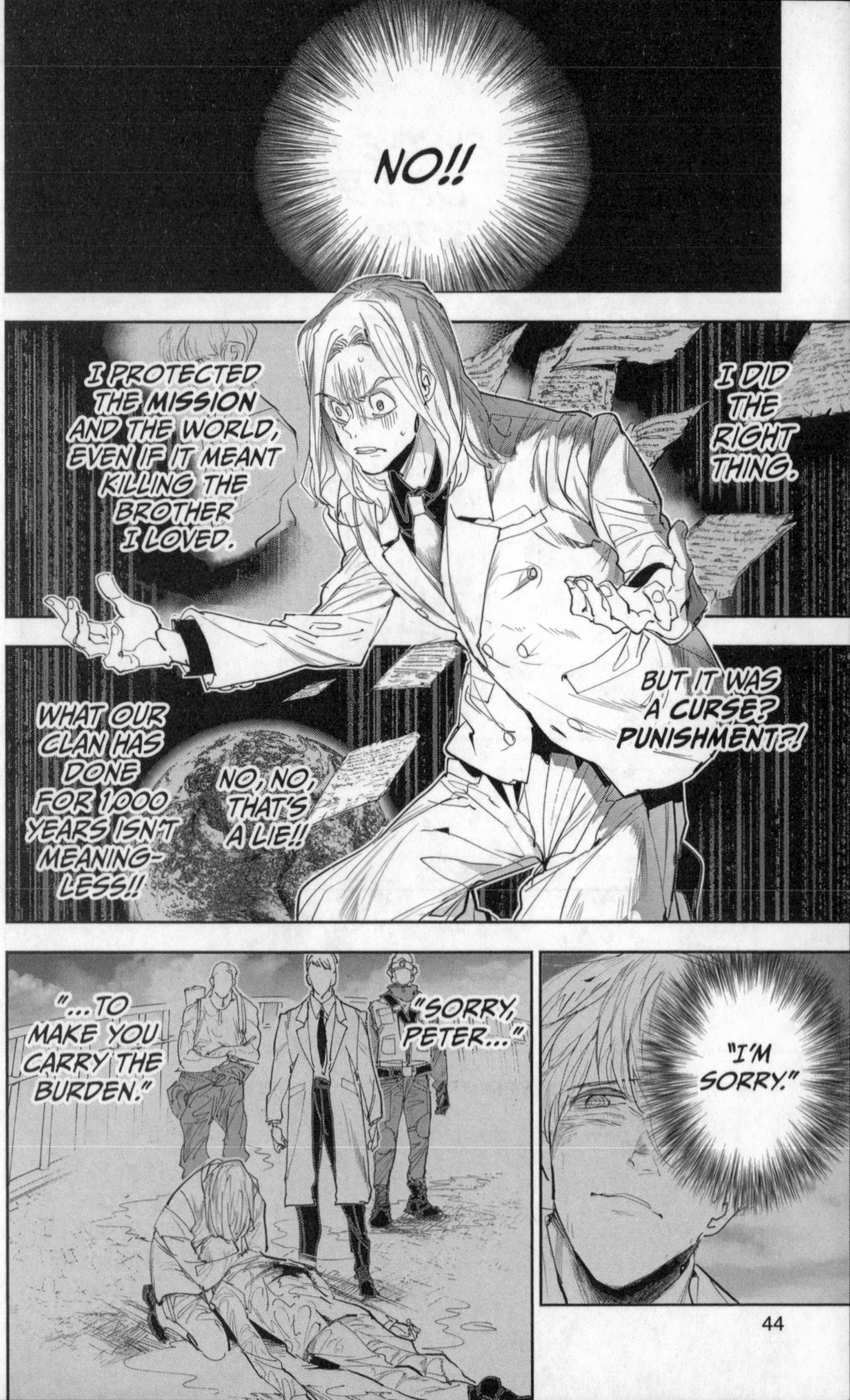

NO!!
I DID THE RIGHT THING.
I PROTECTED THE MISSION AND THE WORLD, EVEN IF IT MEANT KILLING THE BROTHER I LOVED.
BUT IT WAS A CURSE? PUNISHMENT?!
NO, NO, THAT'S A LIE!!
WHAT OUR CLAN HAS DONE FOR 1000 YEARS ISN'T MEANING-LESS!!
"I'M SORRY."
"SORRY, PETER..."
"...TO MAKE YOU CARRY THE BURDEN."

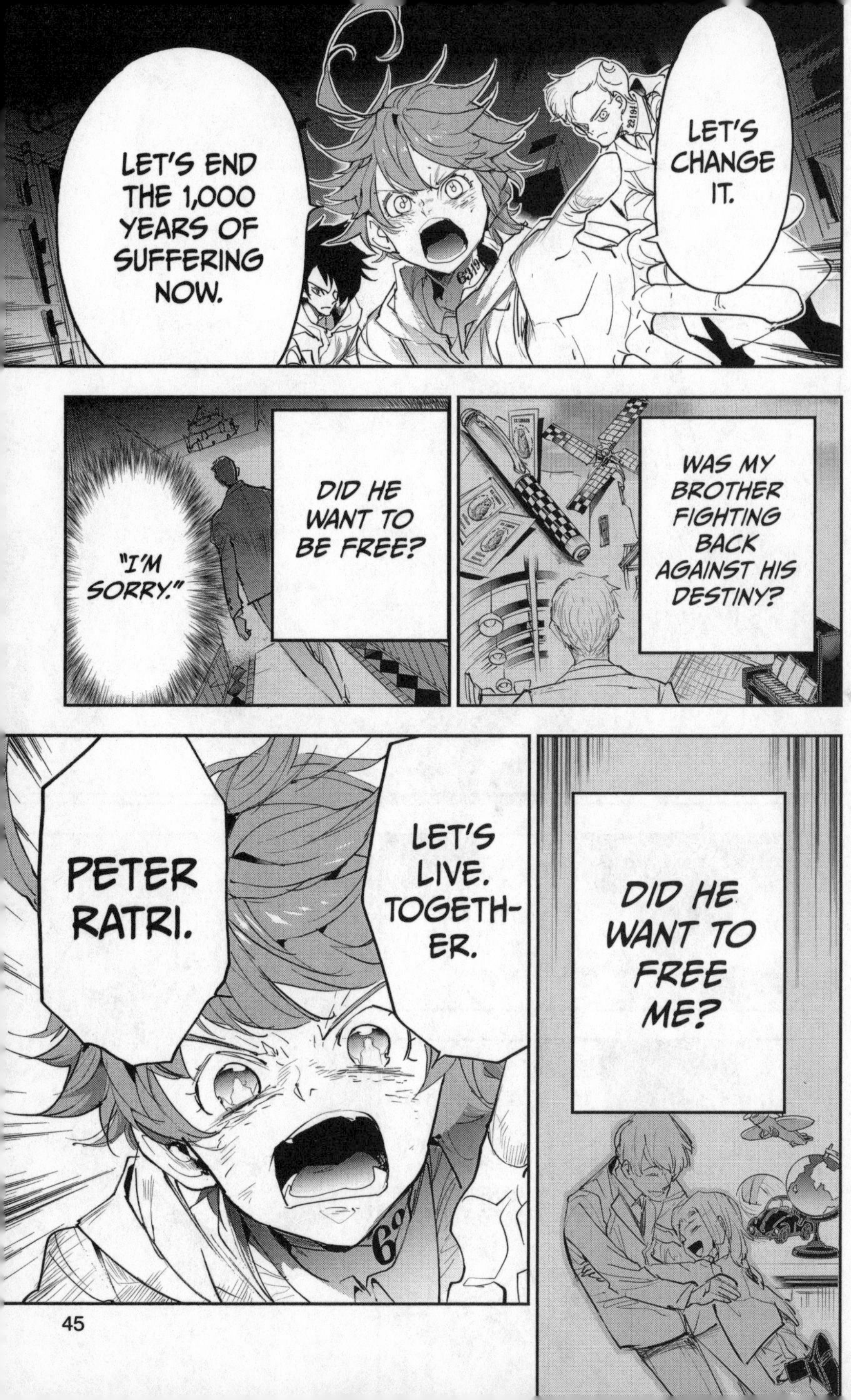
LET'S CHANGE IT.
LET'S END THE 1,000 YEARS OF SUFFERING NOW.
WAS MY BROTHER FIGHTING BACK AGAINST HIS DESTINY?
DID HE WANT TO BE FREE?
"I'M SORRY."
DID HE WANT TO FREE ME?
LET'S LIVE. TOGETH-ER.
PETER RATRI.

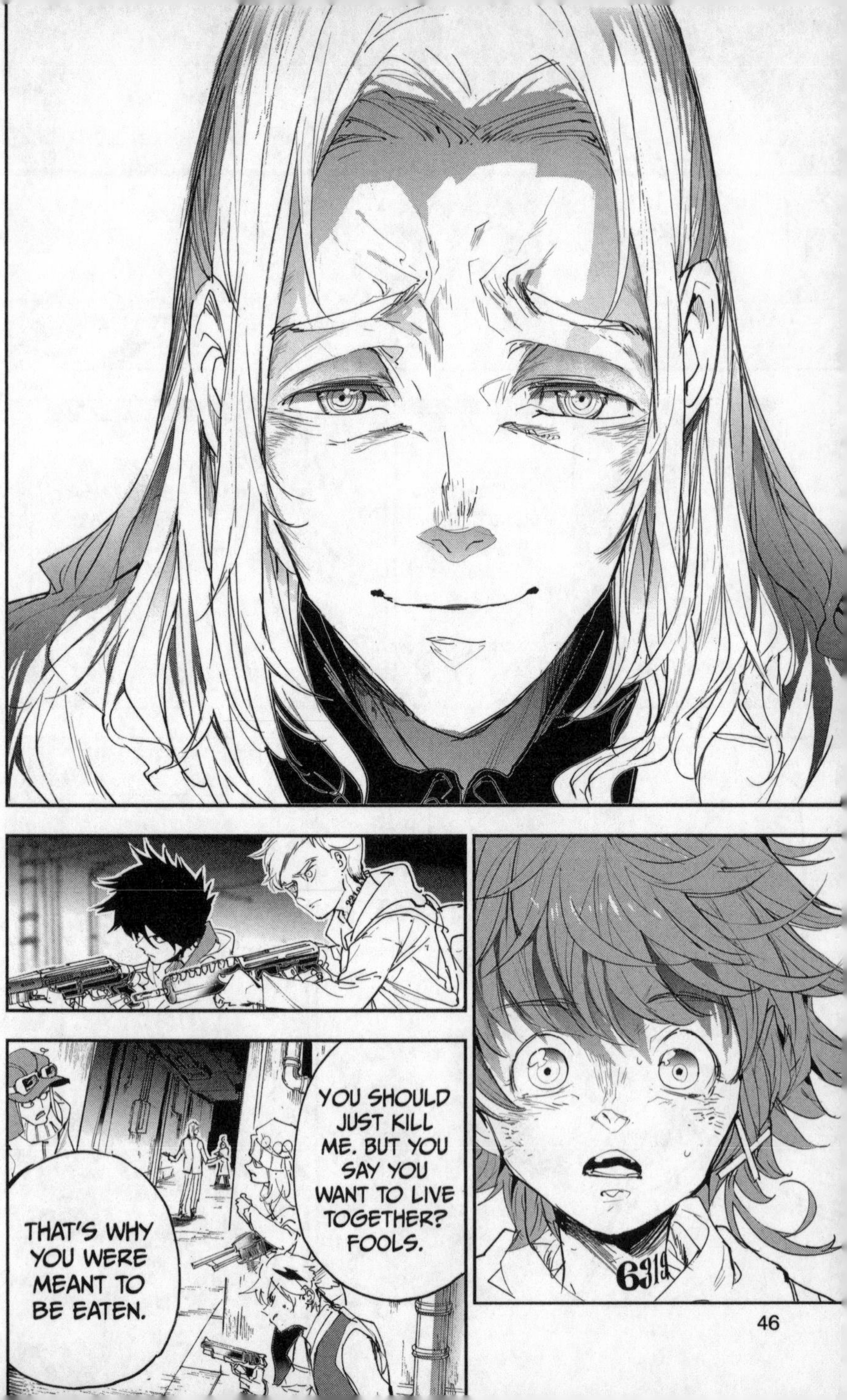
YOU SHOULD JUST KILL ME. BUT YOU SAY YOU WANT TO LIVE TOGETHER? FOOLS.
THAT'S WHY YOU WERE MEANT TO BE EATEN.

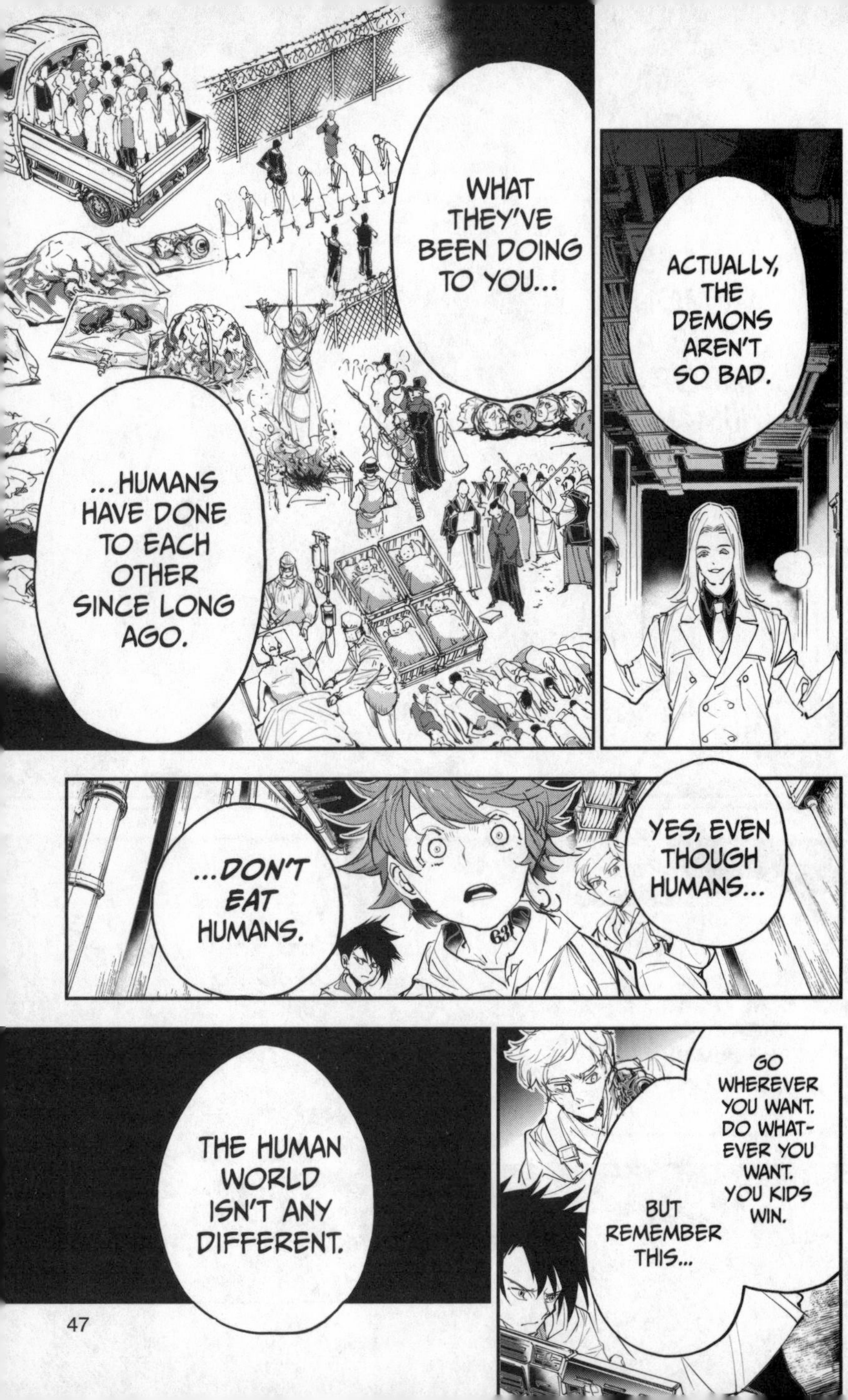
ACTUALLY, THE DEMONS AREN'T SO BAD.
WHAT THEY'VE BEEN DOING TO YOU...
...HUMANS HAVE DONE TO EACH OTHER SINCE LONG AGO.
YES, EVEN THOUGH HUMANS...
...DON'T EAT HUMANS.
GO WHEREVER YOU WANT. DO WHAT-EVER YOU WANT. YOU KIDS WIN.
BUT REMEMBER THIS...
THE HUMAN WORLD ISN'T ANY DIFFERENT.

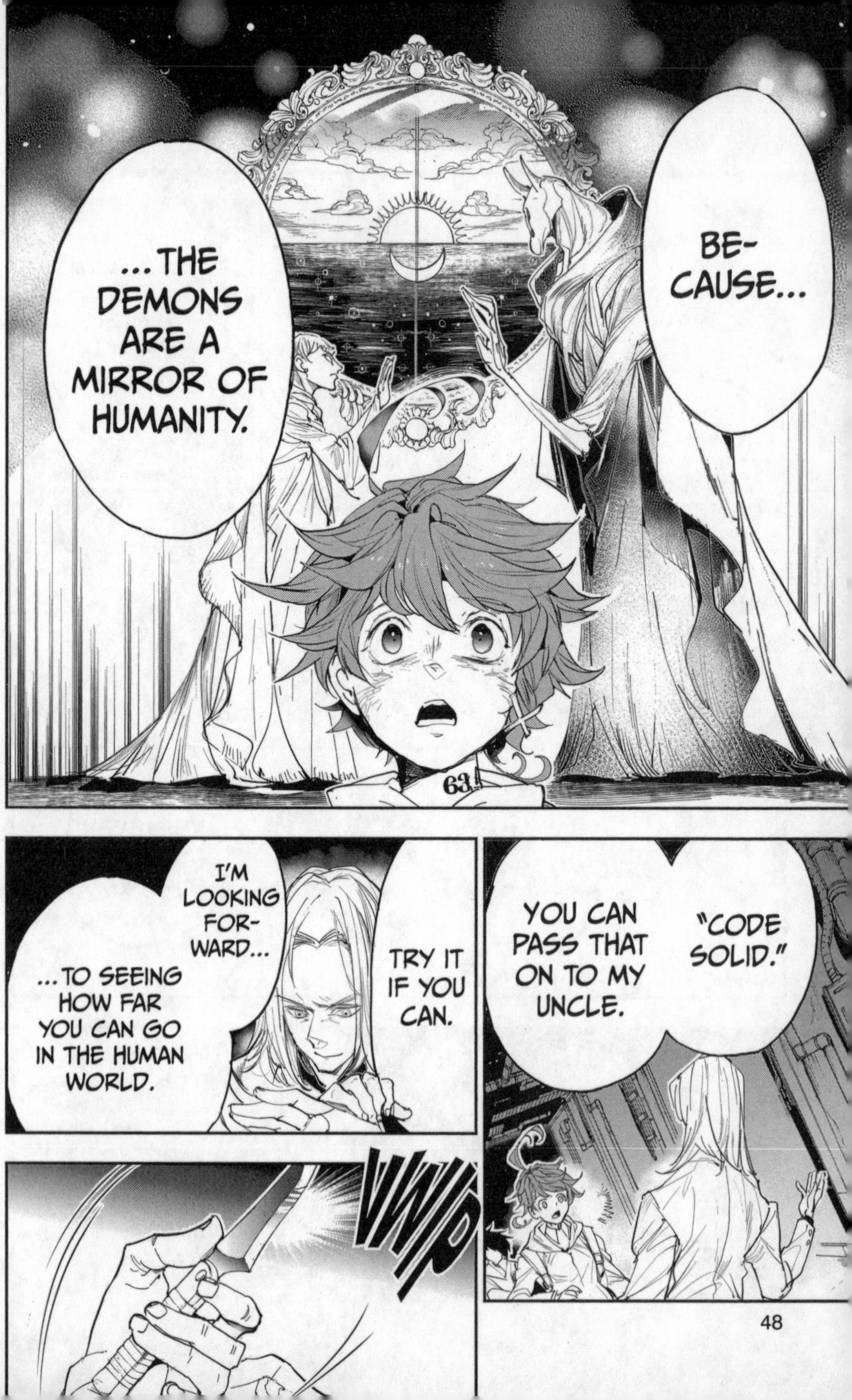
BE-CAUSE...
...THE DEMONS ARE A MIRROR OF HUMANITY.
"CODE SOLID."
YOU CAN PASS THAT ON TO MY UNCLE.
TRY IT IF YOU CAN.
I'M LOOKING FOR-WARD...
...TO SEEING HOW FAR YOU CAN GO IN THE HUMAN WORLD.
VWIP

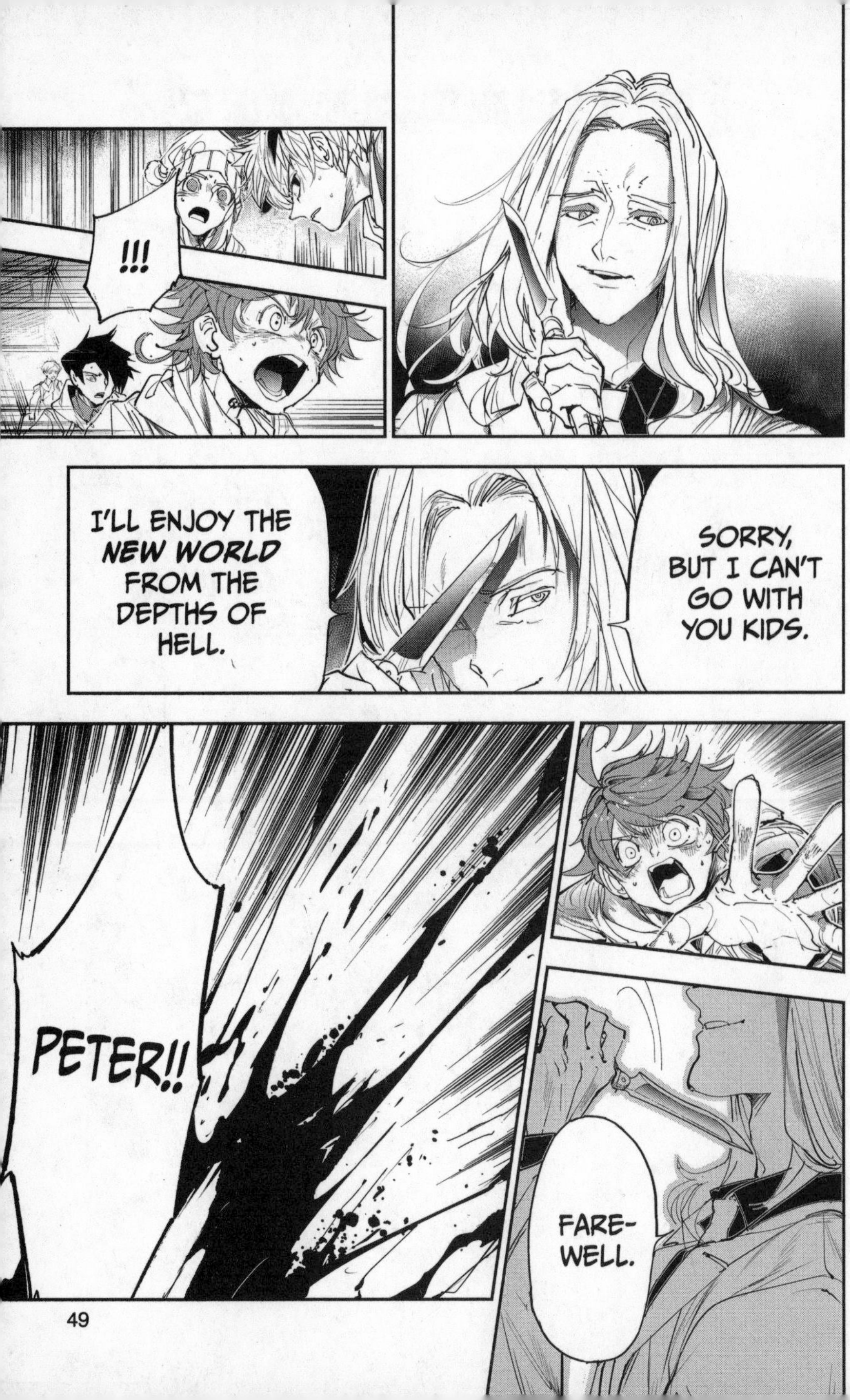
!!!
SORRY, BUT I CAN'T GO WITH YOU KIDS.
I'LL ENJOY THE *NEW WORLD* FROM THE DEPTHS OF HELL.
FARE-WELL.
PETER!!

THE PROMISED NEVERLAND SIDE SCENE 024

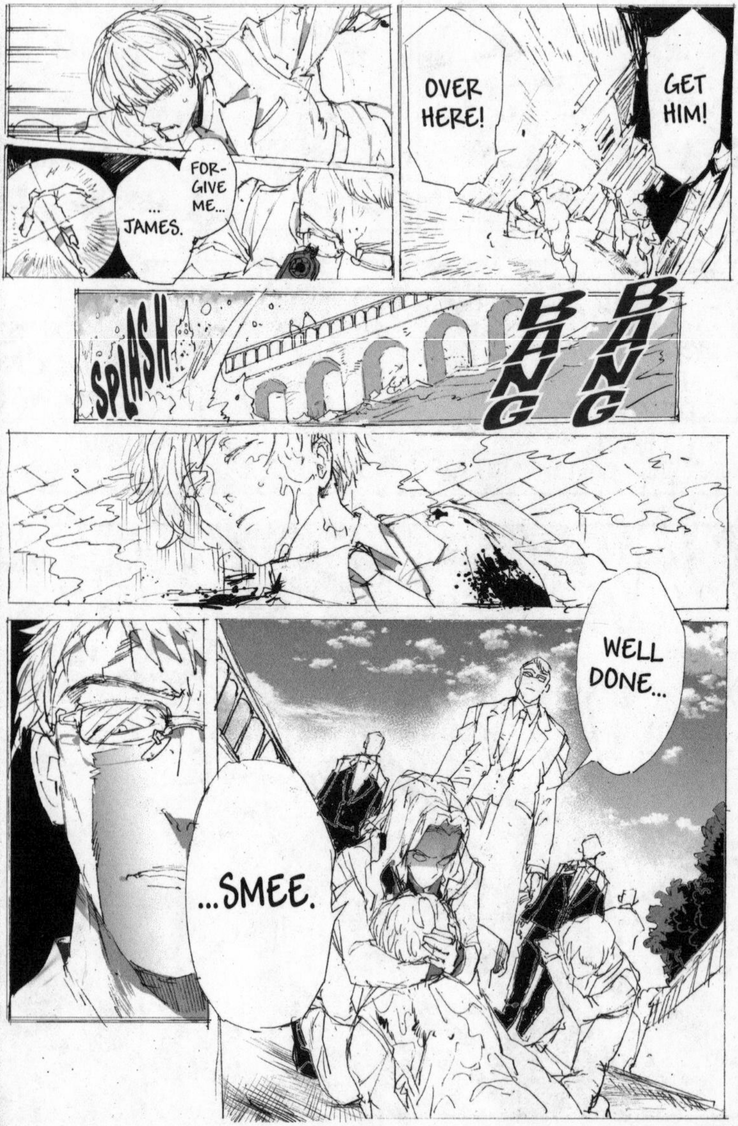
GET HIM!
OVER HERE!
FOR-GIVE ME...
... JAMES.
BANG
BANG
SPLASH
WELL DONE...
...SMEE.

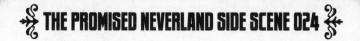

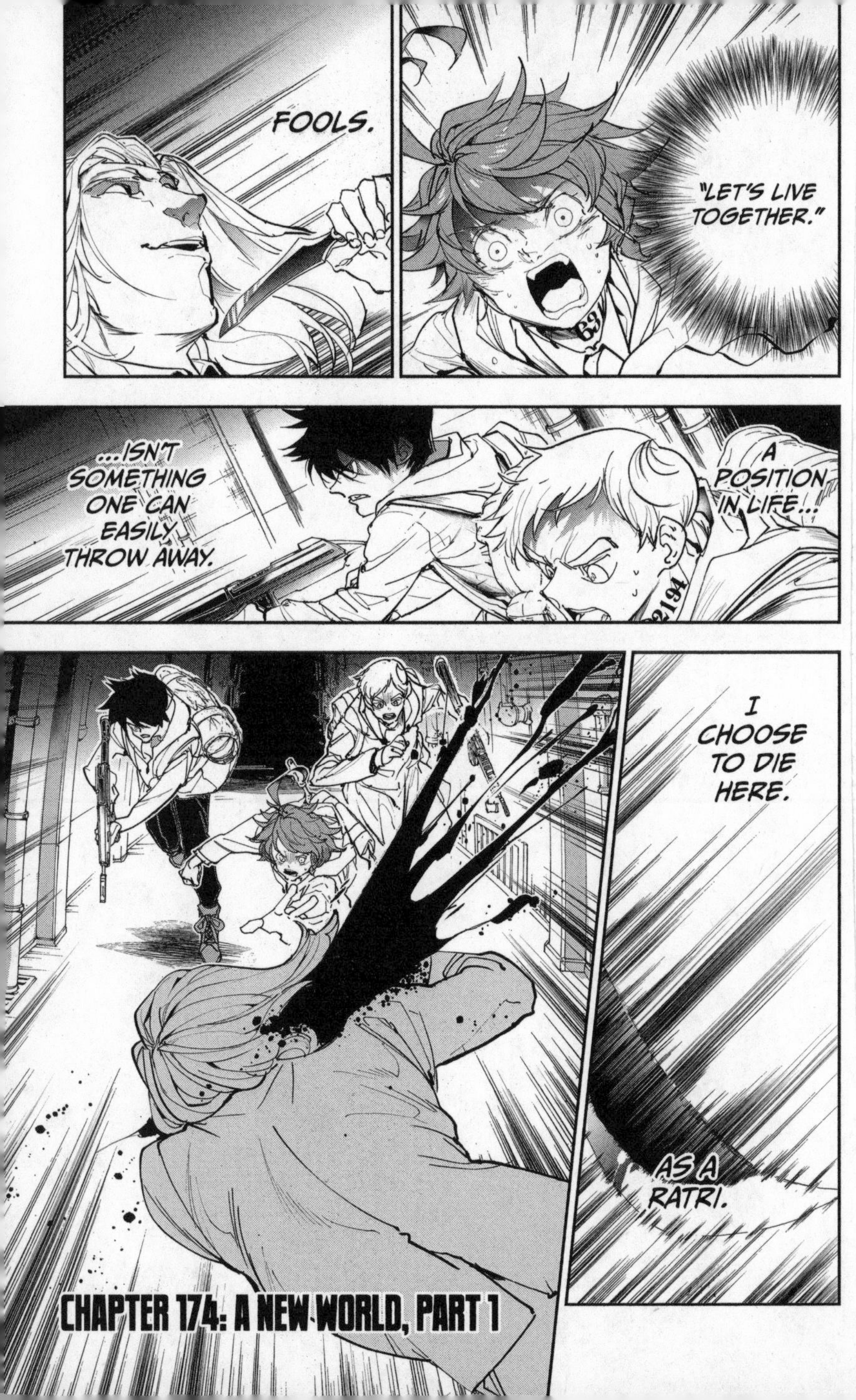
"LET'S LIVE TOGETHER."
FOOLS.
A POSITION IN LIFE...
...ISN'T SOMETHING ONE CAN EASILY THROW AWAY.
I CHOOSE TO DIE HERE.
AS A RATRI.
CHAPTER 174: A NEW WORLD, PART 1

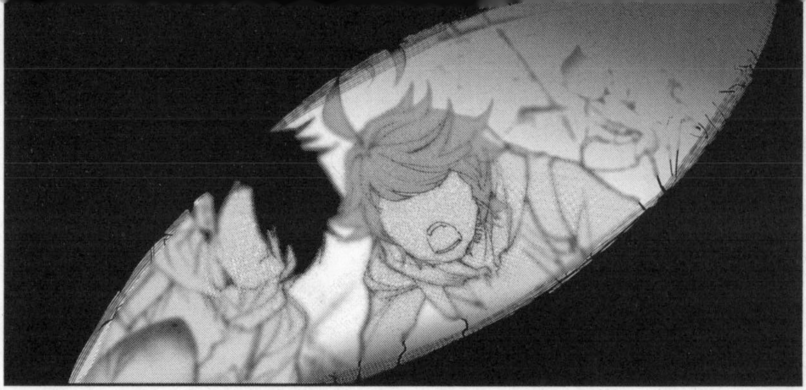

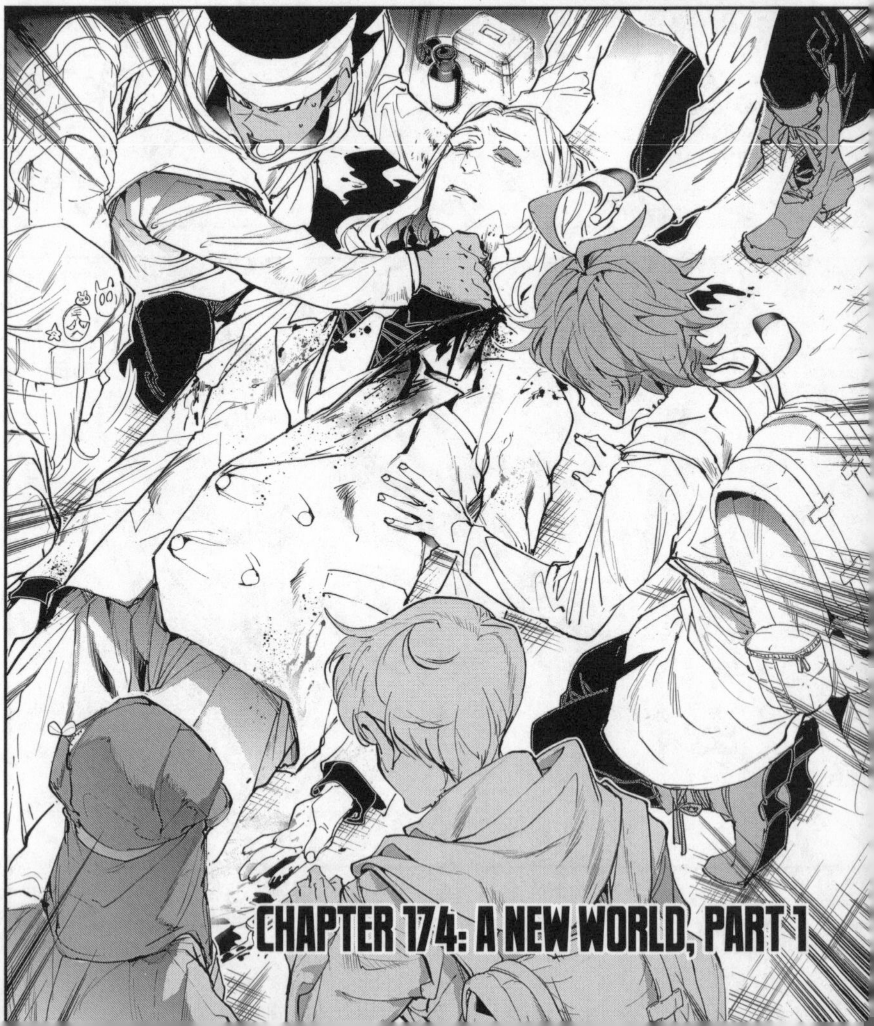
CHAPTER 174: A NEW WORLD, PART 1

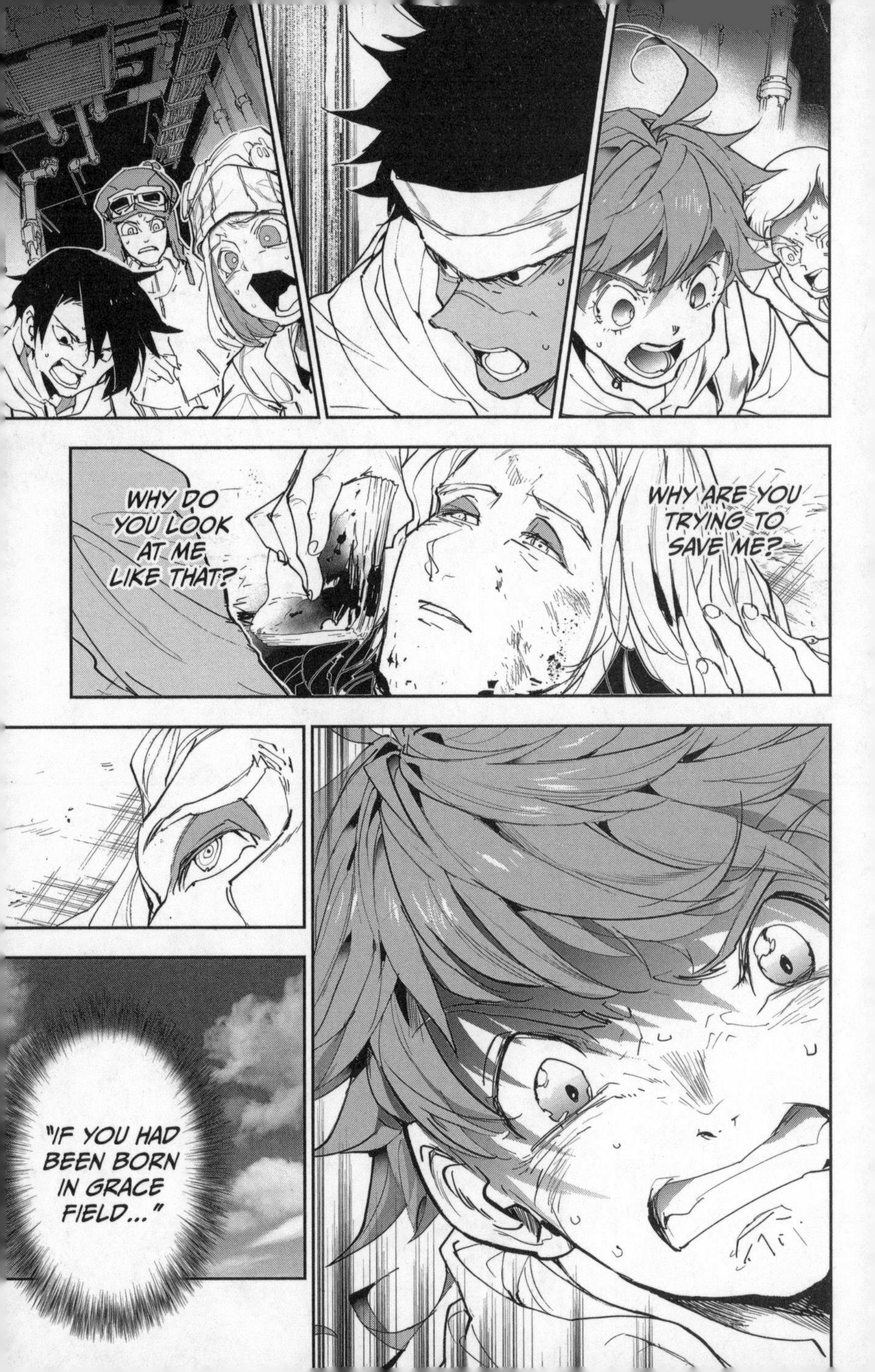
WHY ARE YOU TRYING TO SAVE ME?
WHY DO YOU LOOK AT ME LIKE THAT?
"IF YOU HAD BEEN BORN IN GRACE FIELD..."

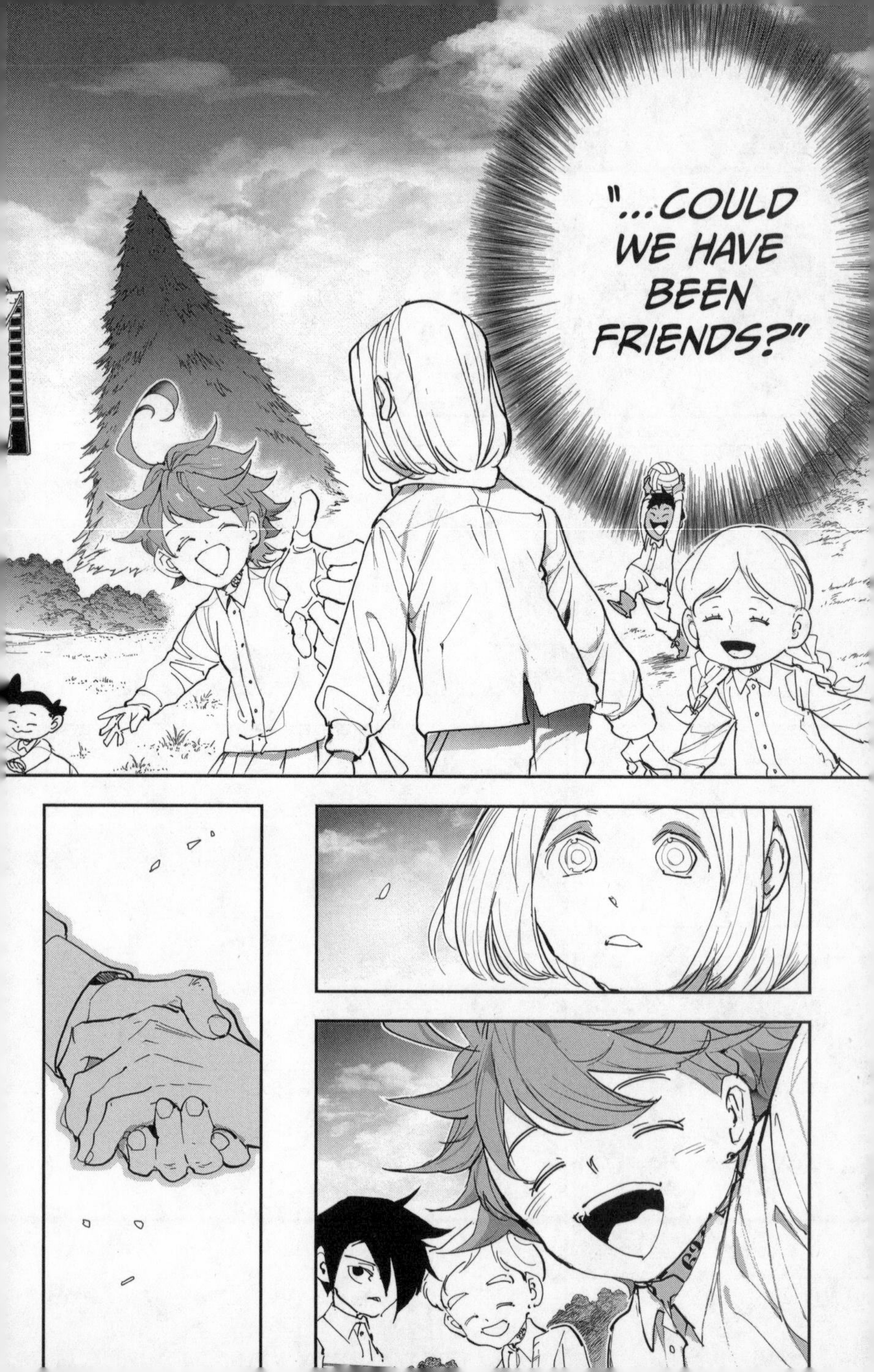
"...COULD WE HAVE BEEN FRIENDS?"

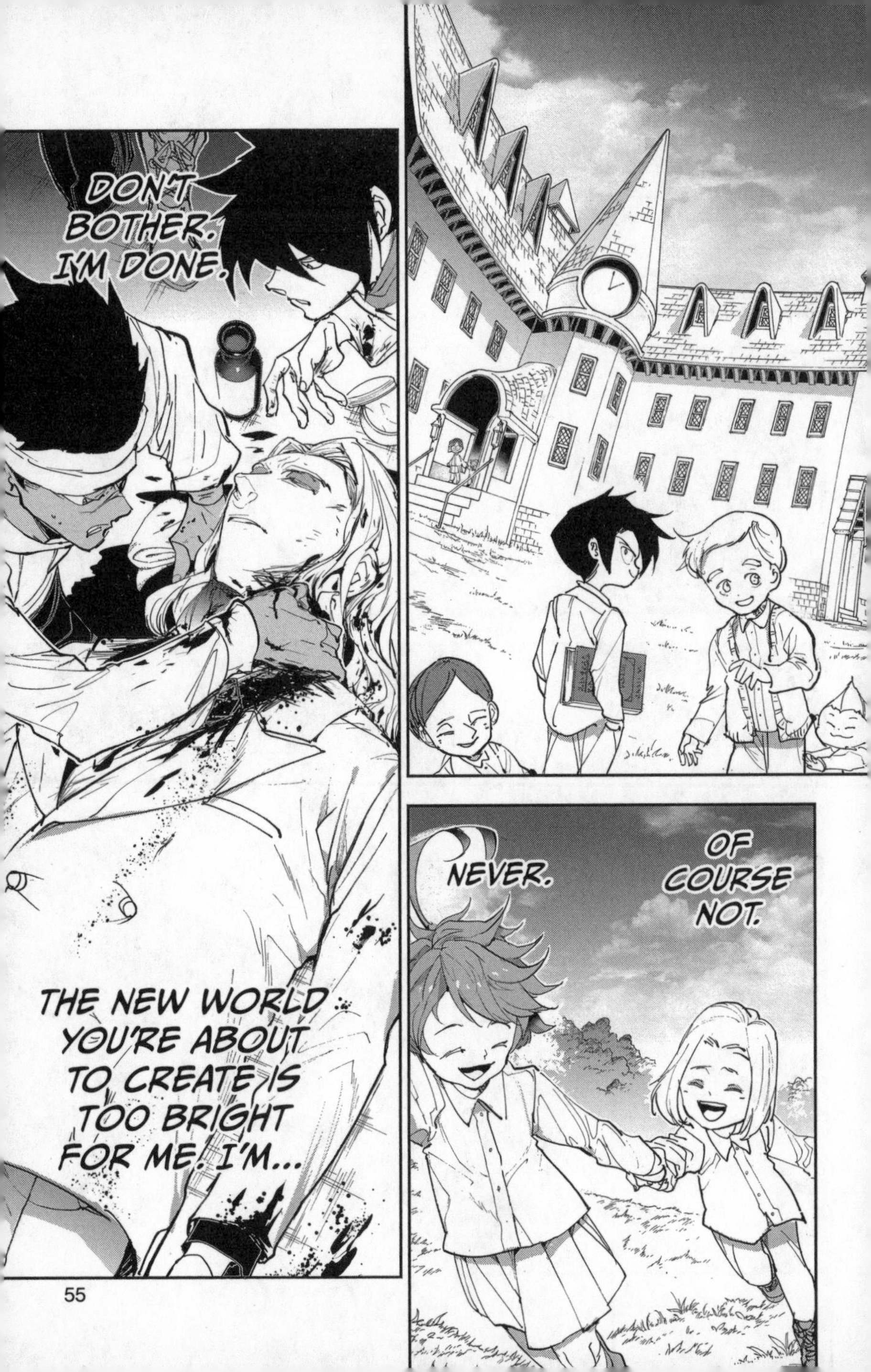
OF COURSE NOT.
NEVER.
DON'T BOTHER. I'M DONE.
THE NEW WORLD YOU'RE ABOUT TO CREATE IS TOO BRIGHT FOR ME. I'M...

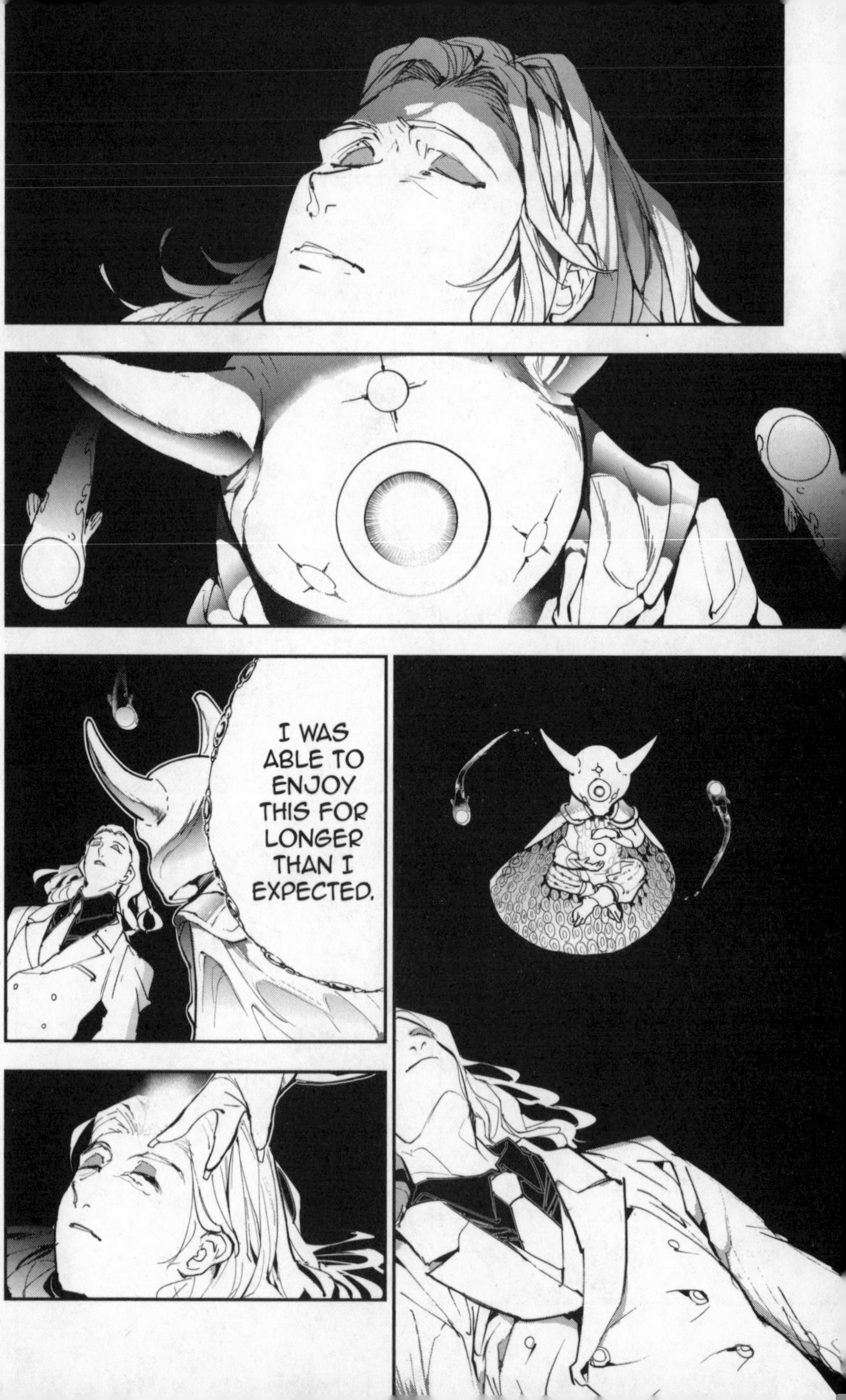
I WAS ABLE TO ENJOY THIS FOR LONGER THAN I EXPECTED.

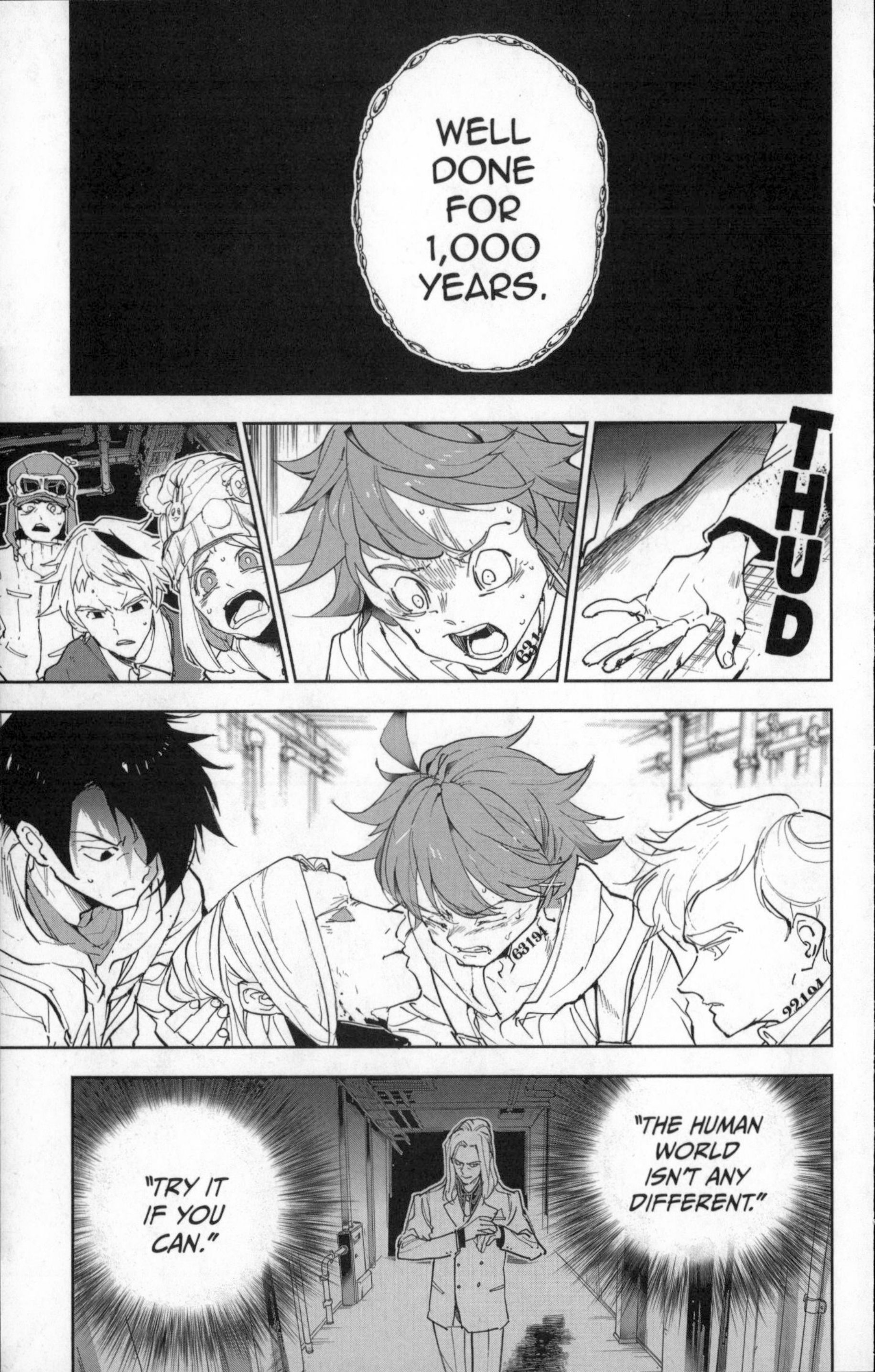
WELL DONE FOR 1,000 YEARS.
THUD
"THE HUMAN WORLD ISN'T ANY DIFFERENT."
"TRY IT IF YOU CAN."

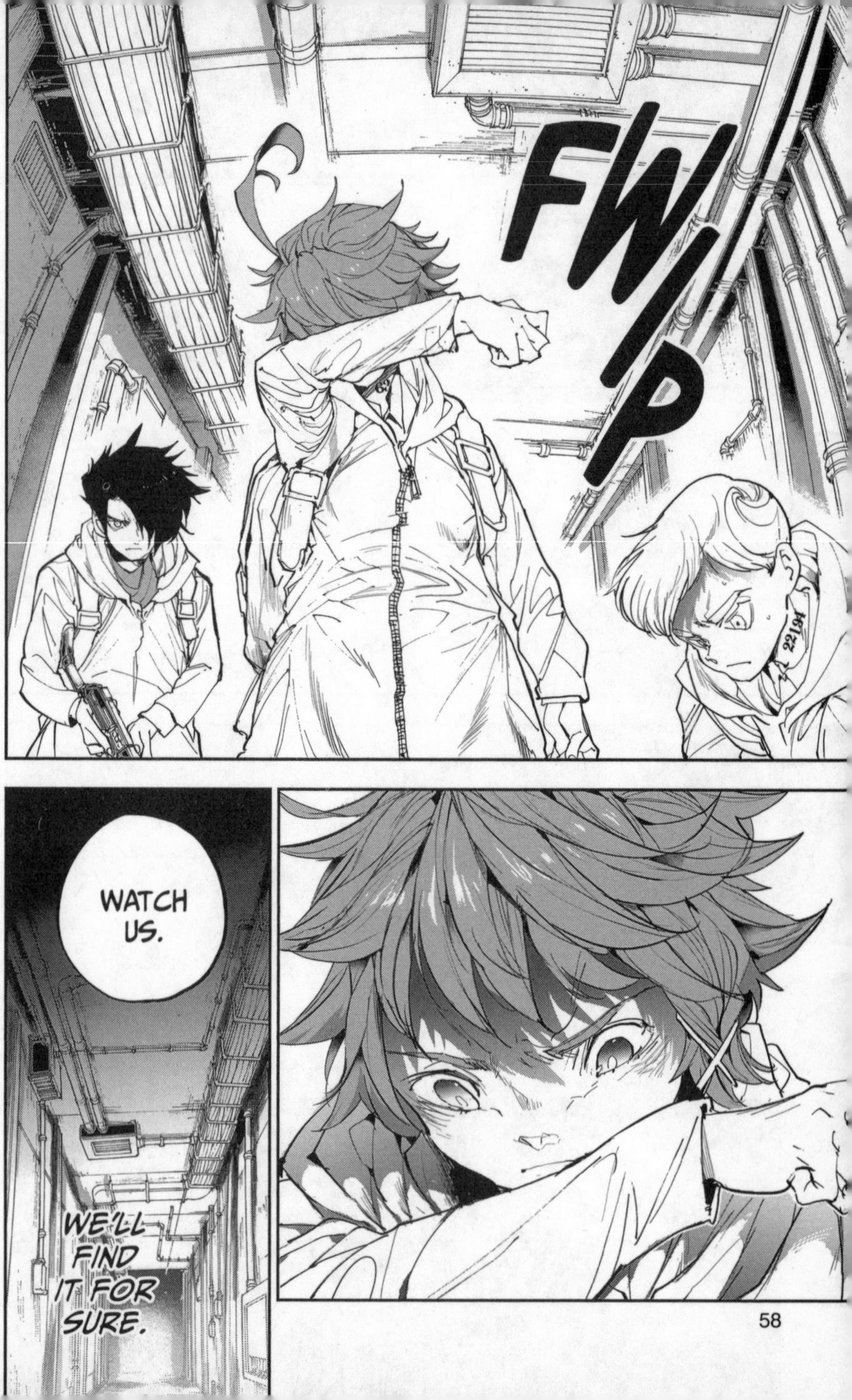
FWIP
WATCH US.
WE'LL FIND IT FOR SURE.

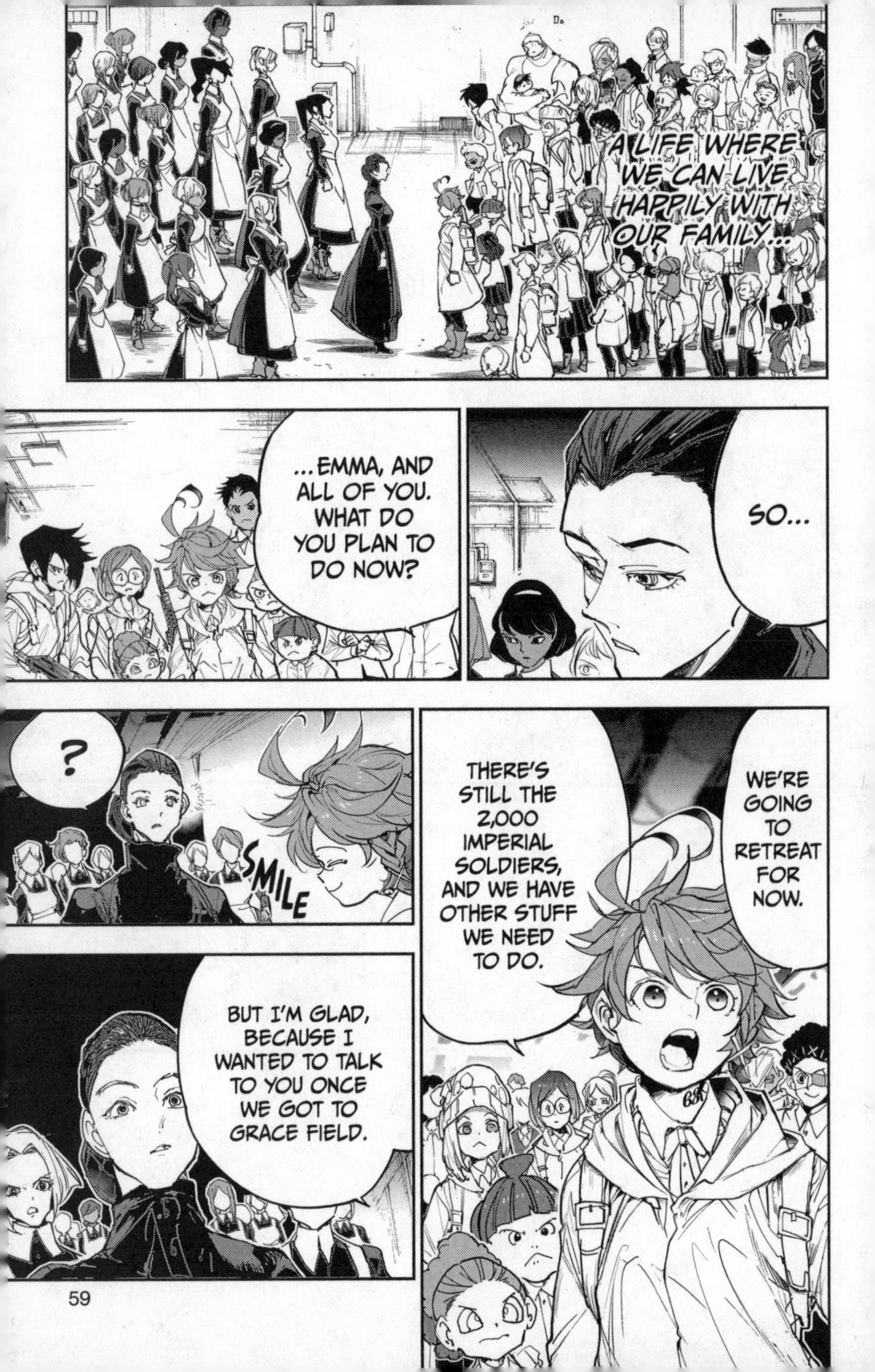

A LIFE WHERE WE CAN LIVE HAPPILY WITH OUR FAMILY...
SO...
...EMMA, AND ALL OF YOU. WHAT DO YOU PLAN TO DO NOW?
WE'RE GOING TO RETREAT FOR NOW.
THERE'S STILL THE 2,000 IMPERIAL SOLDIERS, AND WE HAVE OTHER STUFF WE NEED TO DO.
?
SMILE
BUT I'M GLAD, BECAUSE I WANTED TO TALK TO YOU ONCE WE GOT TO GRACE FIELD.

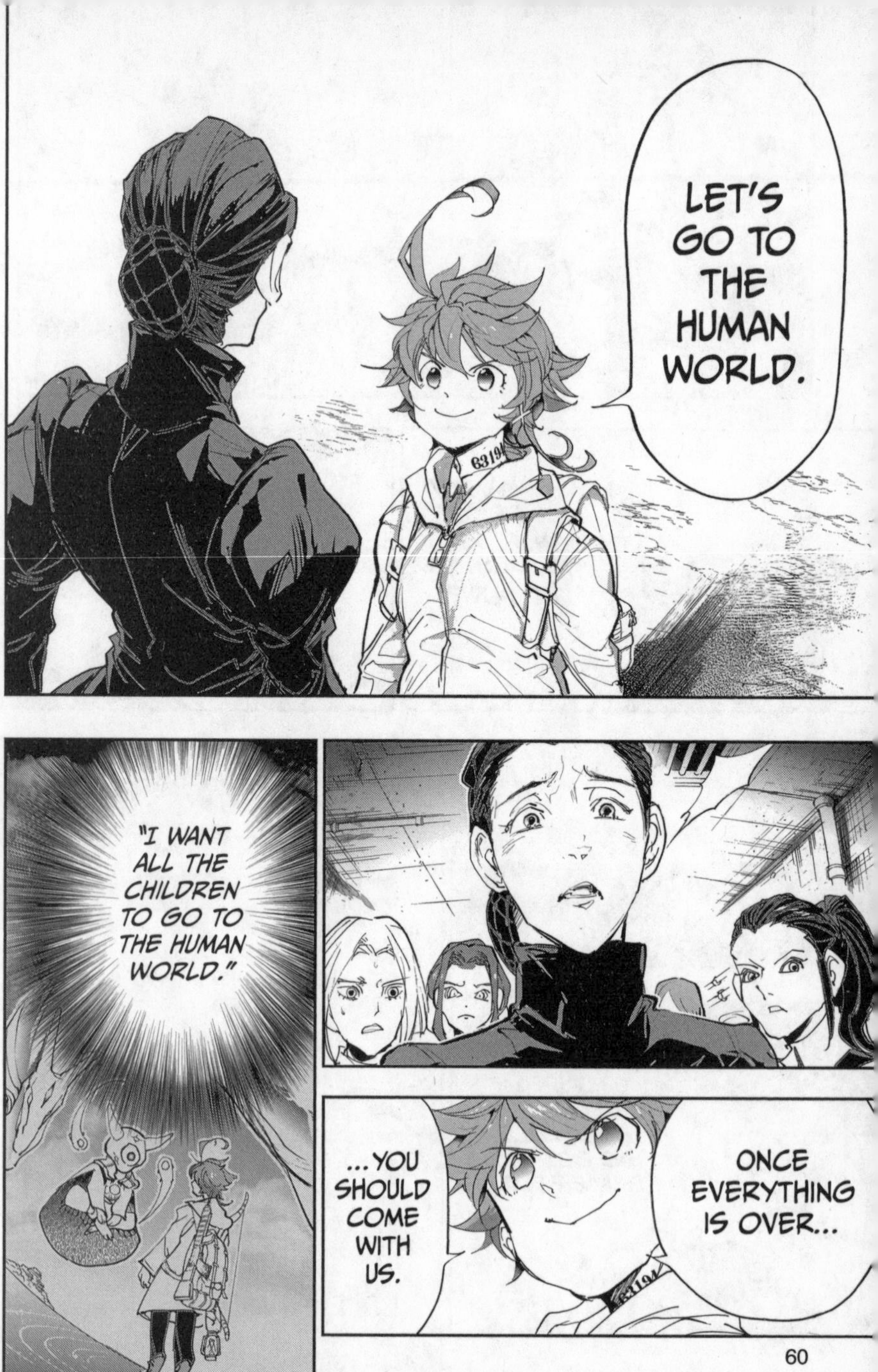
LET'S GO TO THE HUMAN WORLD.
ONCE EVERYTHING IS OVER...
...YOU SHOULD COME WITH US.
"I WANT ALL THE CHILDREN TO GO TO THE HUMAN WORLD."

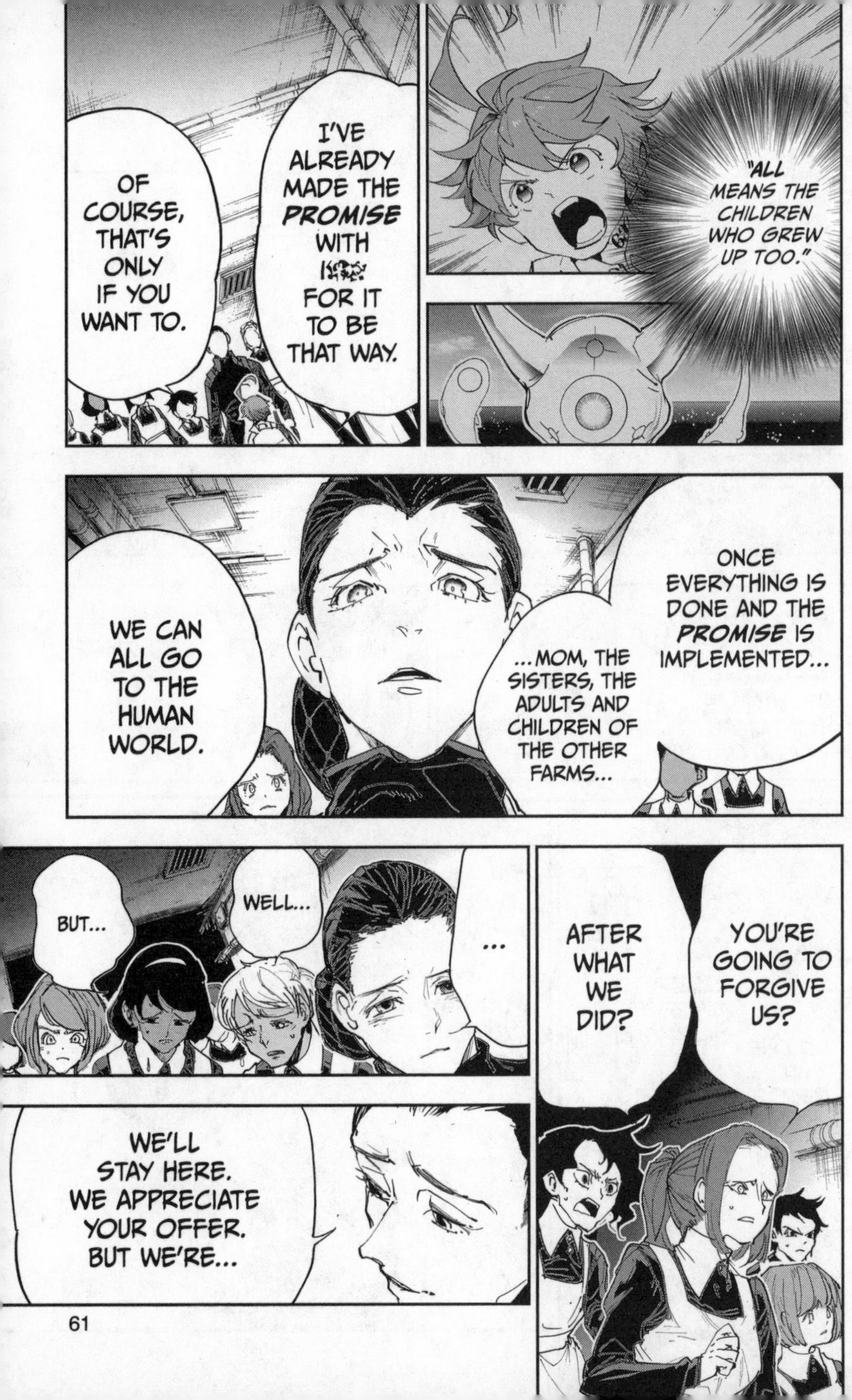
"ALL MEANS THE CHILDREN WHO GREW UP TOO."
I'VE ALREADY MADE THE PROMISE WITH FOR IT TO BE THAT WAY.
OF COURSE, THAT'S ONLY IF YOU WANT TO.
ONCE EVERYTHING IS DONE AND THE PROMISE IS IMPLEMENTED...
...MOM, THE SISTERS, THE ADULTS AND CHILDREN OF THE OTHER FARMS...
WE CAN ALL GO TO THE HUMAN WORLD.
YOU'RE GOING TO FORGIVE US?
AFTER WHAT WE DID?
...
WELL...
BUT...
WE'LL STAY HERE. WE APPRECIATE YOUR OFFER. BUT WE'RE...

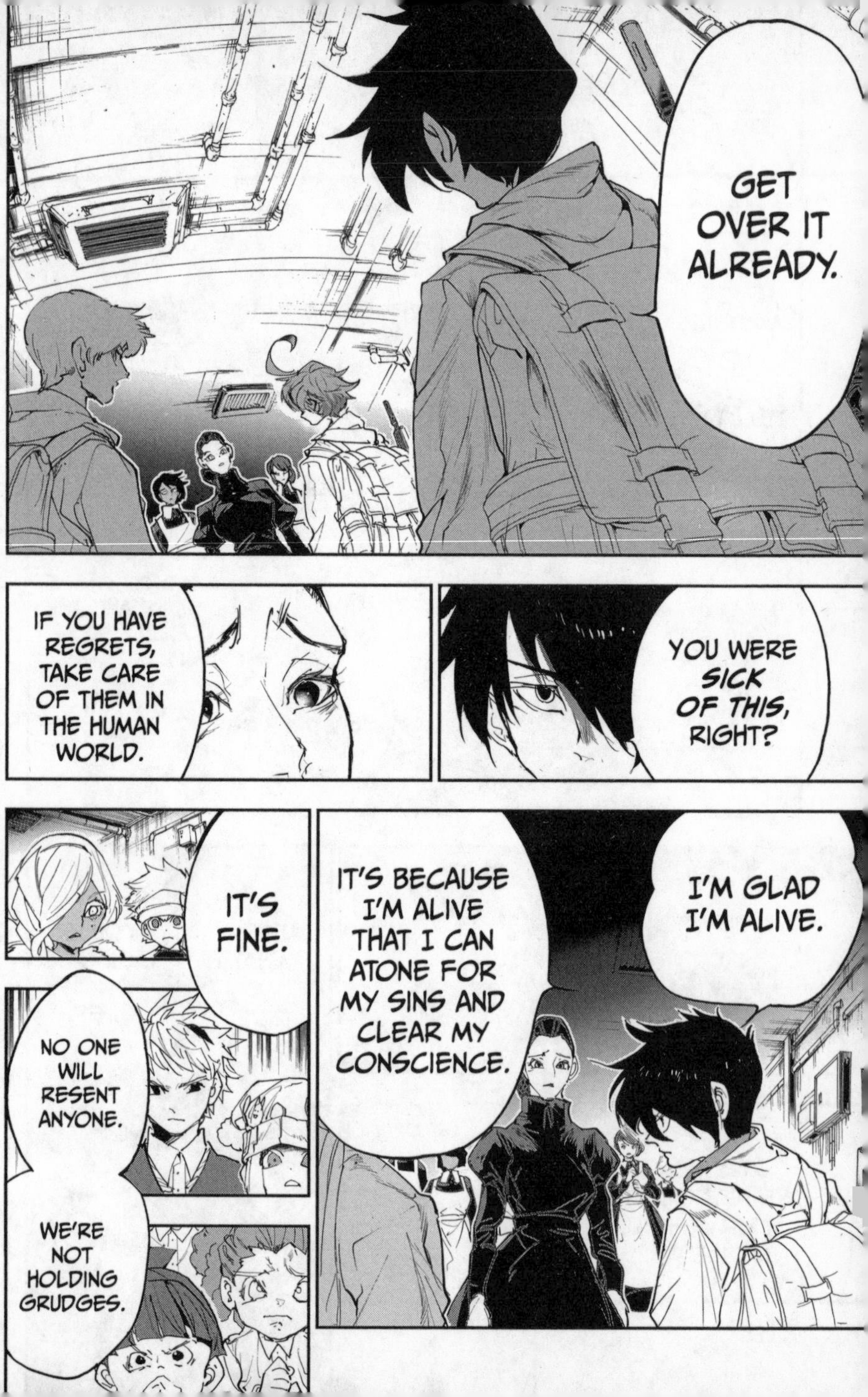
GET OVER IT ALREADY.
YOU WERE SICK OF THIS, RIGHT?
IF YOU HAVE REGRETS, TAKE CARE OF THEM IN THE HUMAN WORLD.
I'M GLAD I'M ALIVE.
IT'S BECAUSE I'M ALIVE THAT I CAN ATONE FOR MY SINS AND CLEAR MY CONSCIENCE.
IT'S FINE.
NO ONE WILL RESENT ANYONE.
WE'RE NOT HOLDING GRUDGES.

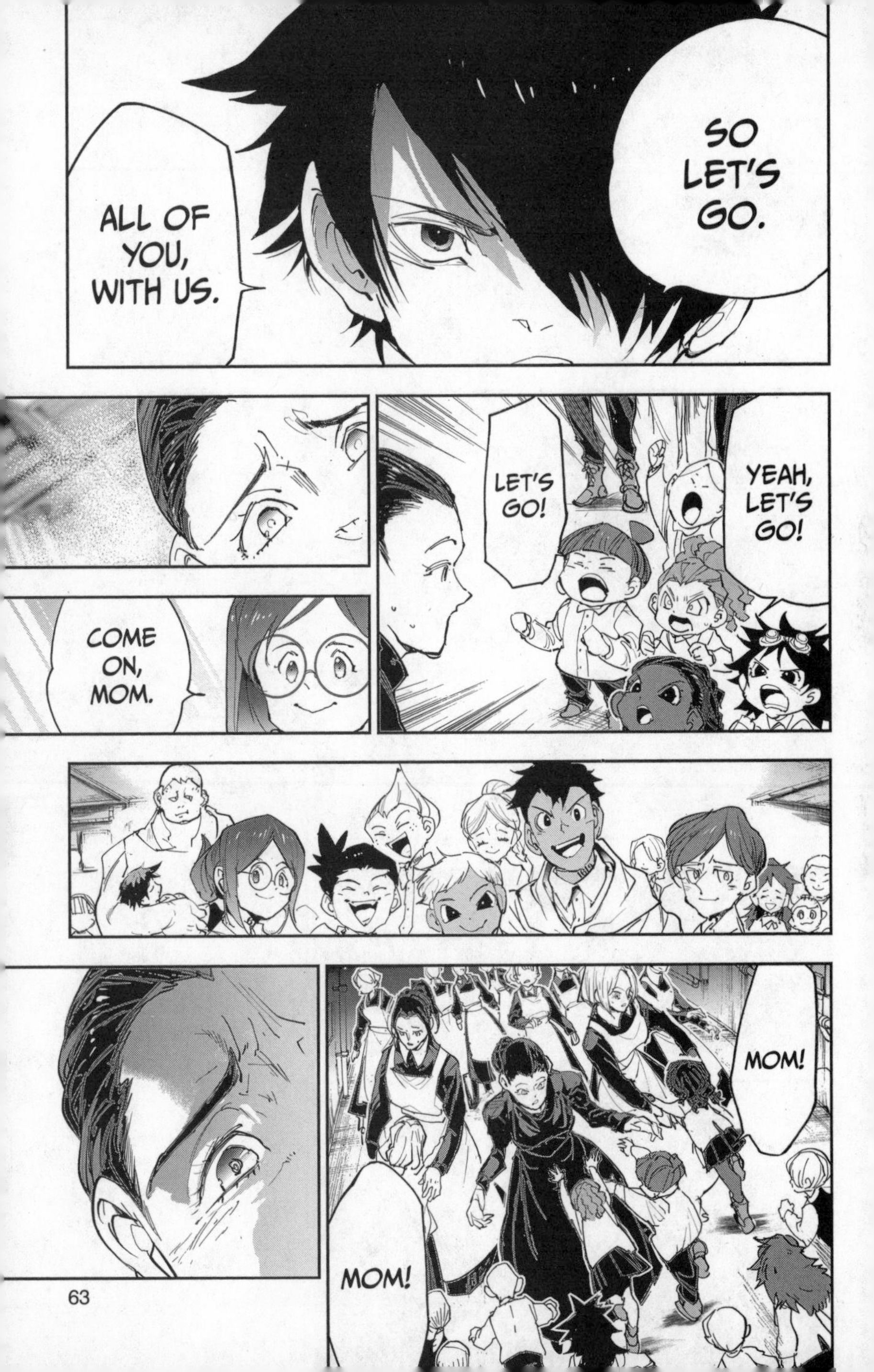
SO LET'S GO.
ALL OF YOU, WITH US.
YEAH, LET'S GO!
LET'S GO!
COME ON, MOM.
MOM!
MOM!

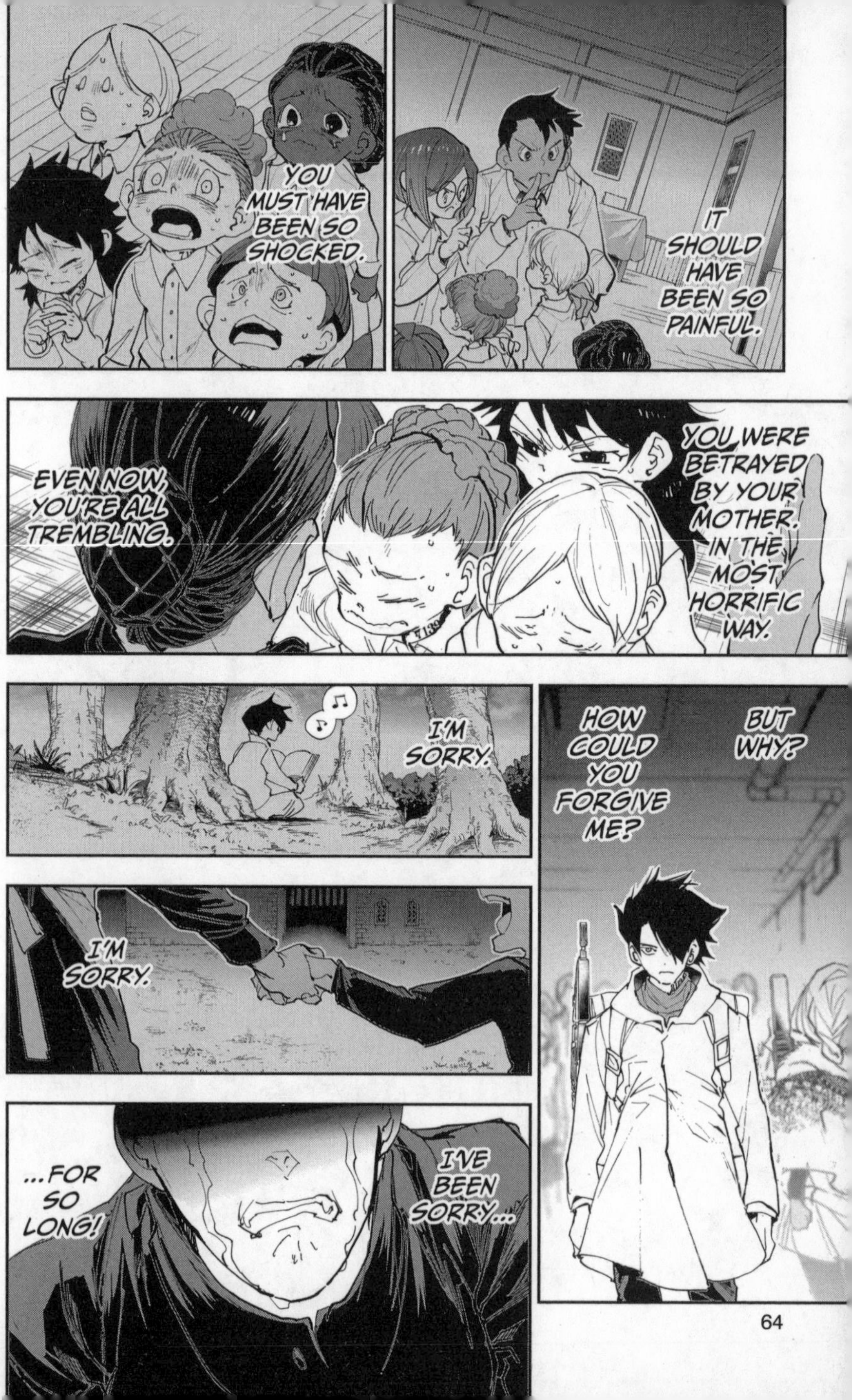
IT SHOULD HAVE BEEN SO PAINFUL.
YOU MUST HAVE BEEN SO SHOCKED.
YOU WERE BETRAYED BY YOUR MOTHER. IN THE MOST HORRIFIC WAY.
EVEN NOW, YOU'RE ALL TREMBLING.
BUT WHY?
HOW COULD YOU FORGIVE ME?
I'M SORRY.
I'M SORRY.
I'VE BEEN SORRY...
...FOR SO LONG!

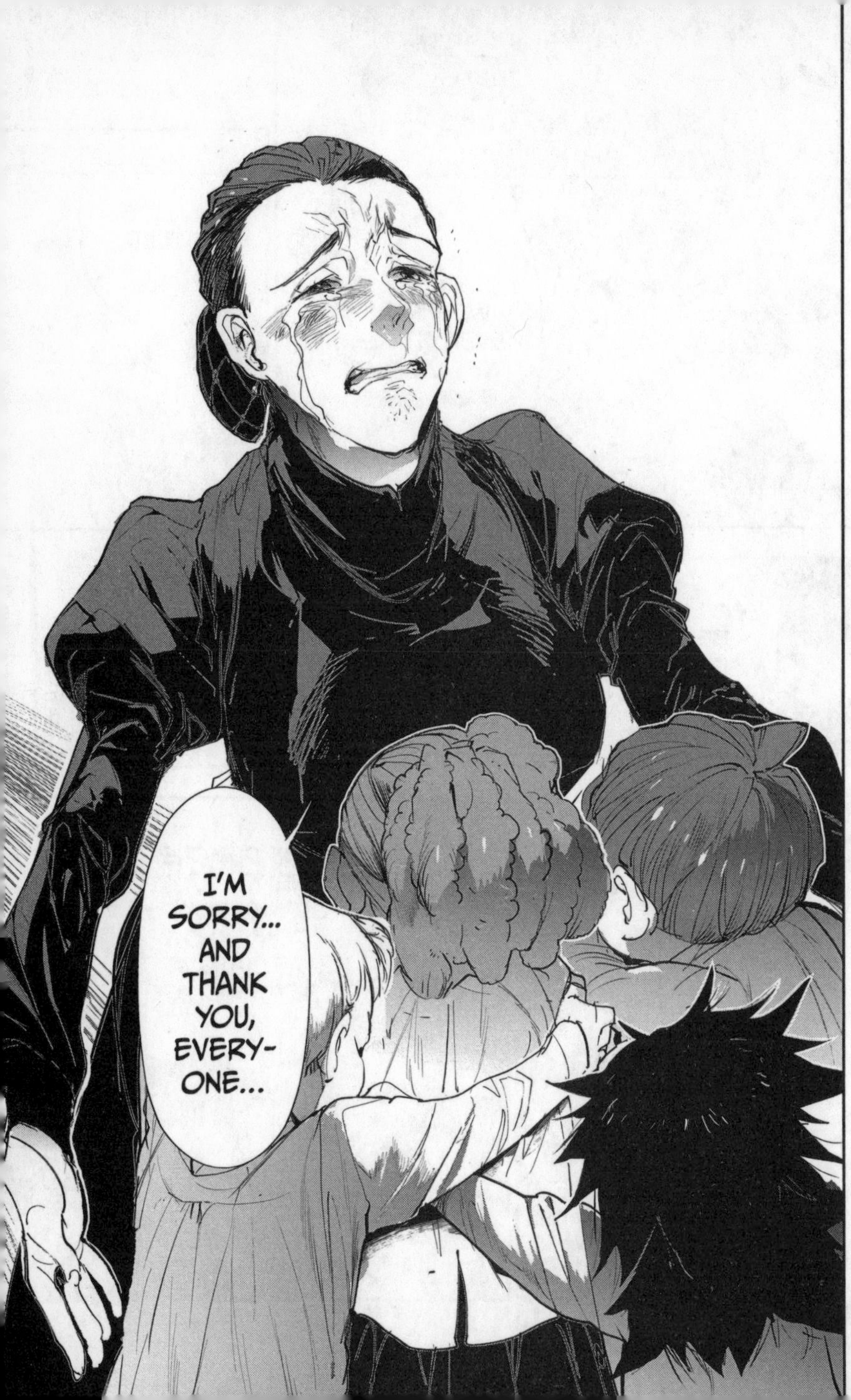
I'M SORRY... AND THANK YOU, EVERY-ONE...

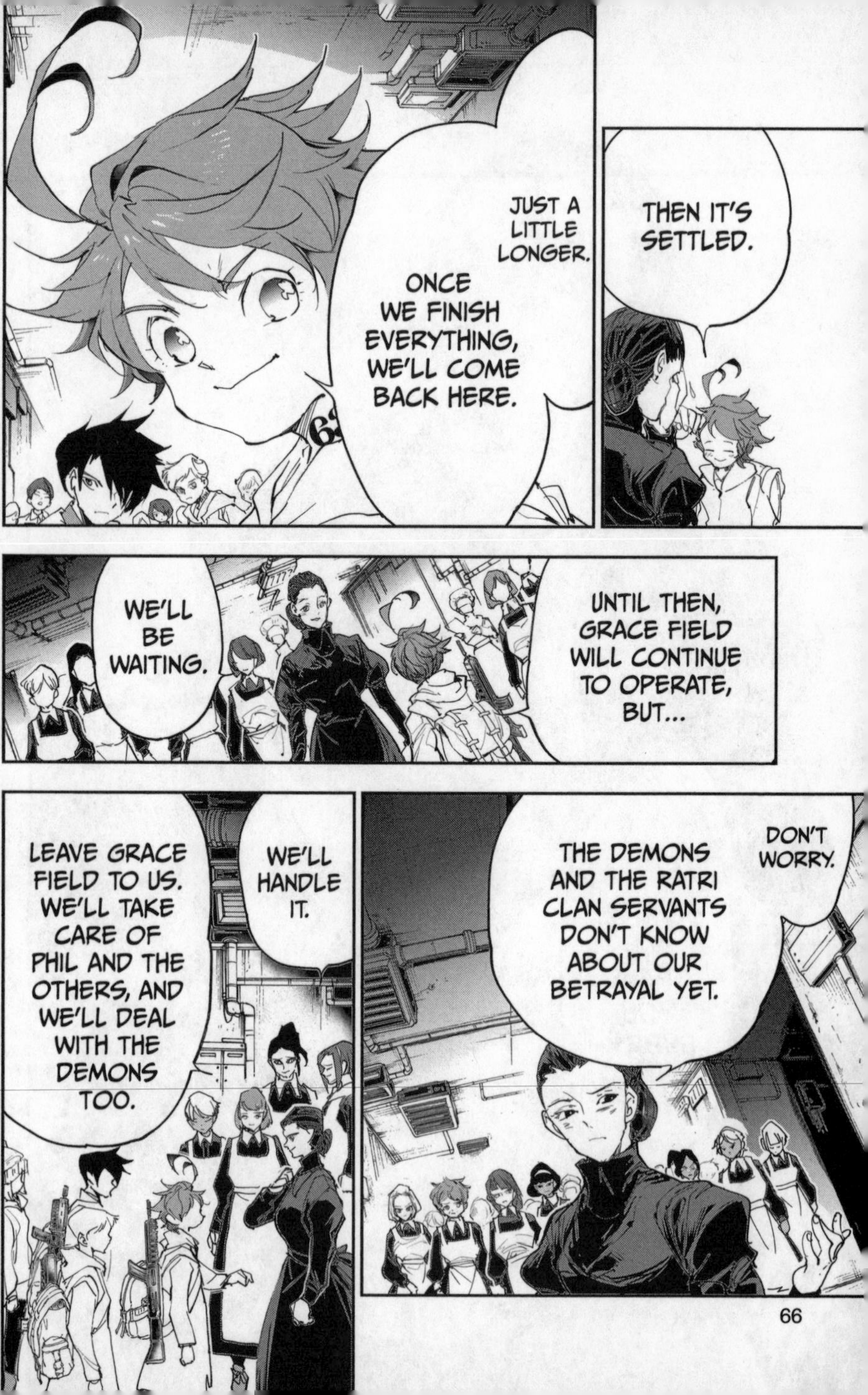
THEN IT'S SETTLED.
JUST A LITTLE LONGER.
ONCE WE FINISH EVERYTHING, WE'LL COME BACK HERE.
UNTIL THEN, GRACE FIELD WILL CONTINUE TO OPERATE, BUT...
WE'LL BE WAITING.
DON'T WORRY.
THE DEMONS AND THE RATRI CLAN SERVANTS DON'T KNOW ABOUT OUR BETRAYAL YET.
WE'LL HANDLE IT.
LEAVE GRACE FIELD TO US. WE'LL TAKE CARE OF PHIL AND THE OTHERS, AND WE'LL DEAL WITH THE DEMONS TOO.

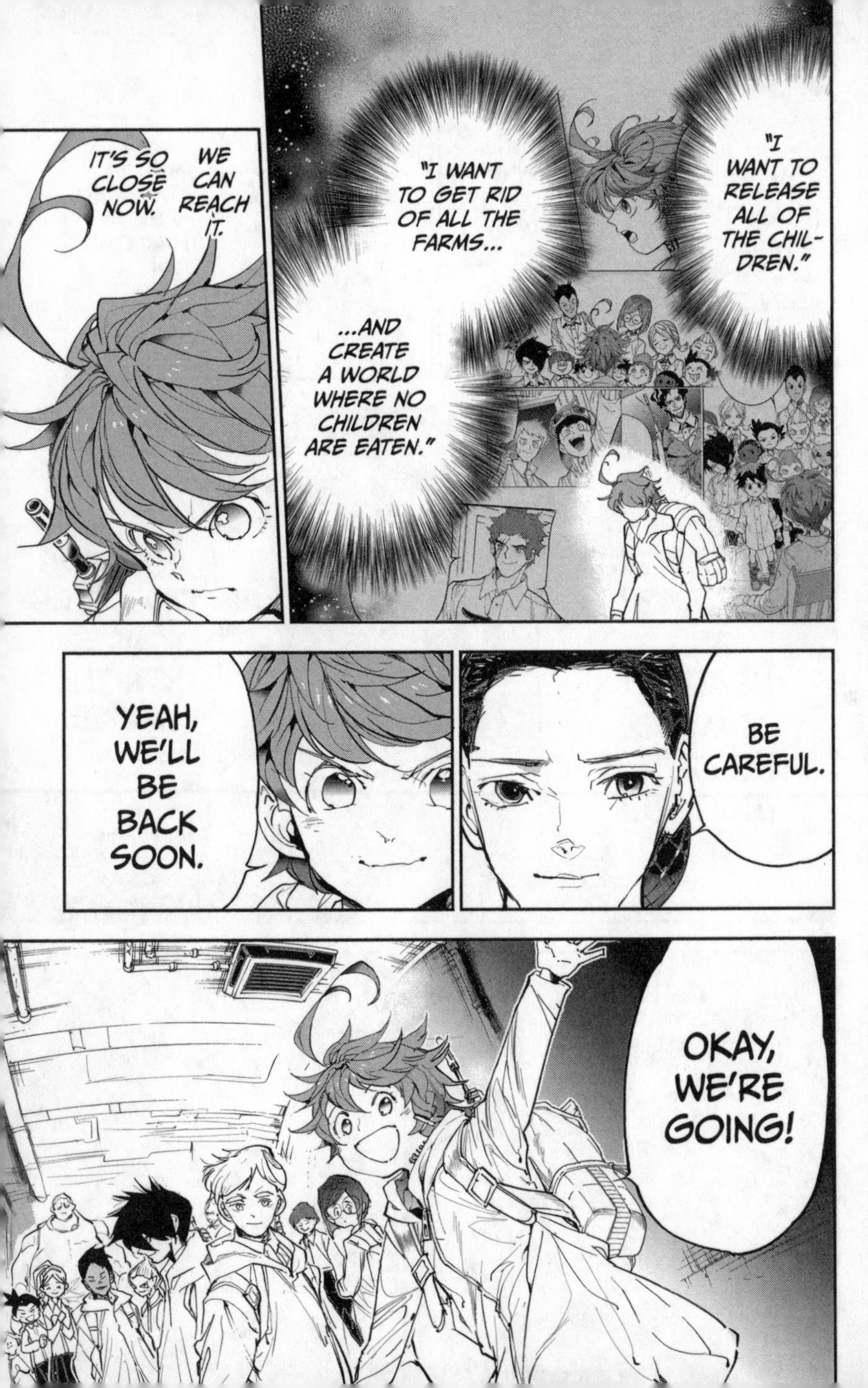
"I WANT TO RELEASE ALL OF THE CHIL-DREN."
"I WANT TO GET RID OF ALL THE FARMS...
...AND CREATE A WORLD WHERE NO CHILDREN ARE EATEN."
WE CAN REACH IT.
IT'S SO CLOSE NOW.
BE CAREFUL.
YEAH, WE'LL BE BACK SOON.
OKAY, WE'RE GOING!

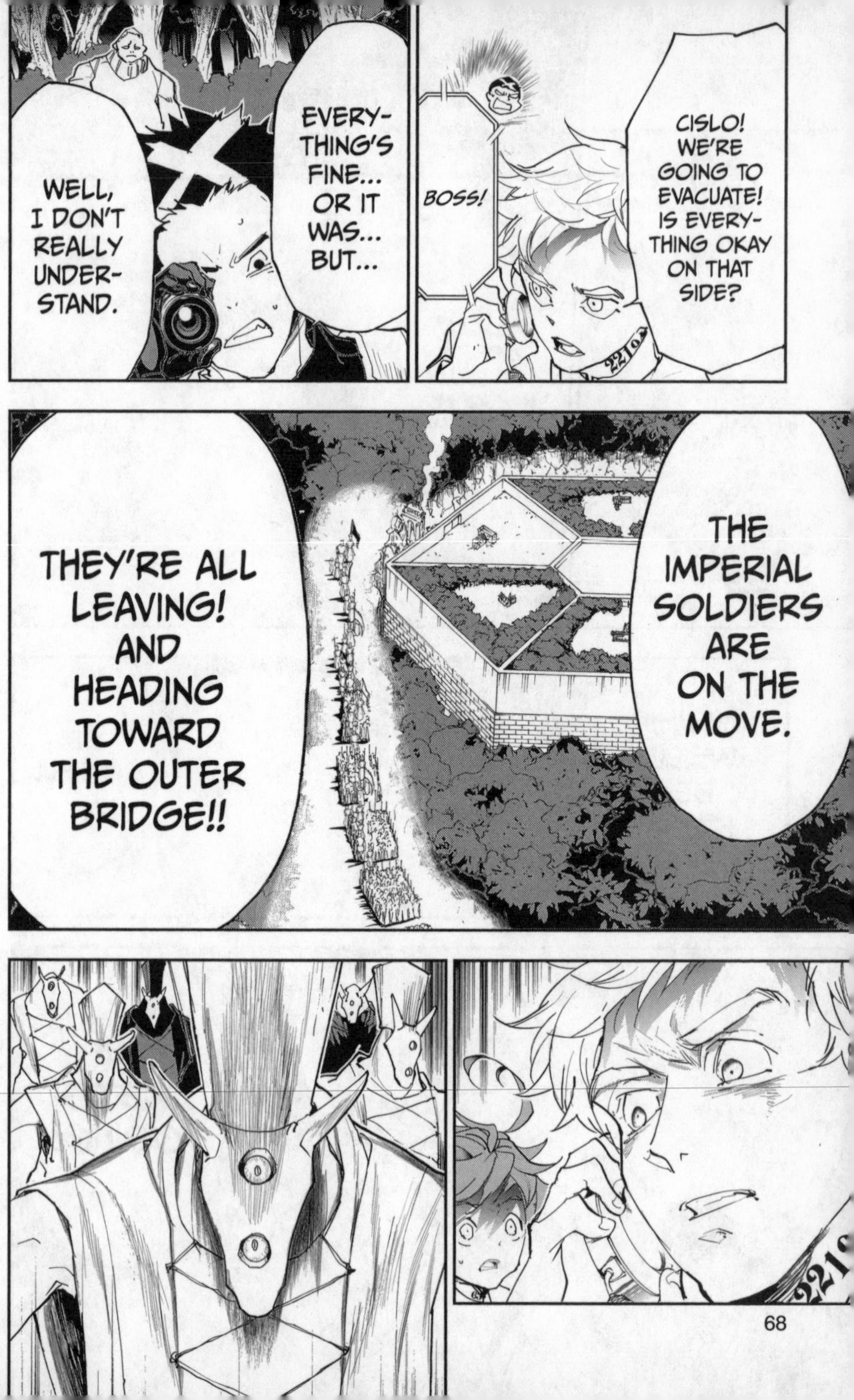
CISLO! WE'RE GOING TO EVACUATE! IS EVERY-THING OKAY ON THAT SIDE?
BOSS!
EVERY-THING'S FINE... OR IT WAS... BUT...
WELL, I DON'T REALLY UNDER-STAND.
THE IMPERIAL SOLDIERS ARE ON THE MOVE.
THEY'RE ALL LEAVING! AND HEADING TOWARD THE OUTER BRIDGE!!

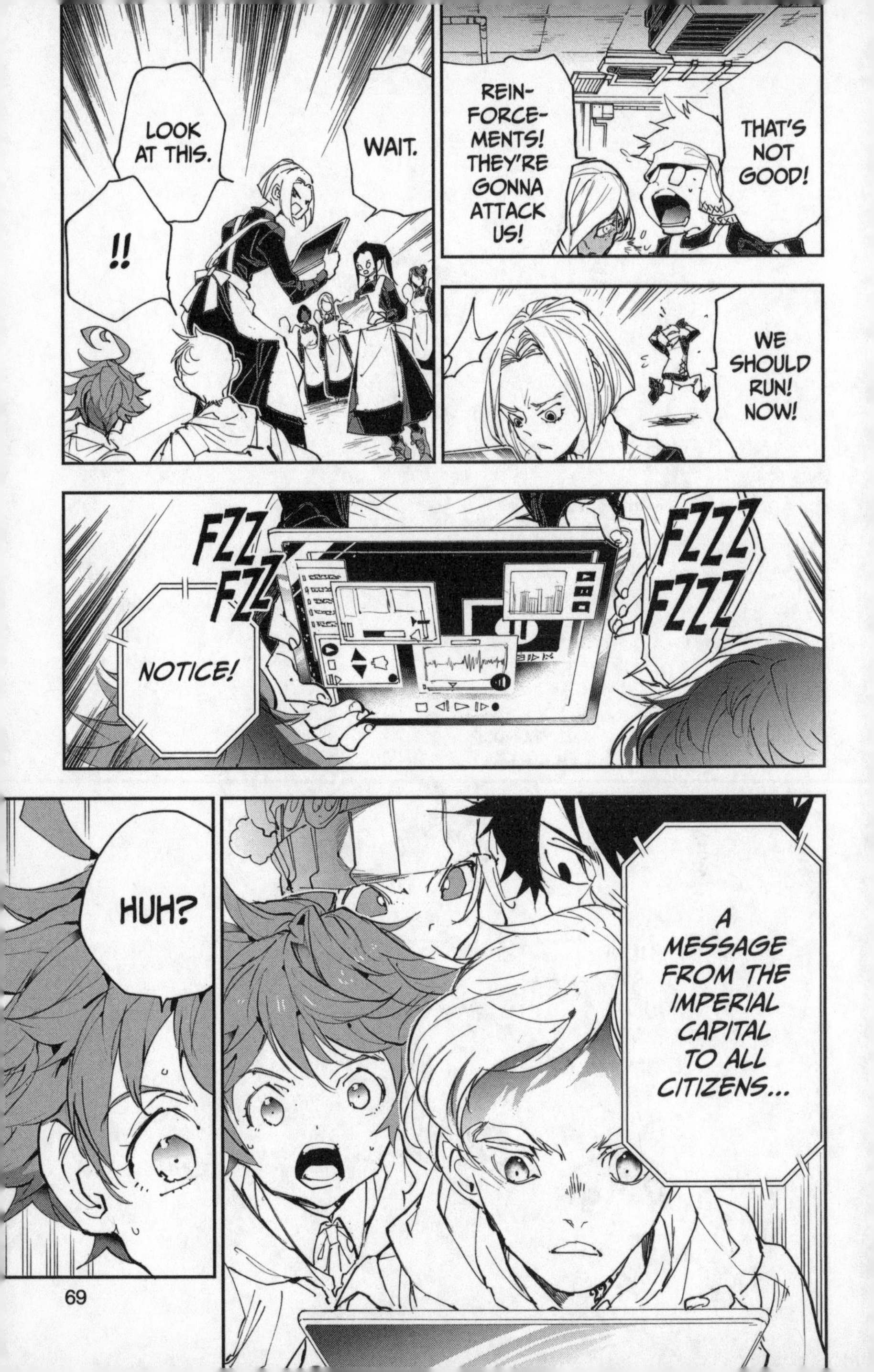
THAT'S NOT GOOD!
REIN-FORCE-MENTS! THEY'RE GONNA ATTACK US!
WE SHOULD RUN! NOW!
WAIT.
LOOK AT THIS.
!!
FZZZ FZZZ
FZZ FZZ
NOTICE!
A MESSAGE FROM THE IMPERIAL CAPITAL TO ALL CITIZENS...
HUH?

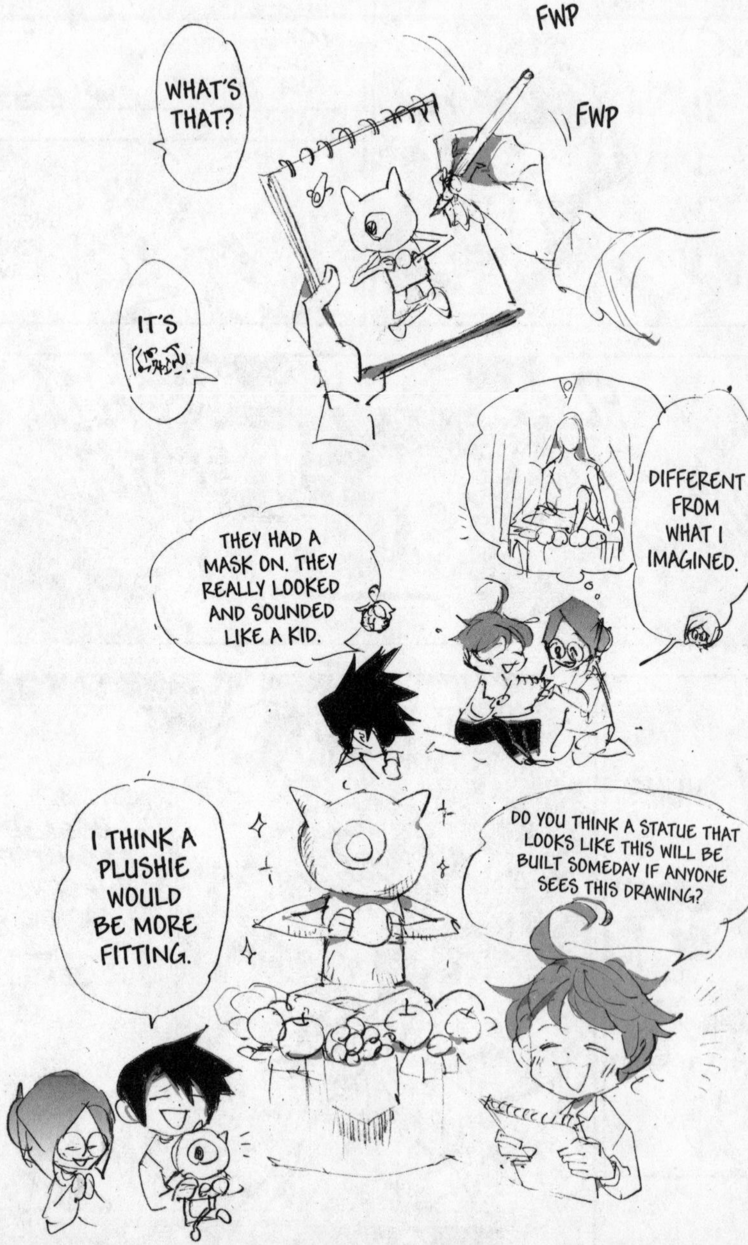
FWP
FWP
WHAT'S THAT?
IT'S
DIFFERENT FROM WHAT I IMAGINED.
THEY HAD A MASK ON. THEY REALLY LOOKED AND SOUNDED LIKE A KID.
DO YOU THINK A STATUE THAT LOOKS LIKE THIS WILL BE BUILT SOMEDAY IF ANYONE SEES THIS DRAWING?
I THINK A PLUSHIE WOULD BE MORE FITTING.

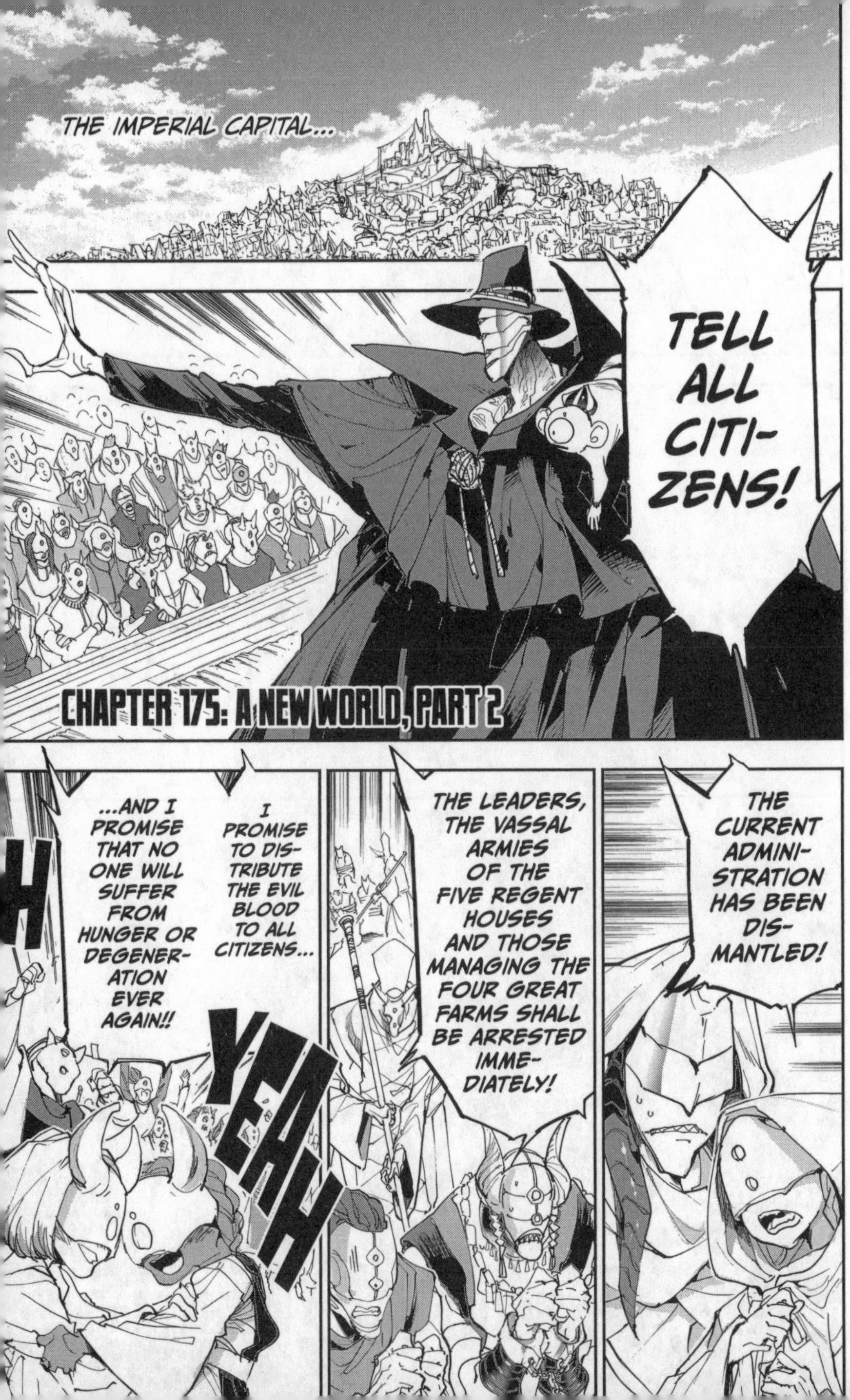
THE IMPERIAL CAPITAL...
TELL ALL CITI-ZENS!
CHAPTER 175: A NEW WORLD, PART 2
THE CURRENT ADMINI-STRATION HAS BEEN DIS-MANTLED!
THE LEADERS, THE VASSAL ARMIES OF THE FIVE REGENT HOUSES AND THOSE MANAGING THE FOUR GREAT FARMS SHALL BE ARRESTED IMME-DIATELY!
I PROMISE TO DIS-TRIBUTE THE EVIL BLOOD TO ALL CITIZENS...
...AND I PROMISE THAT NO ONE WILL SUFFER FROM HUNGER OR DEGENER-ATION EVER AGAIN!!
YEAH

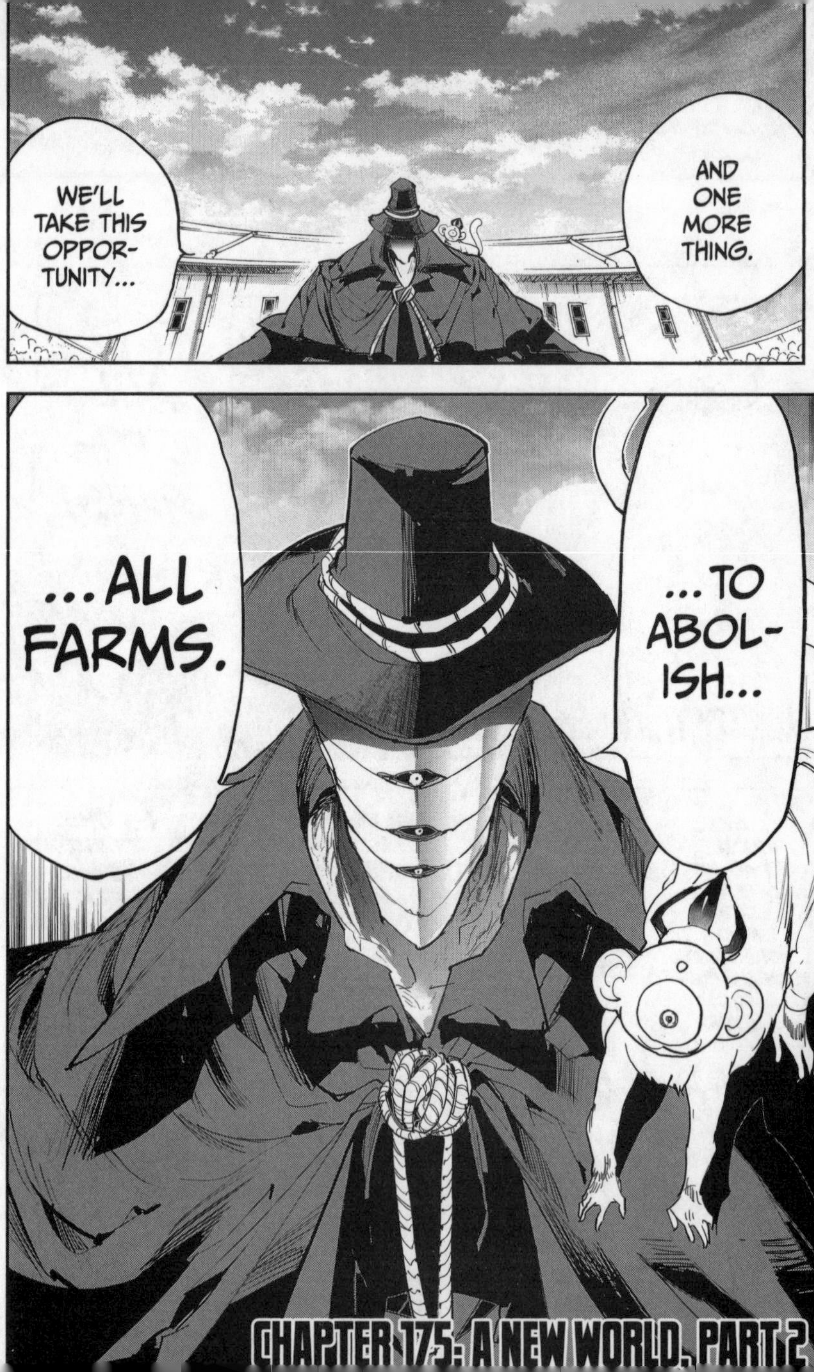
AND ONE MORE THING.
WE'LL TAKE THIS OPPOR-TUNITY...
...TO ABOL-ISH...
...ALL FARMS.
CHAPTER 175: A NEW WORLD, PART 2

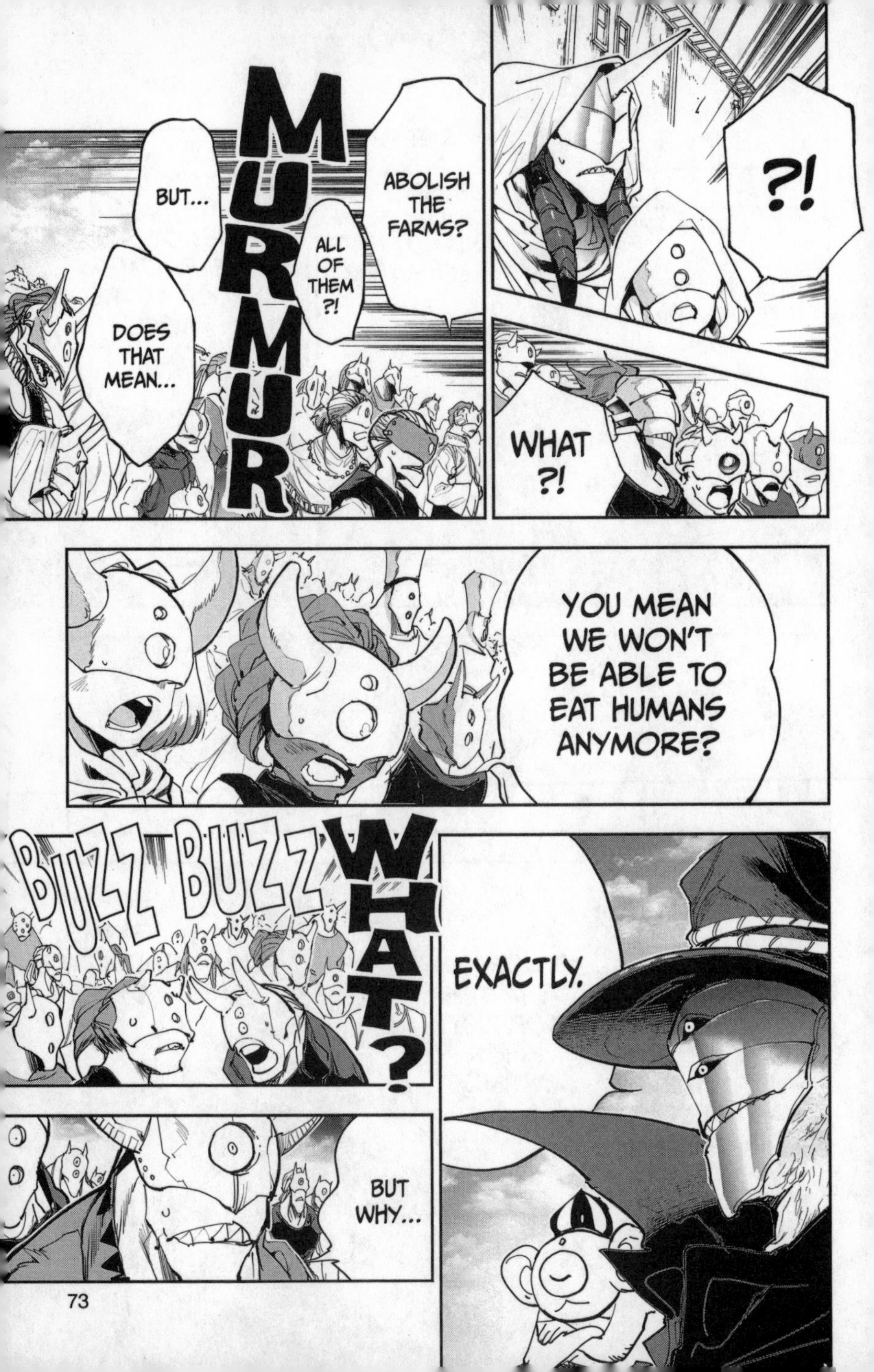
?!
WHAT ?!
ABOLISH THE FARMS?
ALL OF THEM ?!
MURMUR
BUT...
DOES THAT MEAN...
YOU MEAN WE WON'T BE ABLE TO EAT HUMANS ANYMORE?
EXACTLY.
WHAT?
BUZZ BUZZ
BUT WHY...

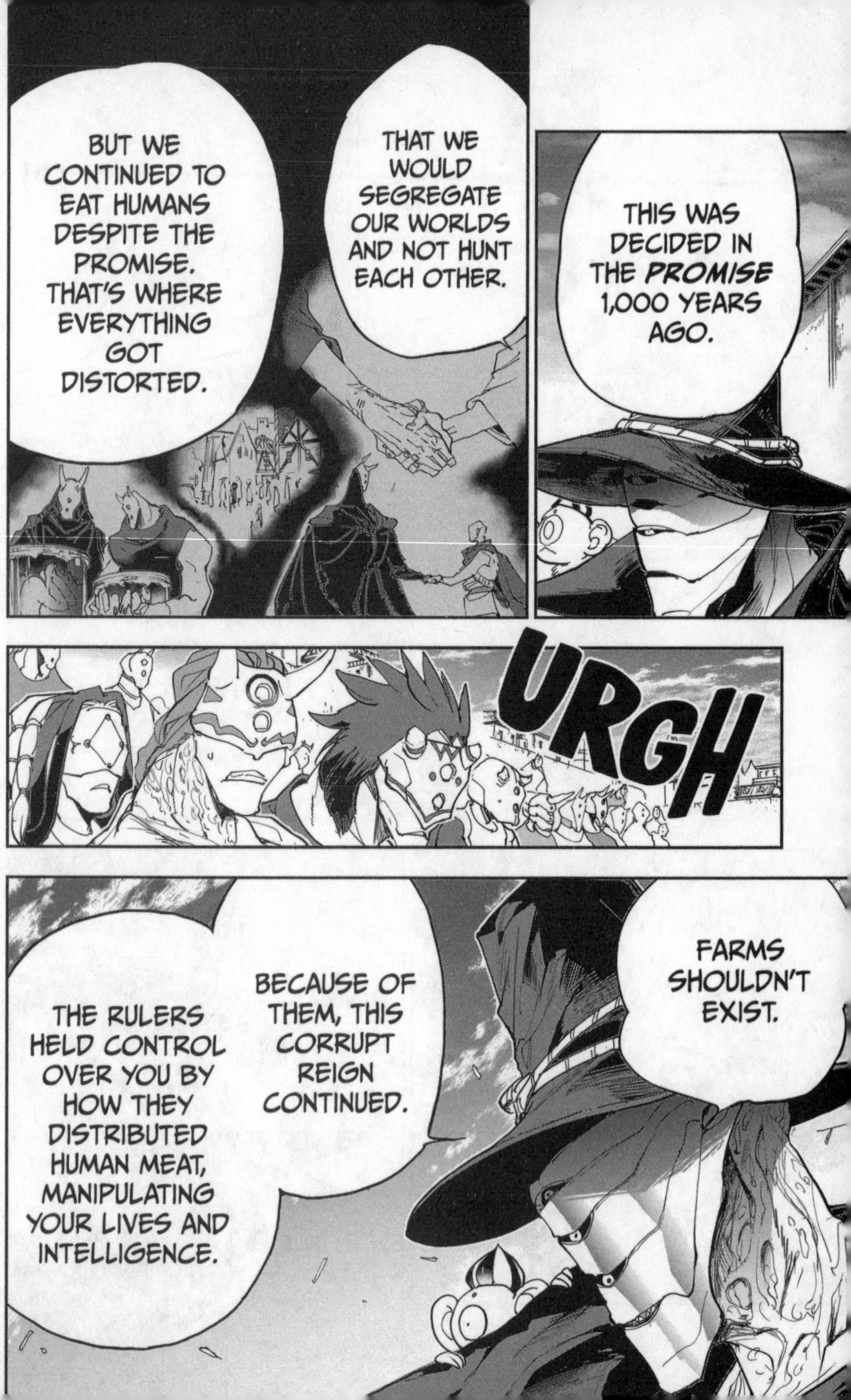
THIS WAS DECIDED IN THE *PROMISE* 1,000 YEARS AGO.
THAT WE WOULD SEGREGATE OUR WORLDS AND NOT HUNT EACH OTHER.
BUT WE CONTINUED TO EAT HUMANS DESPITE THE PROMISE. THAT'S WHERE EVERYTHING GOT DISTORTED.
URGH
FARMS SHOULDN'T EXIST.
BECAUSE OF THEM, THIS CORRUPT REIGN CONTINUED.
THE RULERS HELD CONTROL OVER YOU BY HOW THEY DISTRIBUTED HUMAN MEAT, MANIPULATING YOUR LIVES AND INTELLIGENCE.

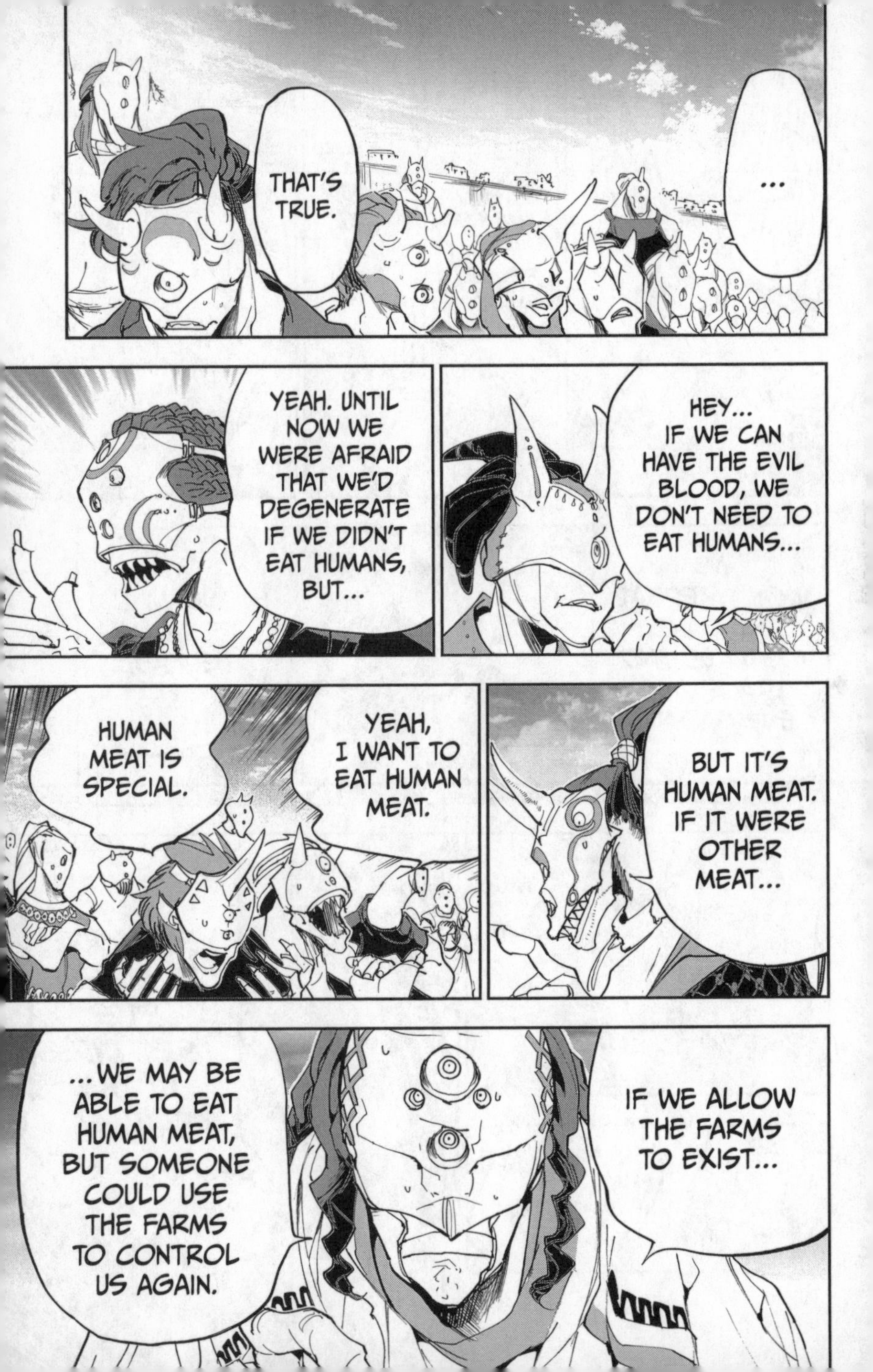
...
THAT'S TRUE.
HEY... IF WE CAN HAVE THE EVIL BLOOD, WE DON'T NEED TO EAT HUMANS...
YEAH. UNTIL NOW WE WERE AFRAID THAT WE'D DEGENERATE IF WE DIDN'T EAT HUMANS, BUT...
BUT IT'S HUMAN MEAT. IF IT WERE OTHER MEAT...
YEAH, I WANT TO EAT HUMAN MEAT.
HUMAN MEAT IS SPECIAL.
IF WE ALLOW THE FARMS TO EXIST...
...WE MAY BE ABLE TO EAT HUMAN MEAT, BUT SOMEONE COULD USE THE FARMS TO CONTROL US AGAIN.

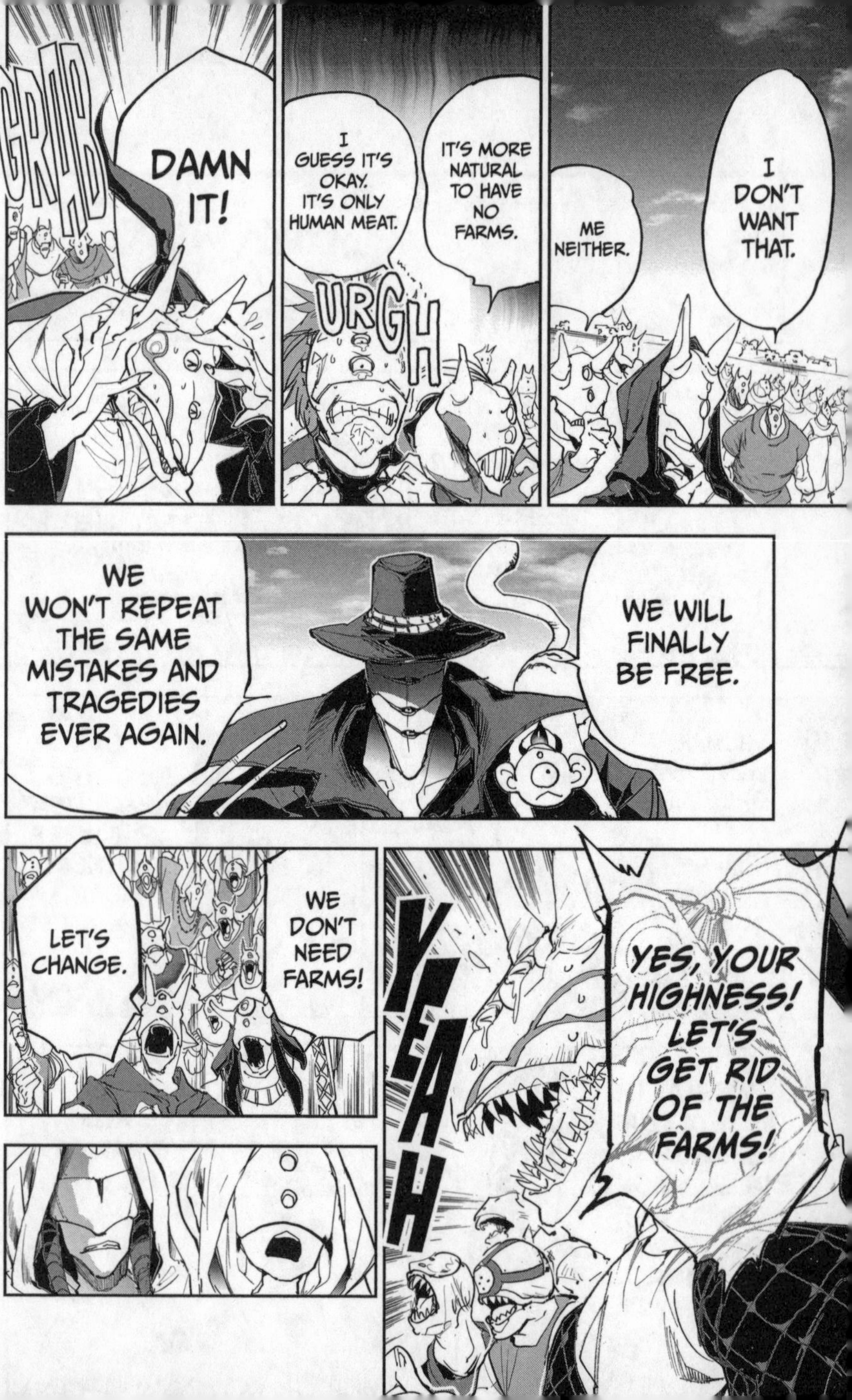
I DON'T WANT THAT.
ME NEITHER.
IT'S MORE NATURAL TO HAVE NO FARMS.
I GUESS IT'S OKAY. IT'S ONLY HUMAN MEAT.
URGH
DAMN IT!
GRIP
WE WILL FINALLY BE FREE.
WE WON'T REPEAT THE SAME MISTAKES AND TRAGEDIES EVER AGAIN.
YES, YOUR HIGHNESS! LET'S GET RID OF THE FARMS!
YEAH
WE DON'T NEED FARMS!
LET'S CHANGE.

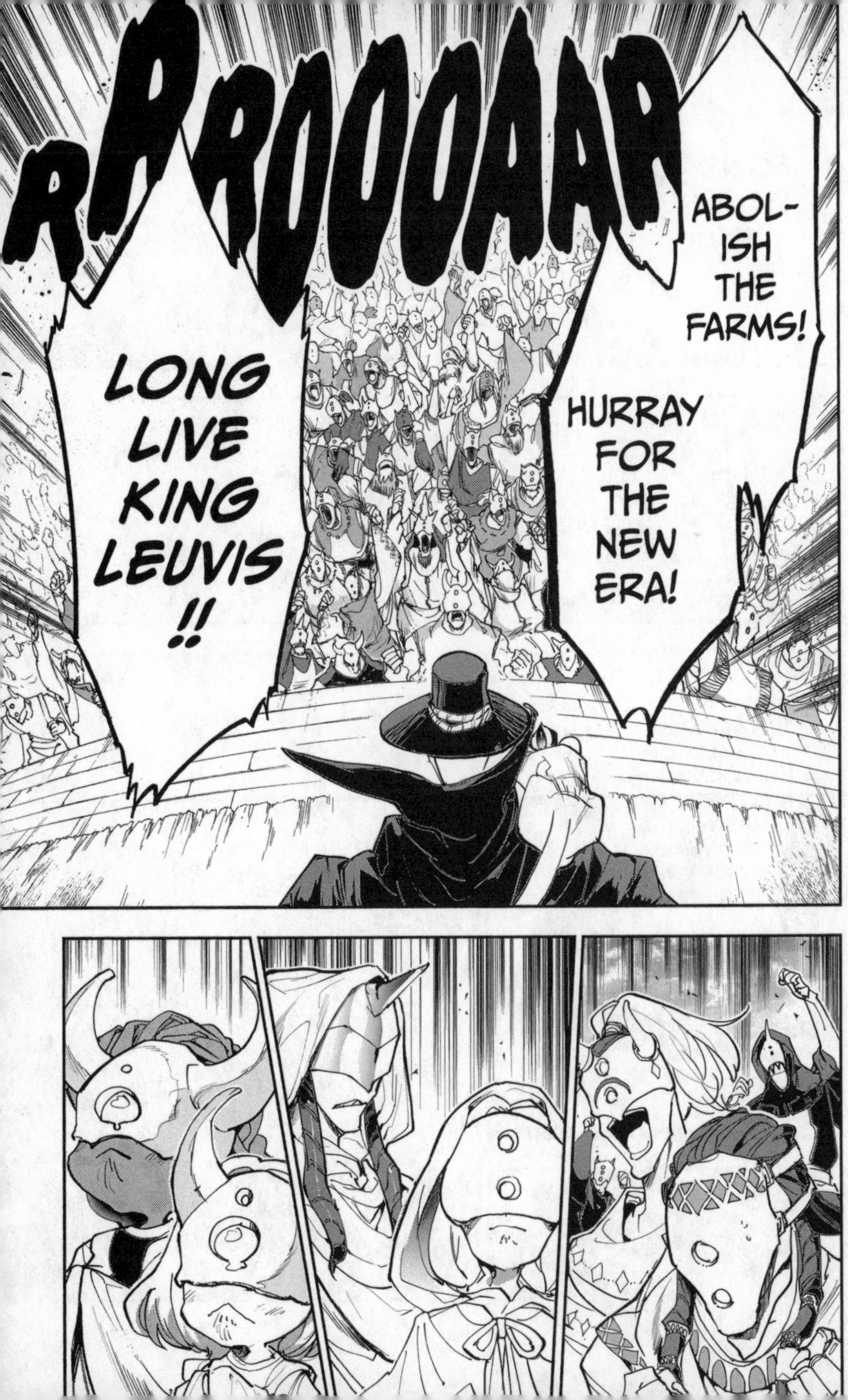
RPROOOAAR
ABOL-
ISH
THE
FARMS!
HURRAY
FOR
THE
NEW
ERA!
LONG
LIVE
KING
LEUVIS
!!

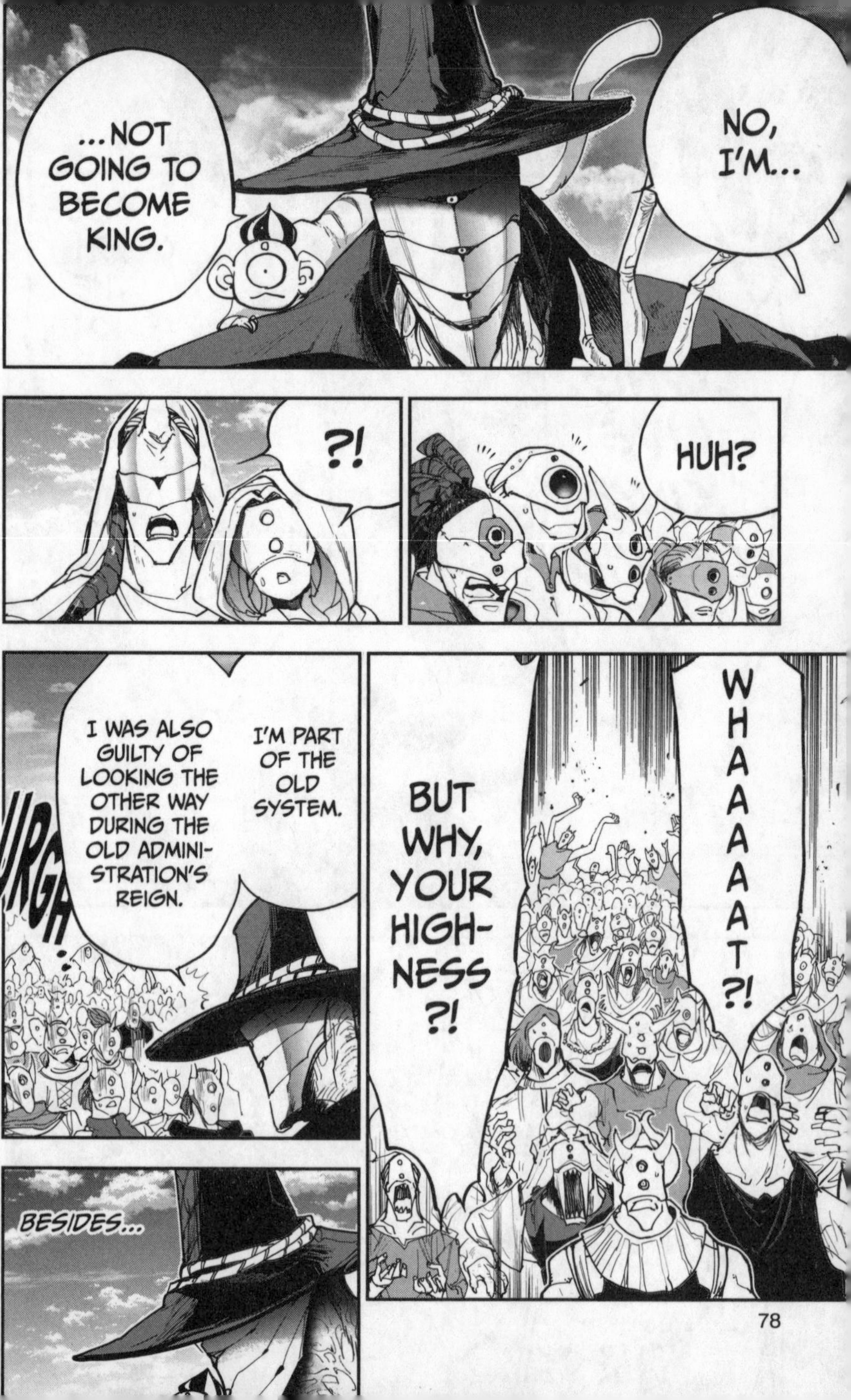
NO, I'M...
...NOT GOING TO BECOME KING.
HUH?
?!
WHAAAAAAT?!
BUT WHY, YOUR HIGHNESS?!
I'M PART OF THE OLD SYSTEM.
I WAS ALSO GUILTY OF LOOKING THE OTHER WAY DURING THE OLD ADMINISTRATION'S REIGN.
URGH
BESIDES...

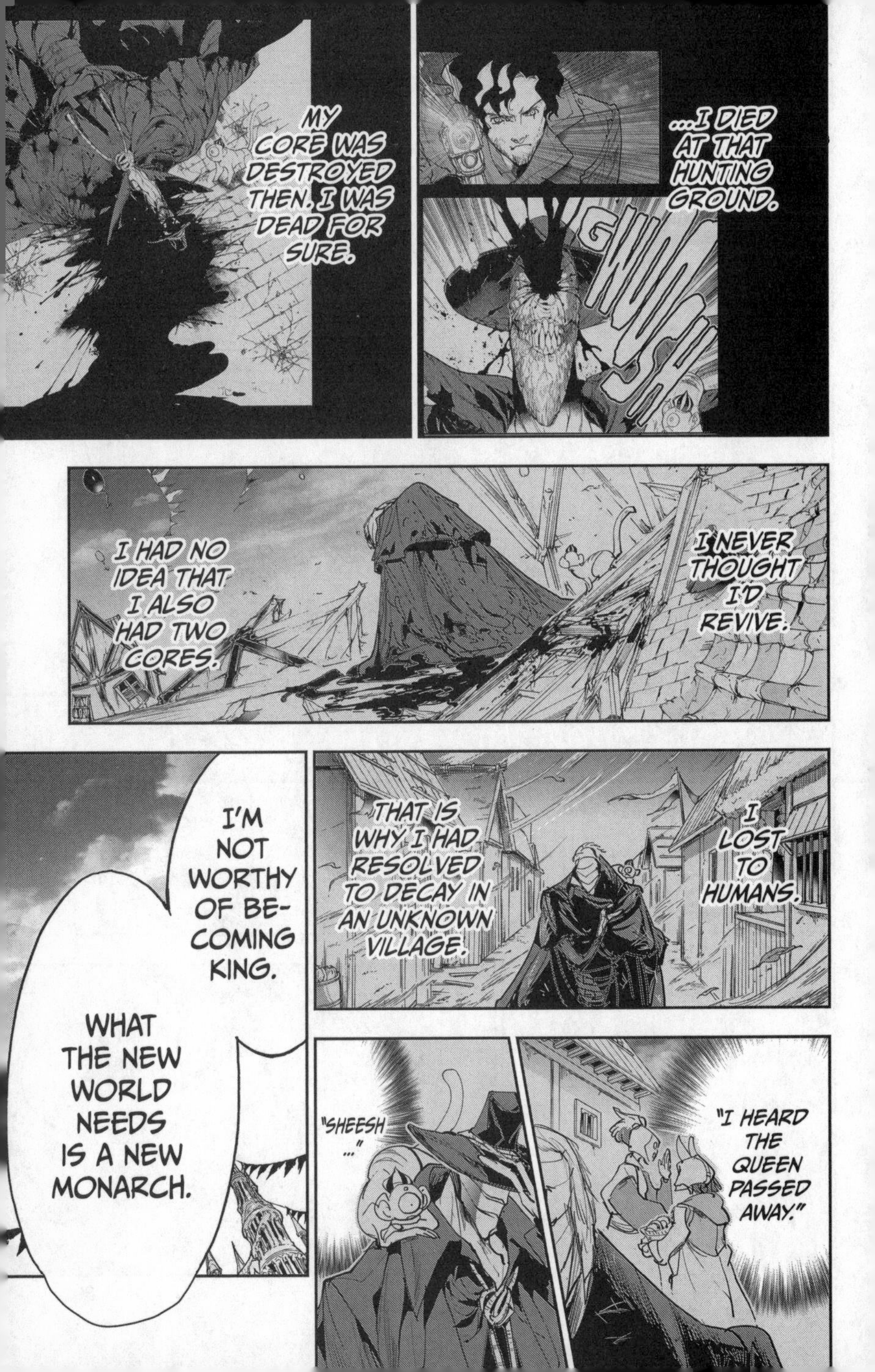
...I DIED AT THAT HUNTING GROUND.
MY CORE WAS DESTROYED THEN. I WAS DEAD FOR SURE.
I NEVER THOUGHT I'D REVIVE.
I HAD NO IDEA THAT I ALSO HAD TWO CORES.
I LOST TO HUMANS.
THAT IS WHY I HAD RESOLVED TO DECAY IN AN UNKNOWN VILLAGE.
"I HEARD THE QUEEN PASSED AWAY."
"SHEESH..."
I'M NOT WORTHY OF BE-COMING KING.
WHAT THE NEW WORLD NEEDS IS A NEW MONARCH.

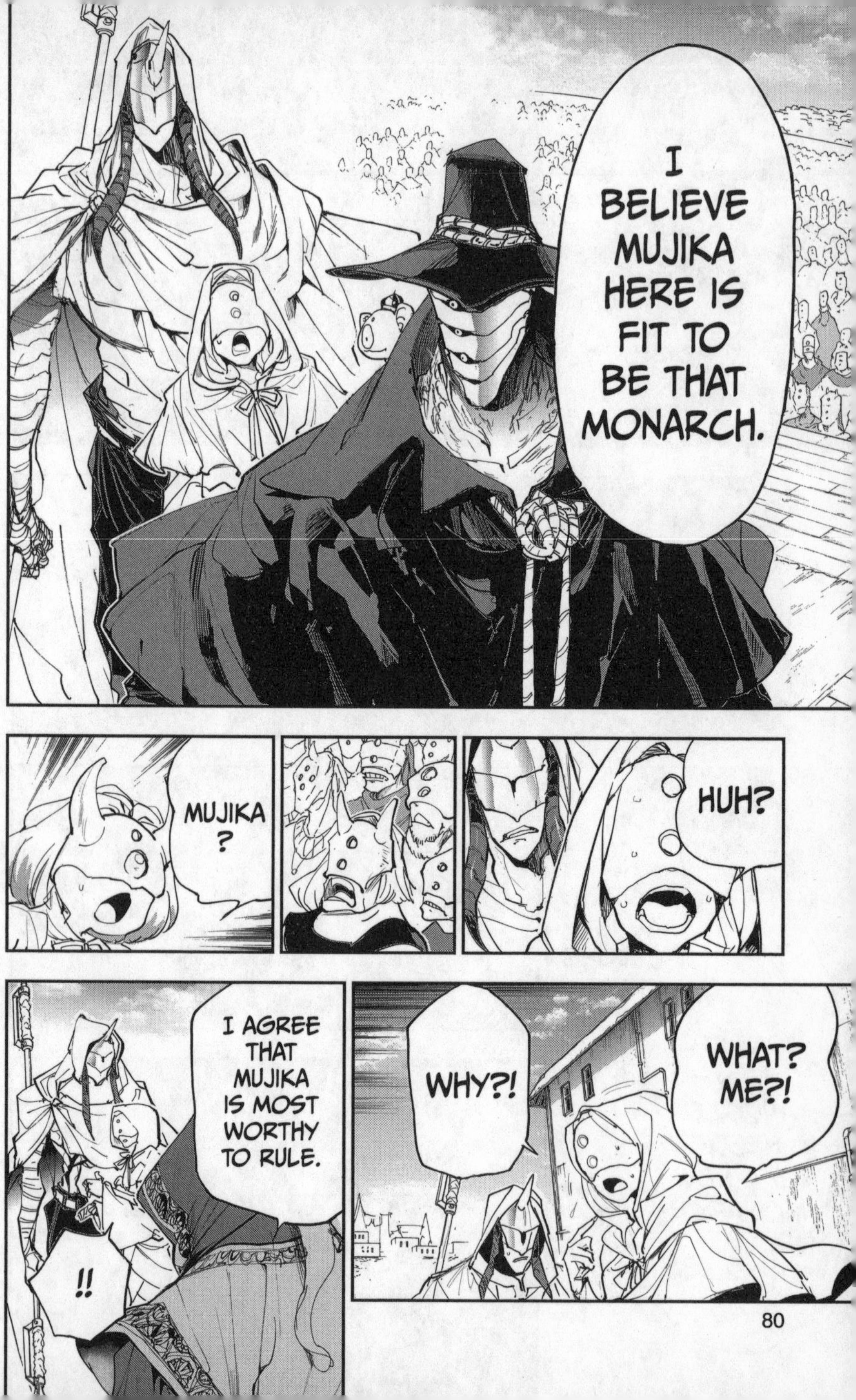
I BELIEVE MUJIKA HERE IS FIT TO BE THAT MONARCH.
HUH?
MUJIKA?
WHAT? ME?!
WHY?!
I AGREE THAT MUJIKA IS MOST WORTHY TO RULE.
!!

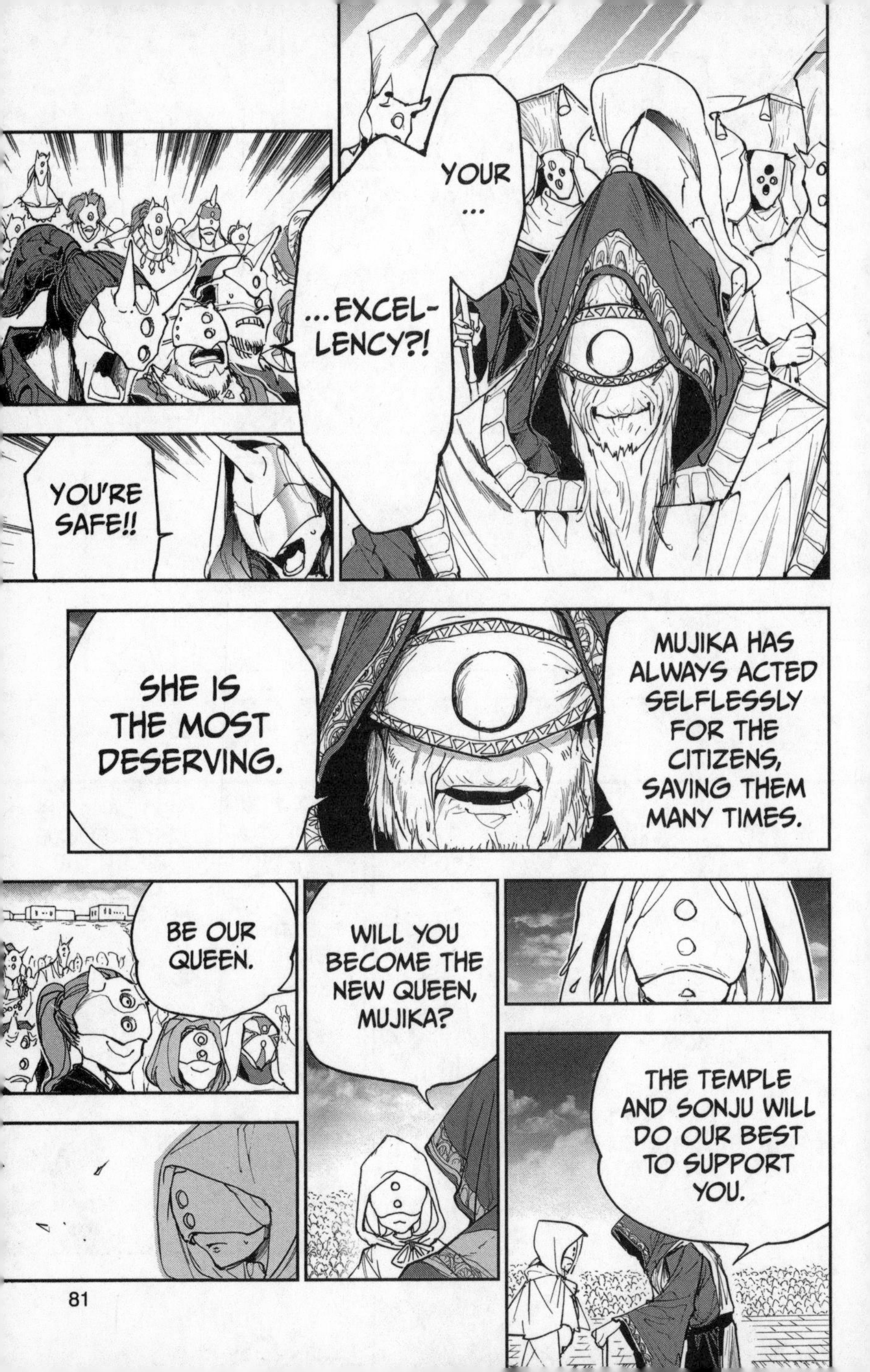
YOUR ...
...EXCEL-LENCY?!
YOU'RE SAFE!!
MUJIKA HAS ALWAYS ACTED SELFLESSLY FOR THE CITIZENS, SAVING THEM MANY TIMES.
SHE IS THE MOST DESERVING.
THE TEMPLE AND SONJU WILL DO OUR BEST TO SUPPORT YOU.
WILL YOU BECOME THE NEW QUEEN, MUJIKA?
BE OUR QUEEN.

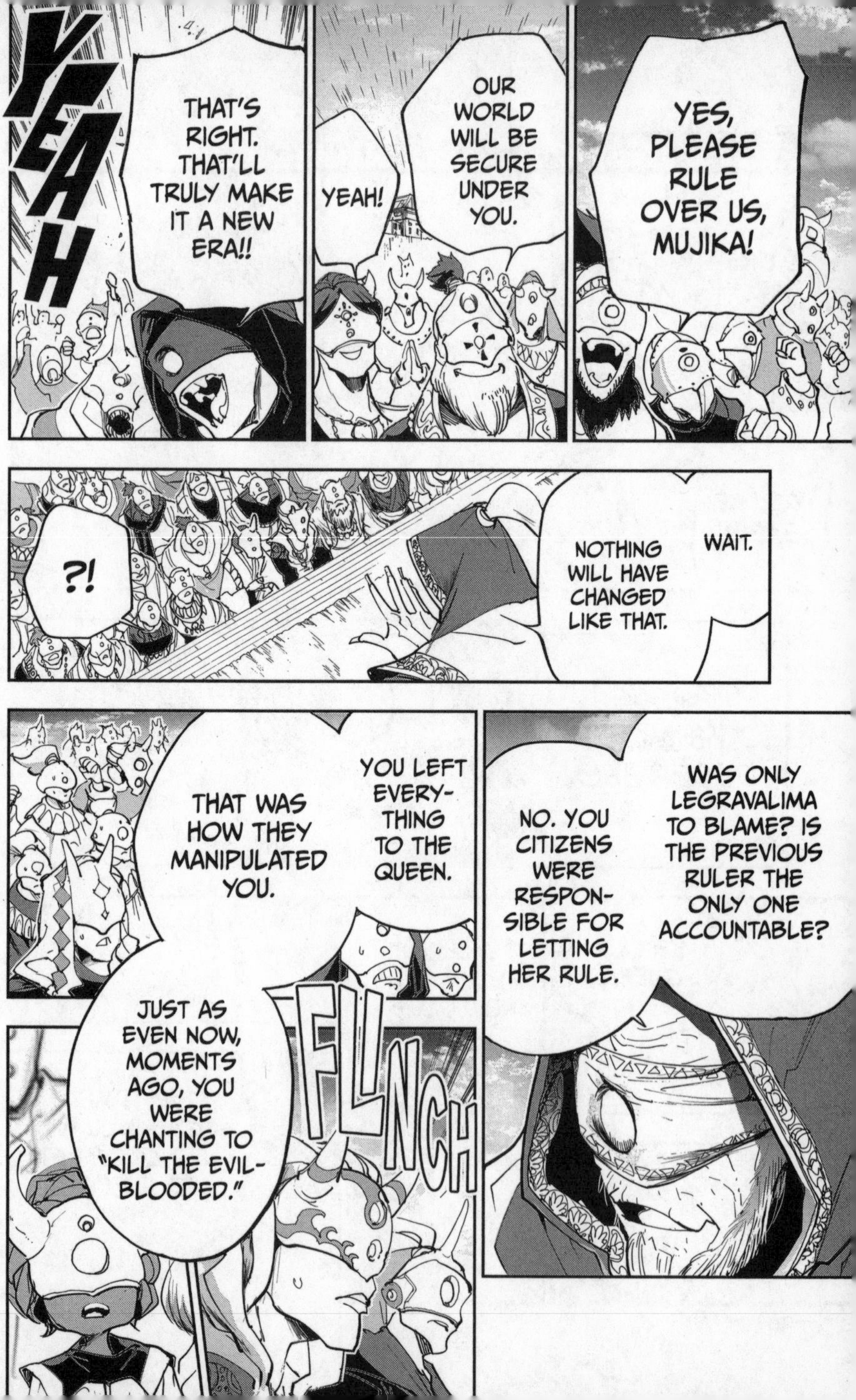
YES, PLEASE RULE OVER US, MUJIKA!
OUR WORLD WILL BE SECURE UNDER YOU.
YEAH!
THAT'S RIGHT. THAT'LL TRULY MAKE IT A NEW ERA!!
YEAH
WAIT.
NOTHING WILL HAVE CHANGED LIKE THAT.
?!
WAS ONLY LEGRAVALIMA TO BLAME? IS THE PREVIOUS RULER THE ONLY ONE ACCOUNTABLE?
NO. YOU CITIZENS WERE RESPON-SIBLE FOR LETTING HER RULE.
YOU LEFT EVERY-THING TO THE QUEEN.
THAT WAS HOW THEY MANIPULATED YOU.
JUST AS EVEN NOW, MOMENTS AGO, YOU WERE CHANTING TO "KILL THE EVIL-BLOODED."
FLINCH

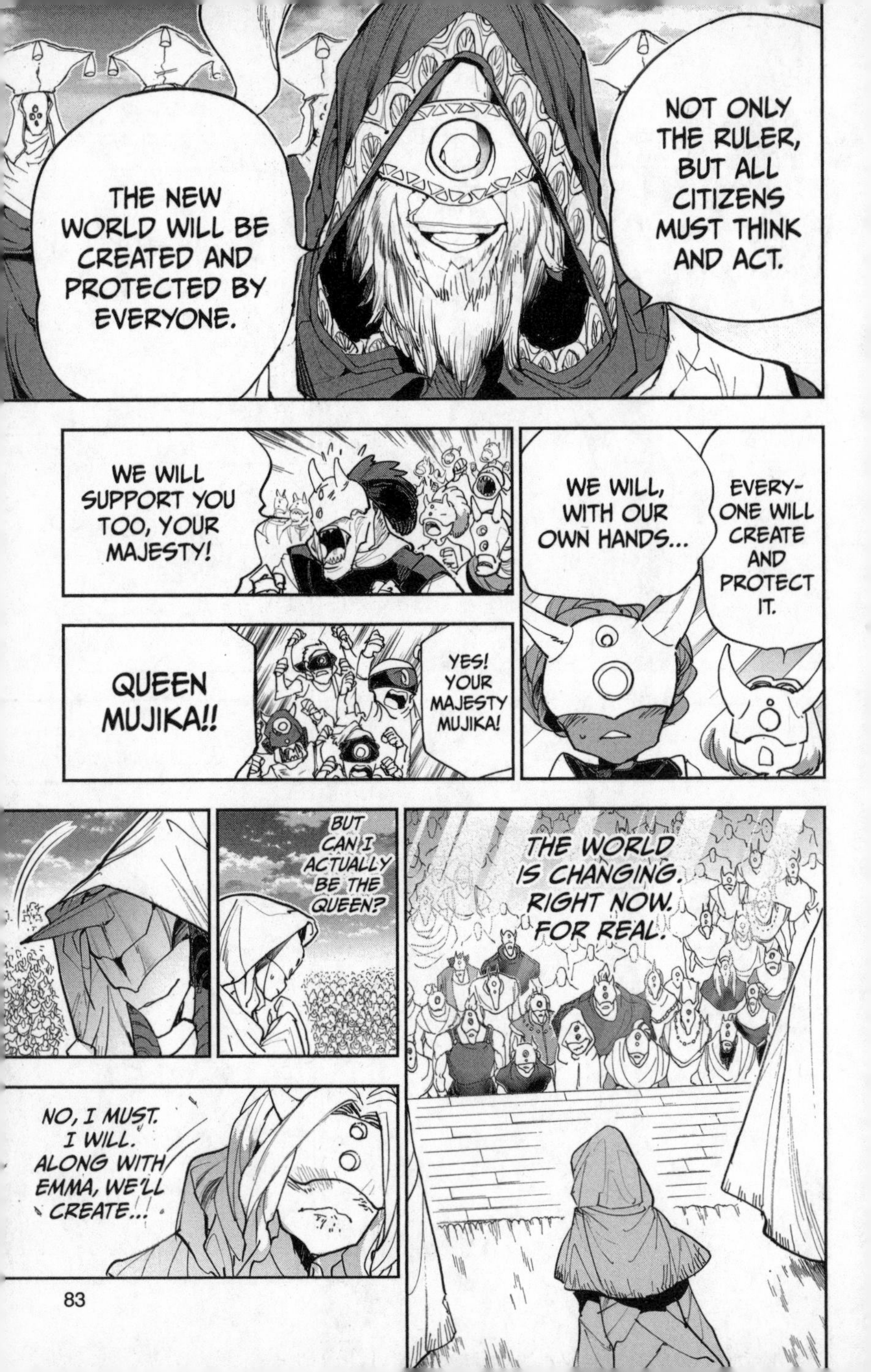
NOT ONLY THE RULER, BUT ALL CITIZENS MUST THINK AND ACT.
THE NEW WORLD WILL BE CREATED AND PROTECTED BY EVERYONE.
EVERY-ONE WILL CREATE AND PROTECT IT.
WE WILL, WITH OUR OWN HANDS...
WE WILL SUPPORT YOU TOO, YOUR MAJESTY!
YES! YOUR MAJESTY MUJIKA!
QUEEN MUJIKA!!
THE WORLD IS CHANGING. RIGHT NOW. FOR REAL.
BUT CAN I ACTUALLY BE THE QUEEN?
NO, I MUST. I WILL. ALONG WITH EMMA, WE'LL CREATE...

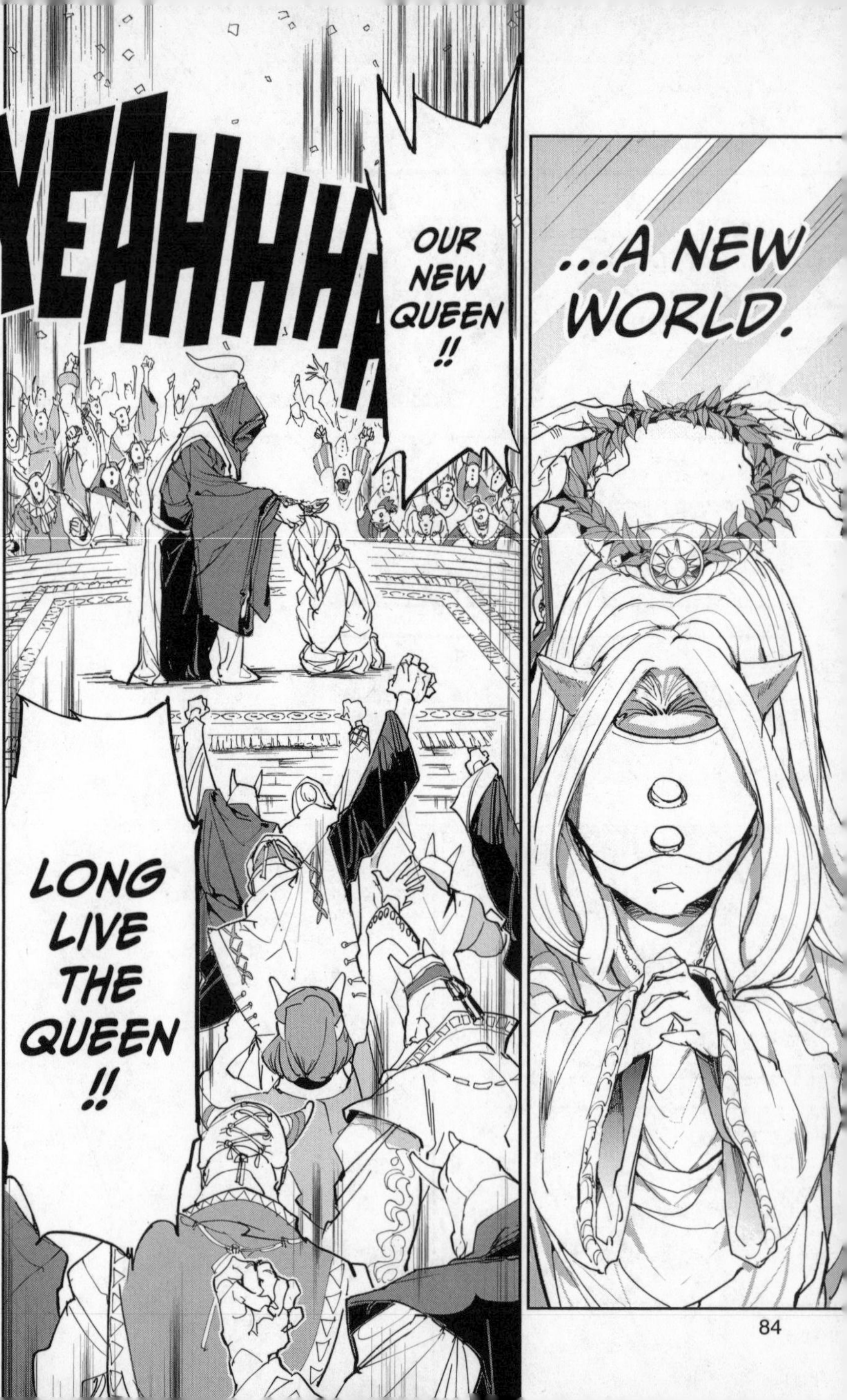
...A NEW WORLD.
YEAHHHA
OUR NEW QUEEN !!
LONG LIVE THE QUEEN !!

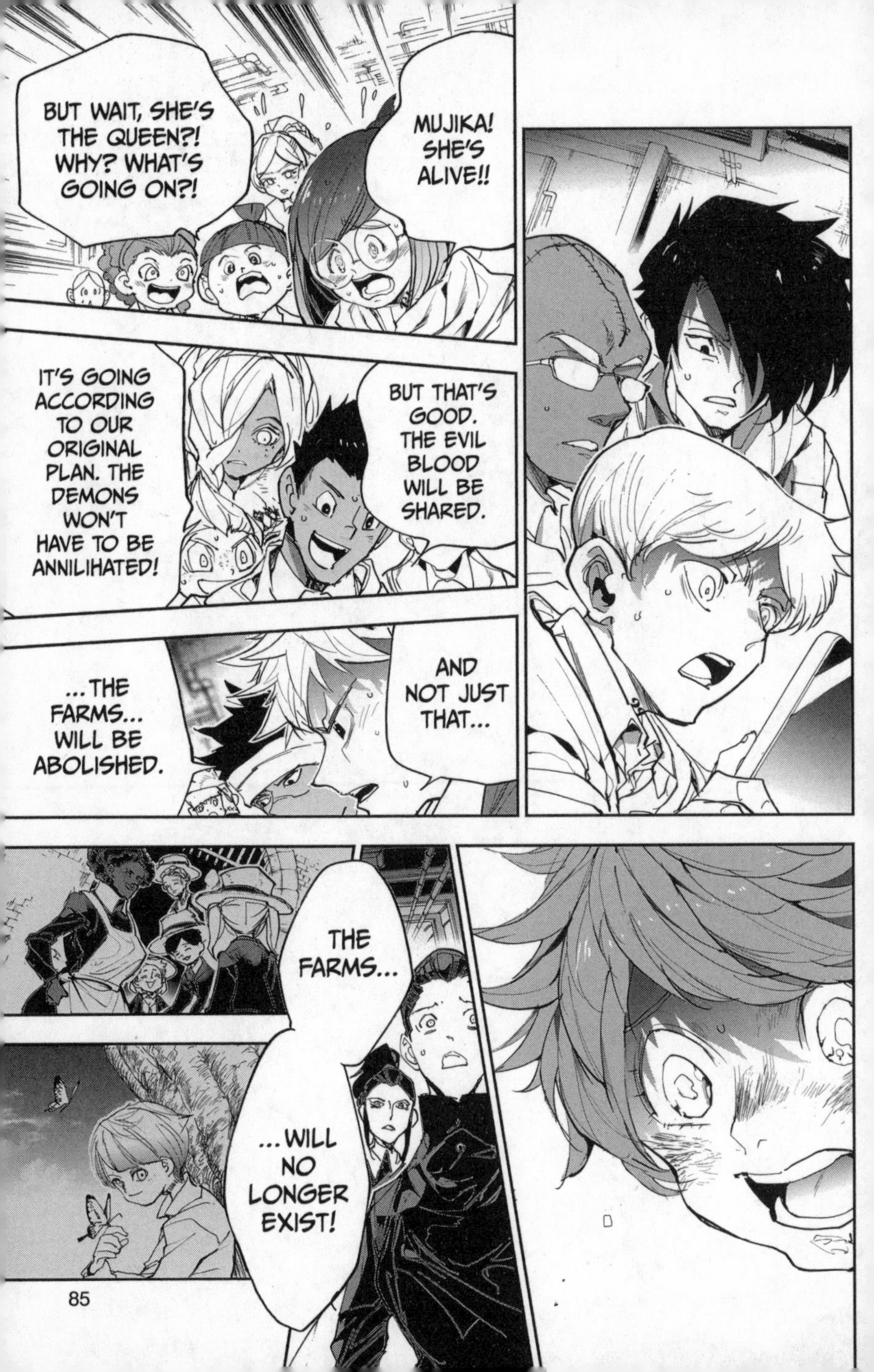
MUJIKA! SHE'S ALIVE!!
BUT WAIT, SHE'S THE QUEEN?! WHY? WHAT'S GOING ON?!
BUT THAT'S GOOD. THE EVIL BLOOD WILL BE SHARED.
IT'S GOING ACCORDING TO OUR ORIGINAL PLAN. THE DEMONS WON'T HAVE TO BE ANNILIHATED!
AND NOT JUST THAT...
...THE FARMS... WILL BE ABOLISHED.
THE FARMS...
...WILL NO LONGER EXIST!

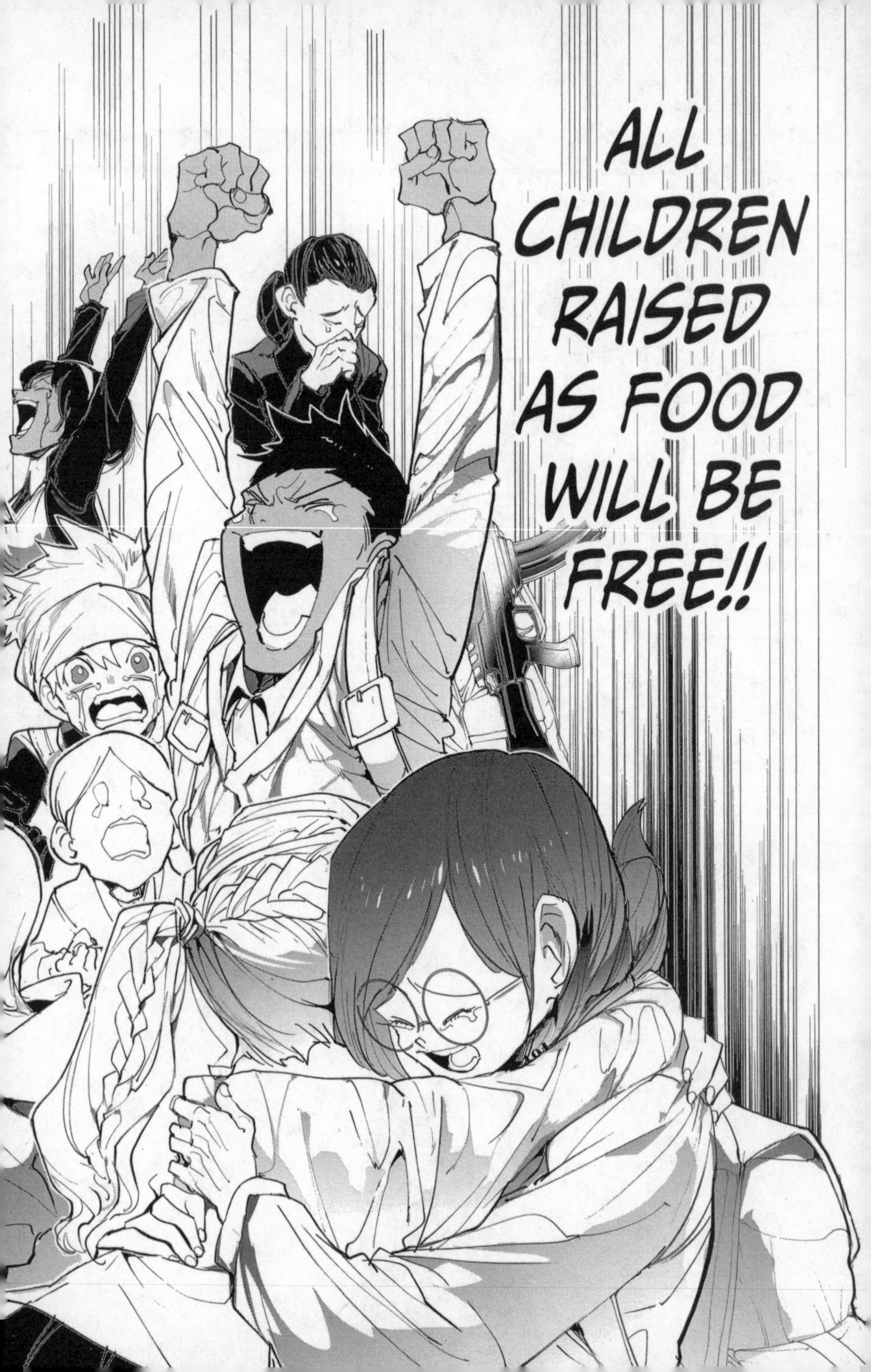
ALL CHILDREN RAISED AS FOOD WILL BE FREE!!

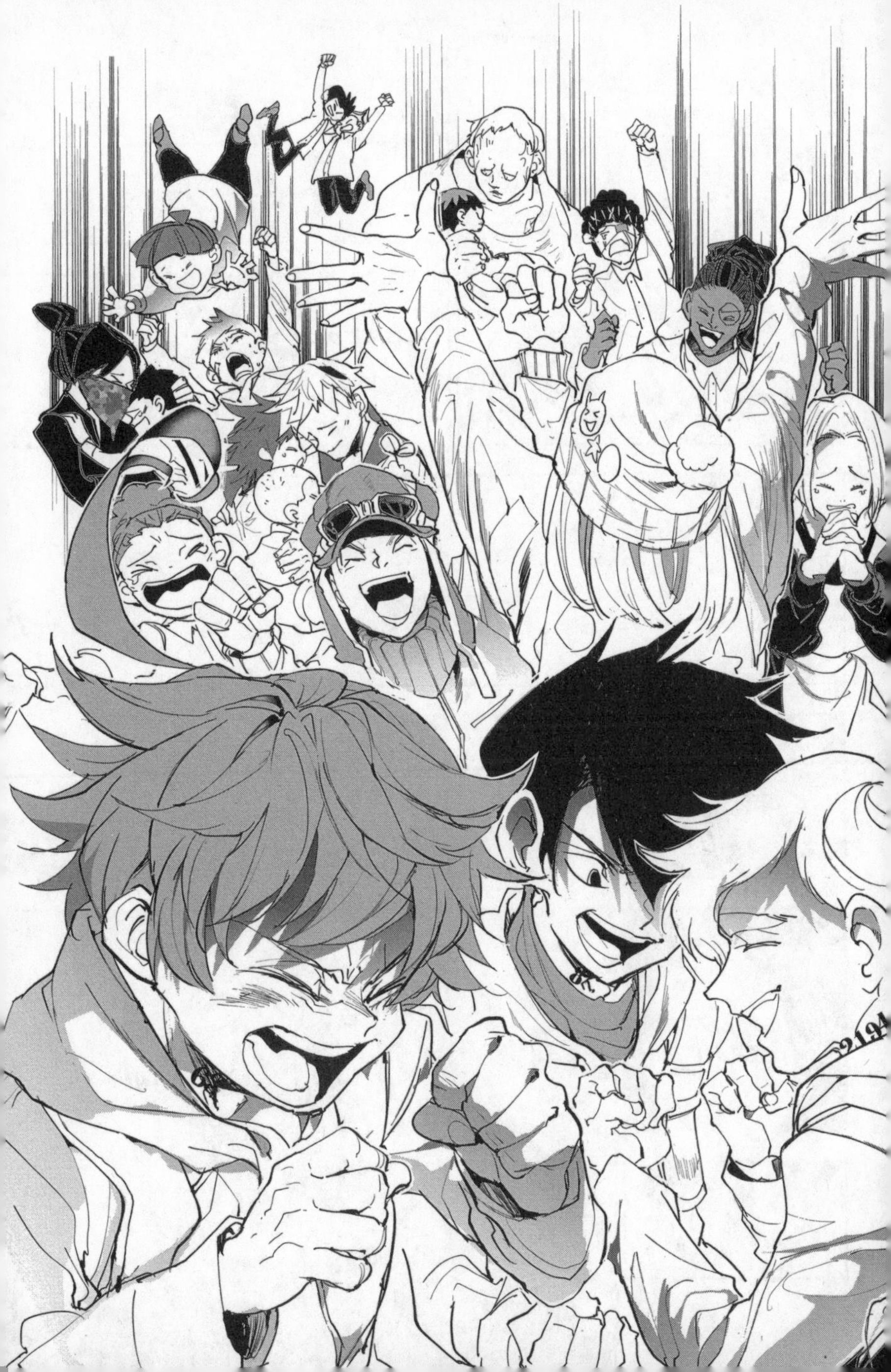

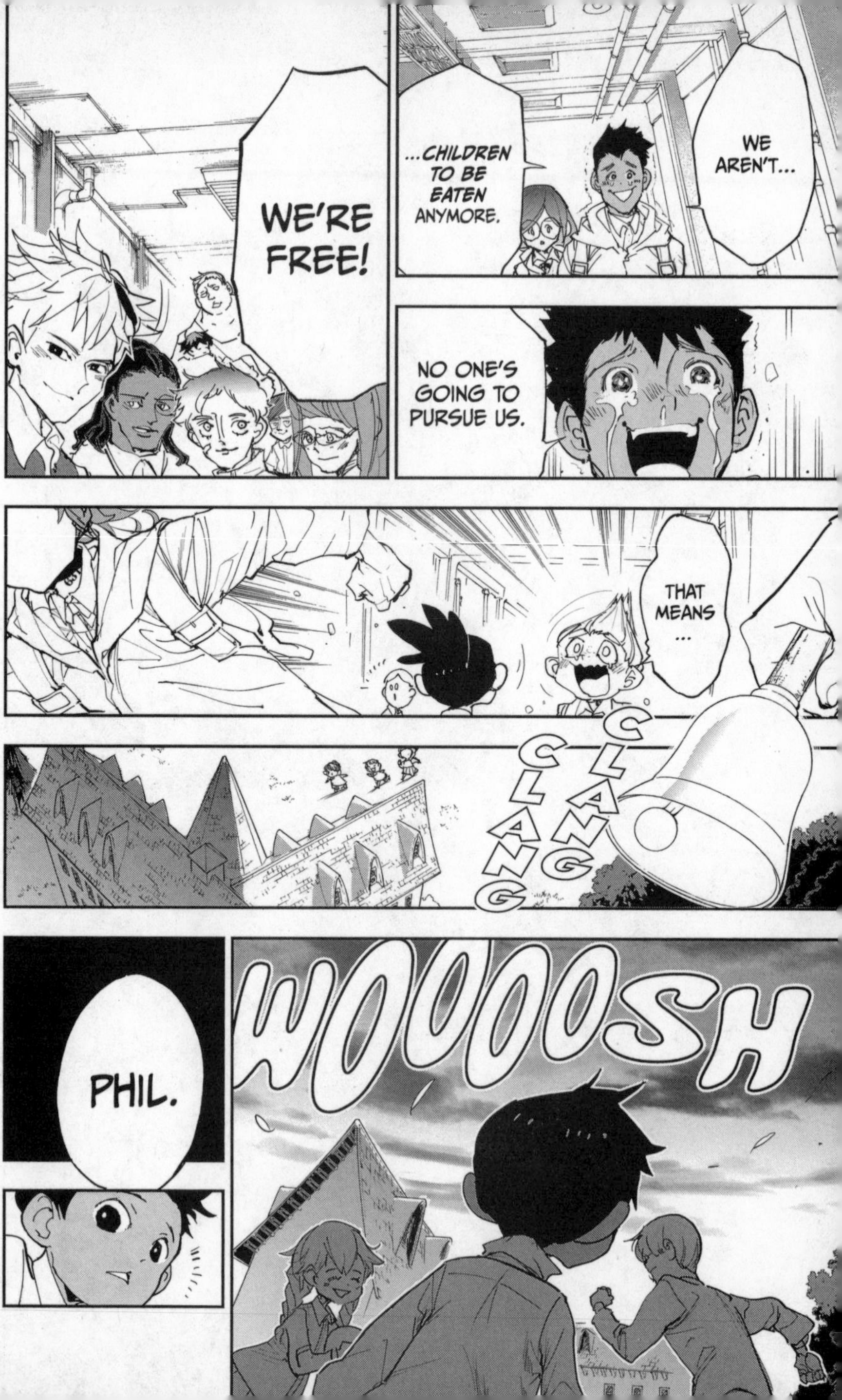
WE AREN'T...
...CHILDREN TO BE EATEN ANYMORE.
NO ONE'S GOING TO PURSUE US.
WE'RE FREE!
THAT MEANS ...
CLANG
CLANG
WOOOOSH
PHIL.

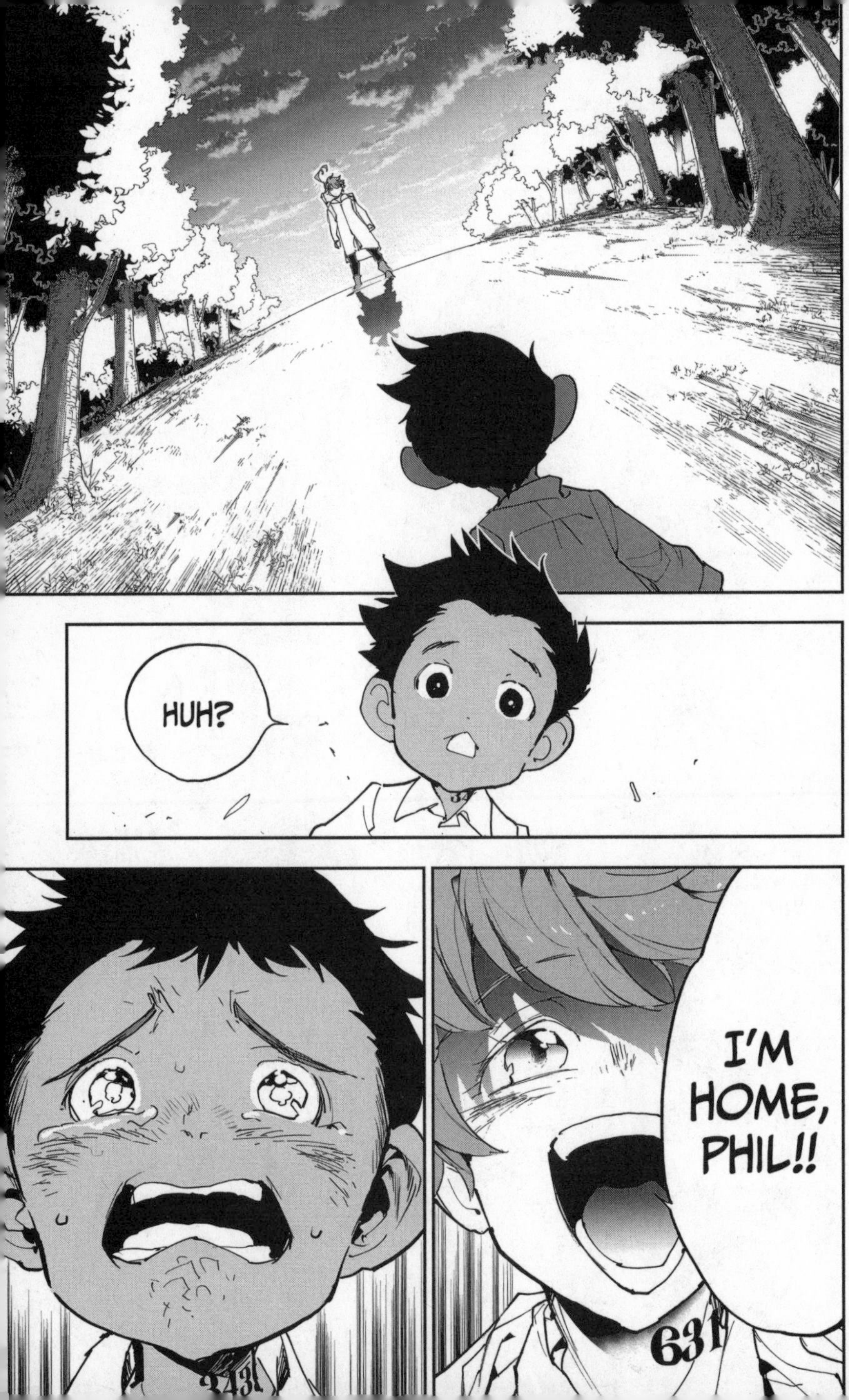
HUH?
I'M HOME, PHIL!!

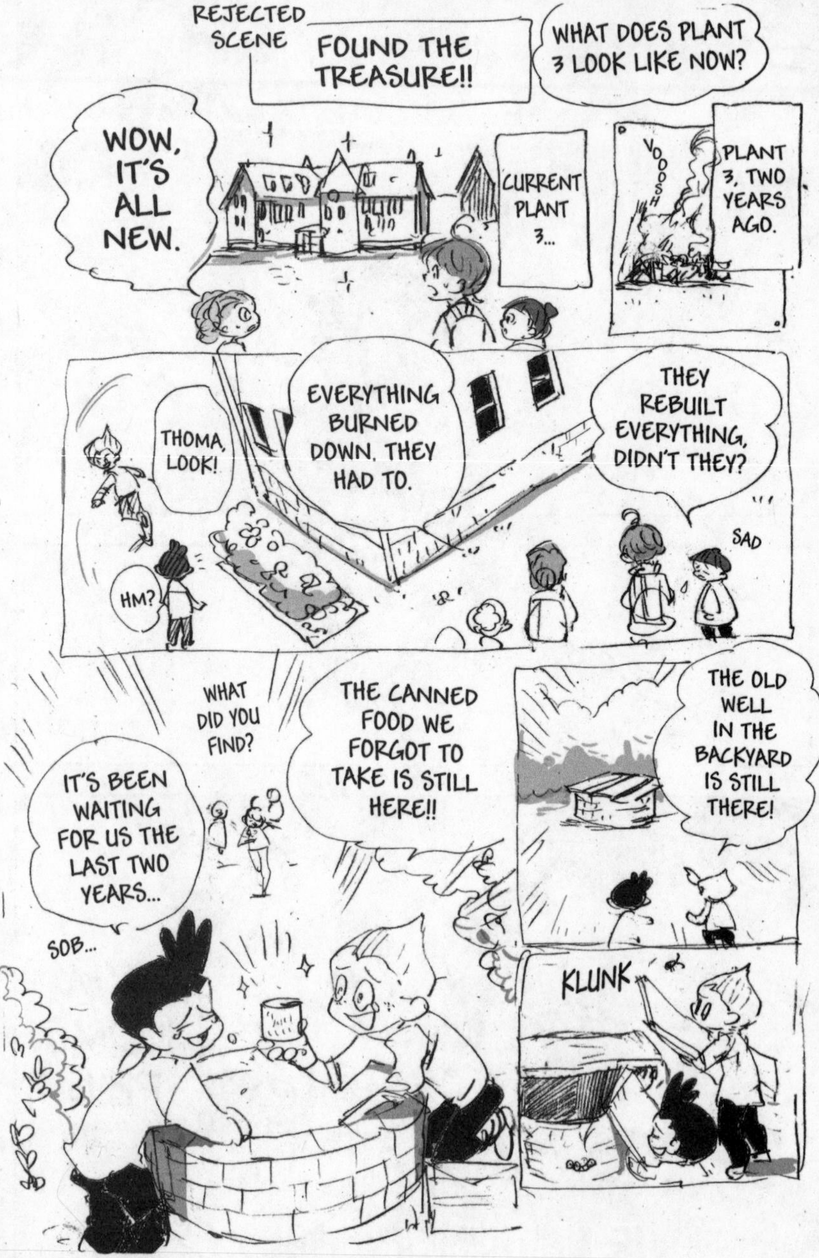
REJECTED SCENE
FOUND THE TREASURE!!
WHAT DOES PLANT 3 LOOK LIKE NOW?
PLANT 3, TWO YEARS AGO.
VOOOSH
CURRENT PLANT 3...
WOW, IT'S ALL NEW.
THEY REBUILT EVERYTHING, DIDN'T THEY?
SAD
EVERYTHING BURNED DOWN. THEY HAD TO.
THOMA, LOOK!
HM?
THE OLD WELL IN THE BACKYARD IS STILL THERE!
KLUNK
THE CANNED FOOD WE FORGOT TO TAKE IS STILL HERE!!
WHAT DID YOU FIND?
IT'S BEEN WAITING FOR US THE LAST TWO YEARS...
SOB...

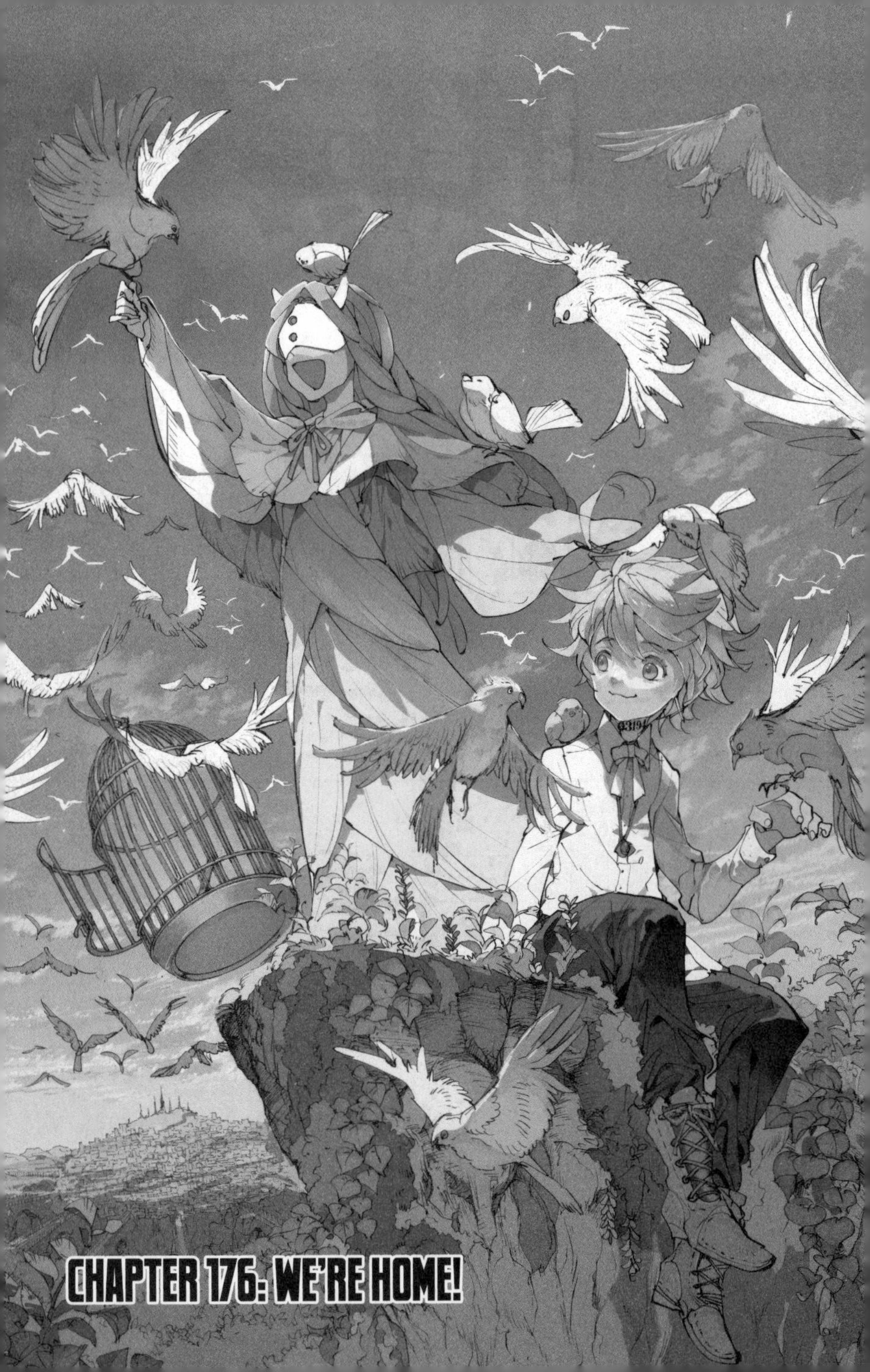
CHAPTER 176: WE'RE HOME!

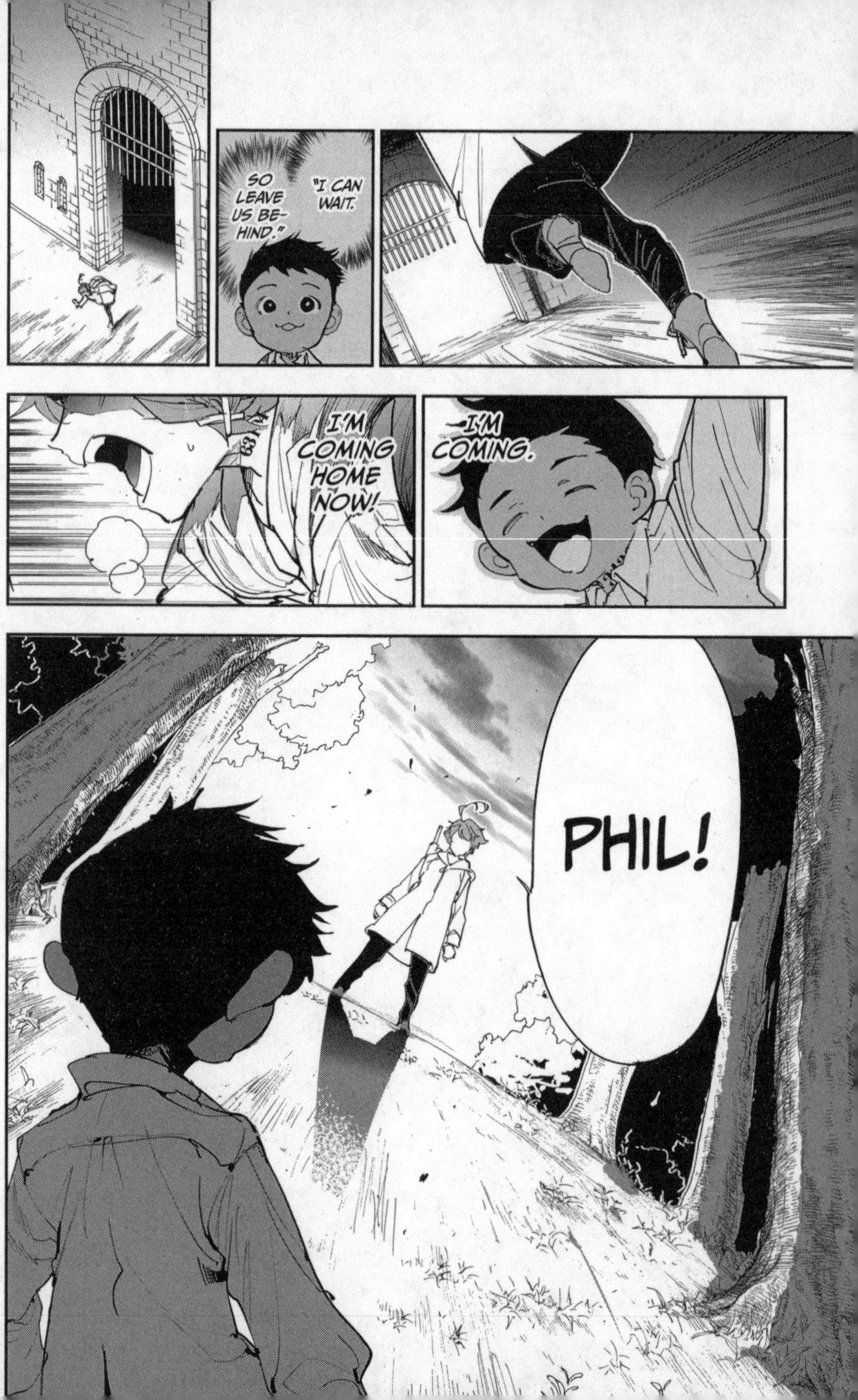
"I CAN WAIT.
SO LEAVE US BE-HIND."
I'M COMING.
I'M COMING HOME NOW!
PHIL!

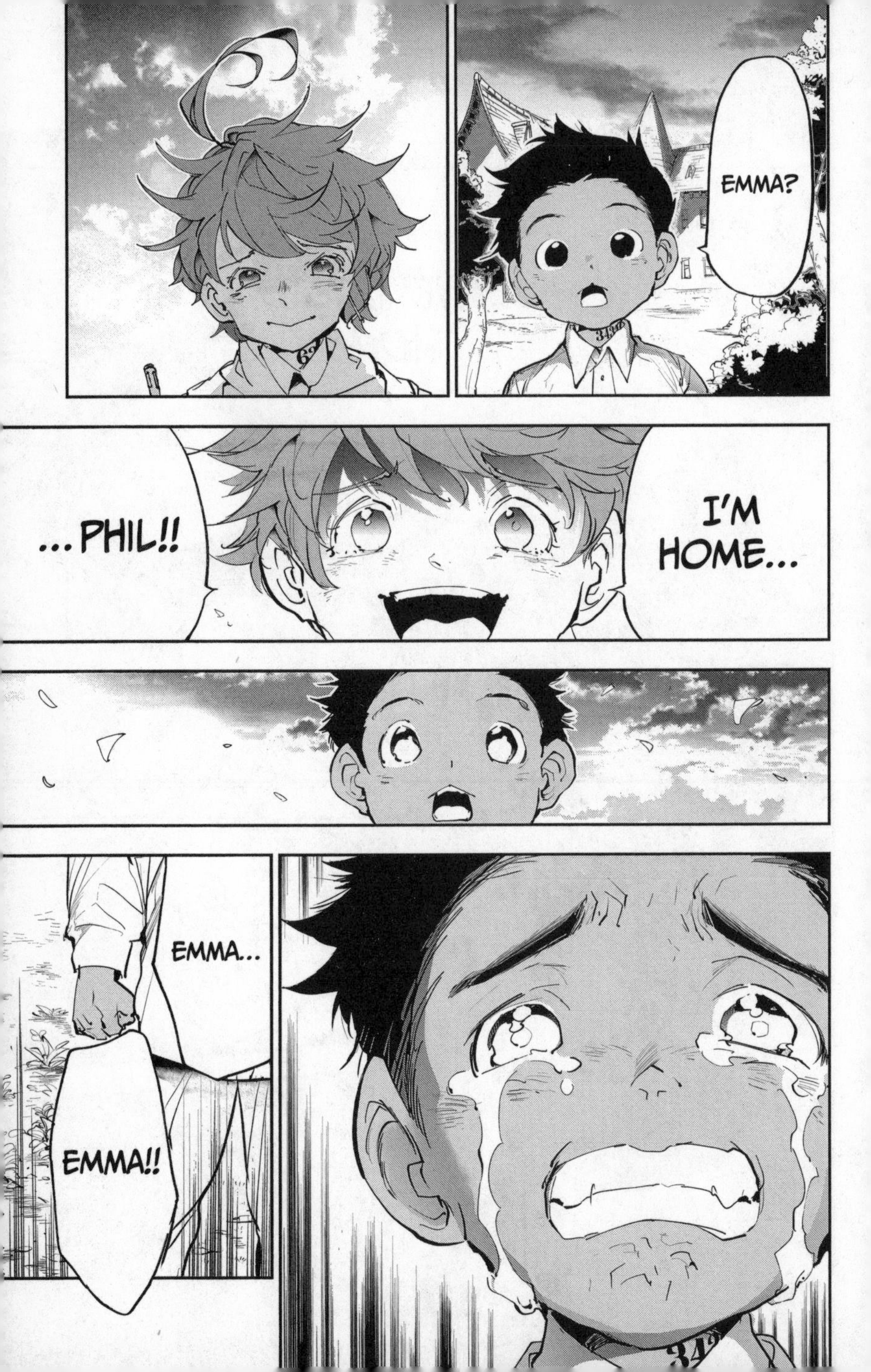
EMMA?
I'M HOME...
...PHIL!!
EMMA...
EMMA!!

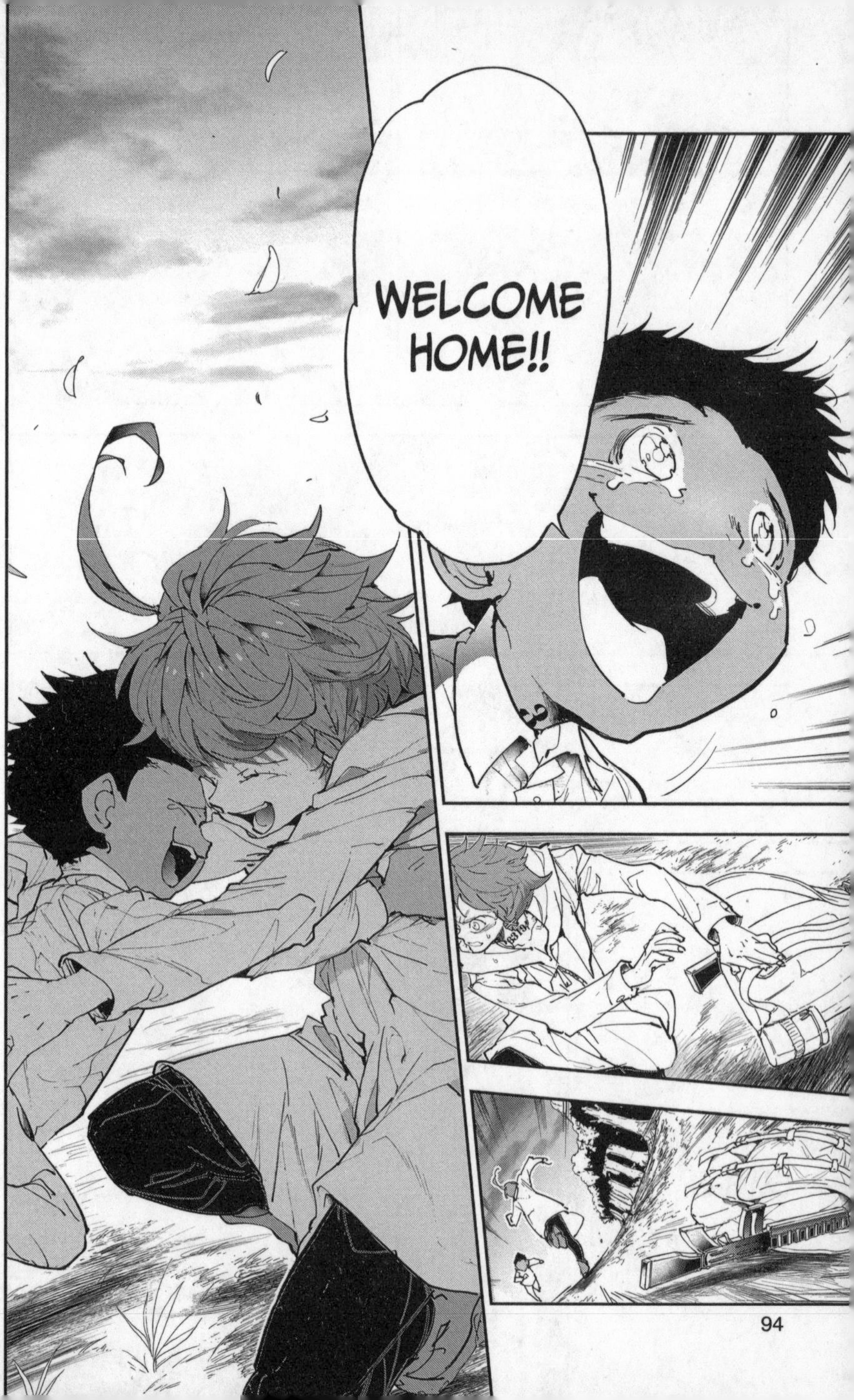
WELCOME HOME!!

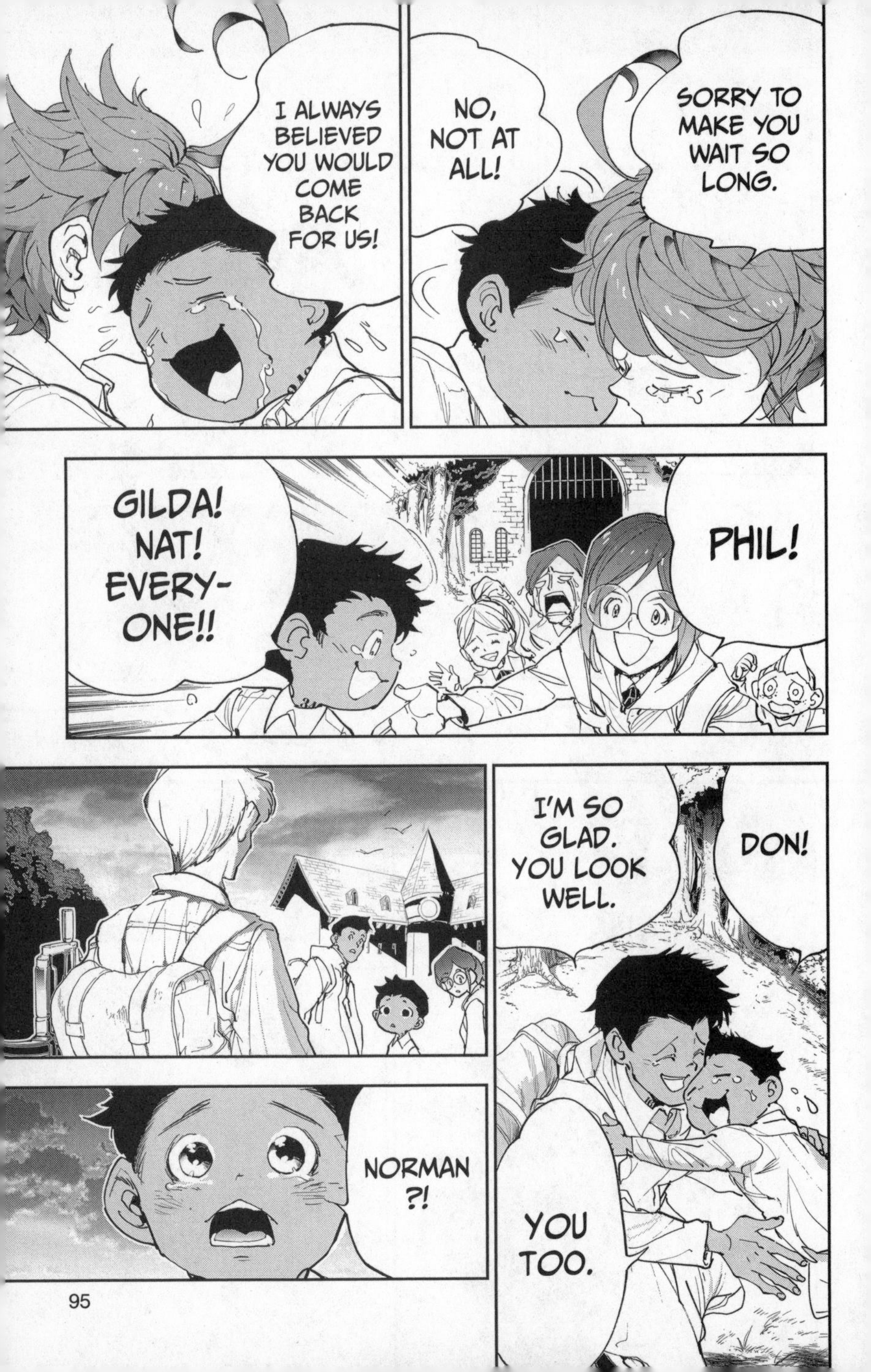
SORRY TO MAKE YOU WAIT SO LONG.
NO, NOT AT ALL!
I ALWAYS BELIEVED YOU WOULD COME BACK FOR US!
PHIL!
GILDA! NAT! EVERY-ONE!!
DON!
I'M SO GLAD. YOU LOOK WELL.
YOU TOO.
NORMAN ?!

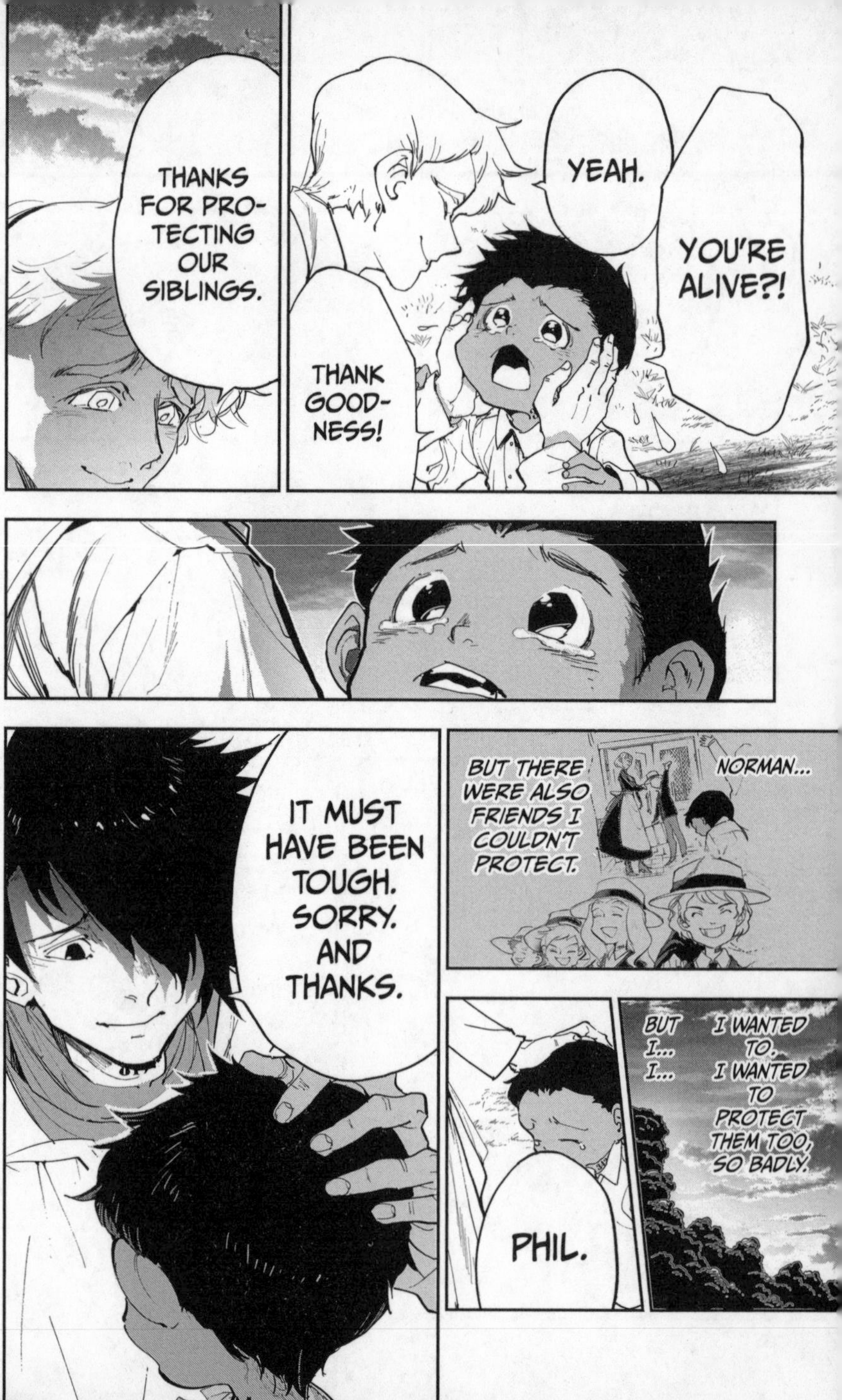
YOU'RE ALIVE?!
YEAH.
THANK GOODNESS!
THANKS FOR PROTECTING OUR SIBLINGS.
NORMAN...
BUT THERE WERE ALSO FRIENDS I COULDN'T PROTECT.
I WANTED TO. I WANTED TO PROTECT THEM TOO, SO BADLY.
BUT I... I...
PHIL.
IT MUST HAVE BEEN TOUGH. SORRY. AND THANKS.

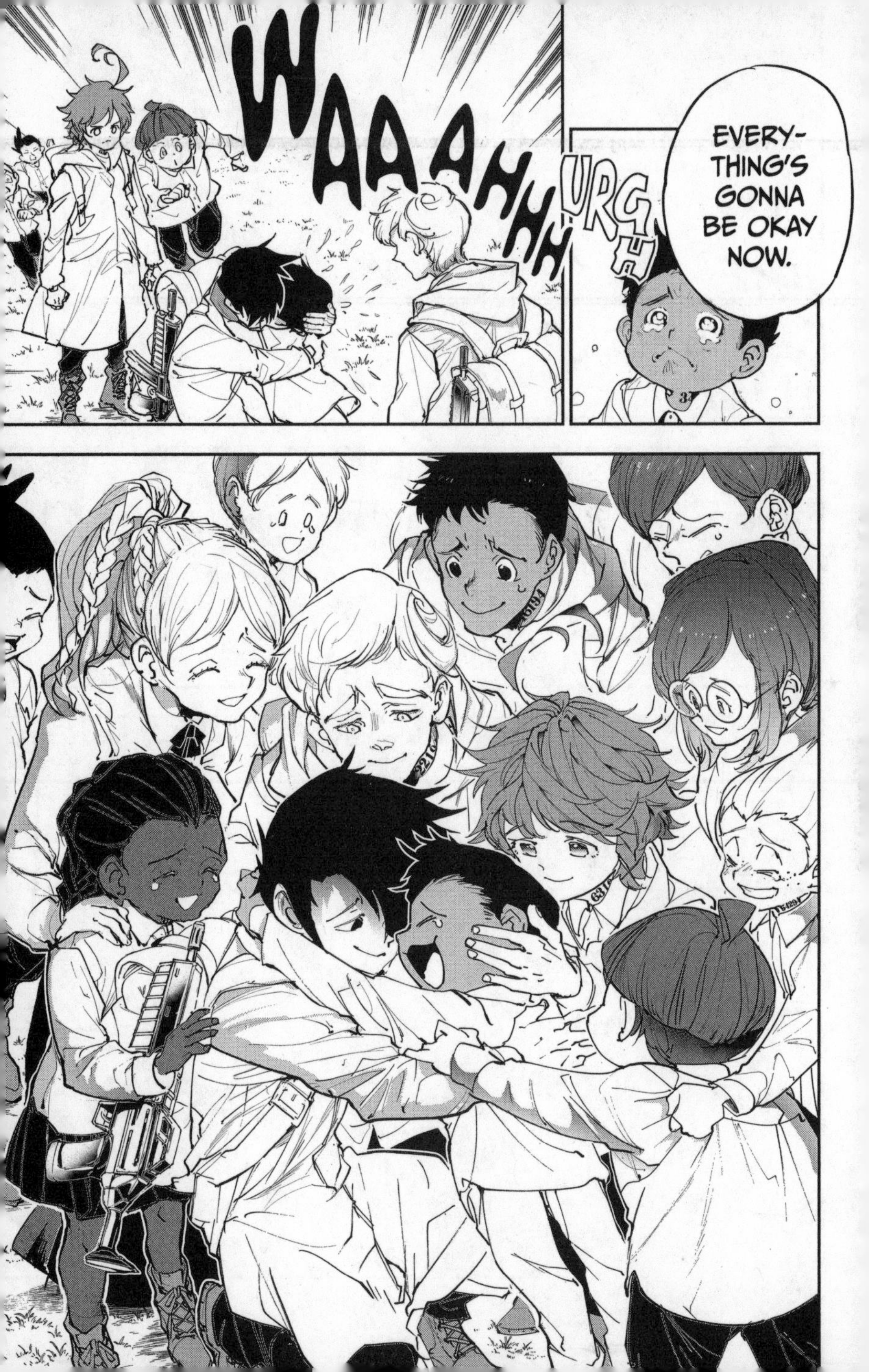
EVERYTHING'S GONNA BE OKAY NOW.
URGH
WAAAHHH

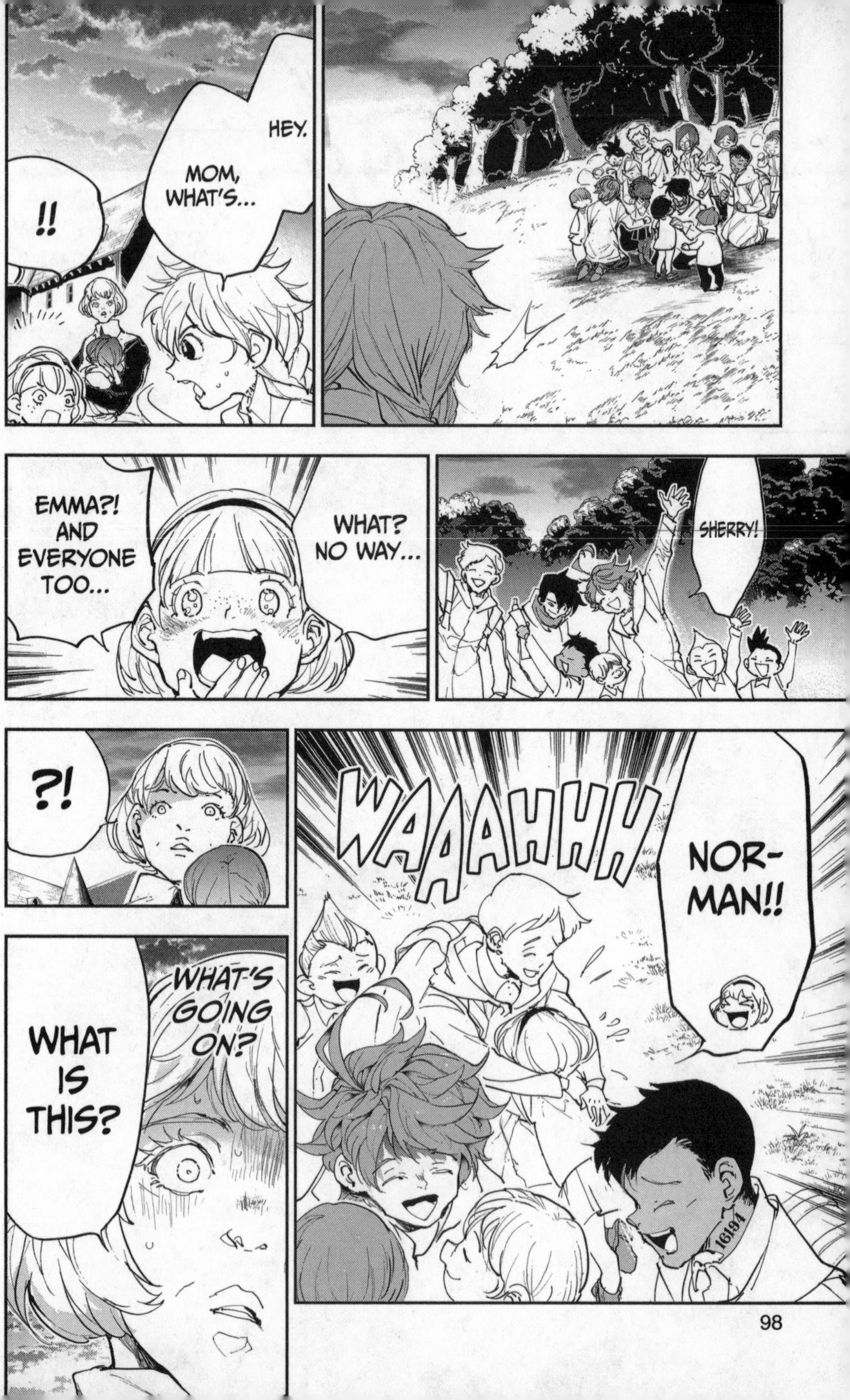
HEY.
MOM, WHAT'S...
!!
SHERRY!
WHAT? NO WAY...
EMMA?! AND EVERYONE TOO...
NOR-MAN!!
WAAAHHH
?!
WHAT'S GOING ON?
WHAT IS THIS?

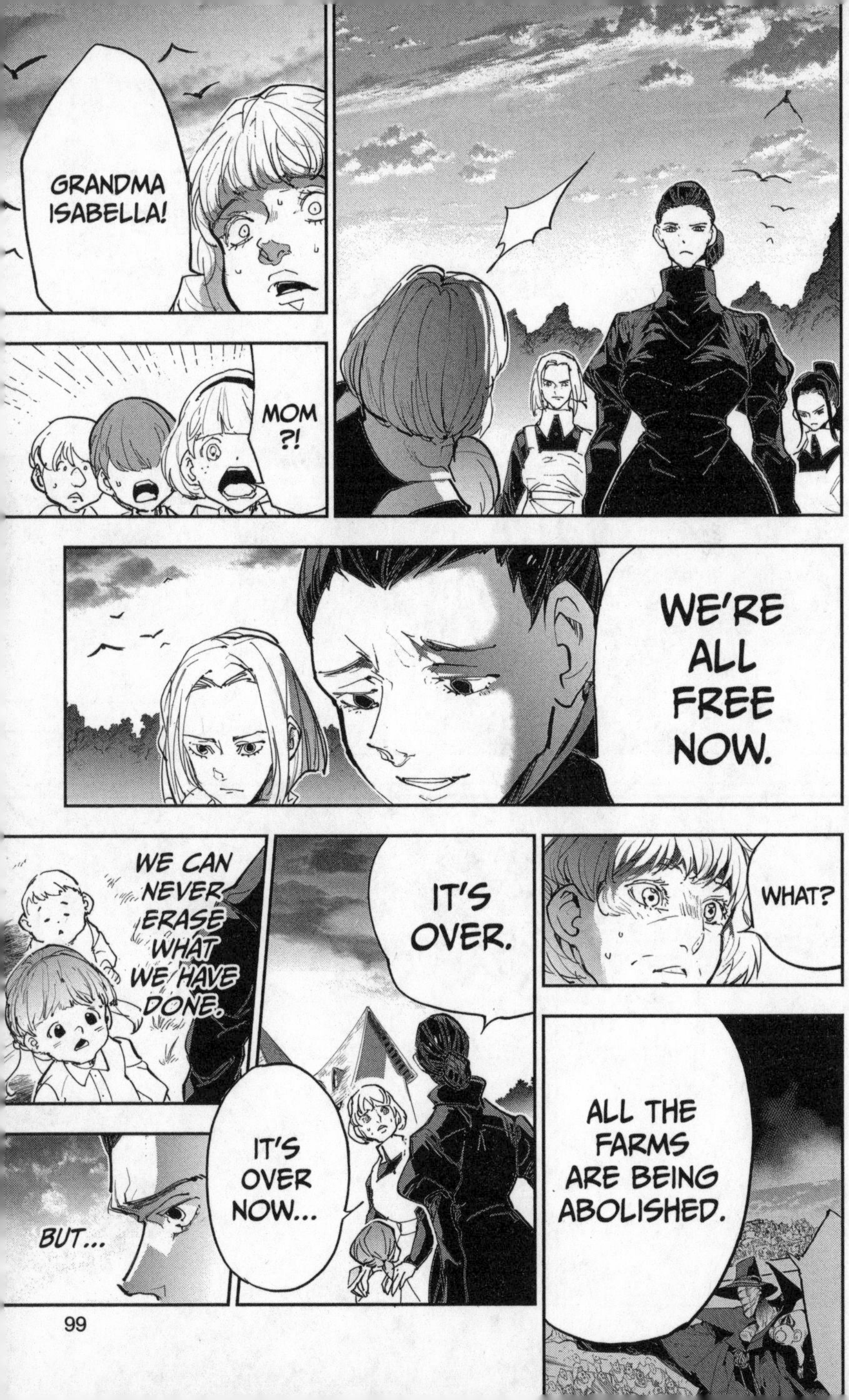
GRANDMA ISABELLA!
MOM ?!
WE'RE ALL FREE NOW.
WHAT?
ALL THE FARMS ARE BEING ABOLISHED.
IT'S OVER.
IT'S OVER NOW...
WE CAN NEVER ERASE WHAT WE HAVE DONE.
BUT...

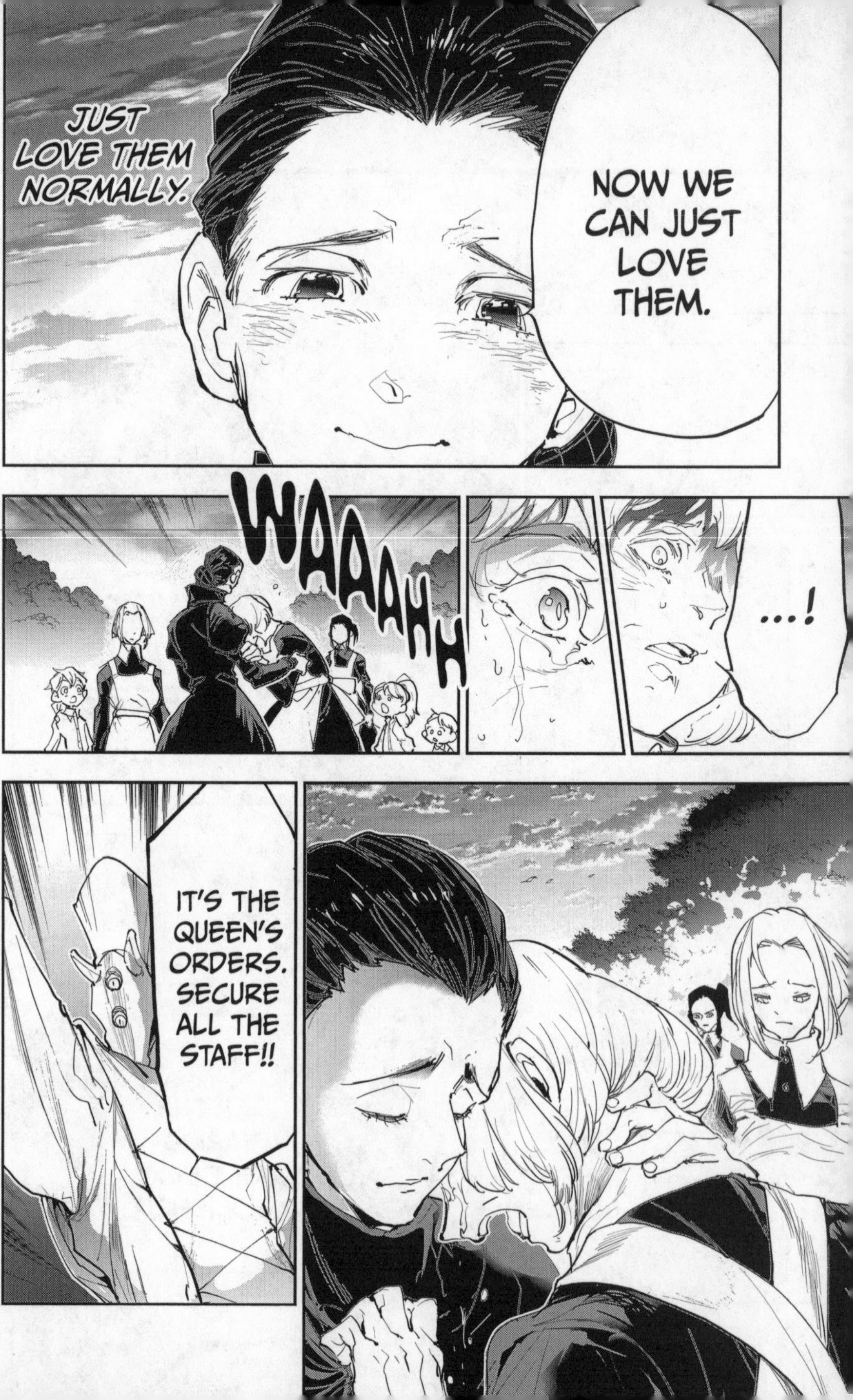
NOW WE CAN JUST LOVE THEM.
JUST LOVE THEM NORMALLY.
...!
WAAAHH
IT'S THE QUEEN'S ORDERS. SECURE ALL THE STAFF!!

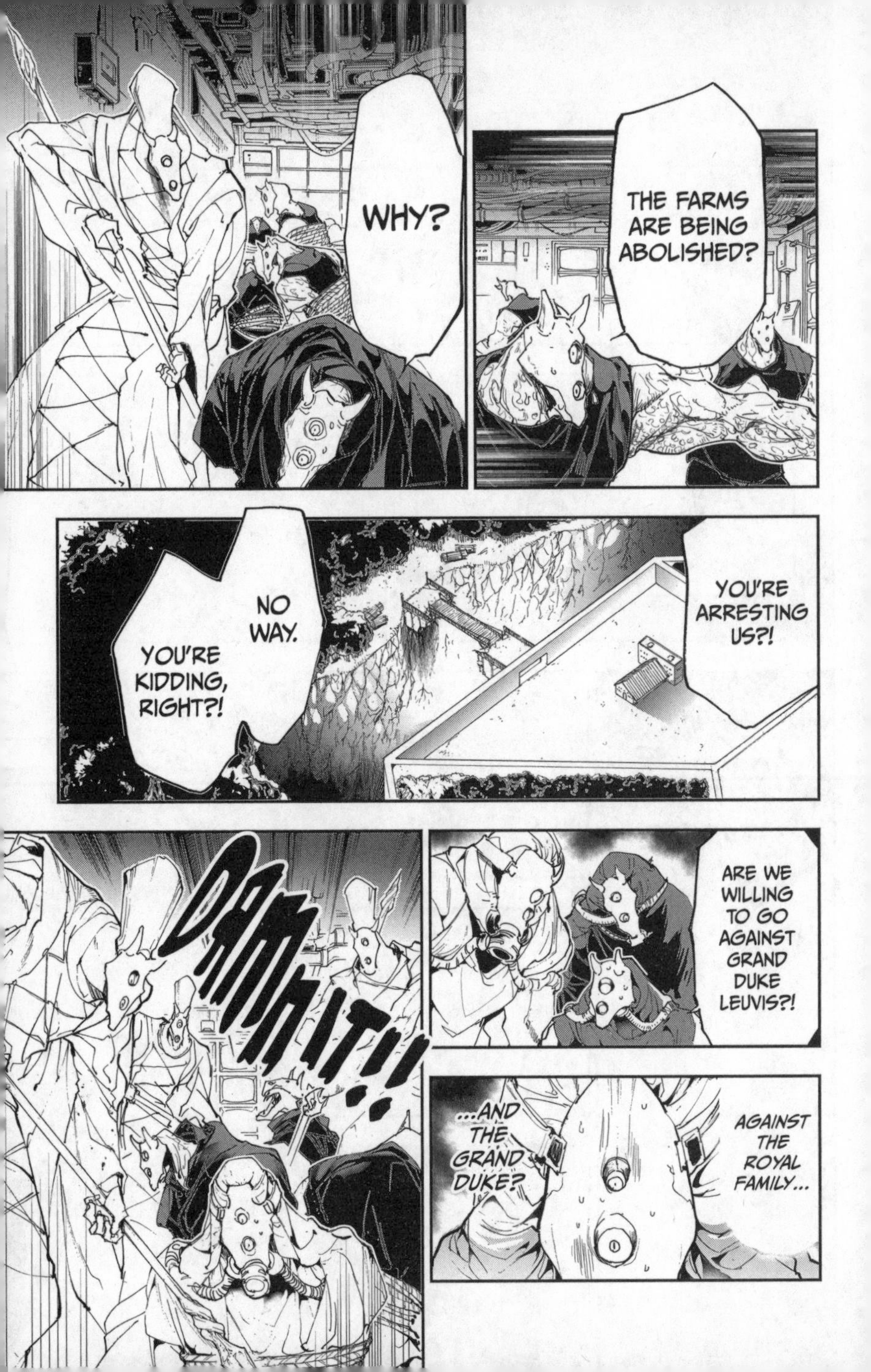
THE FARMS ARE BEING ABOLISHED?
WHY?
YOU'RE ARRESTING US?!
NO WAY.
YOU'RE KIDDING, RIGHT?!
ARE WE WILLING TO GO AGAINST GRAND DUKE LEUVIS?!
AGAINST THE ROYAL FAMILY...
...AND THE GRAND DUKE?
DAMMIT!!

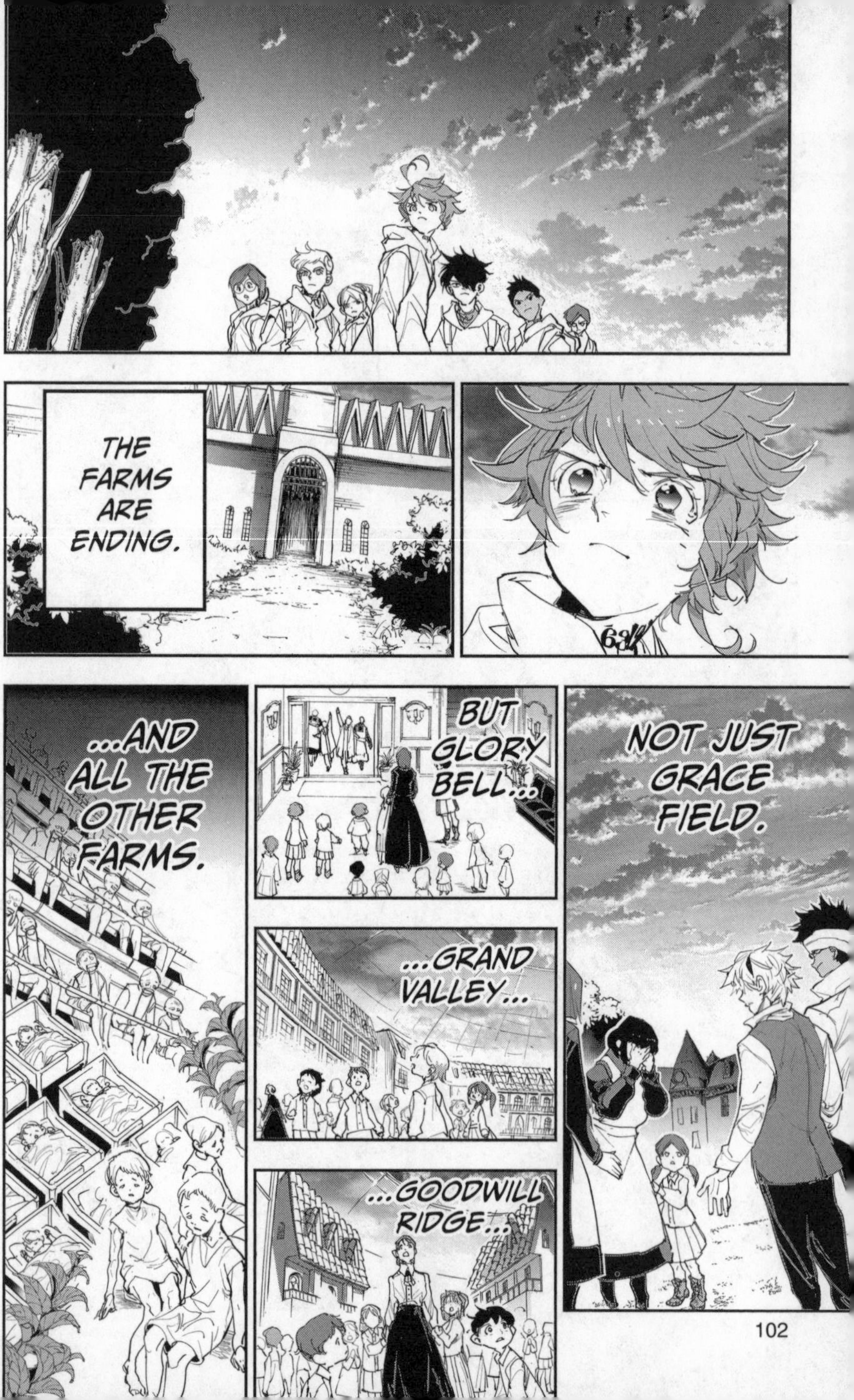
THE FARMS ARE ENDING.
NOT JUST GRACE FIELD.
BUT GLORY BELL...
...GRAND VALLEY...
...GOODWILL RIDGE...
...AND ALL THE OTHER FARMS.

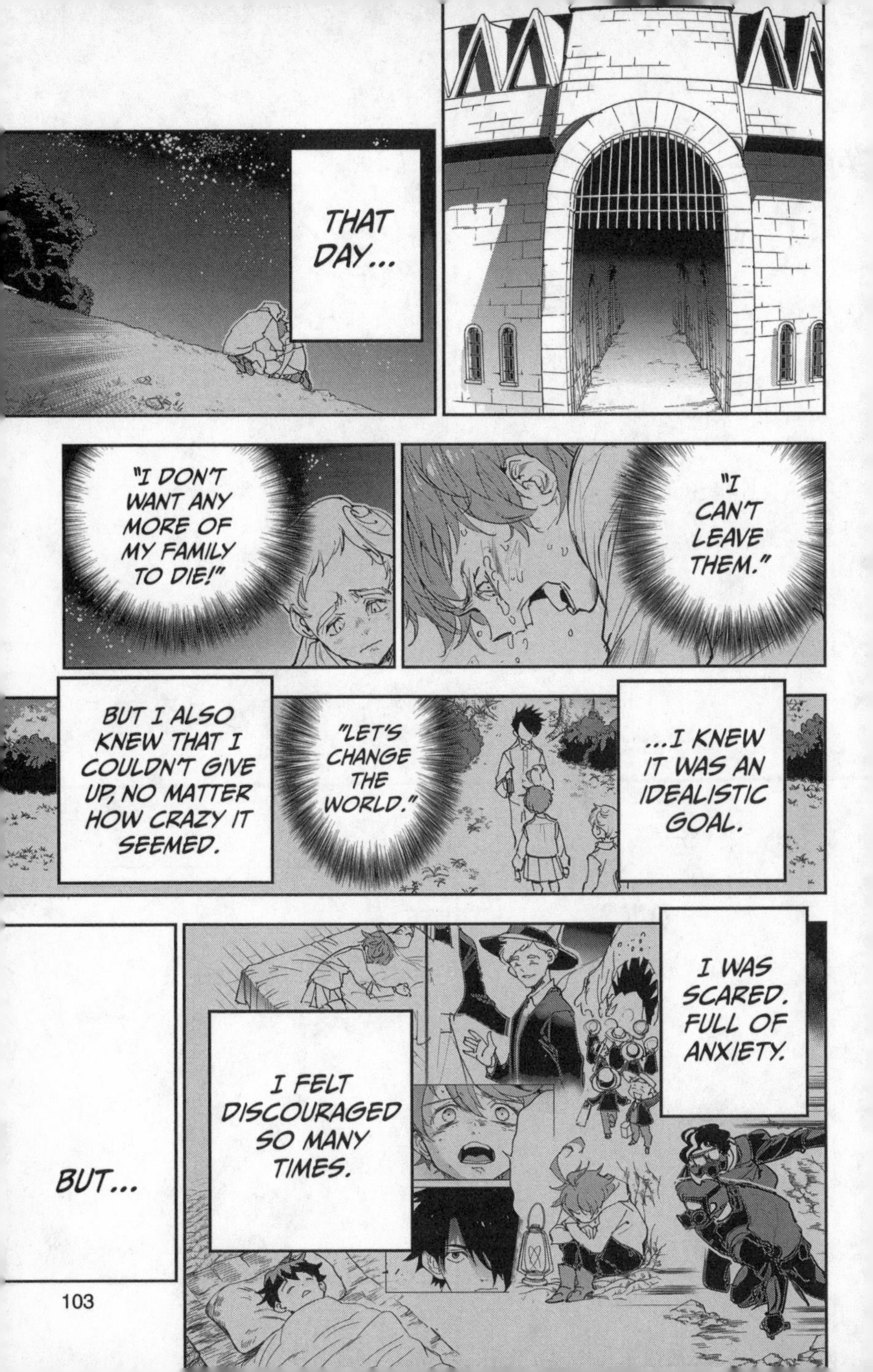
THAT DAY...
"I CAN'T LEAVE THEM."
"I DON'T WANT ANY MORE OF MY FAMILY TO DIE!"
...I KNEW IT WAS AN IDEALISTIC GOAL.
"LET'S CHANGE THE WORLD."
BUT I ALSO KNEW THAT I COULDN'T GIVE UP, NO MATTER HOW CRAZY IT SEEMED.
I WAS SCARED. FULL OF ANXIETY.
I FELT DISCOURAGED SO MANY TIMES.
BUT...

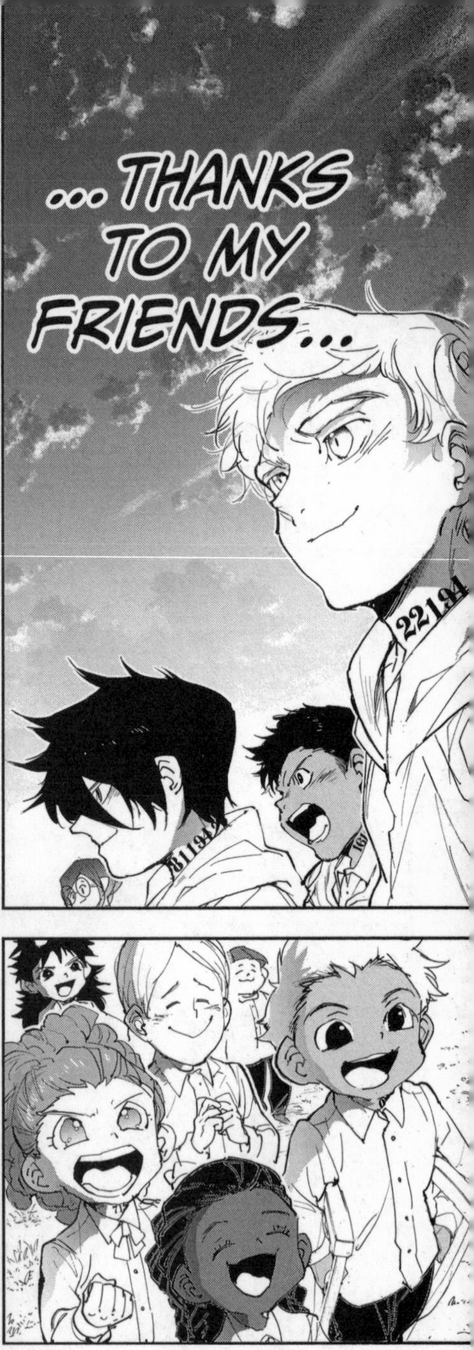
...THANKS TO MY FRIENDS...
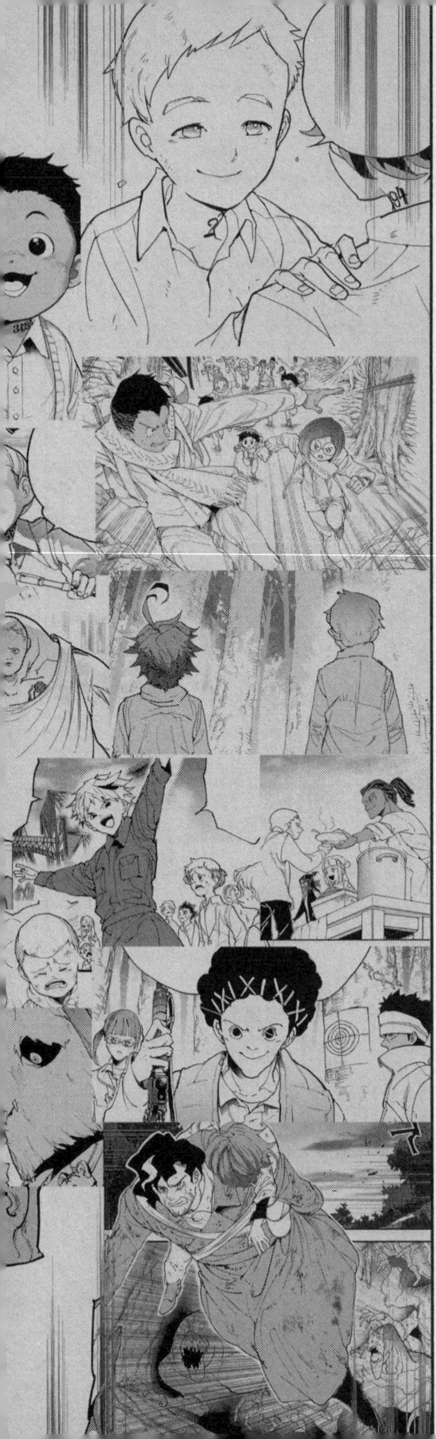

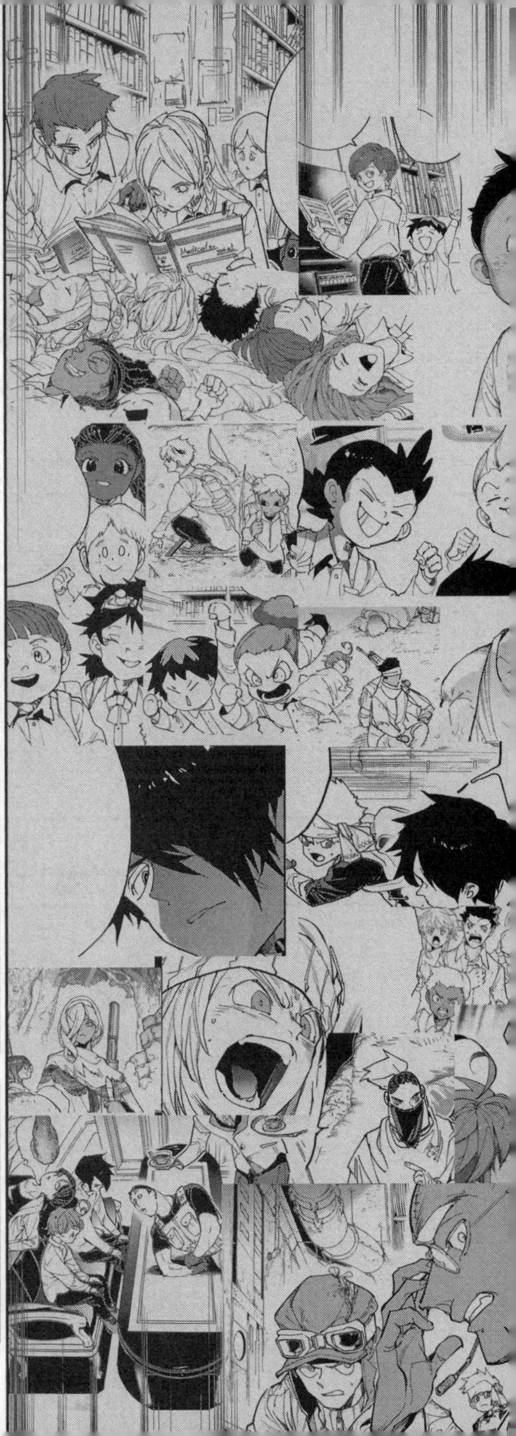

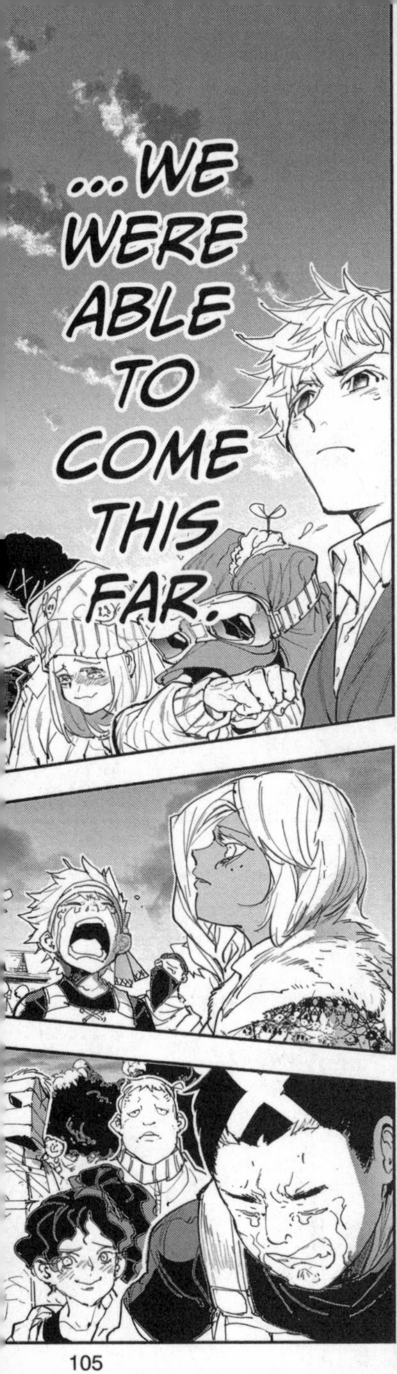
...WE WERE ABLE TO COME THIS FAR.

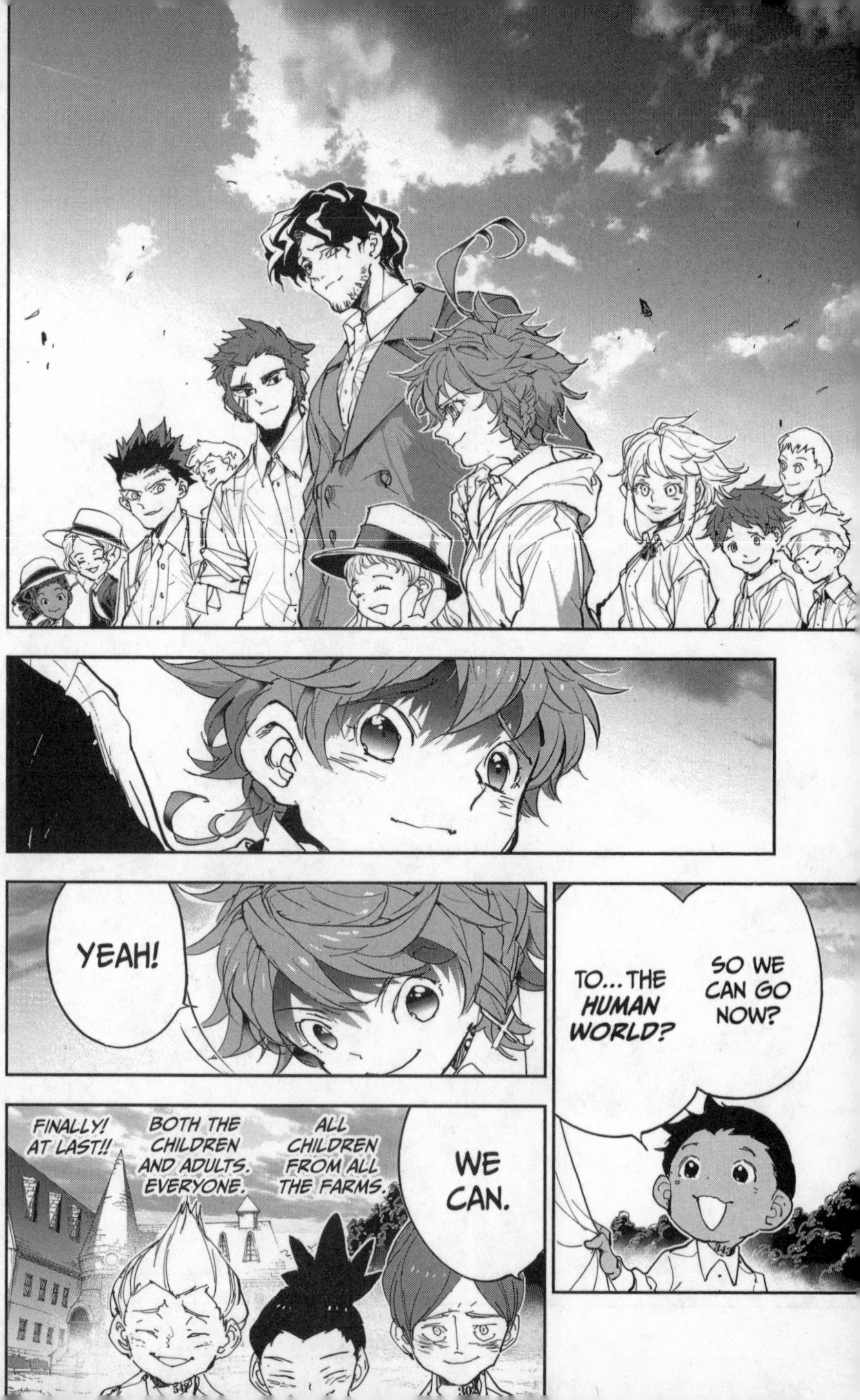
SO WE CAN GO NOW?
TO... THE HUMAN WORLD?
YEAH!
WE CAN.
ALL CHILDREN FROM ALL THE FARMS.
BOTH THE CHILDREN AND ADULTS. EVERYONE.
FINALLY! AT LAST!!

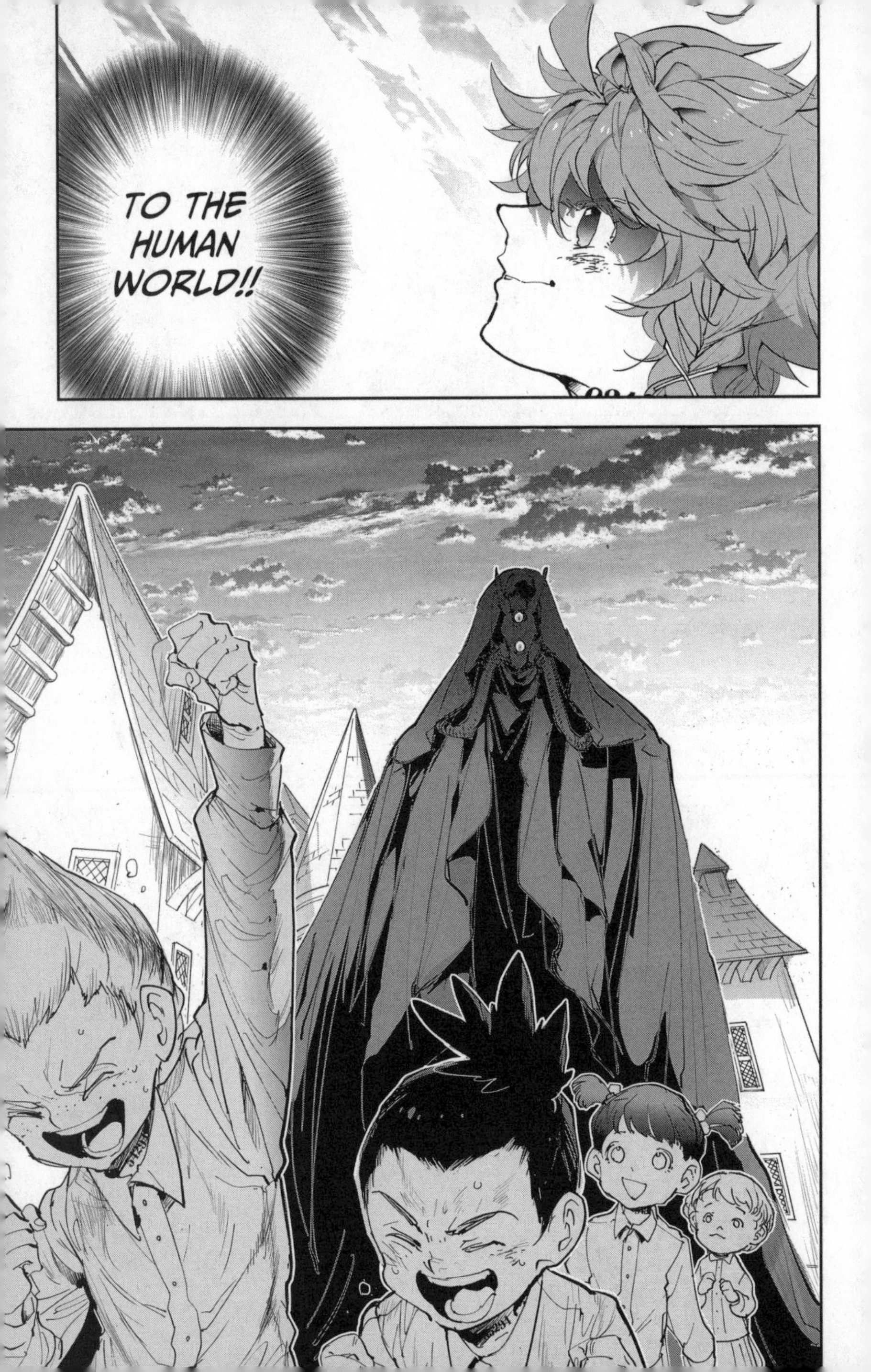
TO THE HUMAN WORLD!!

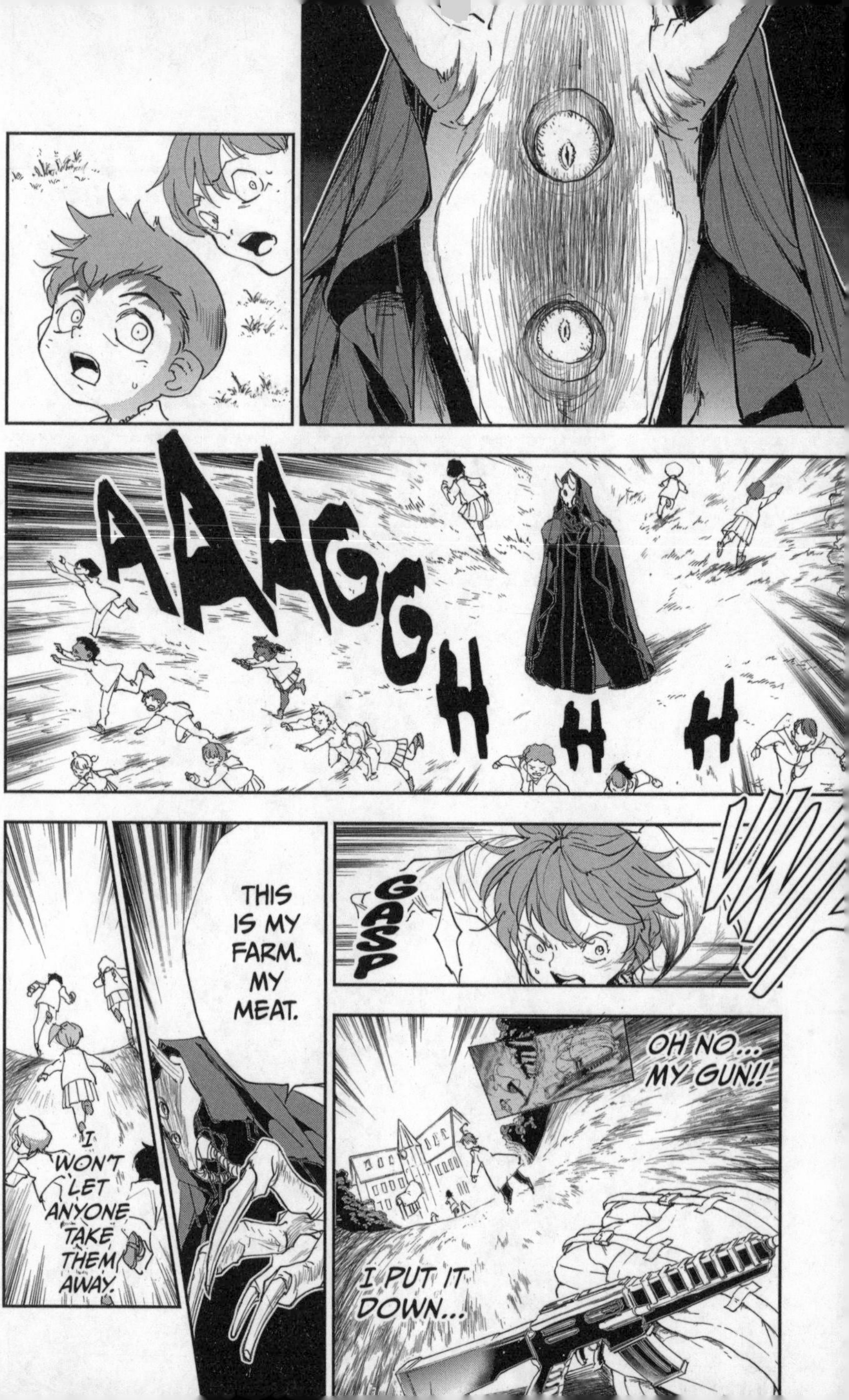

AAAGGHHHH
GASP
OH NO... MY GUN!!
I PUT IT DOWN...
THIS IS MY FARM. MY MEAT.
I WON'T LET ANYONE TAKE THEM AWAY.

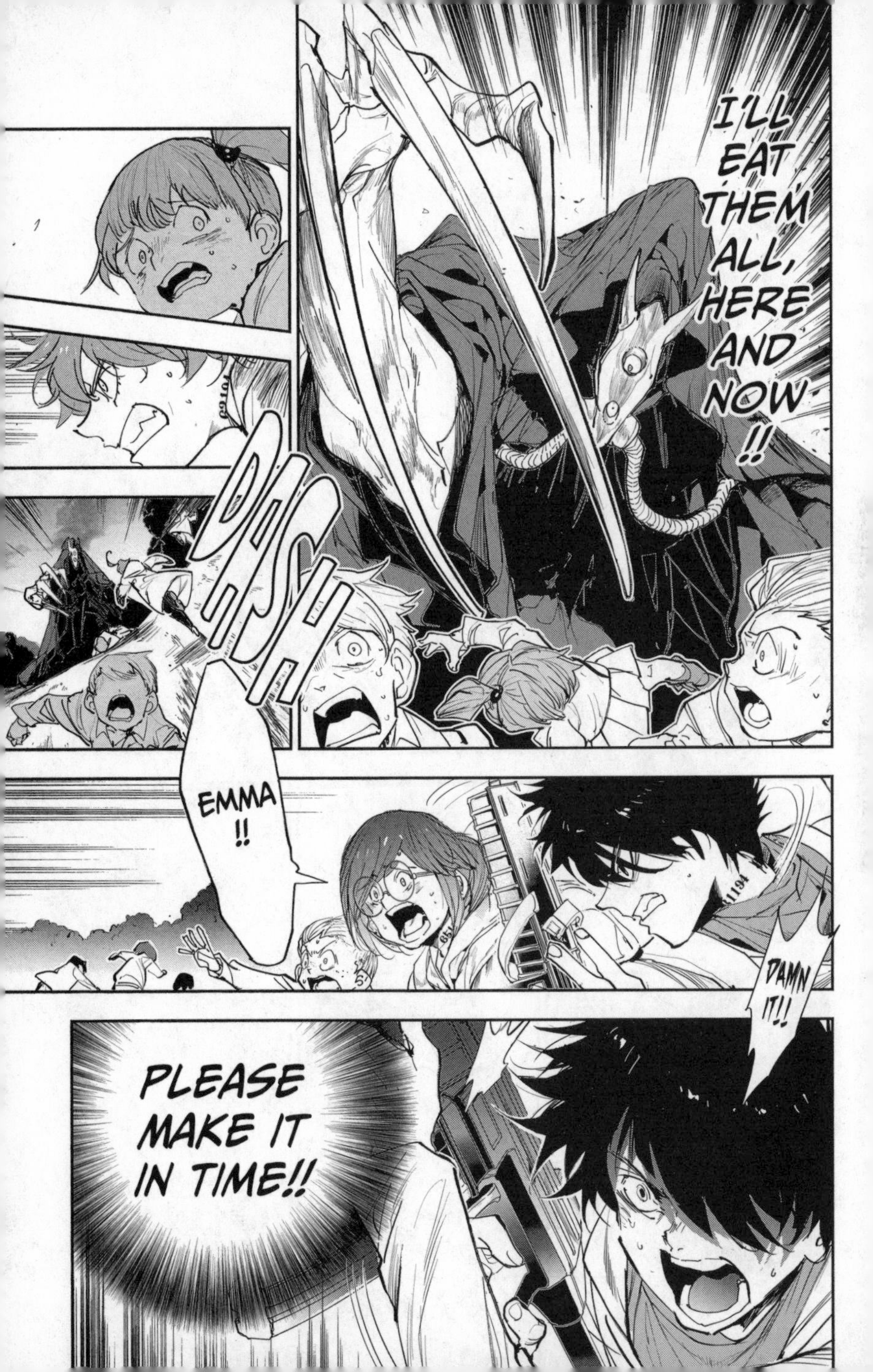
I'LL EAT THEM ALL, HERE AND NOW!!
DISH
EMMA!!
DAMN IT!!
PLEASE MAKE IT IN TIME!!

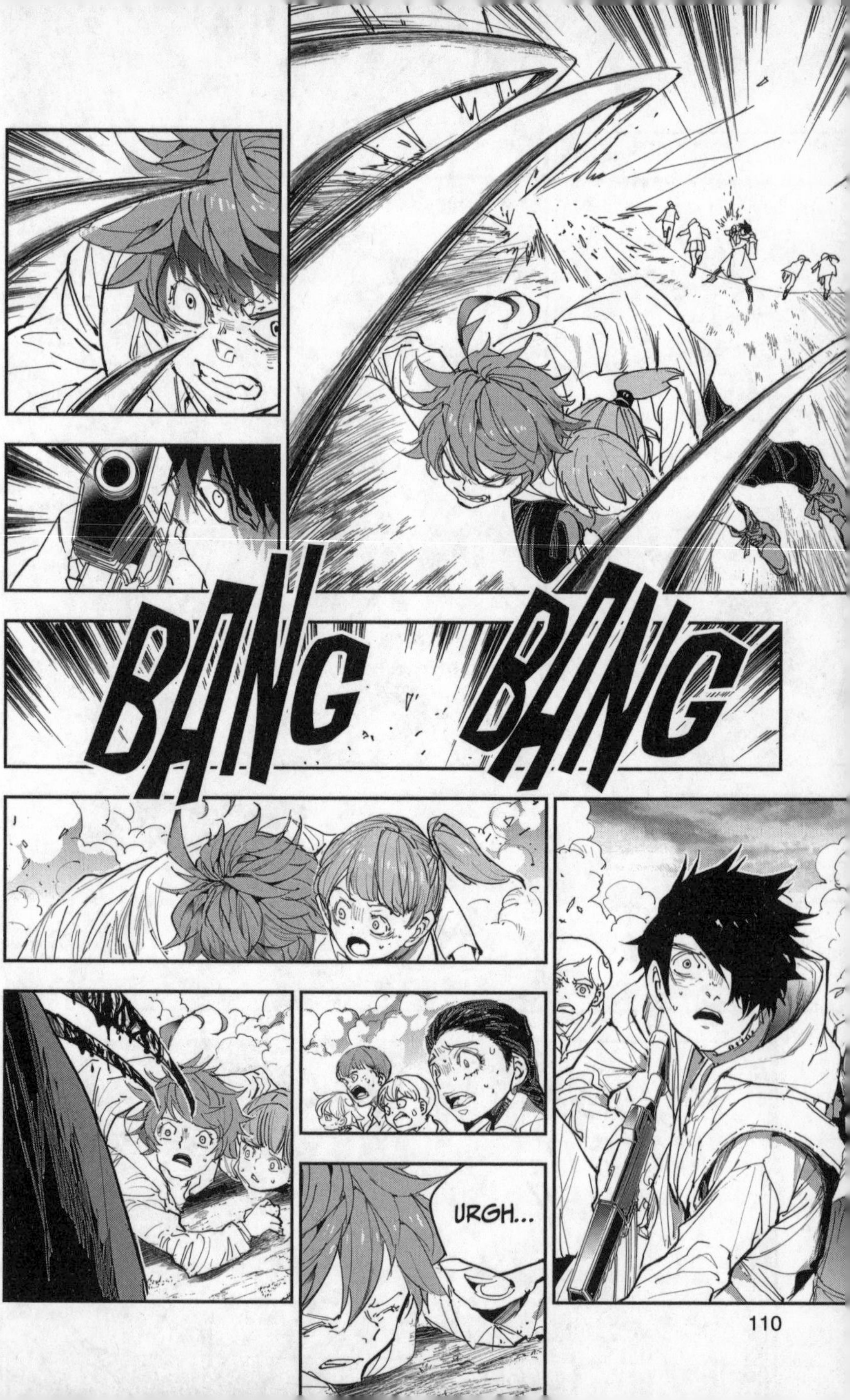

BANG
BANG
URGH...

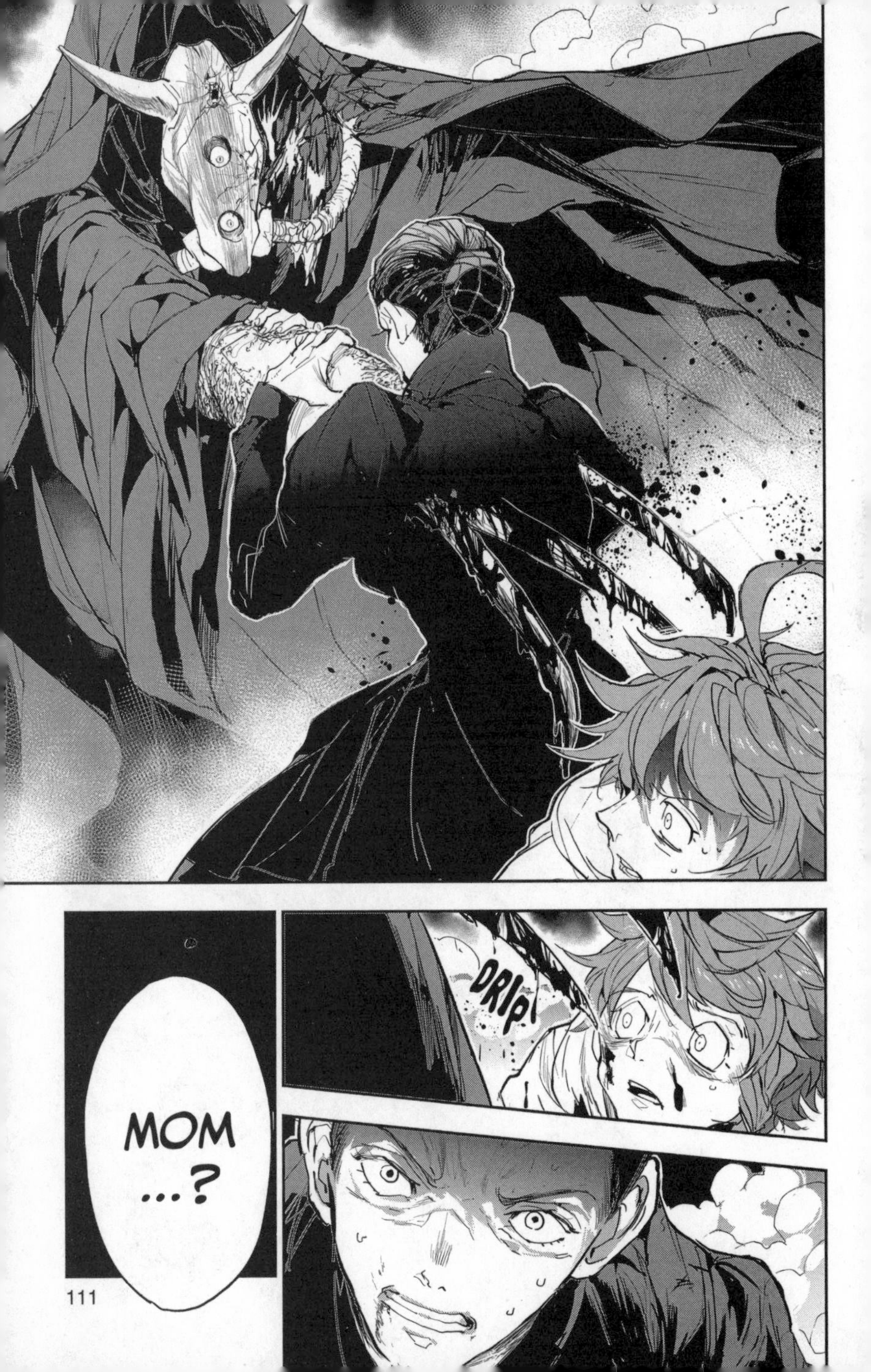
DRIP!
MOM ...?

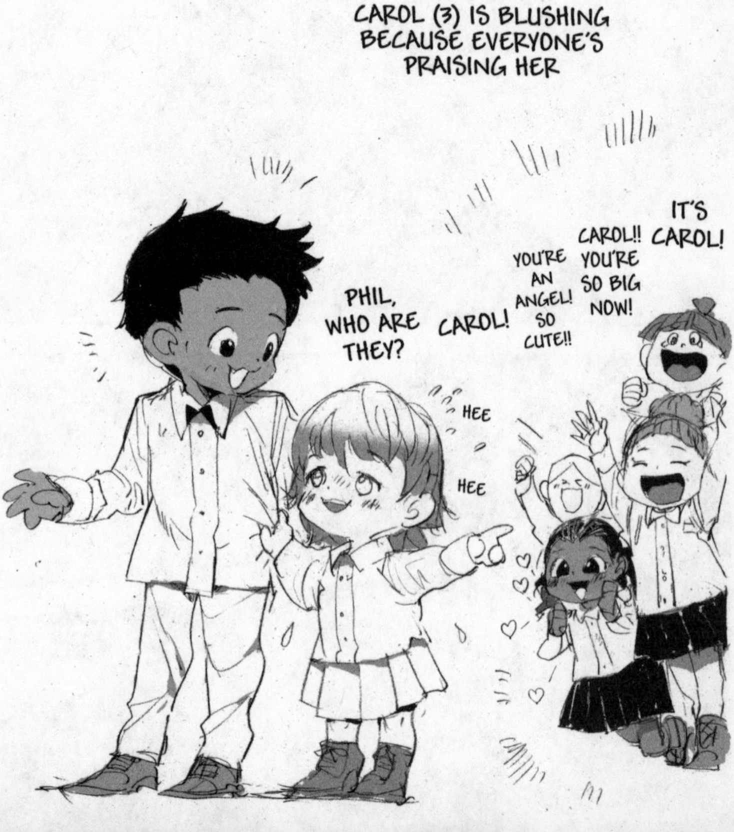
CAROL (3) IS BLUSHING BECAUSE EVERYONE'S PRAISING HER
IT'S CAROL!
CAROL!! YOU'RE SO BIG NOW!
YOU'RE AN ANGEL! SO CUTE!!
CAROL!
PHIL, WHO ARE THEY?
HEE
HEE

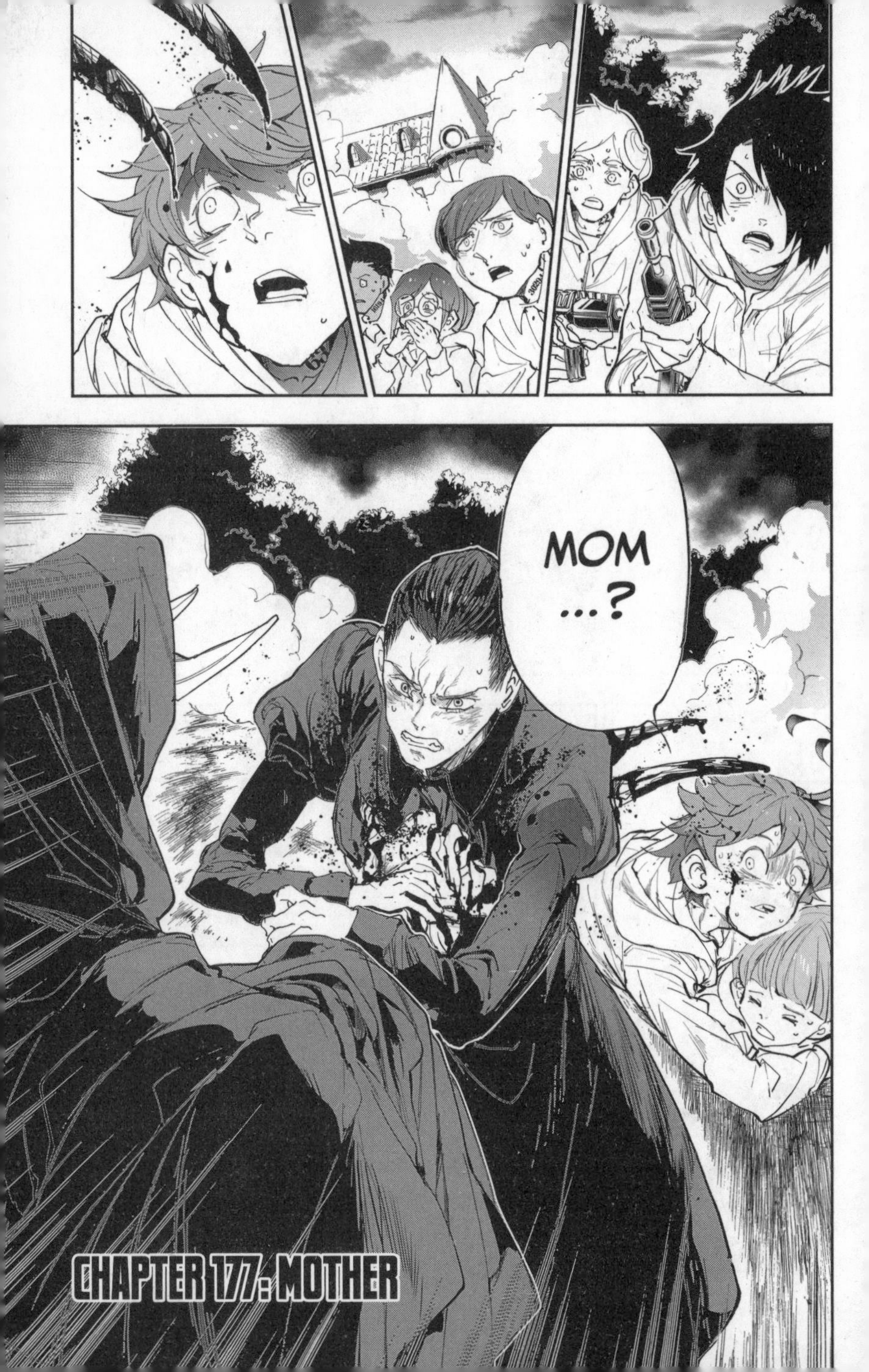
MOM ...?
CHAPTER 177: MOTHER

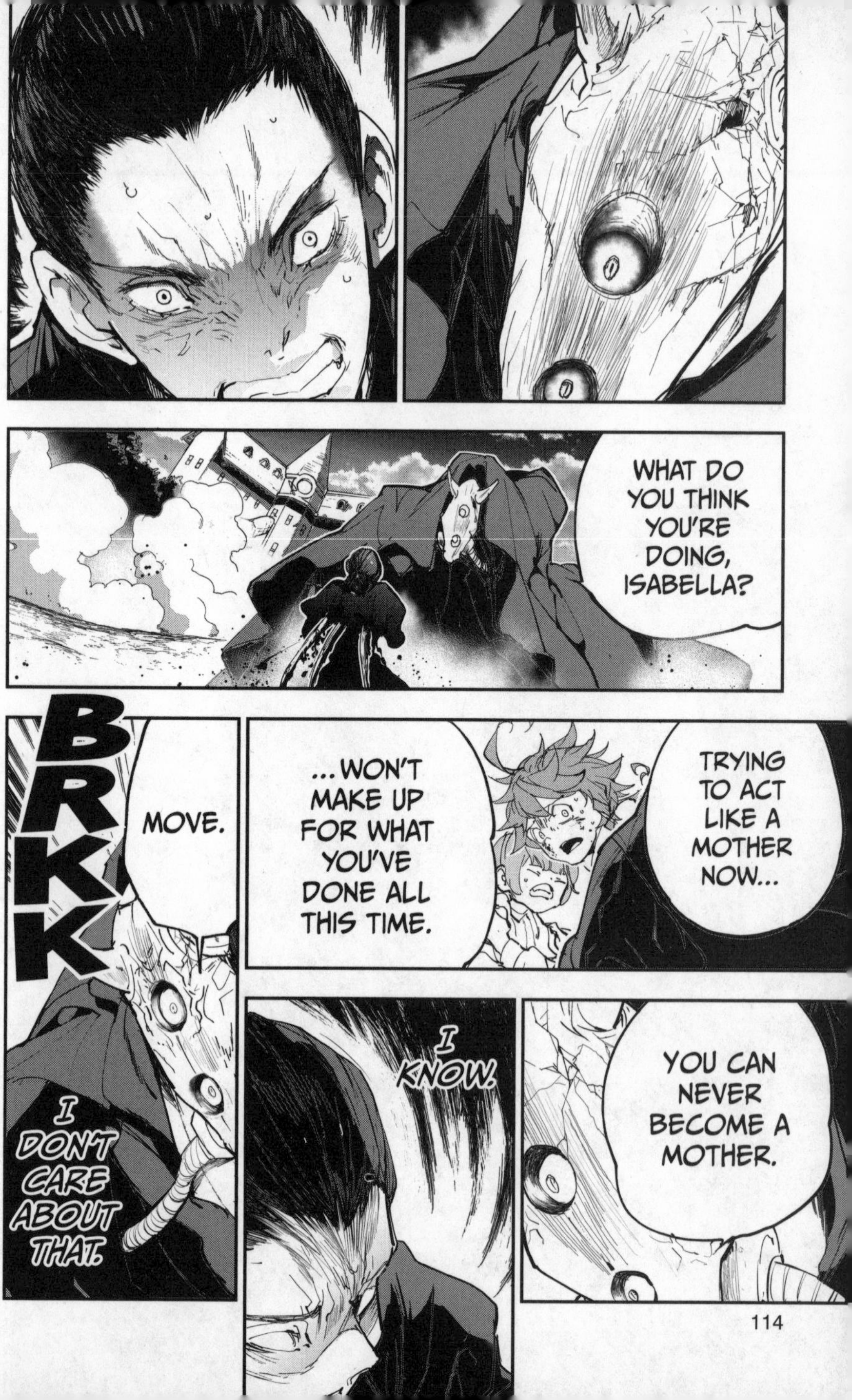
WHAT DO YOU THINK YOU'RE DOING, ISABELLA?
TRYING TO ACT LIKE A MOTHER NOW...
...WON'T MAKE UP FOR WHAT YOU'VE DONE ALL THIS TIME.
YOU CAN NEVER BECOME A MOTHER.
I KNOW.
BRKK
MOVE.
I DON'T CARE ABOUT THAT.

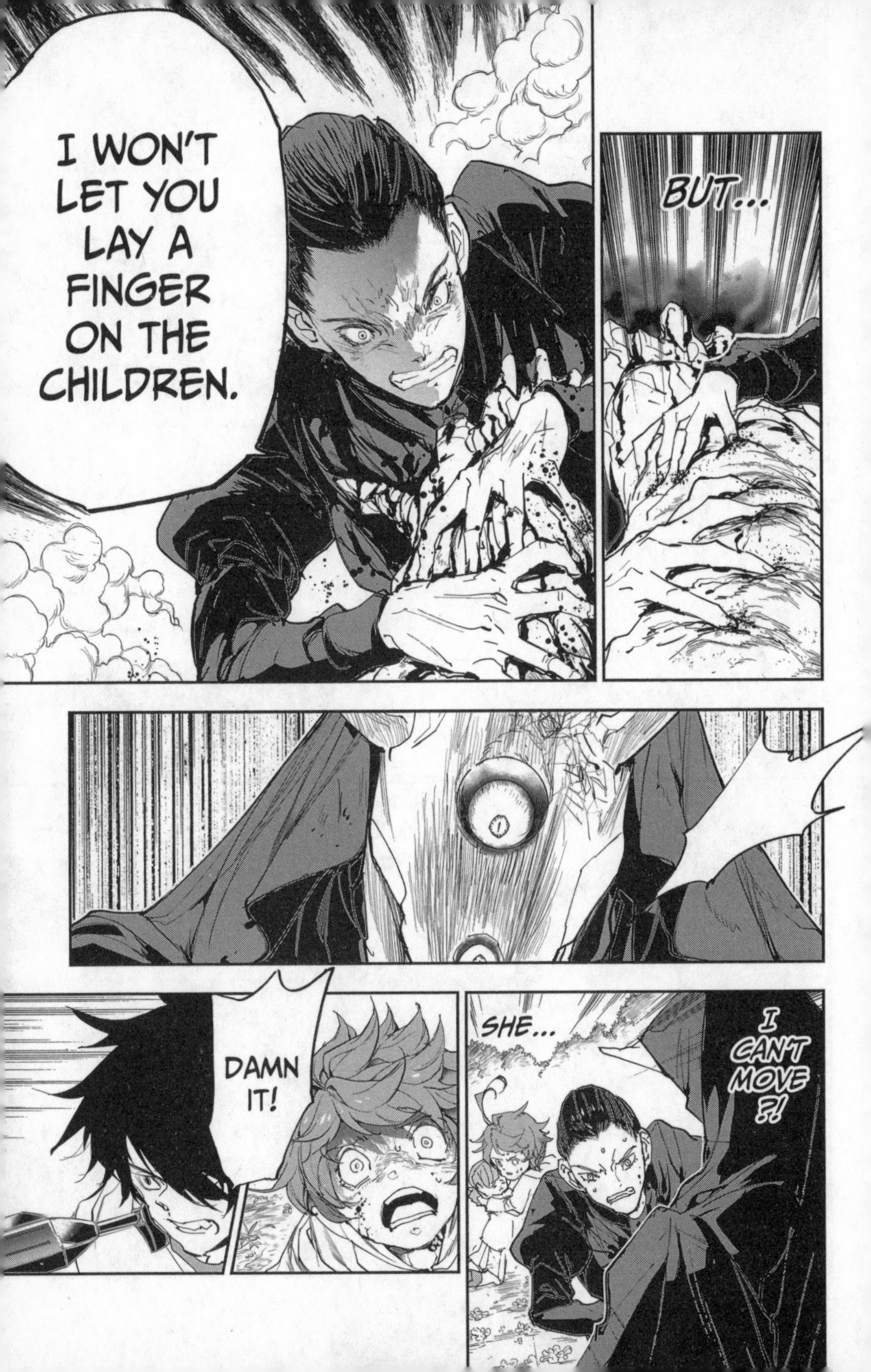
BUT...
I WON'T LET YOU LAY A FINGER ON THE CHILDREN.
SHE...
I CAN'T MOVE ?!
DAMN IT!

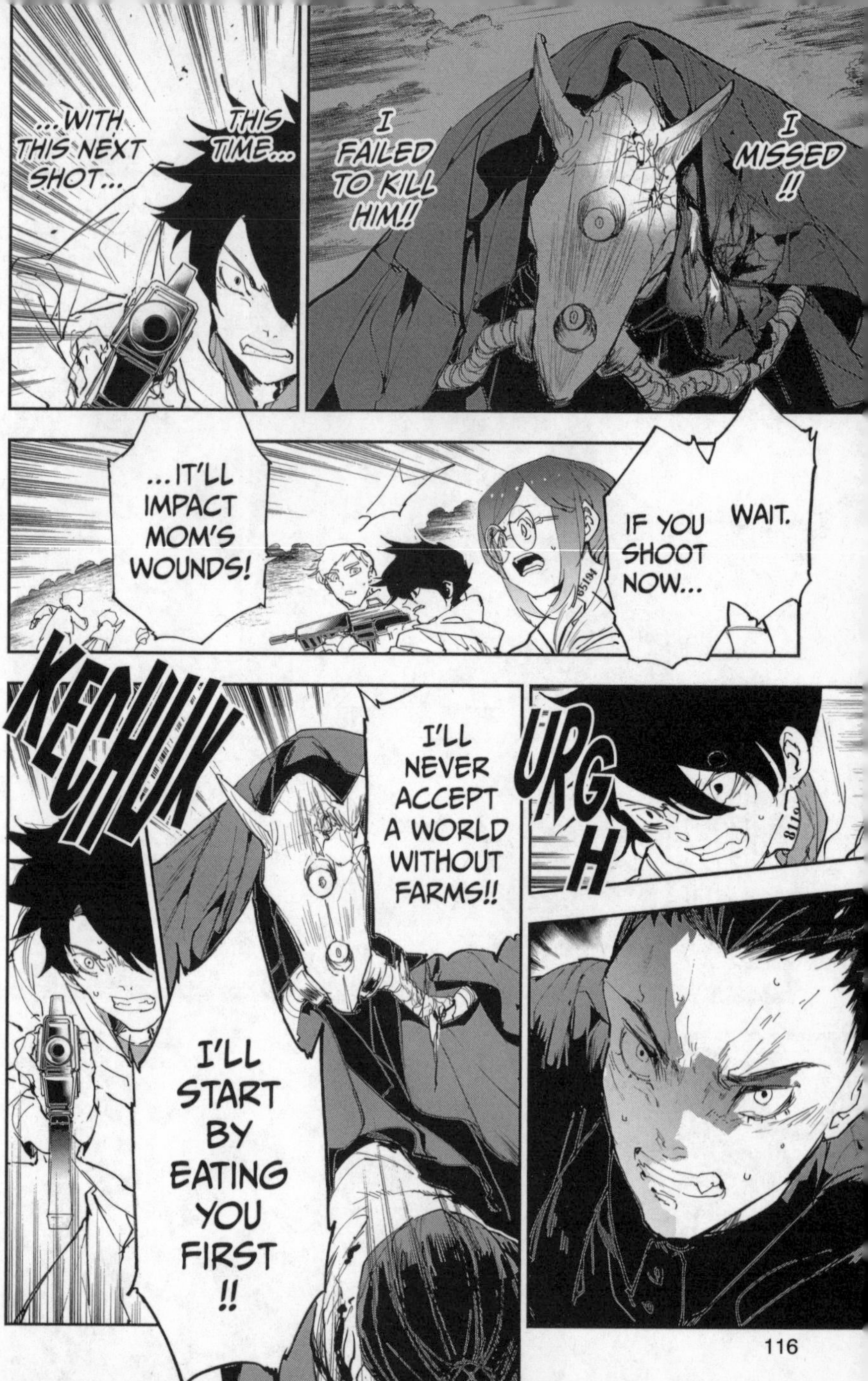
I MISSED!!
I FAILED TO KILL HIM!!
THIS TIME...
...WITH THIS NEXT SHOT...
WAIT.
IF YOU SHOOT NOW...
...IT'LL IMPACT MOM'S WOUNDS!
URGH
KECHUK
I'LL NEVER ACCEPT A WORLD WITHOUT FARMS!!
I'LL START BY EATING YOU FIRST!!

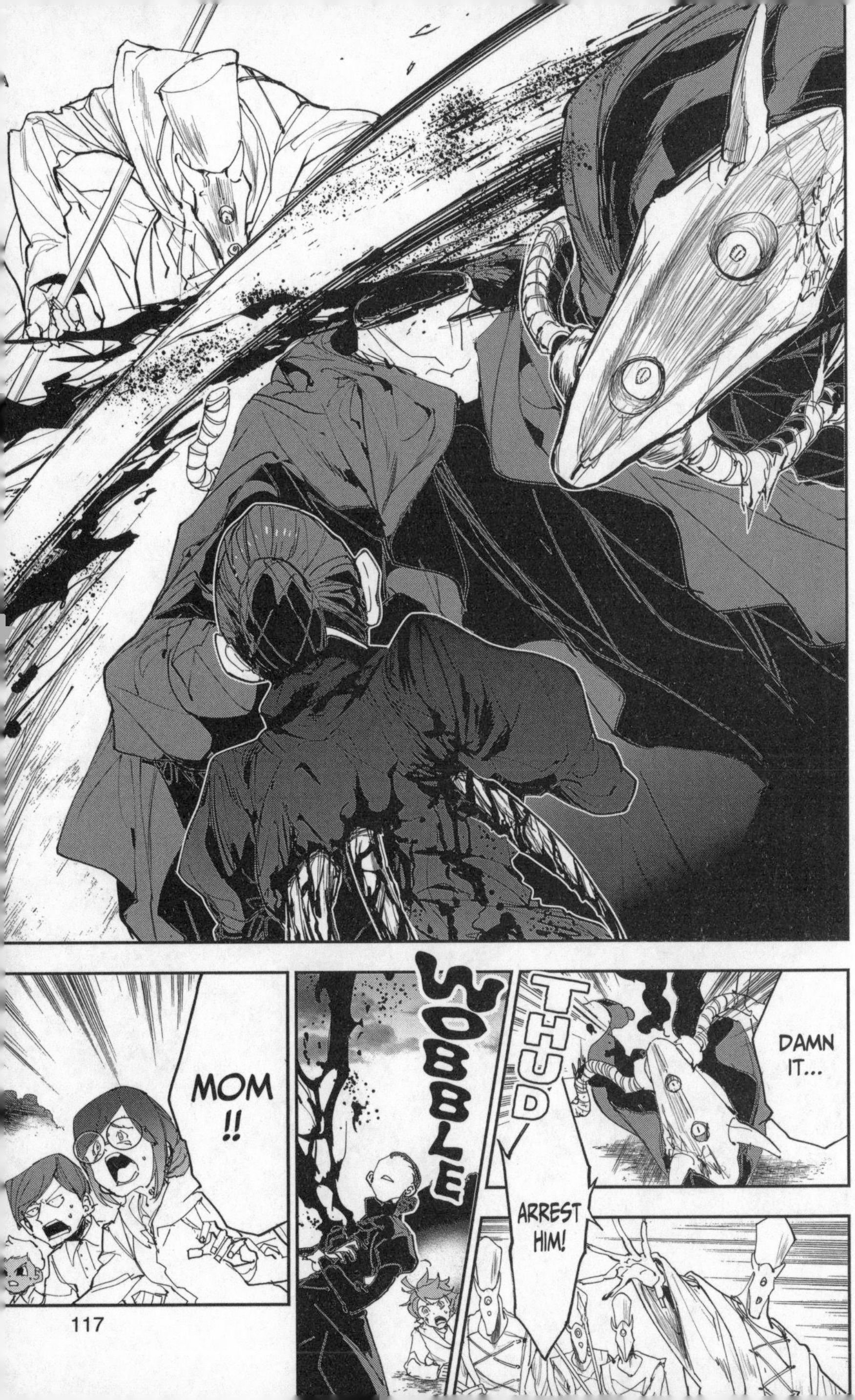
THUD
DAMN IT...
ARREST HIM!
WOBBLE
MOM !!

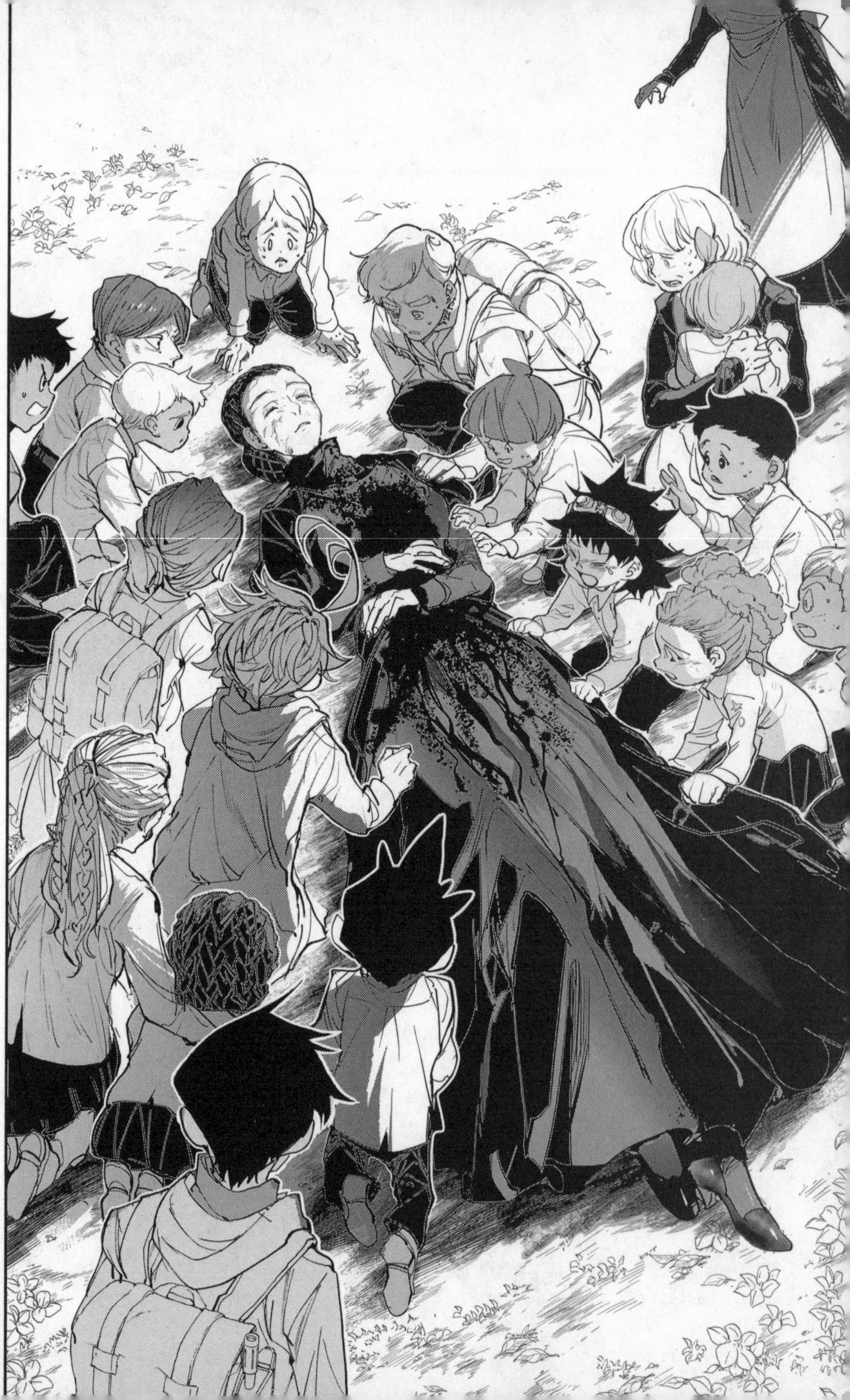

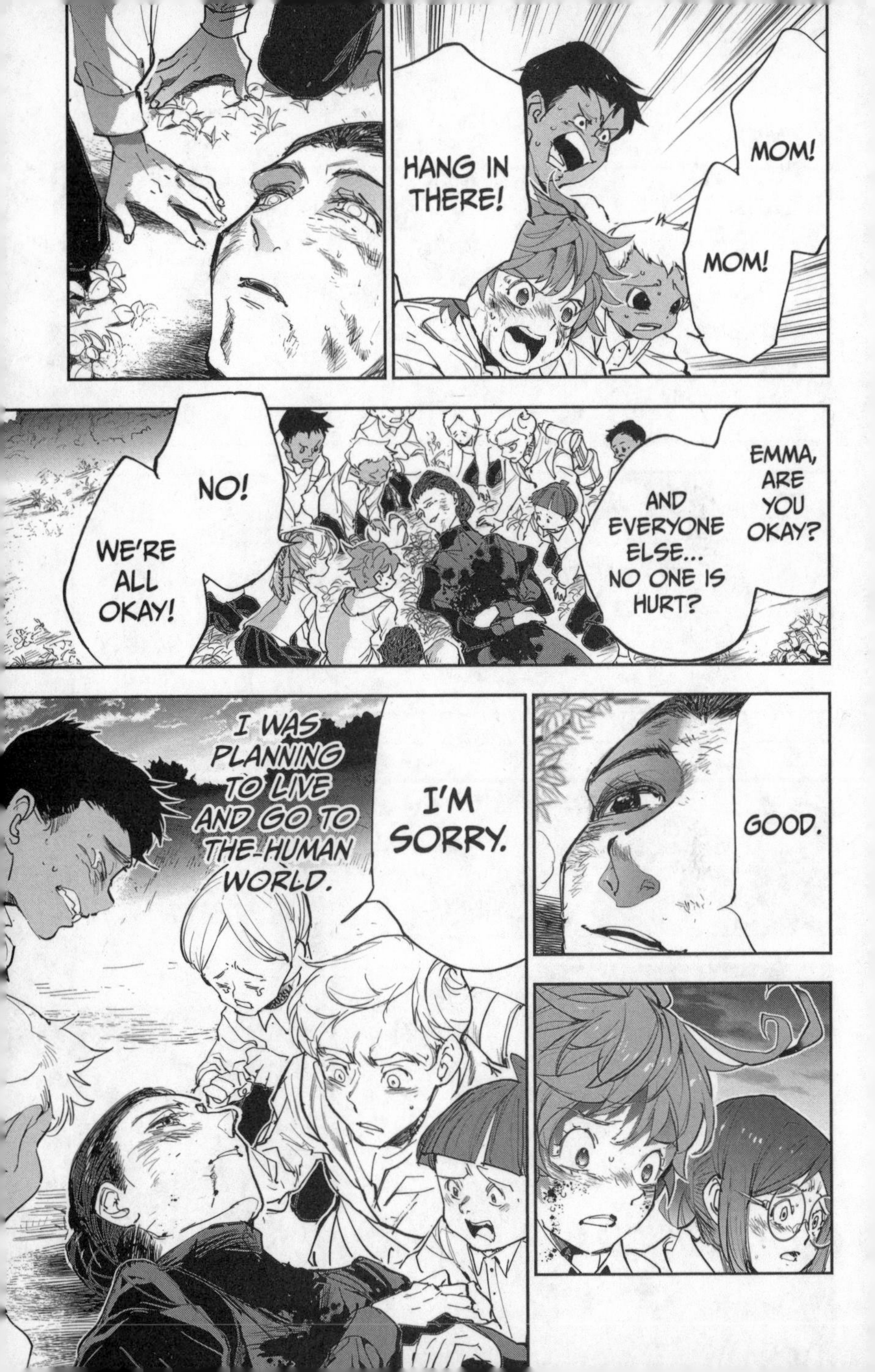
MOM!
MOM!
HANG IN THERE!
EMMA, ARE YOU OKAY?
AND EVERYONE ELSE... NO ONE IS HURT?
NO!
WE'RE ALL OKAY!
GOOD.
I'M SORRY.
I WAS PLANNING TO LIVE AND GO TO THE HUMAN WORLD.

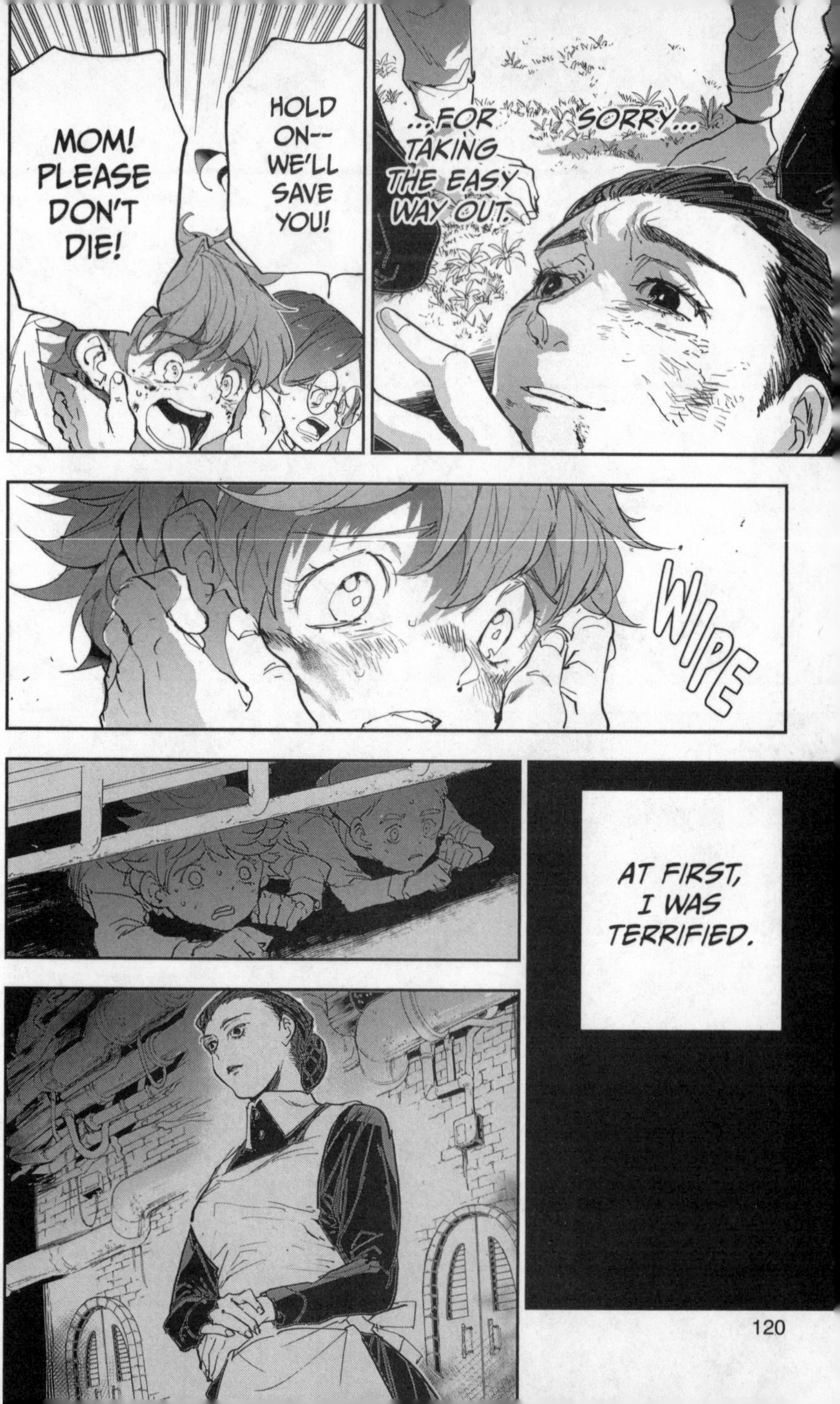
SORRY...
...FOR TAKING THE EASY WAY OUT.
HOLD ON-- WE'LL SAVE YOU!
MOM! PLEASE DON'T DIE!
WIPE
AT FIRST, I WAS TERRIFIED.

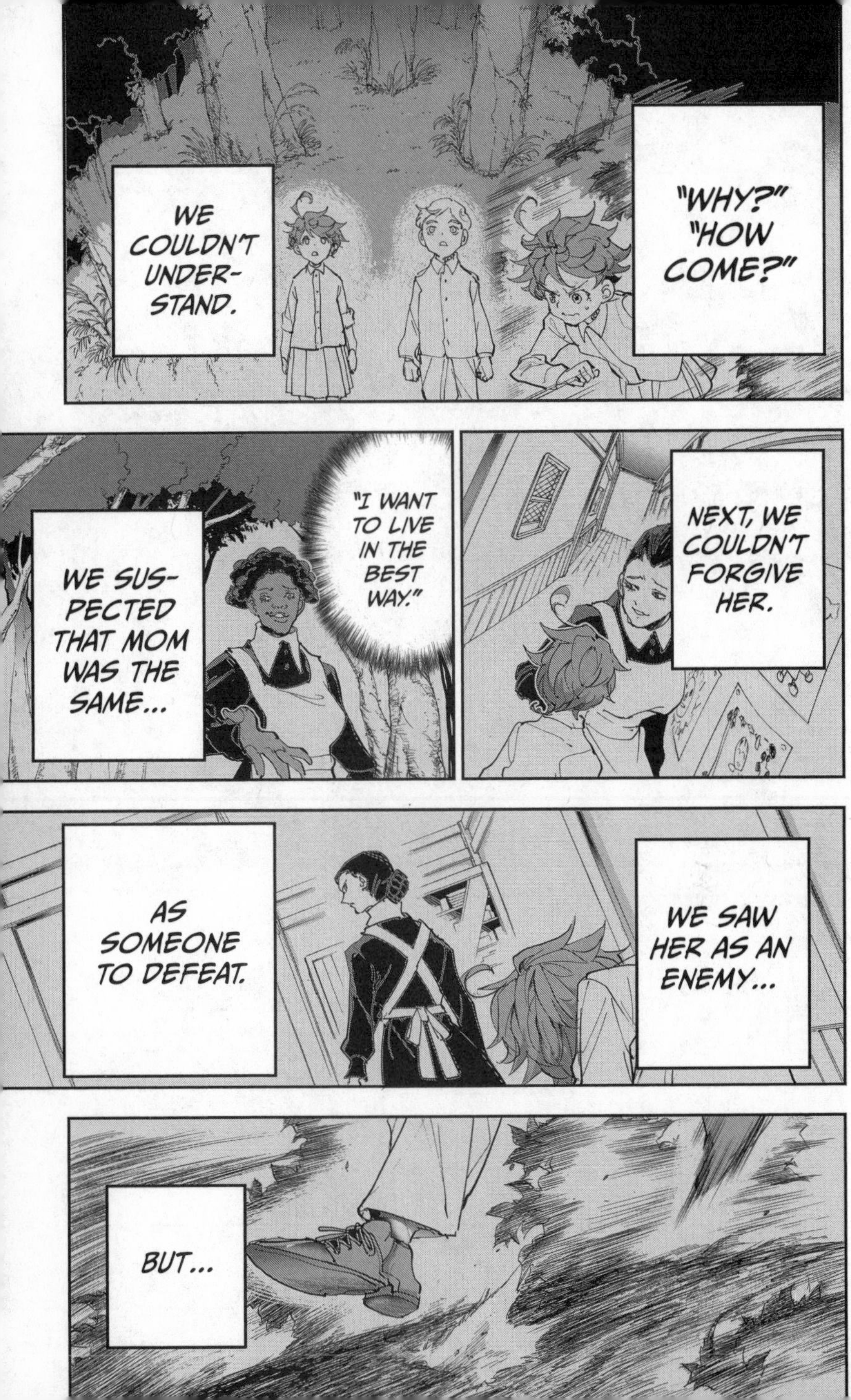
"WHY?" "HOW COME?"
WE COULDN'T UNDER-STAND.
NEXT, WE COULDN'T FORGIVE HER.
"I WANT TO LIVE IN THE BEST WAY."
WE SUS-PECTED THAT MOM WAS THE SAME...
WE SAW HER AS AN ENEMY...
AS SOMEONE TO DEFEAT.
BUT...

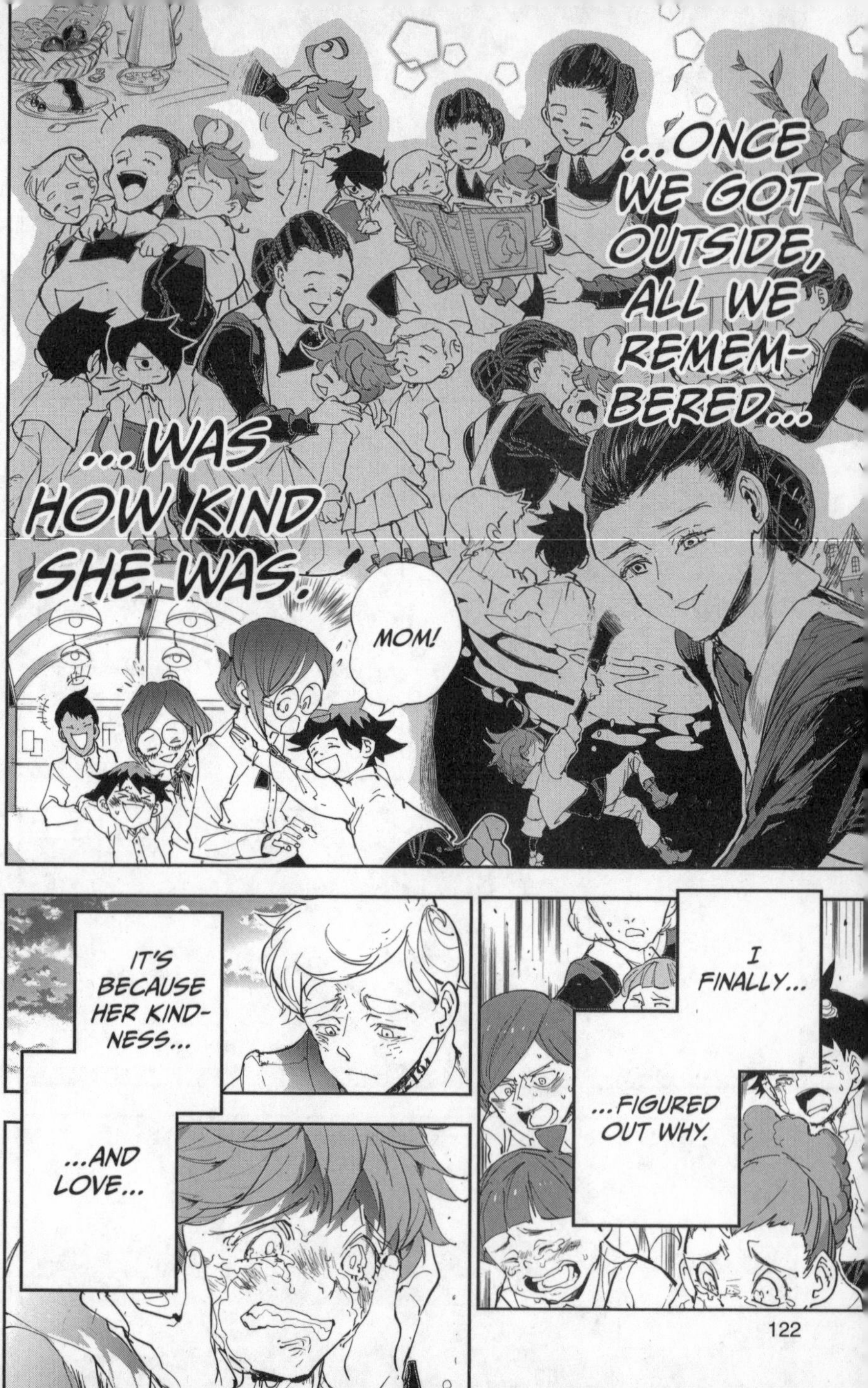
...ONCE WE GOT OUTSIDE, ALL WE REMEMBERED...
...WAS HOW KIND SHE WAS.
MOM!
I FINALLY...
...FIGURED OUT WHY.
IT'S BECAUSE HER KINDNESS...
...AND LOVE...

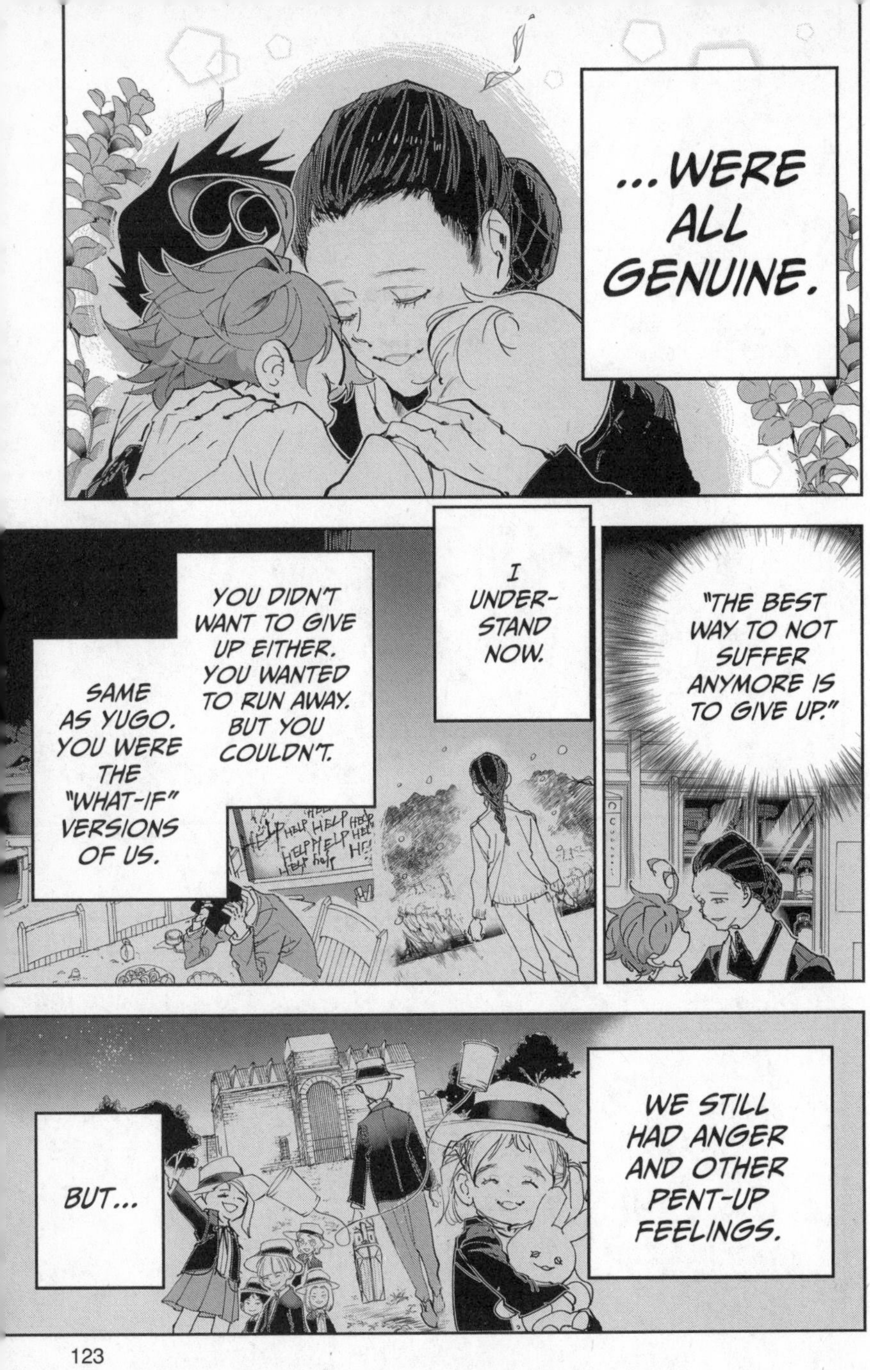
...WERE ALL GENUINE.
"THE BEST WAY TO NOT SUFFER ANYMORE IS TO GIVE UP."
I UNDER-STAND NOW.
YOU DIDN'T WANT TO GIVE UP EITHER. YOU WANTED TO RUN AWAY. BUT YOU COULDN'T.
SAME AS YUGO. YOU WERE THE "WHAT-IF" VERSIONS OF US.
WE STILL HAD ANGER AND OTHER PENT-UP FEELINGS.
BUT...

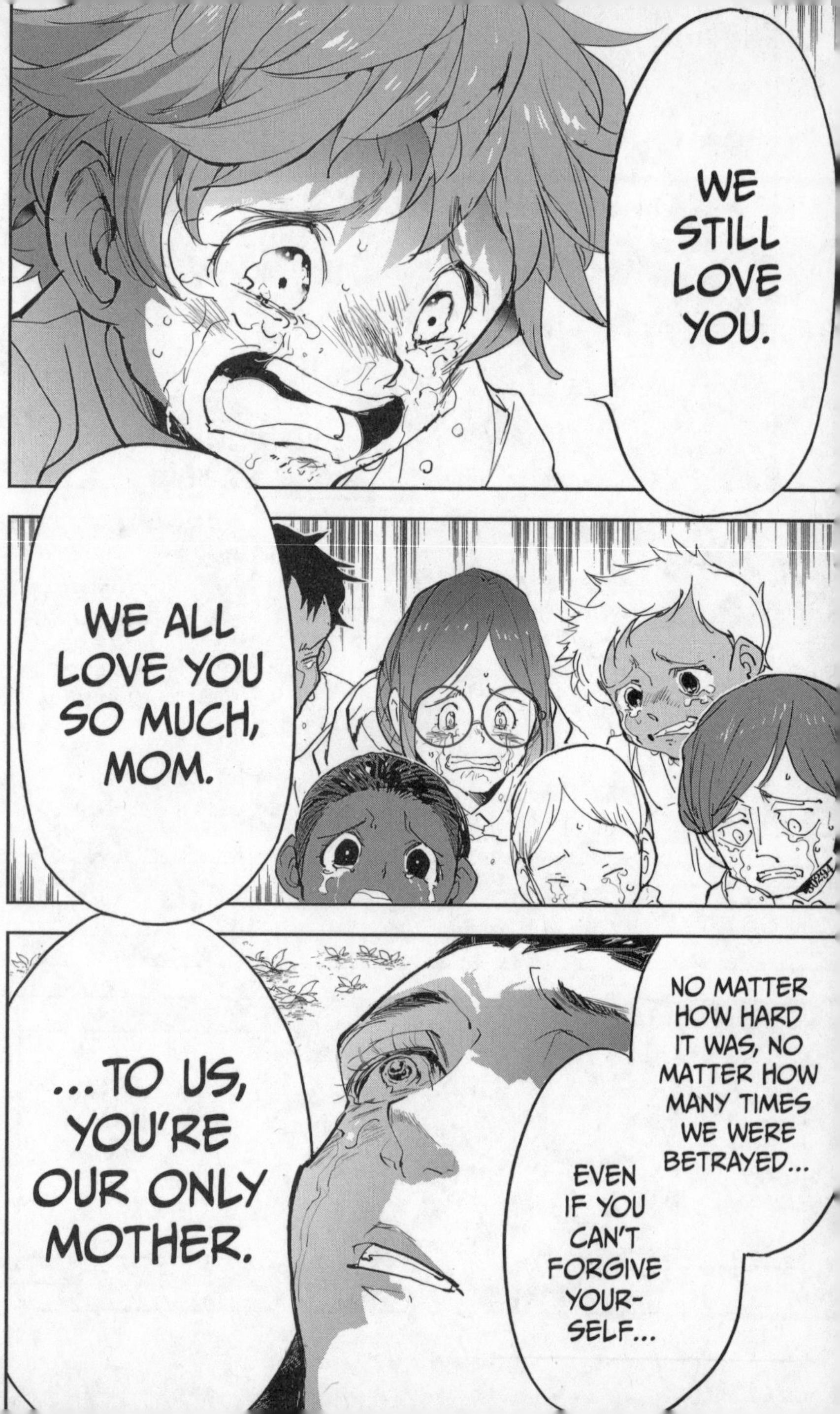
WE STILL LOVE YOU.
WE ALL LOVE YOU SO MUCH, MOM.
NO MATTER HOW HARD IT WAS, NO MATTER HOW MANY TIMES WE WERE BETRAYED...
EVEN IF YOU CAN'T FORGIVE YOUR-SELF...
...TO US, YOU'RE OUR ONLY MOTHER.

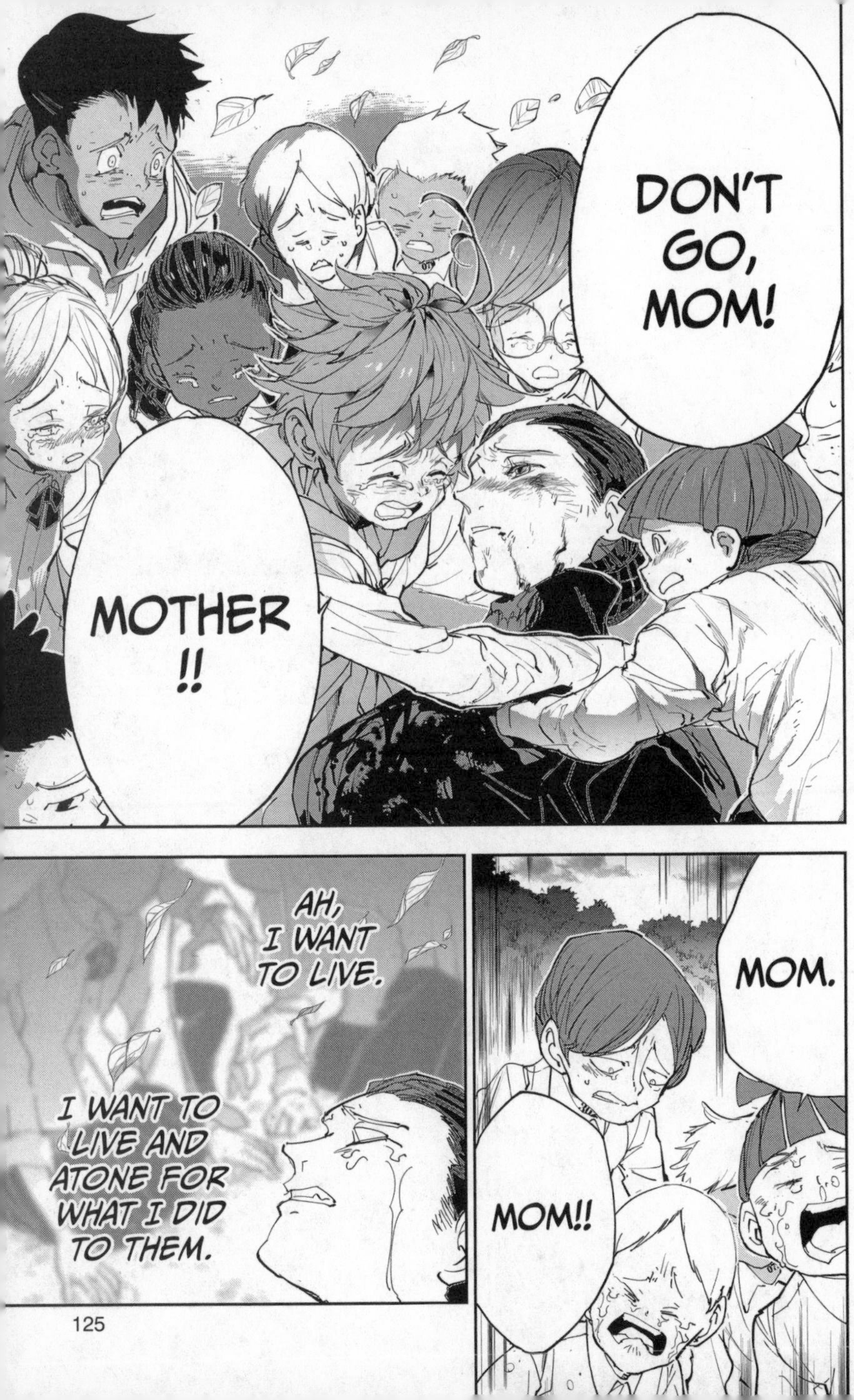
DON'T GO, MOM!
MOTHER !!
MOM.
MOM!!
AH, I WANT TO LIVE.
I WANT TO LIVE AND ATONE FOR WHAT I DID TO THEM.

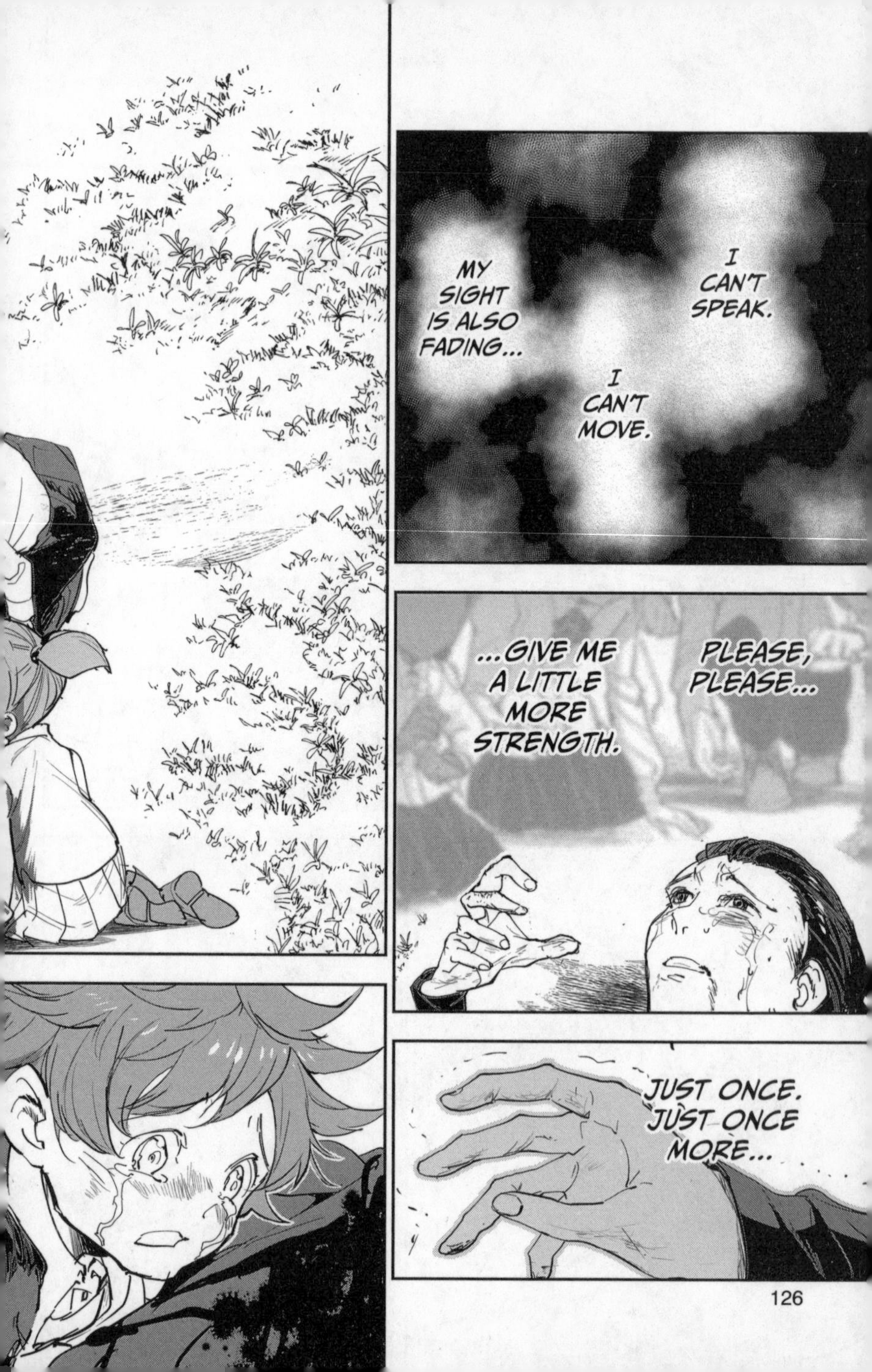
I CAN'T SPEAK.
MY SIGHT IS ALSO FADING...
I CAN'T MOVE.
PLEASE, PLEASE...
...GIVE ME A LITTLE MORE STRENGTH.
JUST ONCE. JUST ONCE MORE...

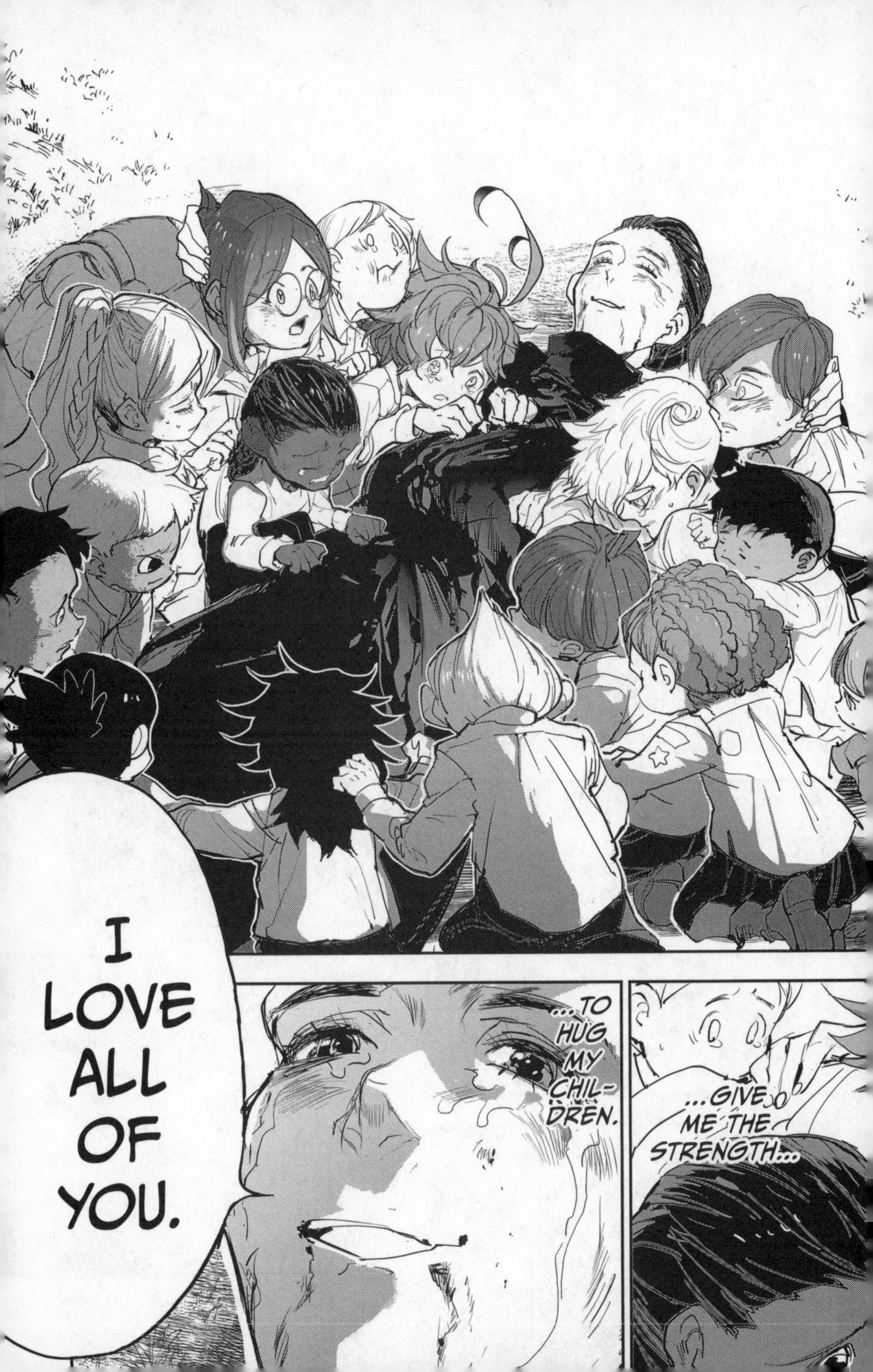
...GIVE ME THE STRENGTH...
...TO HUG MY CHIL-DREN.
I LOVE ALL OF YOU.

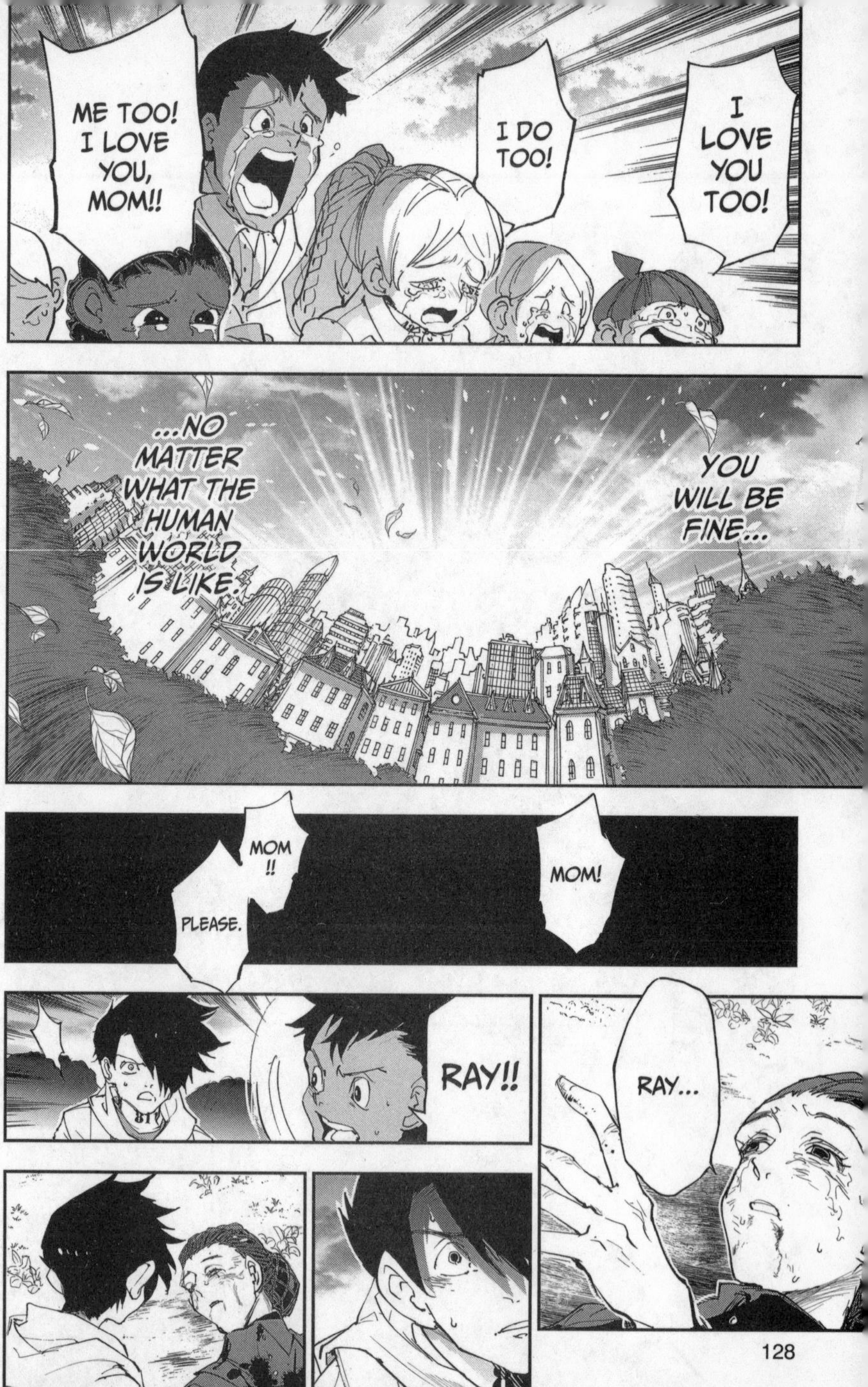
I LOVE YOU TOO!
I DO TOO!
ME TOO! I LOVE YOU, MOM!!
YOU WILL BE FINE...
...NO MATTER WHAT THE HUMAN WORLD IS LIKE.
MOM!
MOM !!
PLEASE.
RAY...
RAY!!

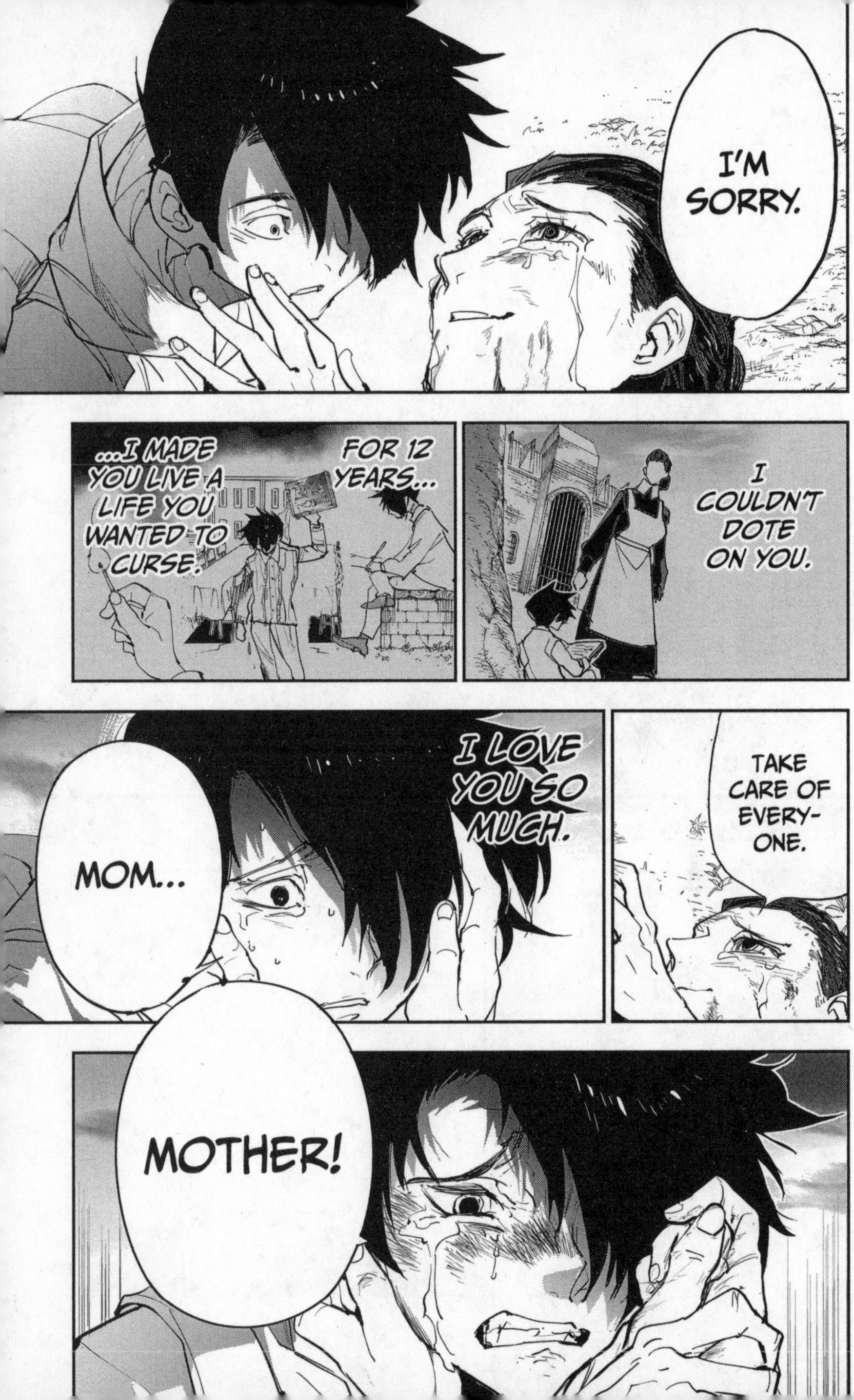
I'M SORRY.
I COULDN'T DOTE ON YOU.
FOR 12 YEARS...
...I MADE YOU LIVE A LIFE YOU WANTED TO CURSE.
TAKE CARE OF EVERY-ONE.
I LOVE YOU SO MUCH.
MOM...
MOTHER!

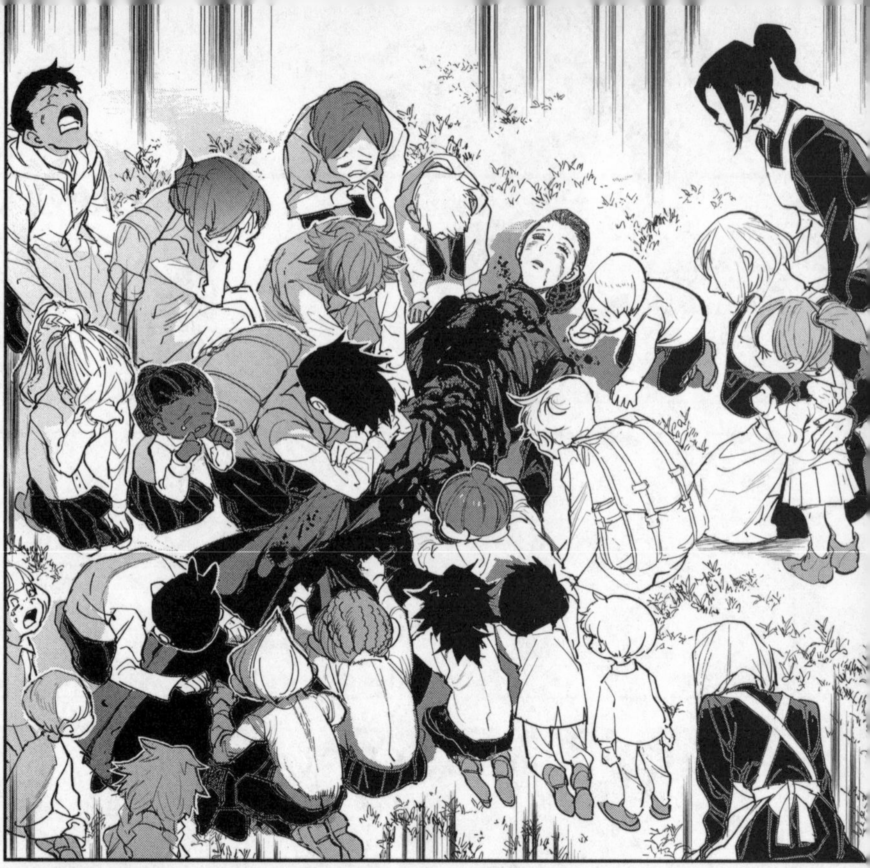
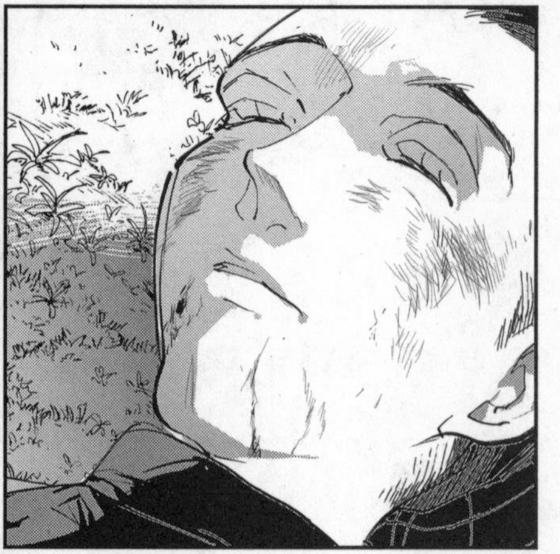
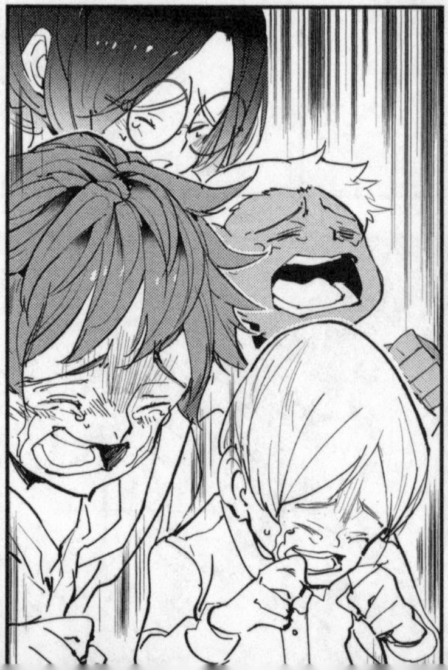

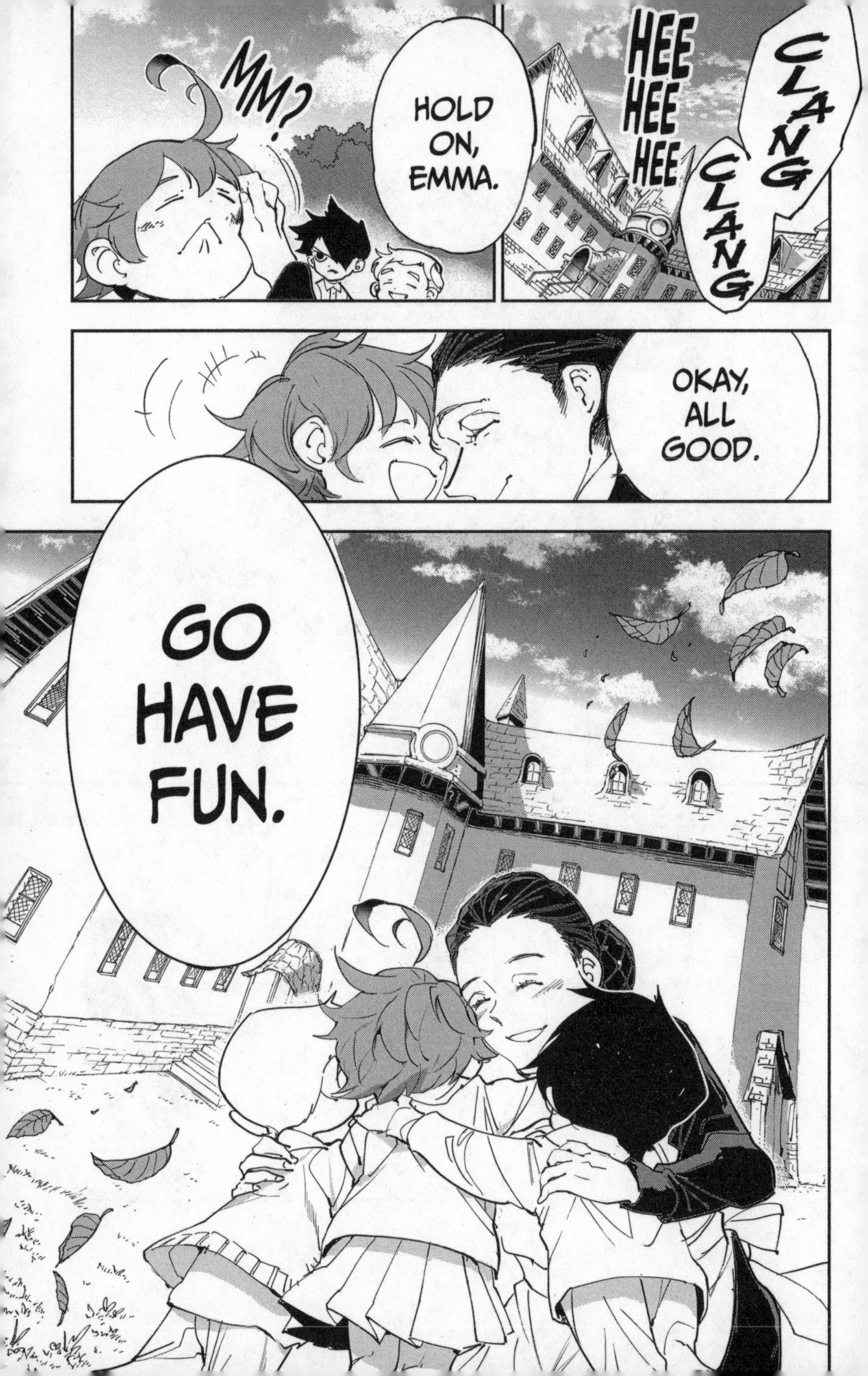
CLANG
CLANG
HEE HEE HEE
HOLD ON, EMMA.
MM?
OKAY, ALL GOOD.
GO HAVE FUN.

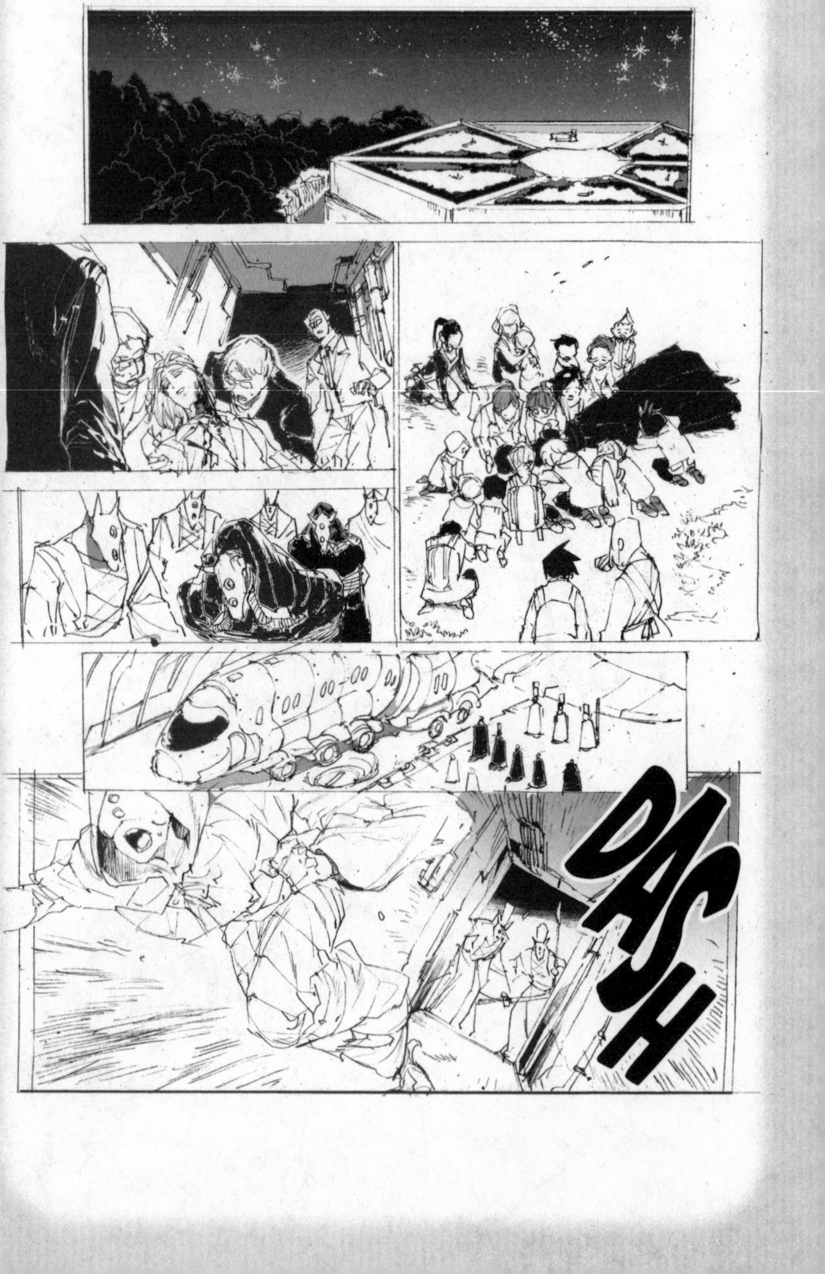
DASH

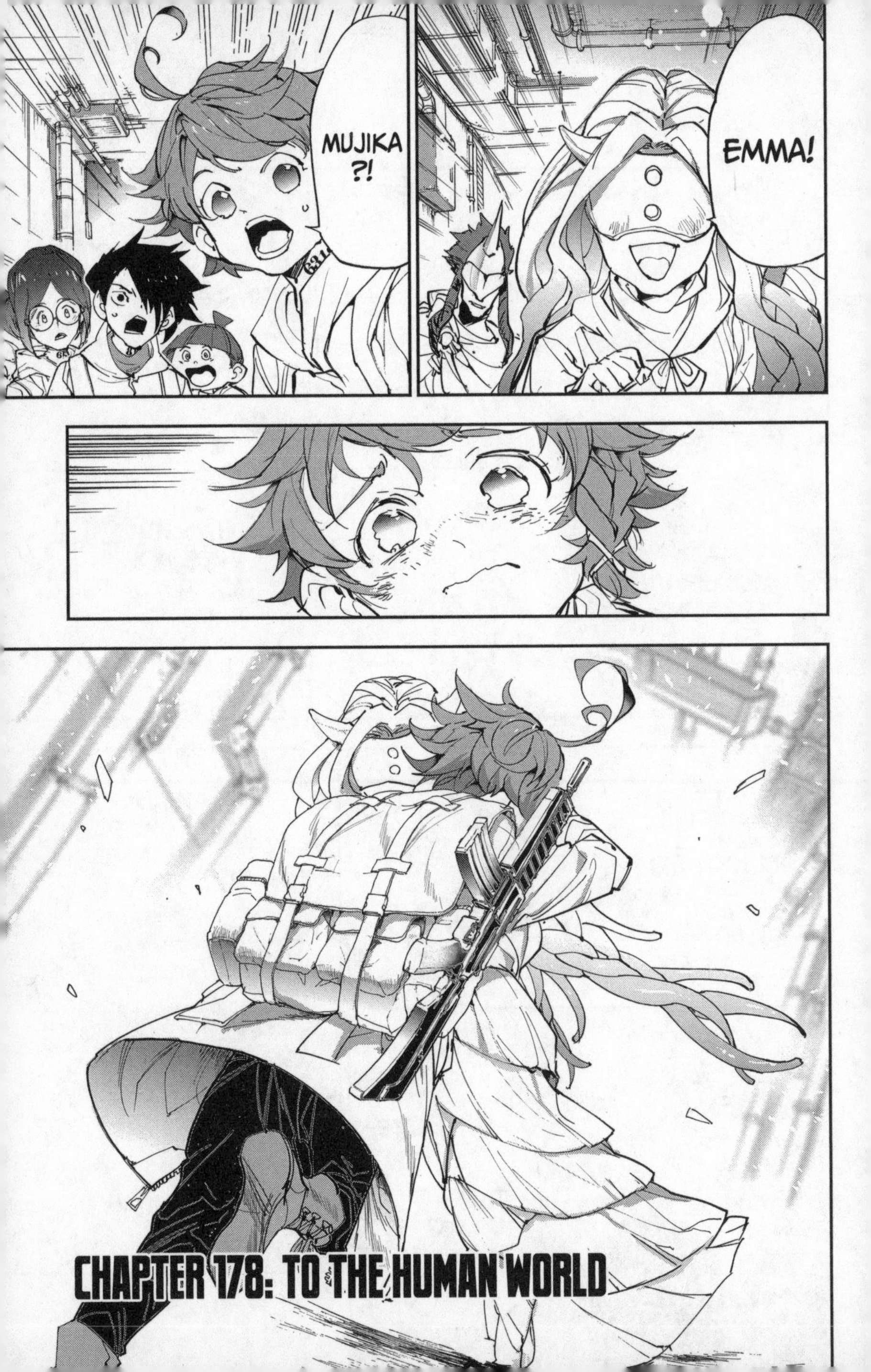
EMMA!
MUJIKA ?!
CHAPTER 178: TO THE HUMAN WORLD

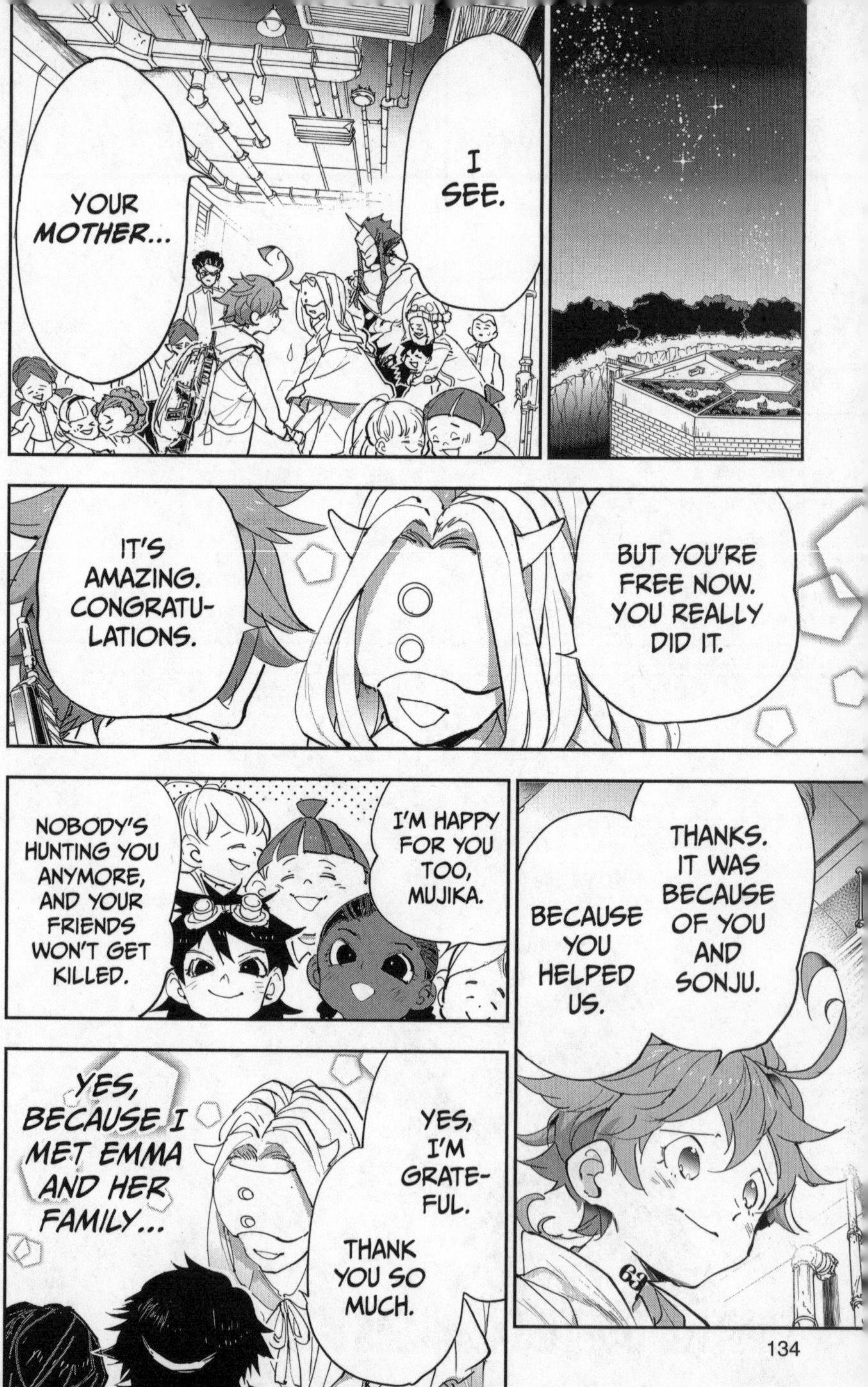
I SEE.
YOUR MOTHER...
BUT YOU'RE FREE NOW. YOU REALLY DID IT.
IT'S AMAZING. CONGRATU-LATIONS.
THANKS. IT WAS BECAUSE OF YOU AND SONJU.
BECAUSE YOU HELPED US.
I'M HAPPY FOR YOU TOO, MUJIKA.
NOBODY'S HUNTING YOU ANYMORE, AND YOUR FRIENDS WON'T GET KILLED.
YES, I'M GRATE-FUL.
THANK YOU SO MUCH.
YES, BECAUSE I MET EMMA AND HER FAMILY...

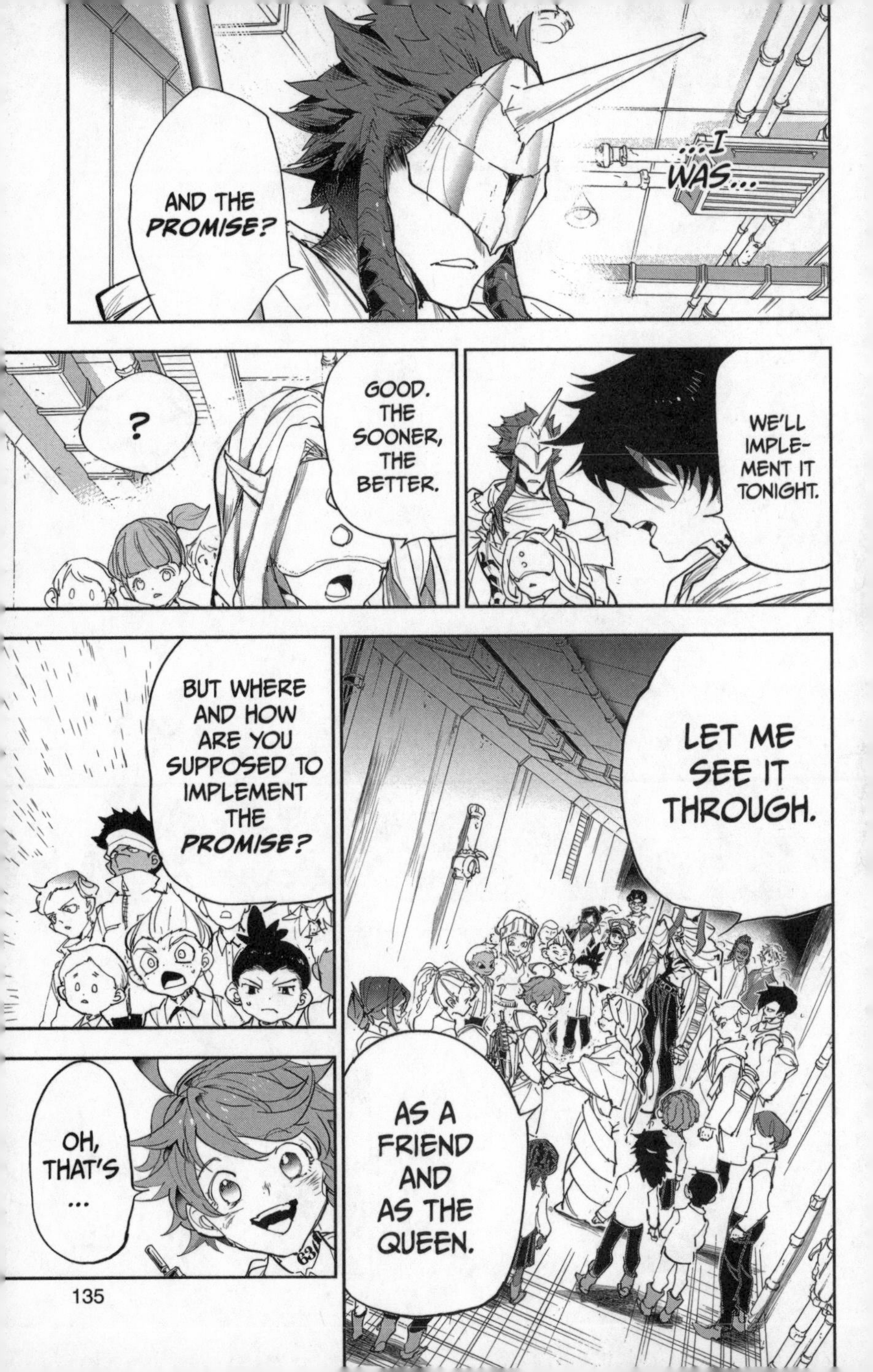
...I WAS...
AND THE PROMISE?
WE'LL IMPLEMENT IT TONIGHT.
GOOD. THE SOONER, THE BETTER.
?
LET ME SEE IT THROUGH.
AS A FRIEND AND AS THE QUEEN.
BUT WHERE AND HOW ARE YOU SUPPOSED TO IMPLEMENT THE PROMISE?
OH, THAT'S ...

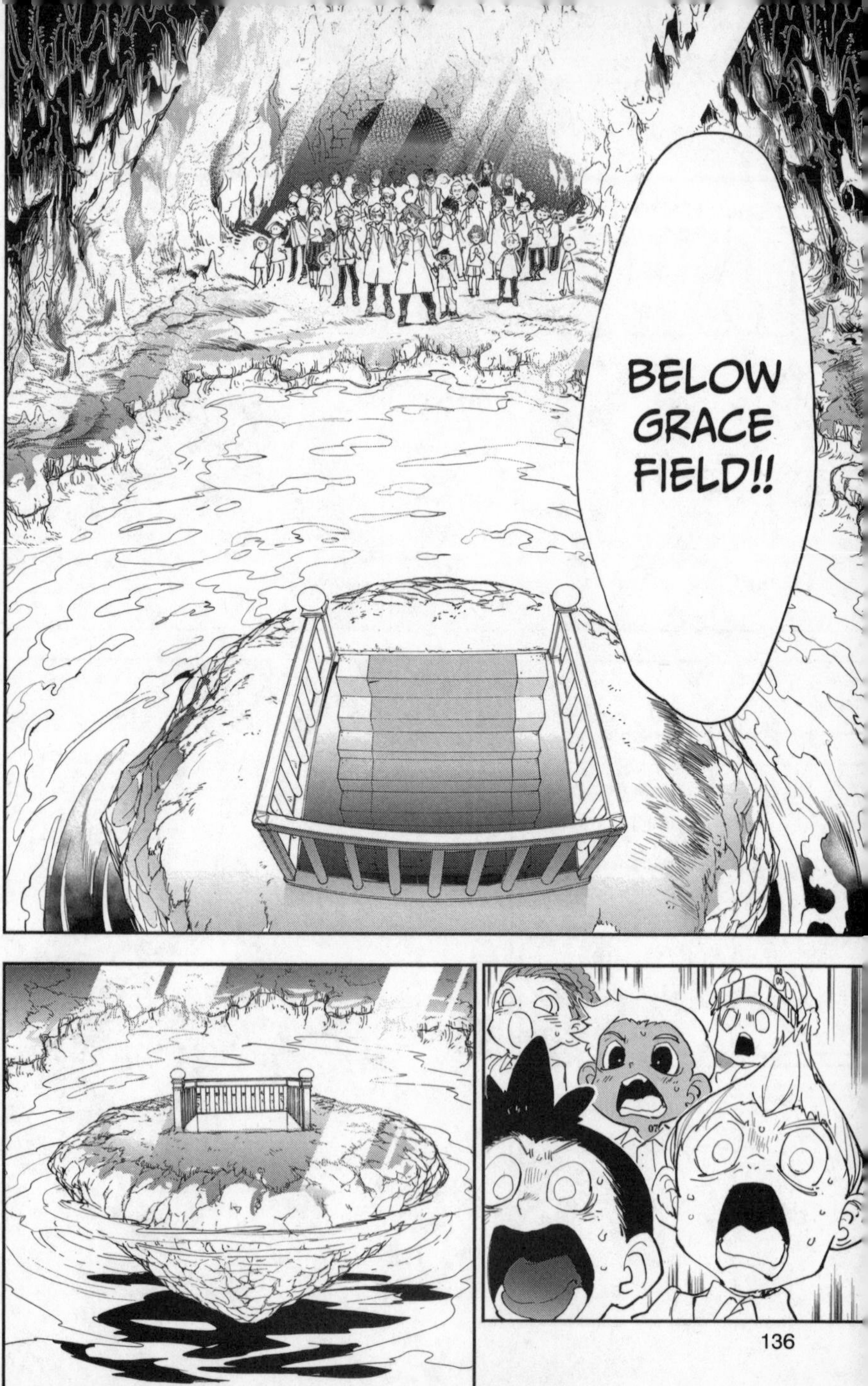
BELOW GRACE FIELD!!

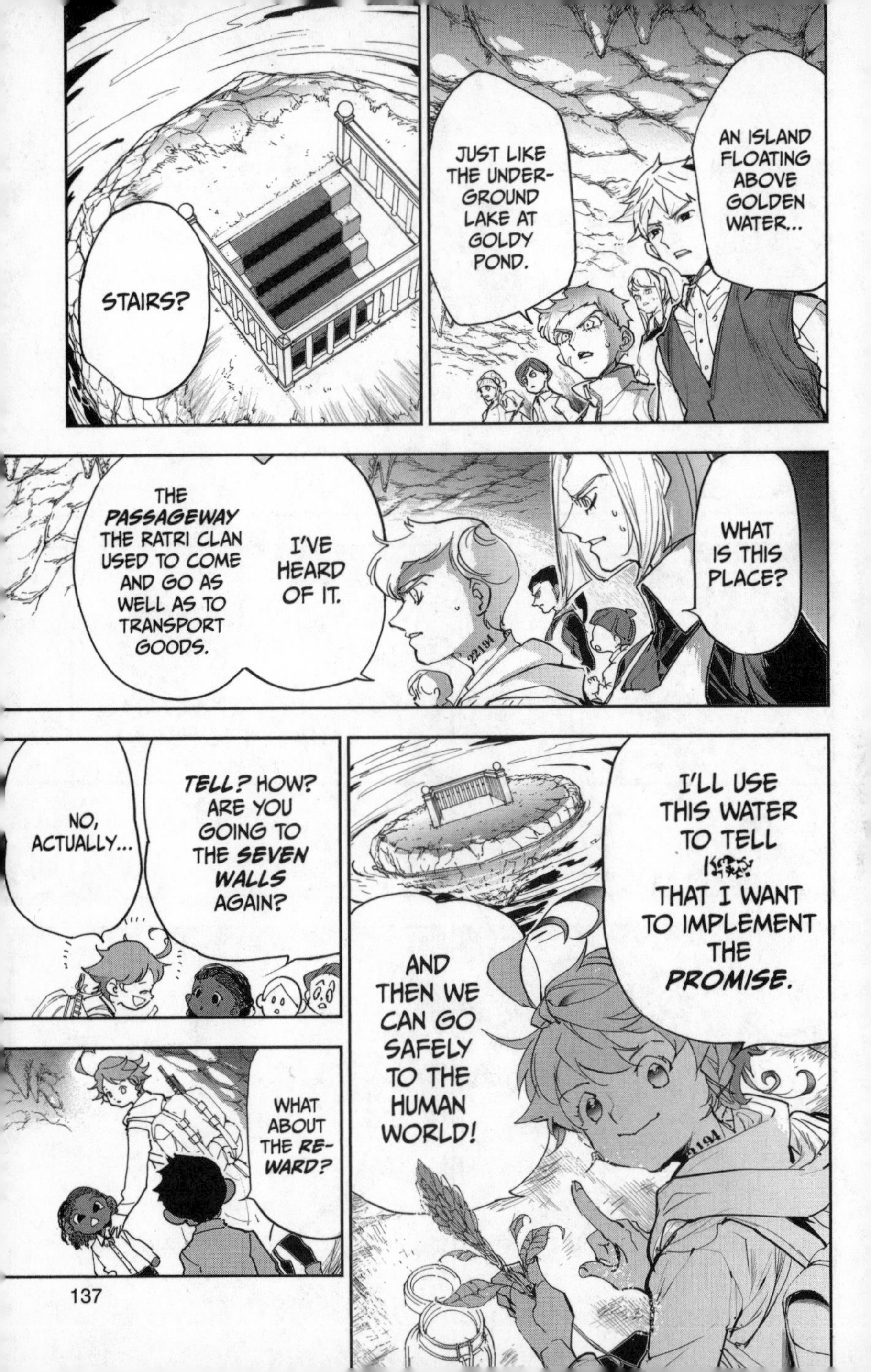
AN ISLAND FLOATING ABOVE GOLDEN WATER...
JUST LIKE THE UNDER-GROUND LAKE AT GOLDY POND.
STAIRS?
WHAT IS THIS PLACE?
I'VE HEARD OF IT.
THE *PASSAGEWAY* THE RATRI CLAN USED TO COME AND GO AS WELL AS TO TRANSPORT GOODS.
I'LL USE THIS WATER TO TELL THAT I WANT TO IMPLEMENT THE *PROMISE*.
AND THEN WE CAN GO SAFELY TO THE HUMAN WORLD!
TELL? HOW? ARE YOU GOING TO THE *SEVEN WALLS* AGAIN?
NO, ACTUALLY...
WHAT ABOUT THE *RE-WARD?*

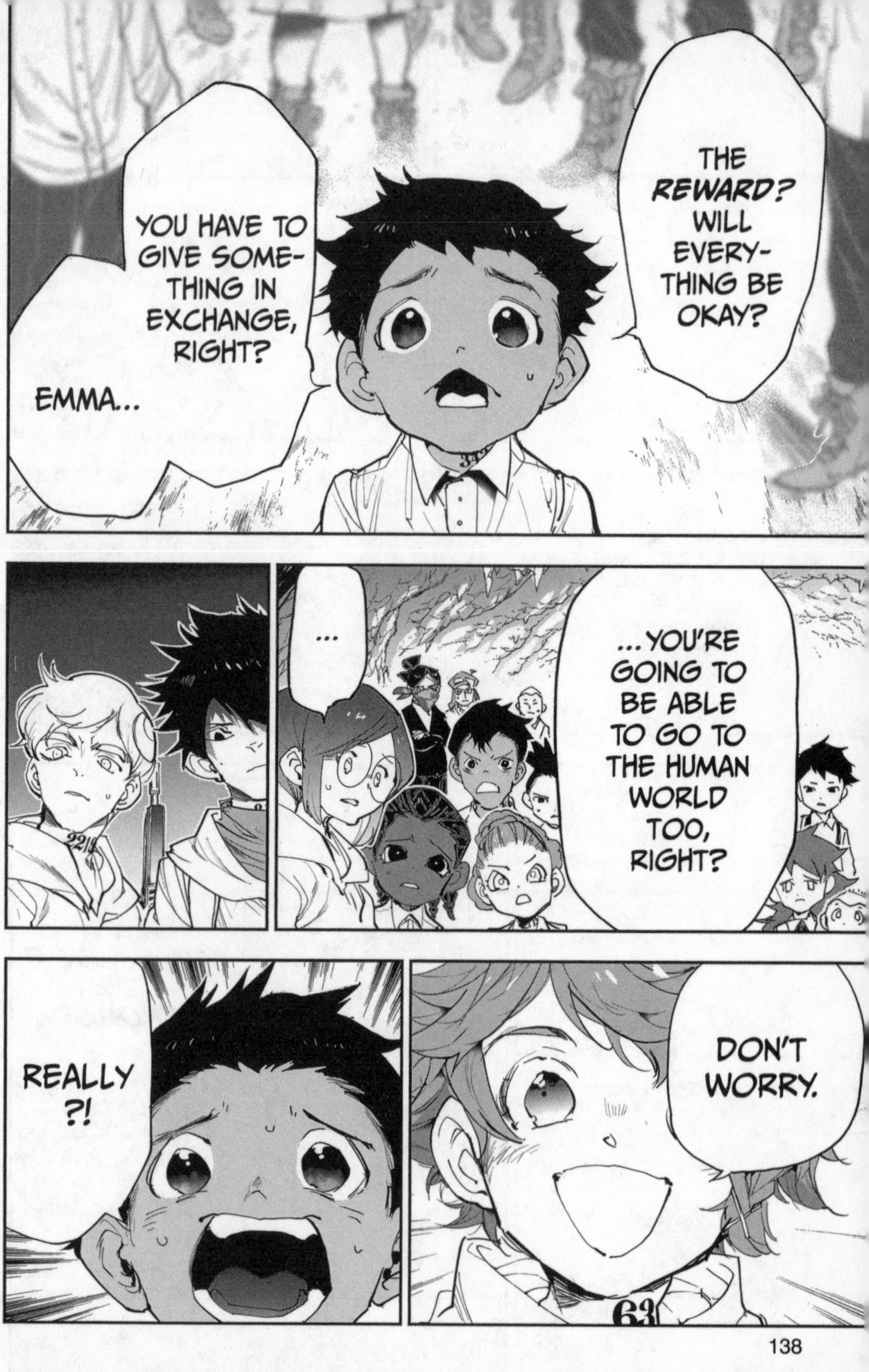
THE REWARD? WILL EVERYTHING BE OKAY?
YOU HAVE TO GIVE SOMETHING IN EXCHANGE, RIGHT?
EMMA...
...YOU'RE GOING TO BE ABLE TO GO TO THE HUMAN WORLD TOO, RIGHT?
...
DON'T WORRY.
REALLY?!

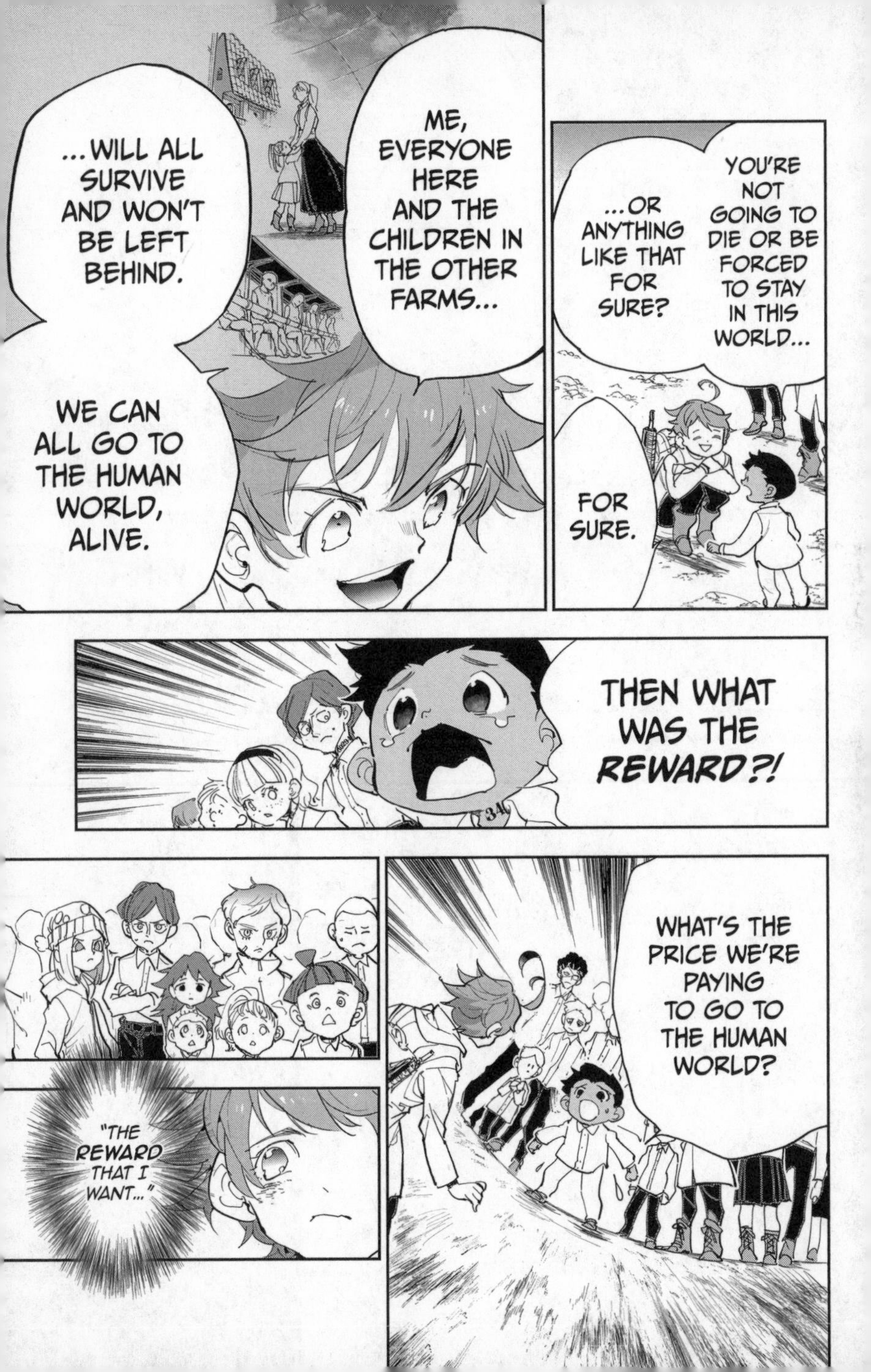
YOU'RE NOT GOING TO DIE OR BE FORCED TO STAY IN THIS WORLD...
...OR ANYTHING LIKE THAT FOR SURE?
FOR SURE.
ME, EVERYONE HERE AND THE CHILDREN IN THE OTHER FARMS...
...WILL ALL SURVIVE AND WON'T BE LEFT BEHIND.
WE CAN ALL GO TO THE HUMAN WORLD, ALIVE.
THEN WHAT WAS THE *REWARD*?!
WHAT'S THE PRICE WE'RE PAYING TO GO TO THE HUMAN WORLD?
"THE REWARD THAT I WANT..."

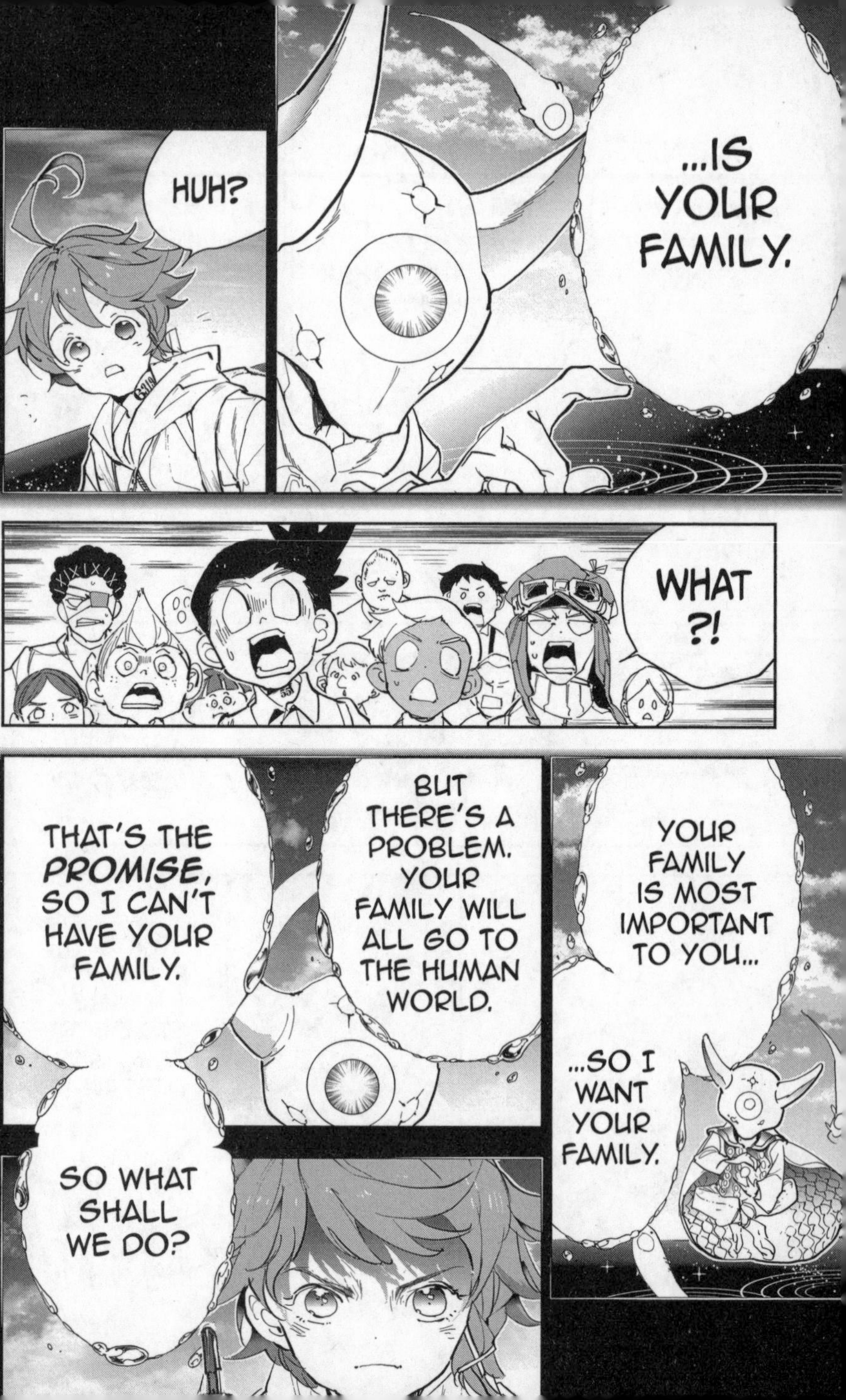
...IS YOUR FAMILY.
HUH?
WHAT ?!
YOUR FAMILY IS MOST IMPORTANT TO YOU...
...SO I WANT YOUR FAMILY.
BUT THERE'S A PROBLEM. YOUR FAMILY WILL ALL GO TO THE HUMAN WORLD.
THAT'S THE *PROMISE*, SO I CAN'T HAVE YOUR FAMILY.
SO WHAT SHALL WE DO?

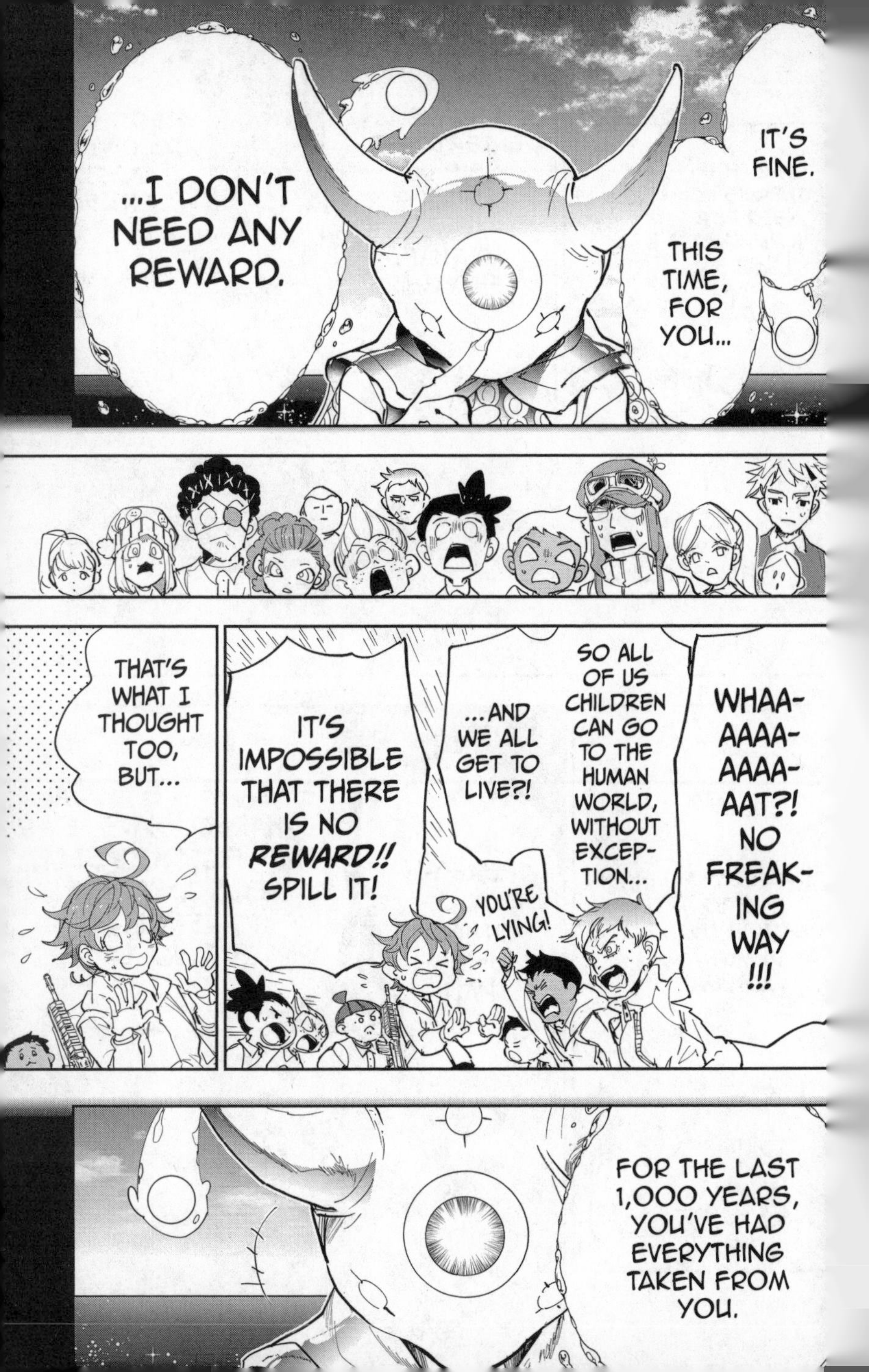
IT'S FINE.
THIS TIME, FOR YOU...
...I DON'T NEED ANY REWARD.
WHAA-AAAA-AAAA-AAT?! NO FREAK-ING WAY!!!
SO ALL OF US CHILDREN CAN GO TO THE HUMAN WORLD, WITHOUT EXCEP-TION...
...AND WE ALL GET TO LIVE?!
IT'S IMPOSSIBLE THAT THERE IS NO *REWARD!!* SPILL IT!
YOU'RE LYING!
THAT'S WHAT I THOUGHT TOO, BUT...
FOR THE LAST 1,000 YEARS, YOU'VE HAD EVERYTHING TAKEN FROM YOU.

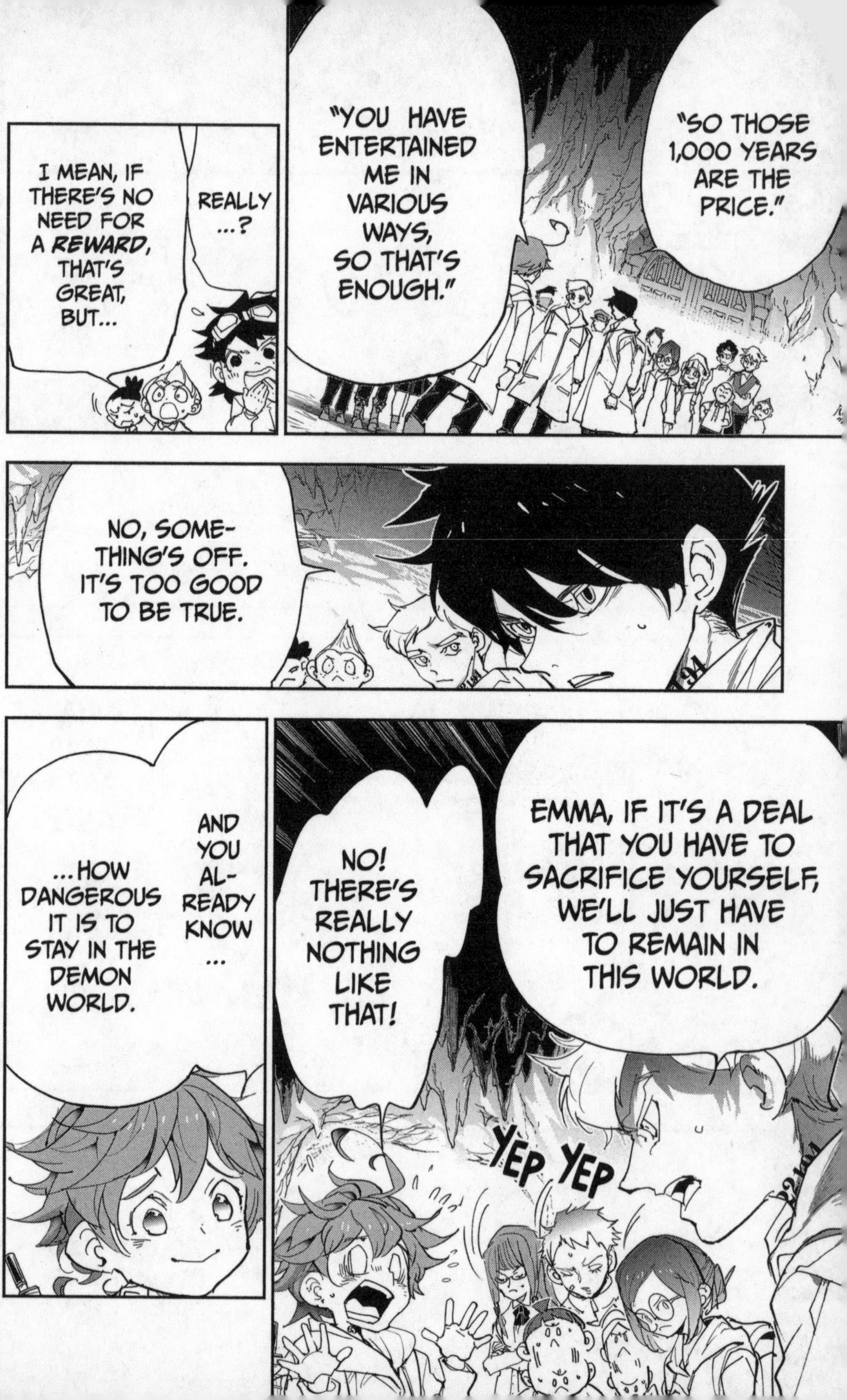
"SO THOSE 1,000 YEARS ARE THE PRICE."
"YOU HAVE ENTERTAINED ME IN VARIOUS WAYS, SO THAT'S ENOUGH."
REALLY ...?
I MEAN, IF THERE'S NO NEED FOR A *REWARD*, THAT'S GREAT, BUT...
NO, SOME-THING'S OFF. IT'S TOO GOOD TO BE TRUE.
EMMA, IF IT'S A DEAL THAT YOU HAVE TO SACRIFICE YOURSELF, WE'LL JUST HAVE TO REMAIN IN THIS WORLD.
YEP YEP
NO! THERE'S REALLY NOTHING LIKE THAT!
AND YOU AL-READY KNOW ...
...HOW DANGEROUS IT IS TO STAY IN THE DEMON WORLD.

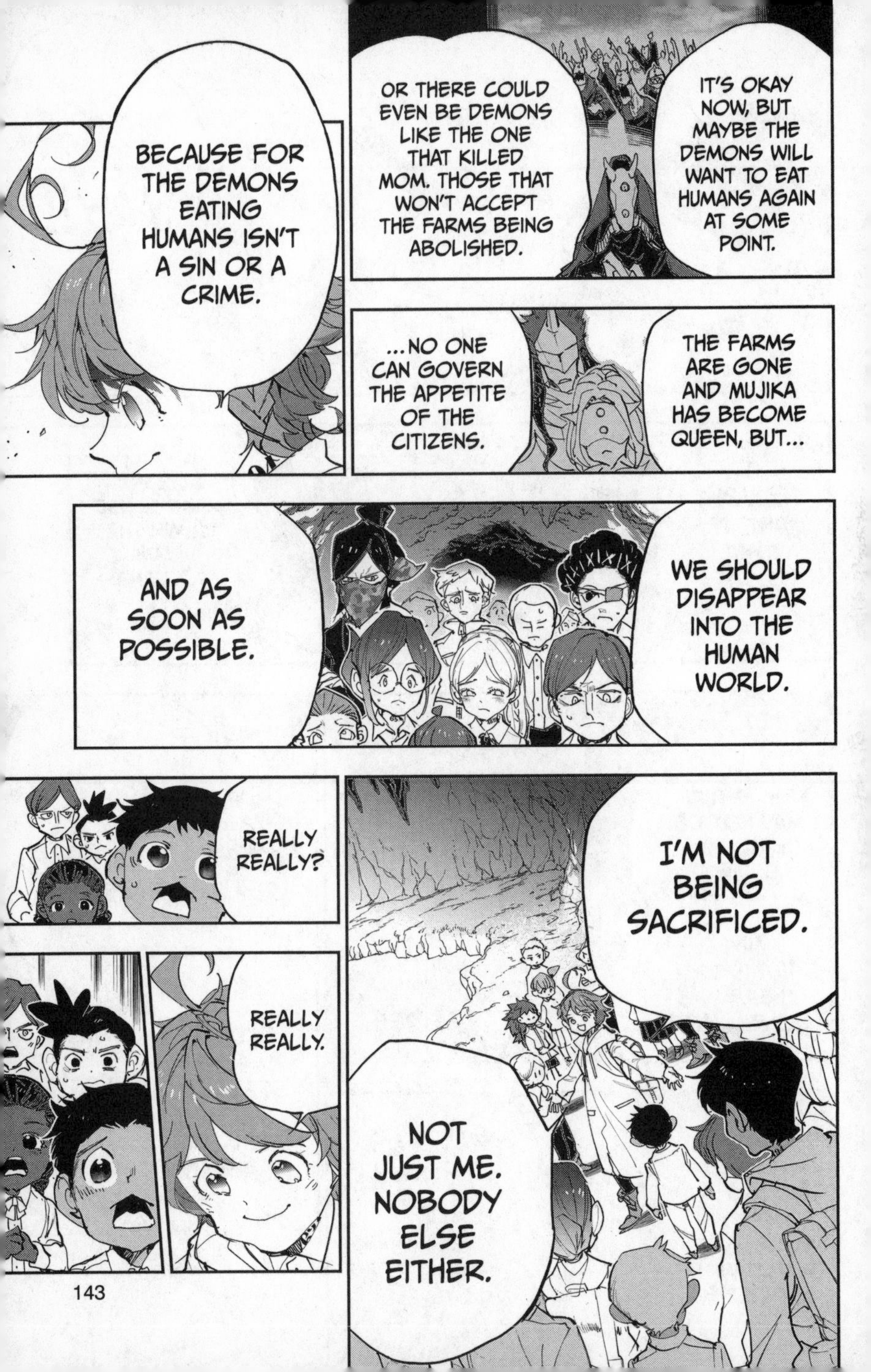
IT'S OKAY NOW, BUT MAYBE THE DEMONS WILL WANT TO EAT HUMANS AGAIN AT SOME POINT.
OR THERE COULD EVEN BE DEMONS LIKE THE ONE THAT KILLED MOM. THOSE THAT WON'T ACCEPT THE FARMS BEING ABOLISHED.
THE FARMS ARE GONE AND MUJIKA HAS BECOME QUEEN, BUT...
...NO ONE CAN GOVERN THE APPETITE OF THE CITIZENS.
BECAUSE FOR THE DEMONS EATING HUMANS ISN'T A SIN OR A CRIME.
WE SHOULD DISAPPEAR INTO THE HUMAN WORLD.
AND AS SOON AS POSSIBLE.
I'M NOT BEING SACRIFICED.
NOT JUST ME. NOBODY ELSE EITHER.
REALLY REALLY?
REALLY REALLY.

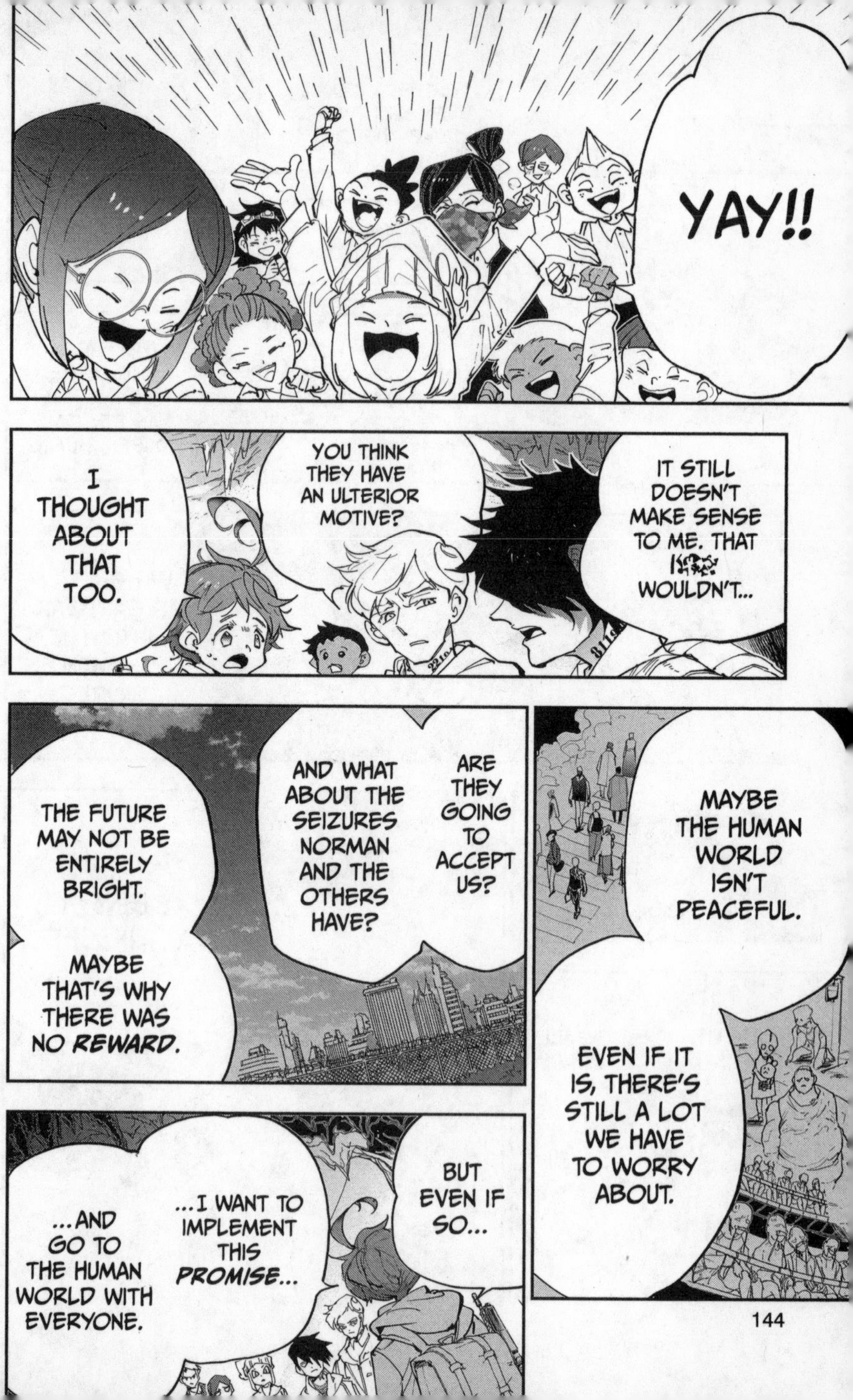
YAY!!
IT STILL DOESN'T MAKE SENSE TO ME. THAT
WOULDN'T...
YOU THINK THEY HAVE AN ULTERIOR MOTIVE?
I THOUGHT ABOUT THAT TOO.
MAYBE THE HUMAN WORLD ISN'T PEACEFUL.
EVEN IF IT IS, THERE'S STILL A LOT WE HAVE TO WORRY ABOUT.
ARE THEY GOING TO ACCEPT US?
AND WHAT ABOUT THE SEIZURES NORMAN AND THE OTHERS HAVE?
THE FUTURE MAY NOT BE ENTIRELY BRIGHT.
MAYBE THAT'S WHY THERE WAS NO *REWARD*.
BUT EVEN IF SO...
...I WANT TO IMPLEMENT THIS *PROMISE*...
...AND GO TO THE HUMAN WORLD WITH EVERYONE.

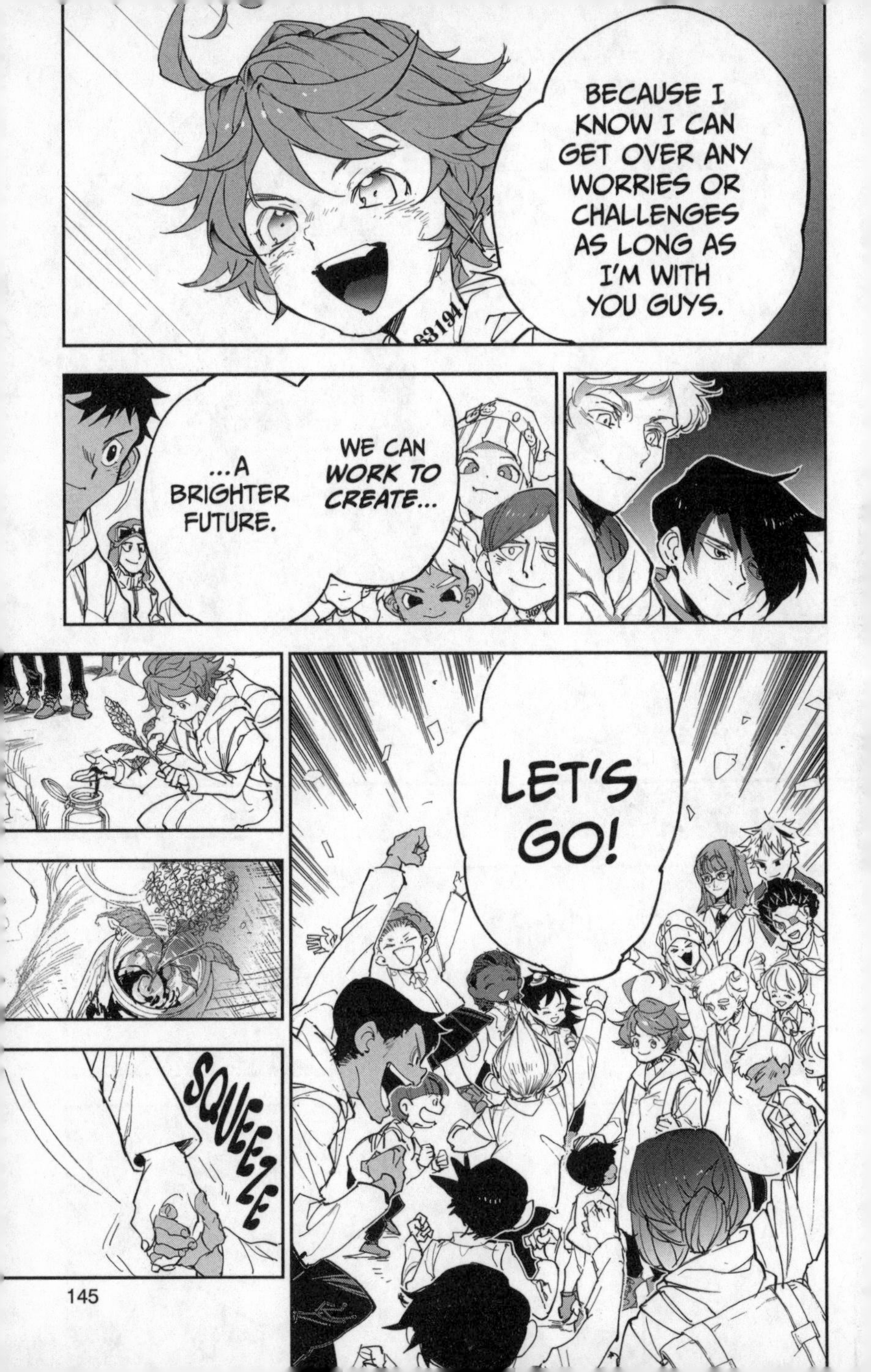
BECAUSE I KNOW I CAN GET OVER ANY WORRIES OR CHALLENGES AS LONG AS I'M WITH YOU GUYS.
WE CAN *WORK* TO *CREATE*...
...A BRIGHTER FUTURE.
LET'S GO!
SQUEEEZE

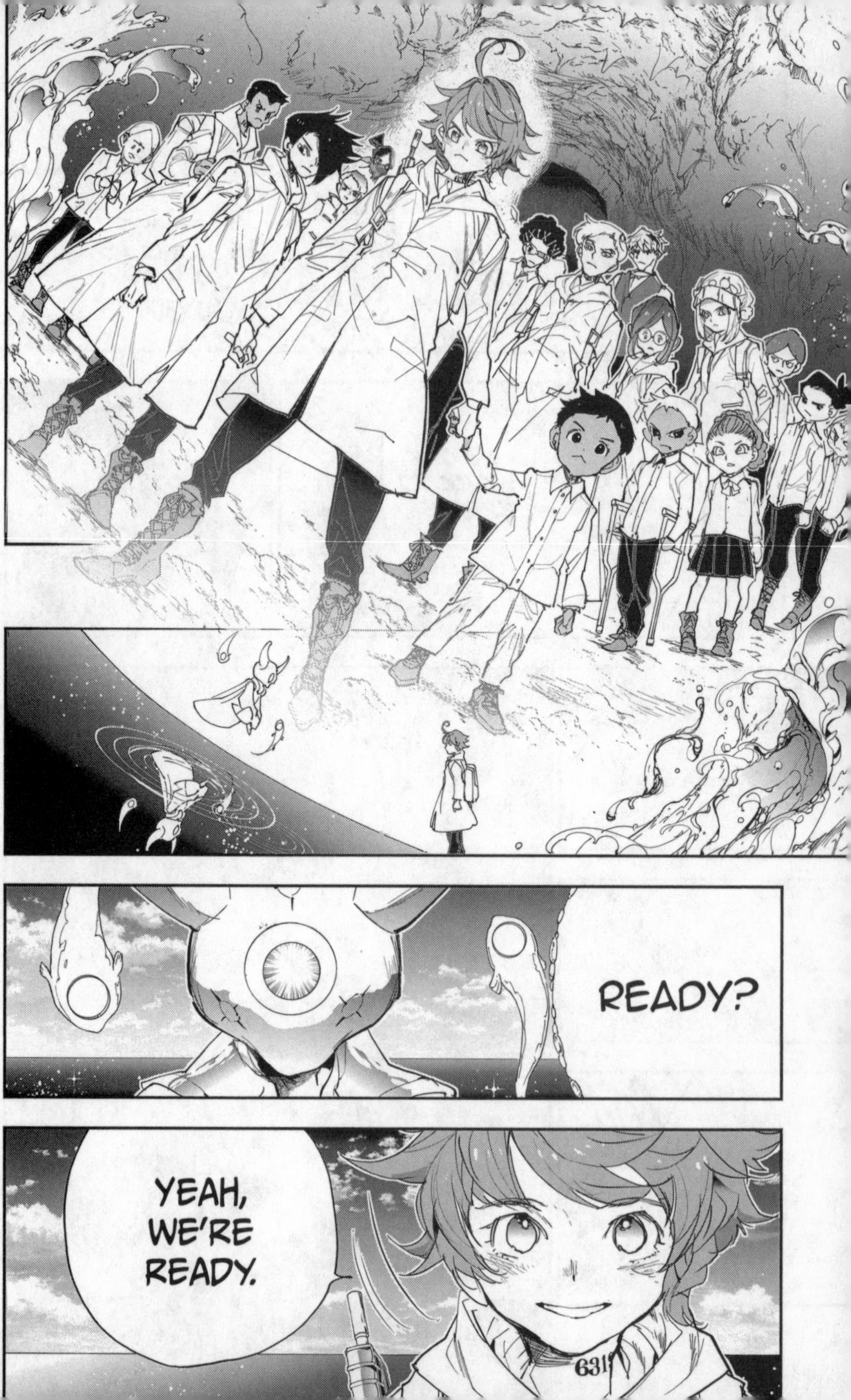
READY?
YEAH, WE'RE READY.

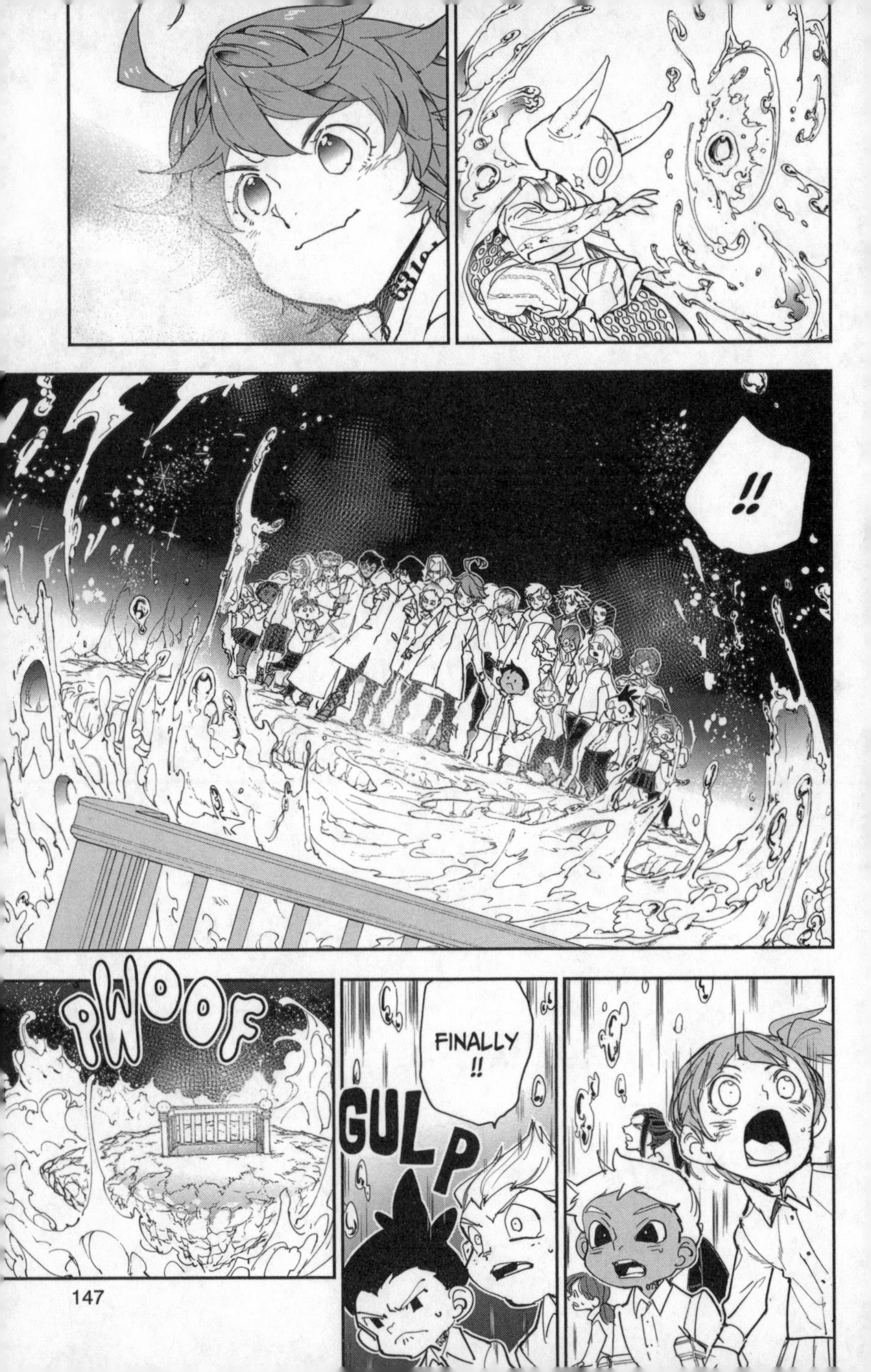
!!
FINALLY !!
GULP
PWOOF

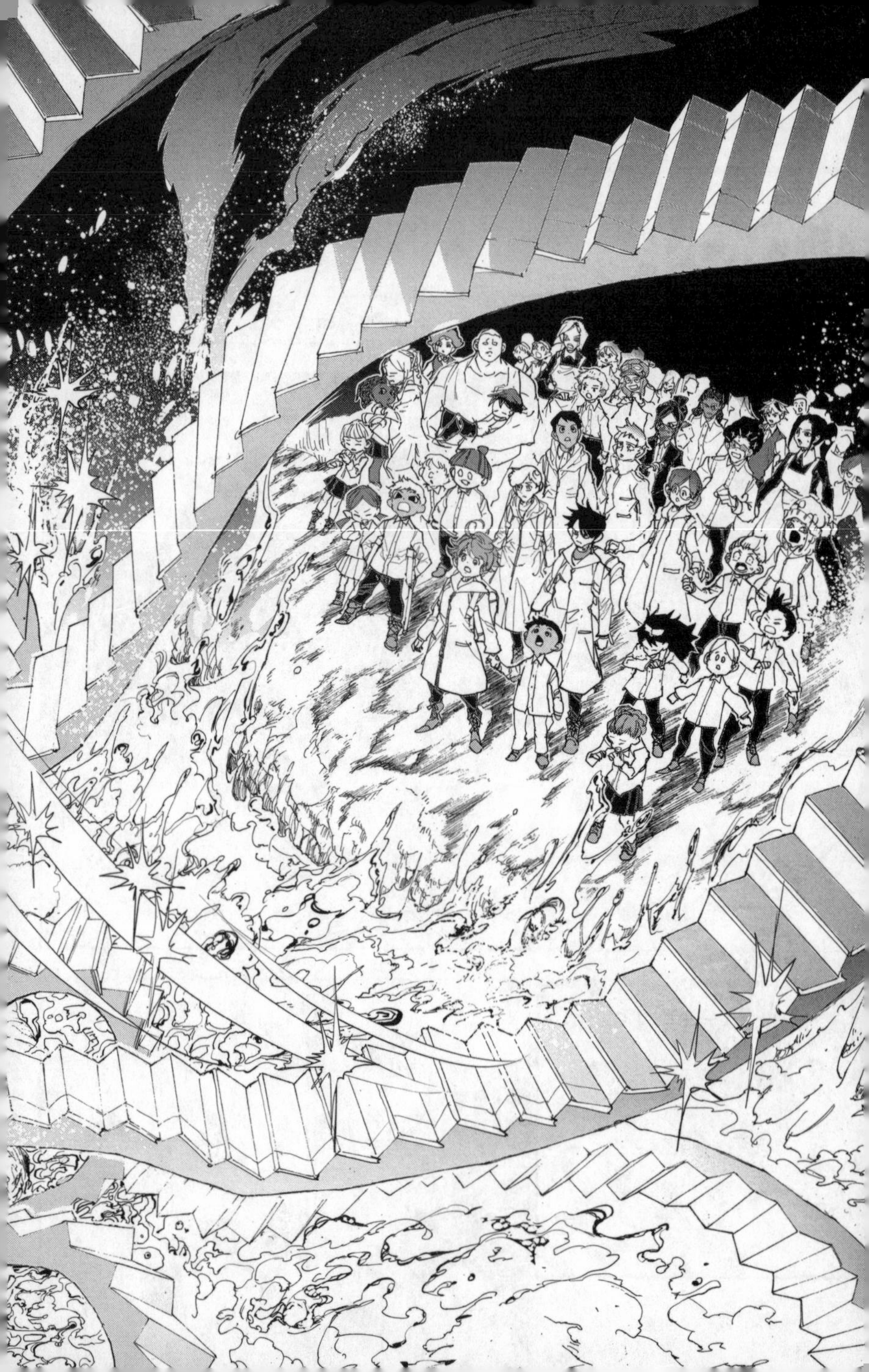

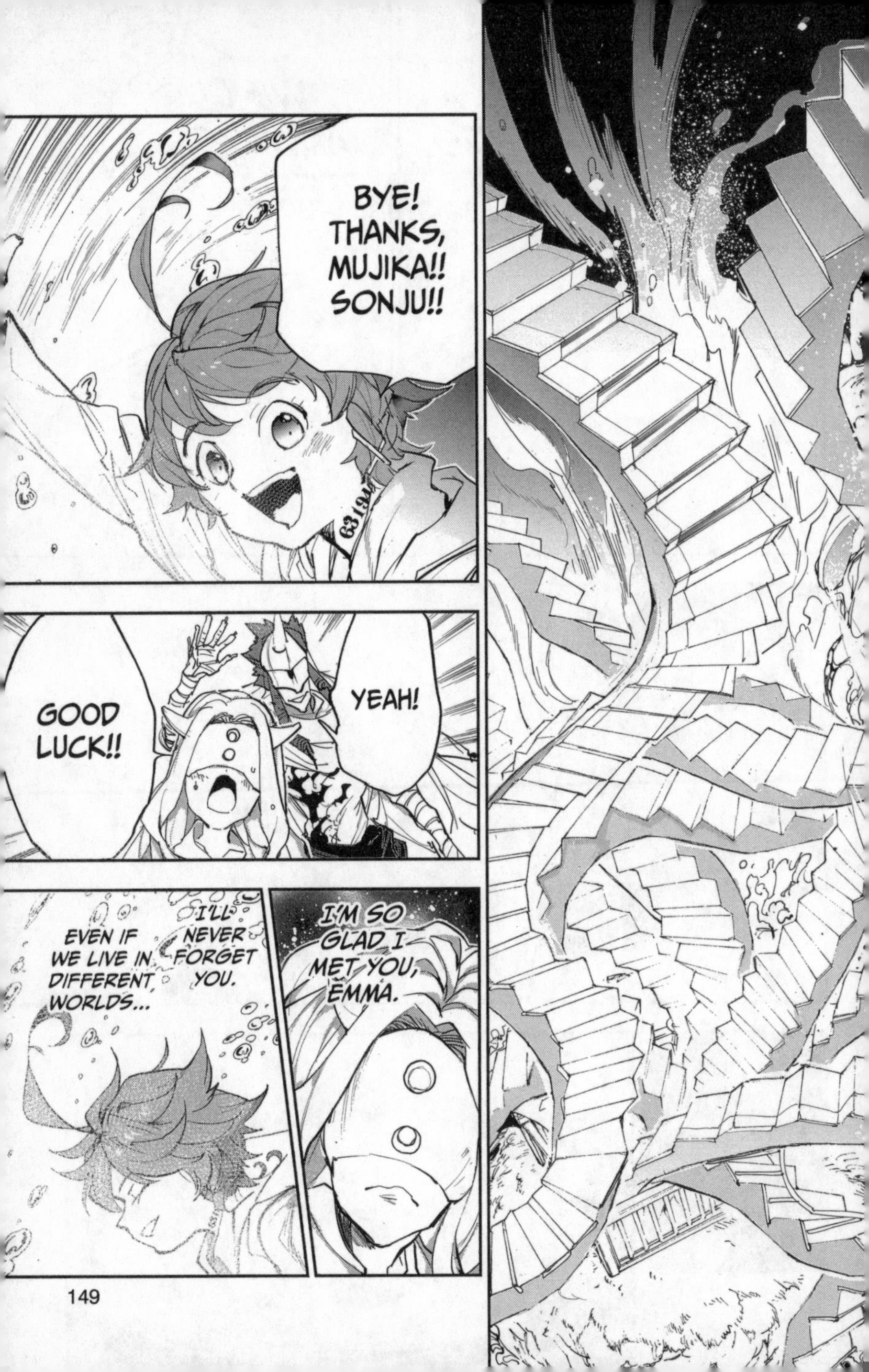
BYE! THANKS, MUJIKA!! SONJU!!
YEAH!
GOOD LUCK!!
I'M SO GLAD I MET YOU, EMMA.
I'LL NEVER FORGET YOU.
EVEN IF WE LIVE IN DIFFERENT WORLDS...

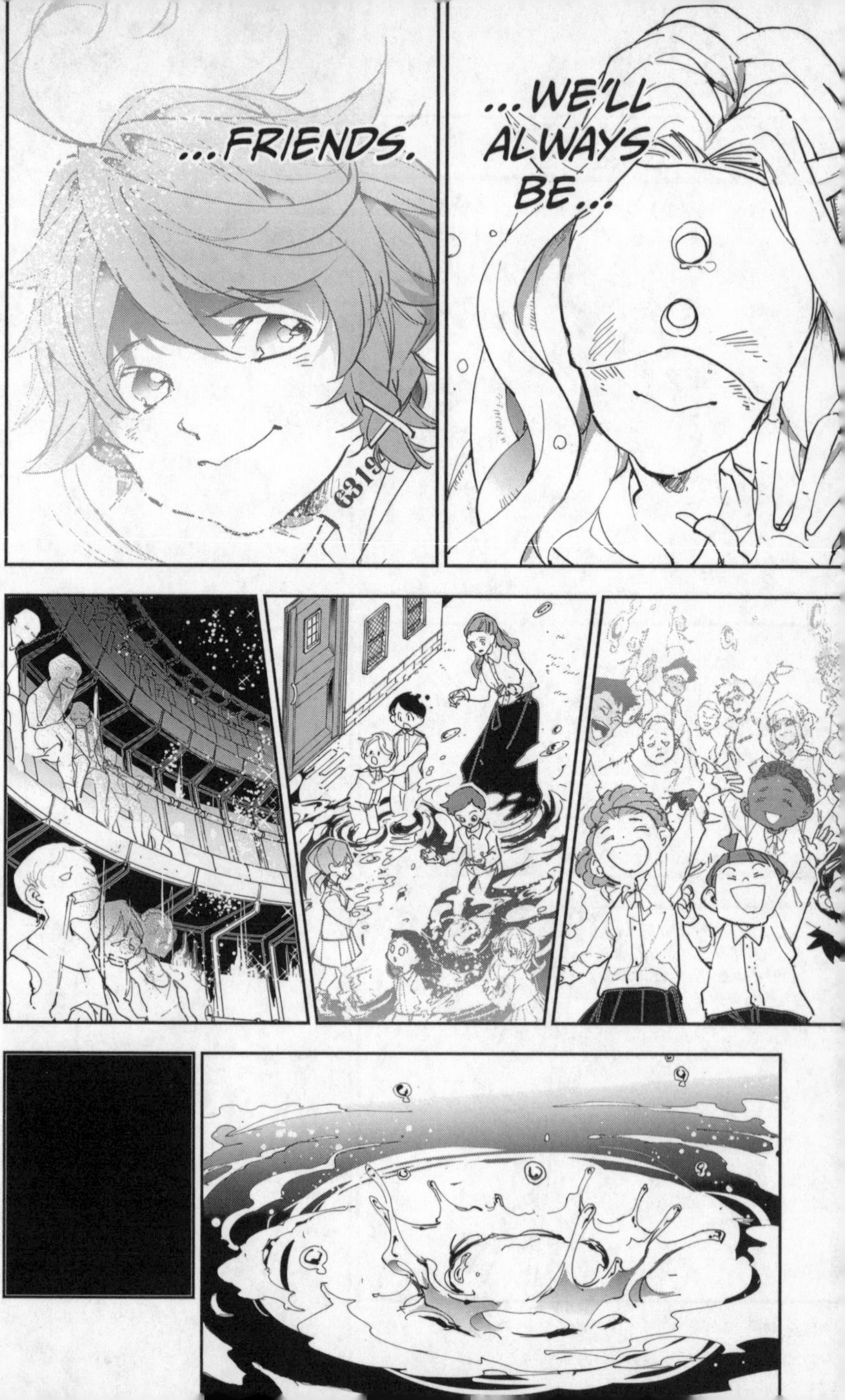
...WE'LL ALWAYS BE...
...FRIENDS.

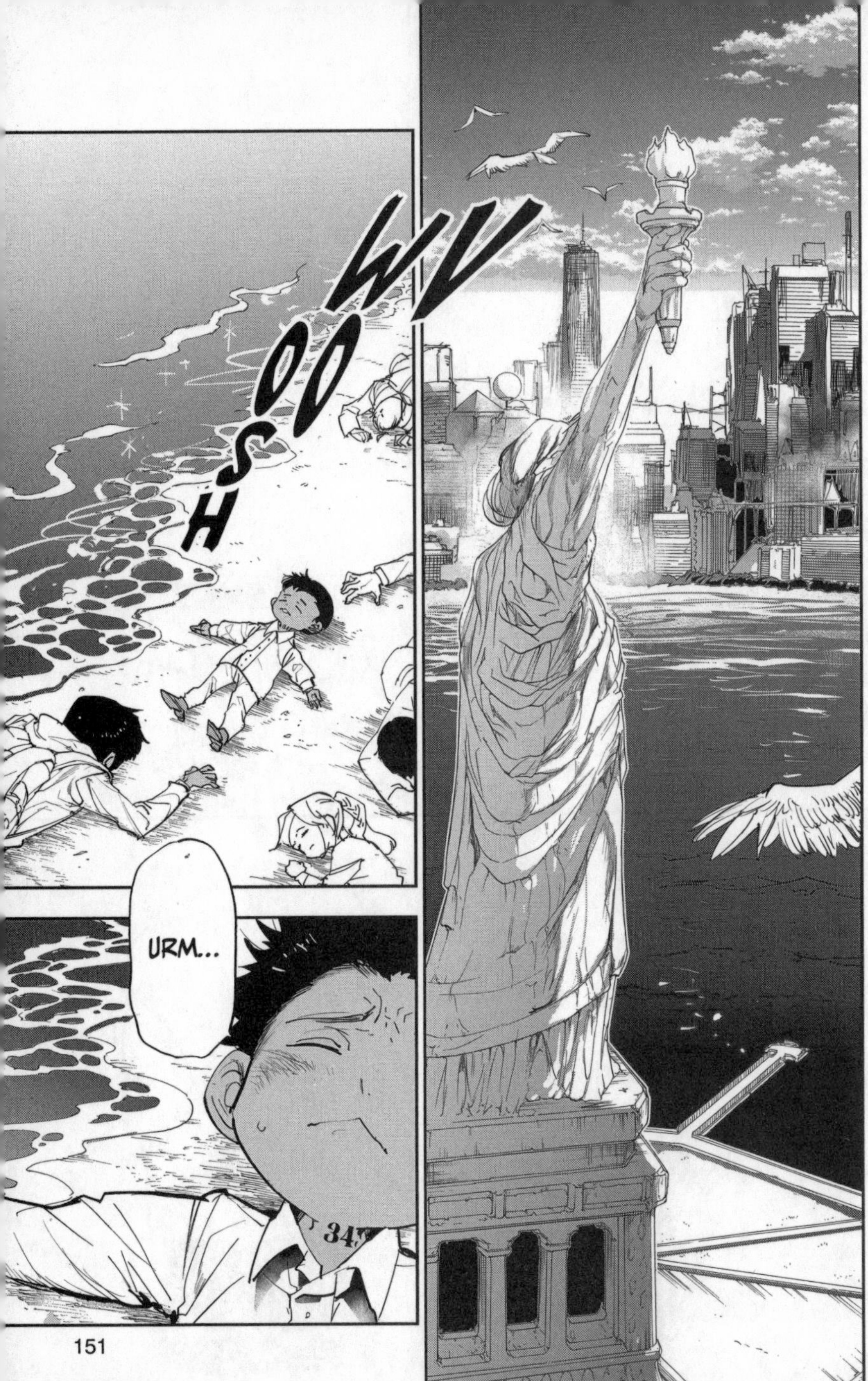
WOOSH
URM...

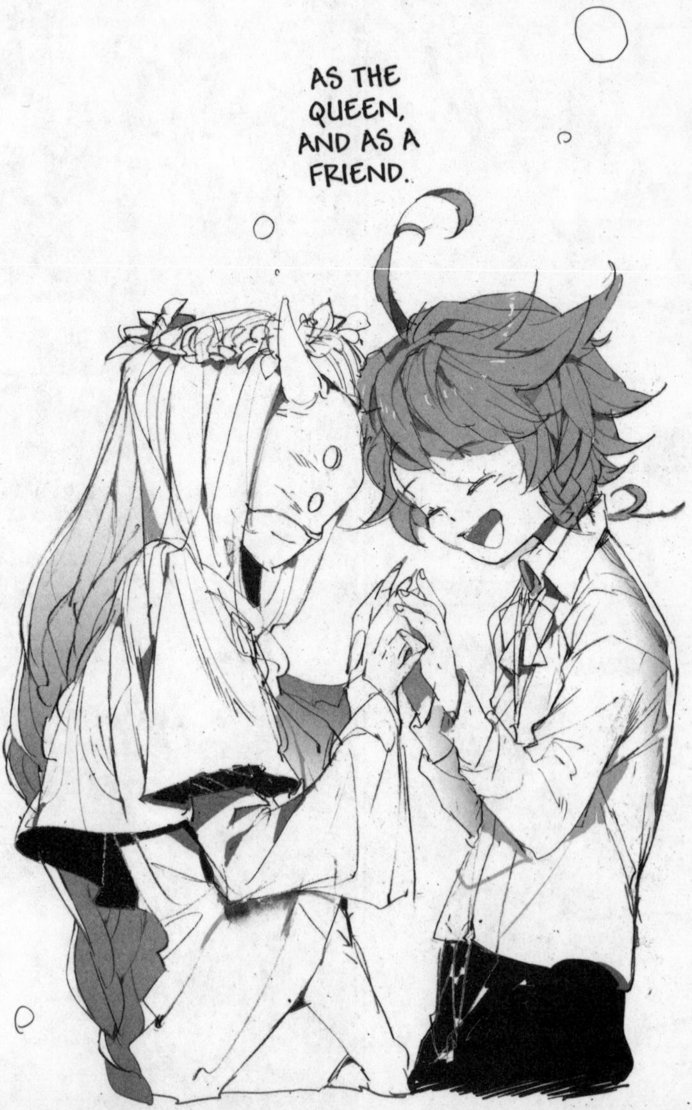
AS THE QUEEN, AND AS A FRIEND.

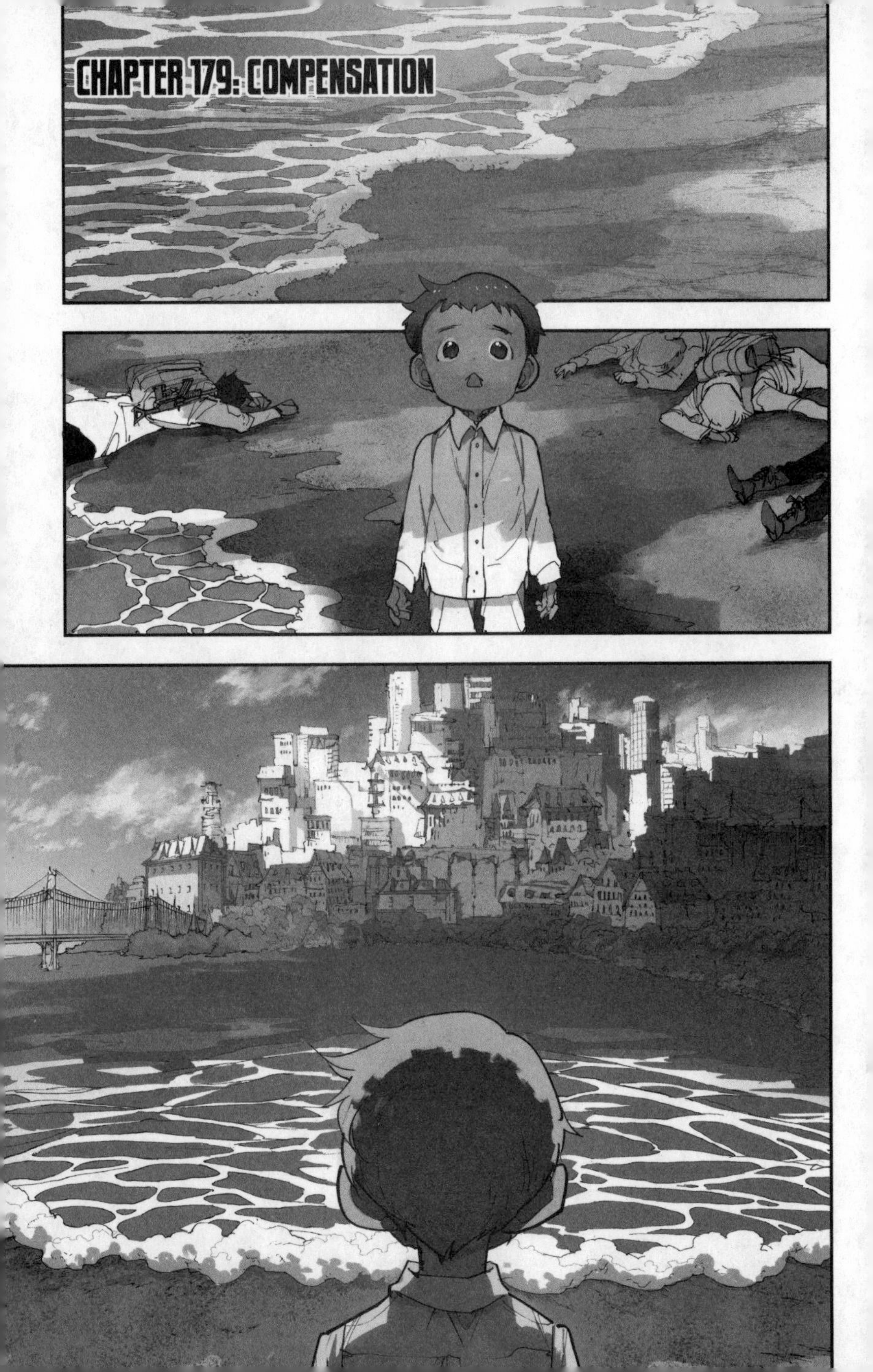
CHAPTER 179: COMPENSATION

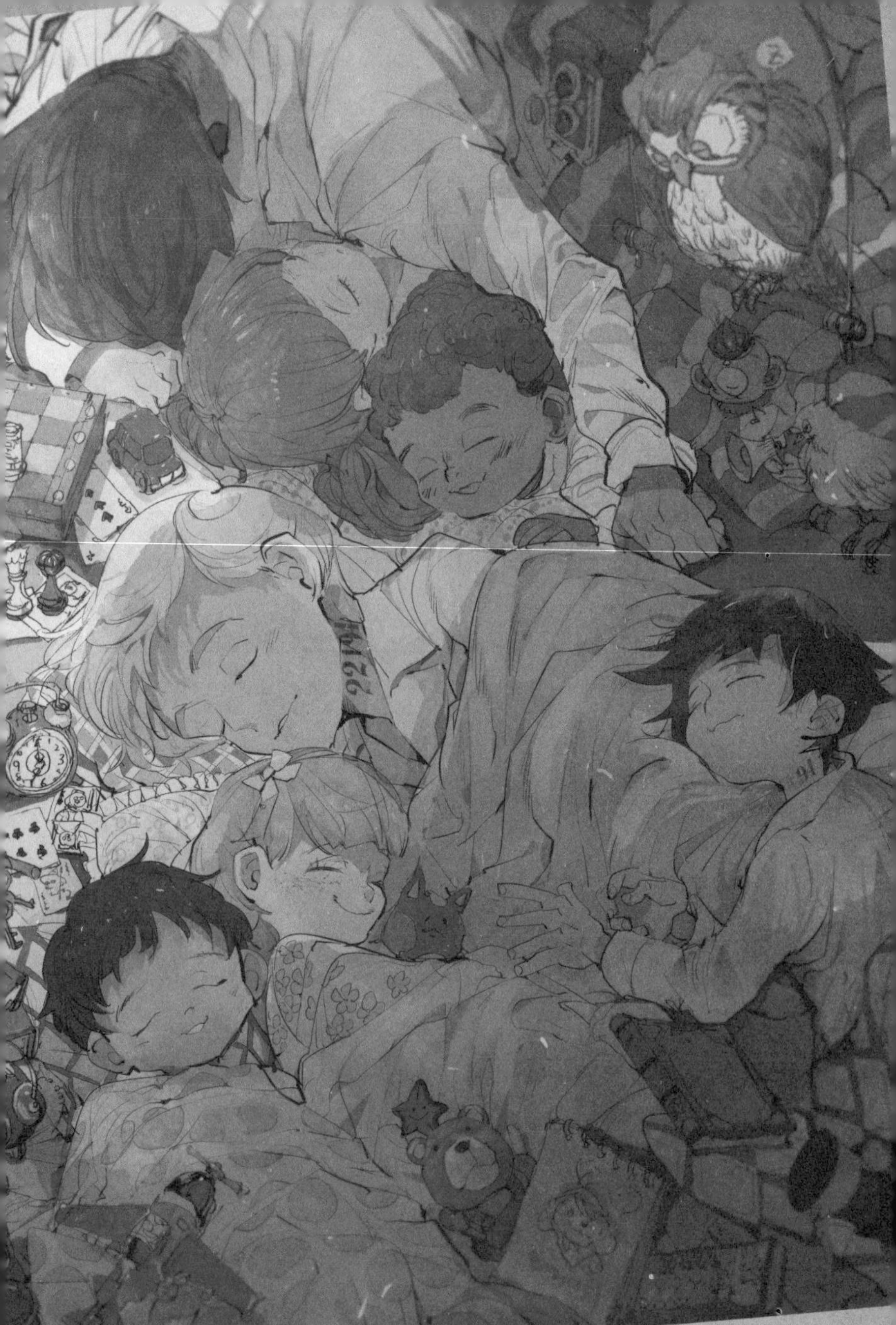

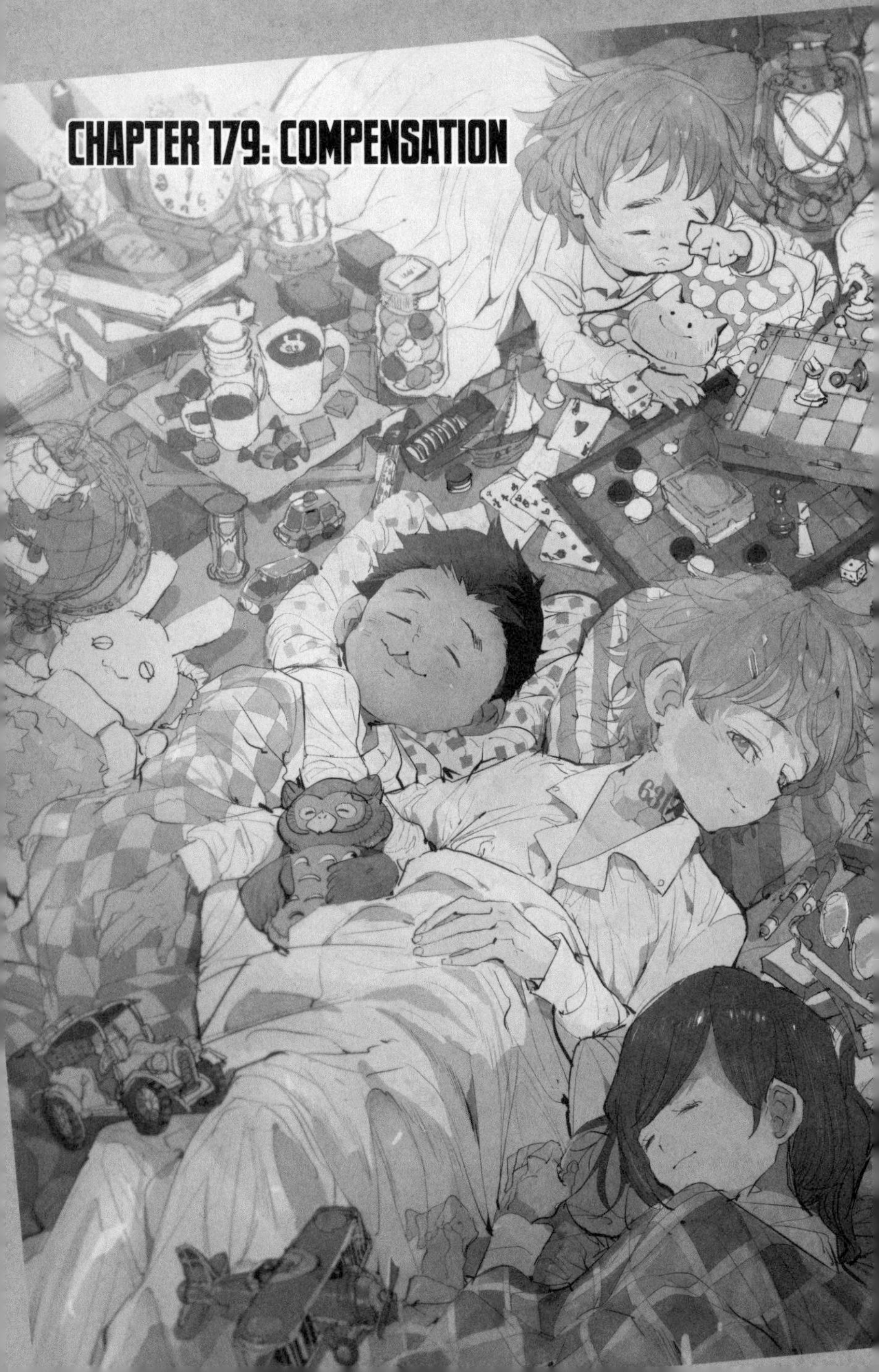
CHAPTER 179: COMPENSATION

REUNIONS

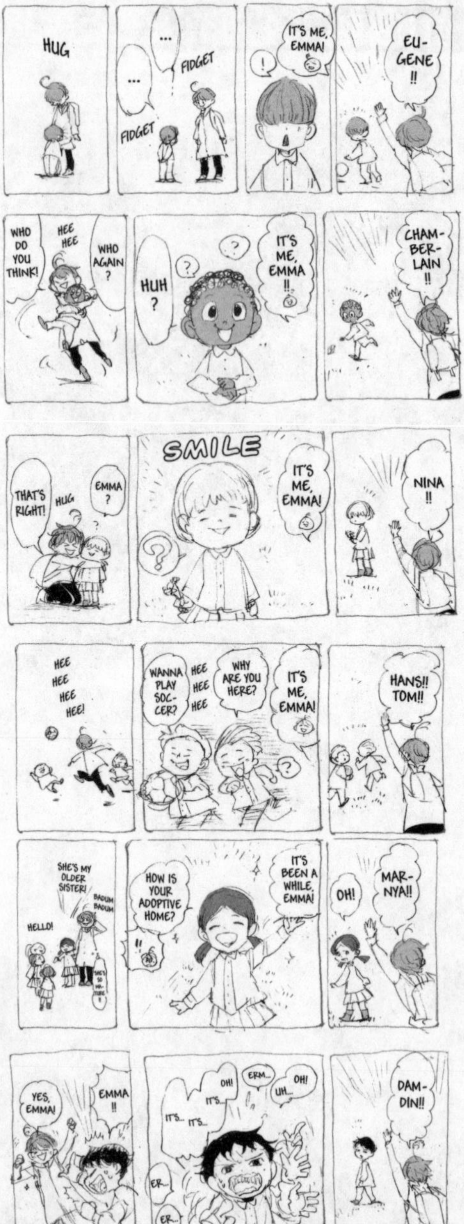
EU-GENE!!
IT'S ME, EMMA!
!
...
FIDGET
...
FIDGET
HUG
CHAM-BER-LAIN!!
IT'S ME, EMMA!!
?
?
HUH?
WHO AGAIN?
HEE HEE
WHO DO YOU THINK!
NINA!!
SMILE
IT'S ME, EMMA!
?
EMMA?
?
HUG
THAT'S RIGHT!
HANS!! TOM!!
IT'S ME, EMMA!
?
WHY ARE YOU HERE?
HEE HEE HEE
WANNA PLAY SOC-CER?
HEE HEE HEE HEE!
MAR-NYA!!
OH!
IT'S BEEN A WHILE, EMMA!
HOW IS YOUR ADOPTIVE HOME?
!!
SHE'S MY OLDER SISTER!
BADUM BADUM
SHE'S SO MA-TURE!!
HELLO!
DAM-DIN!!
OH!
UH...
ERM...
OH!
IT'S...
IT'S...
IT'S...
ER...
ER...
EMMA!!
YES, EMMA!

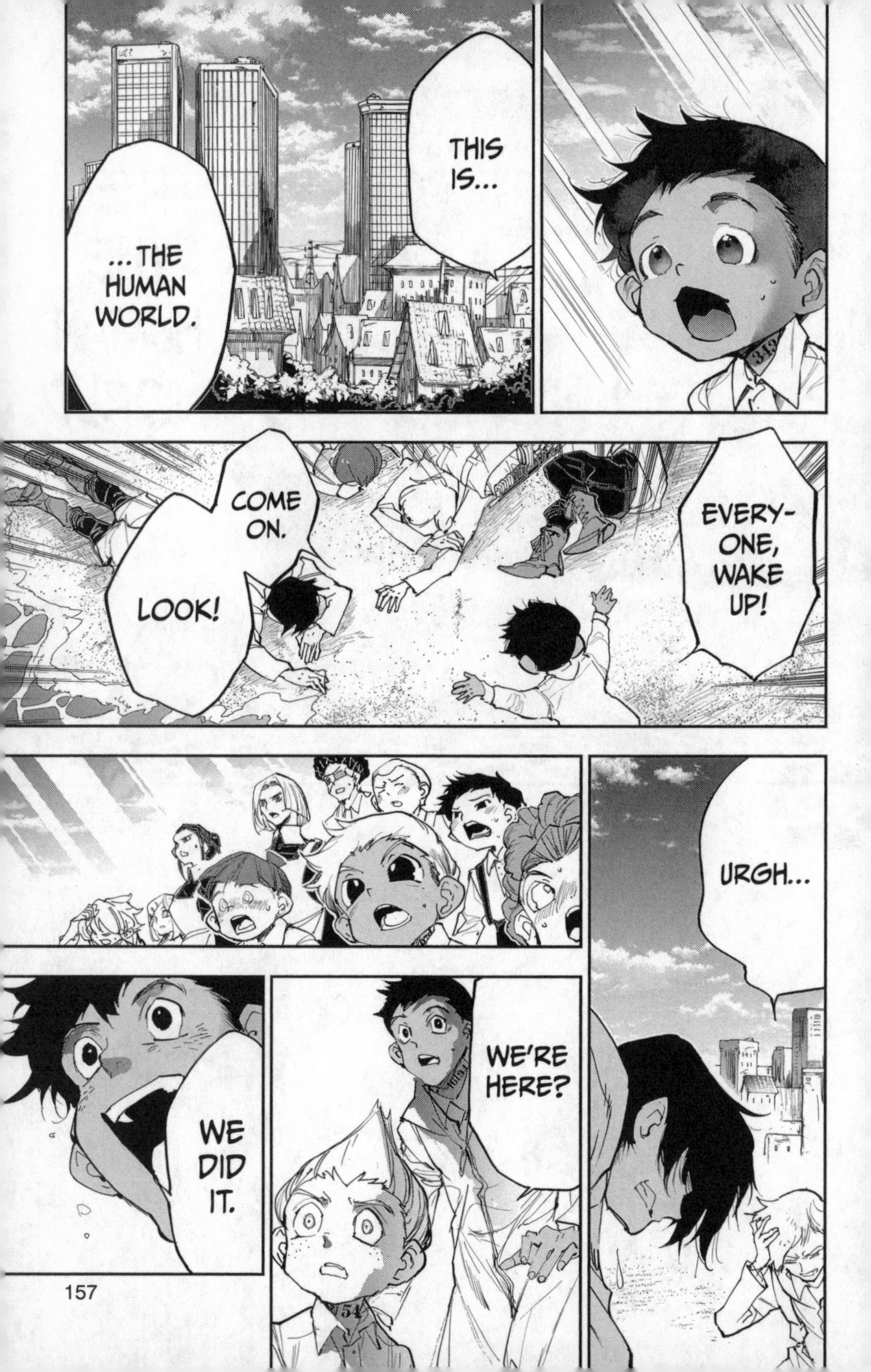
THIS IS...
...THE HUMAN WORLD.
EVERY-ONE, WAKE UP!
COME ON.
LOOK!
URGH...
WE'RE HERE?
WE DID IT.

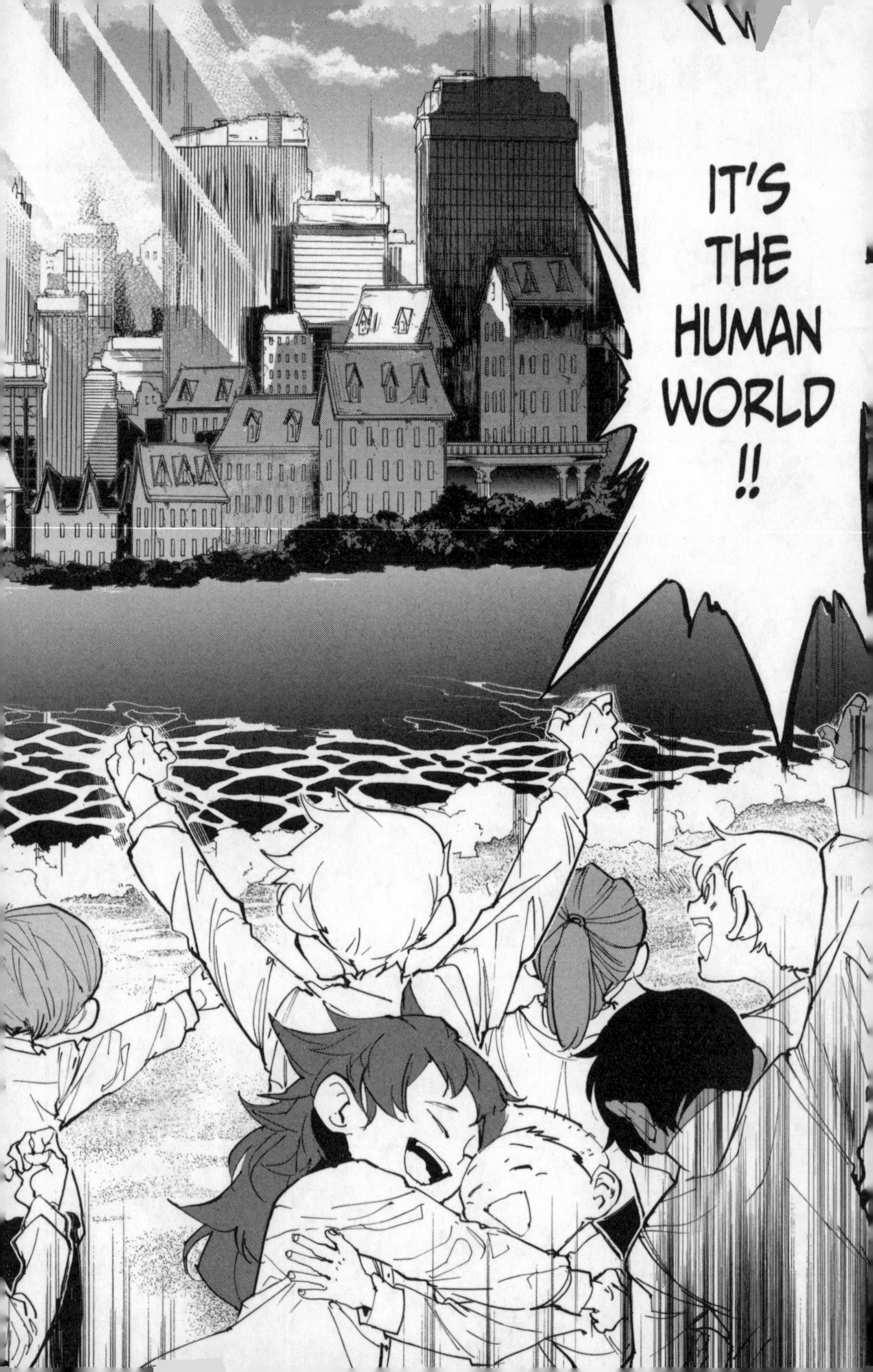
IT'S THE HUMAN WORLD !!

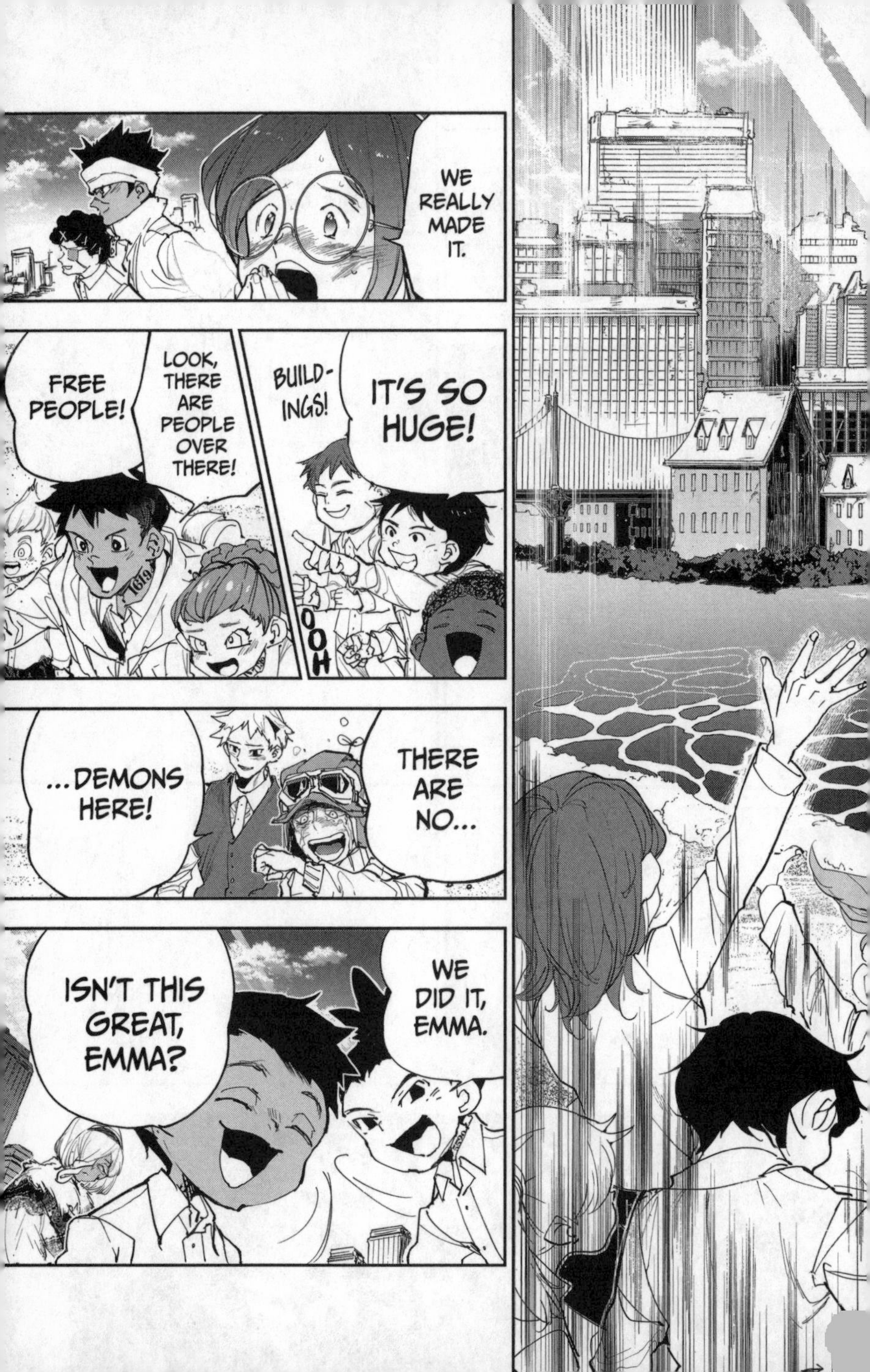
WE REALLY MADE IT.
IT'S SO HUGE!
BUILD-INGS!
OOH
LOOK, THERE ARE PEOPLE OVER THERE!
FREE PEOPLE!
THERE ARE NO...
...DEMONS HERE!
WE DID IT, EMMA.
ISN'T THIS GREAT, EMMA?

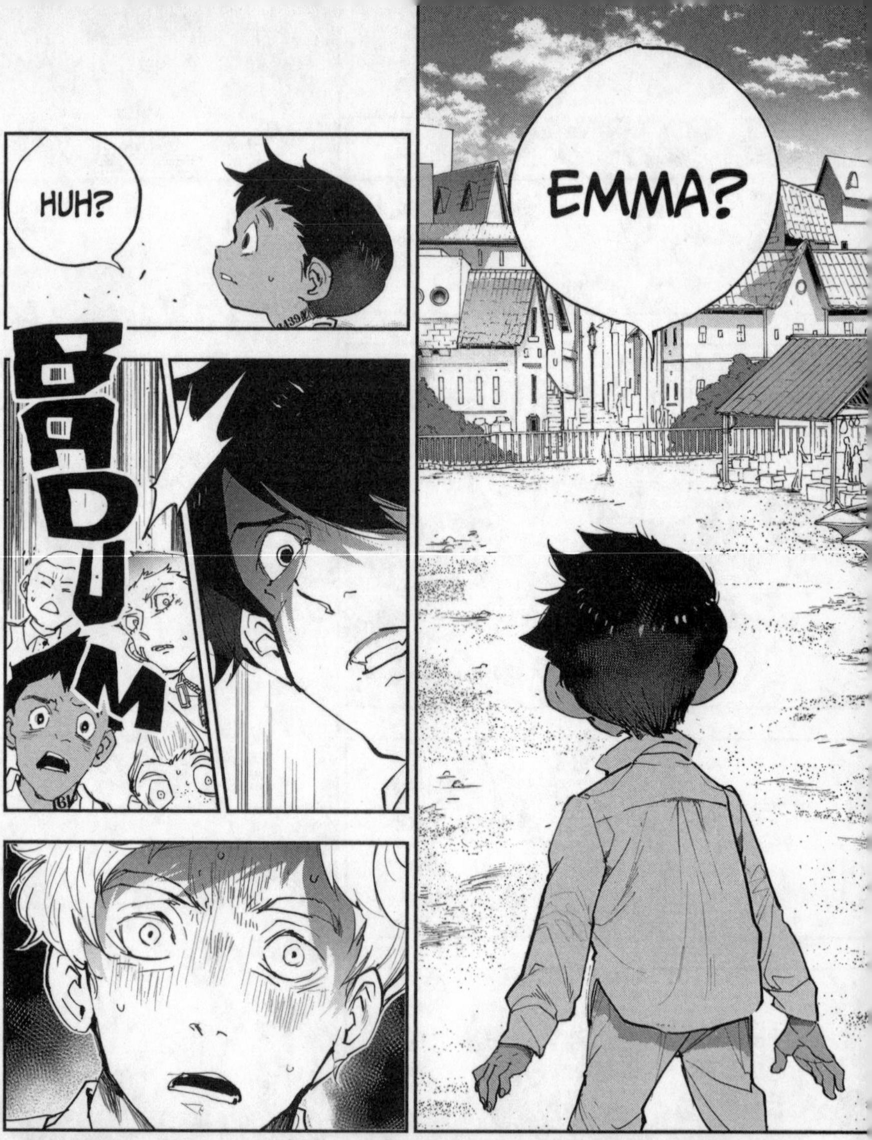
EMMA?
HUH?
BADUM

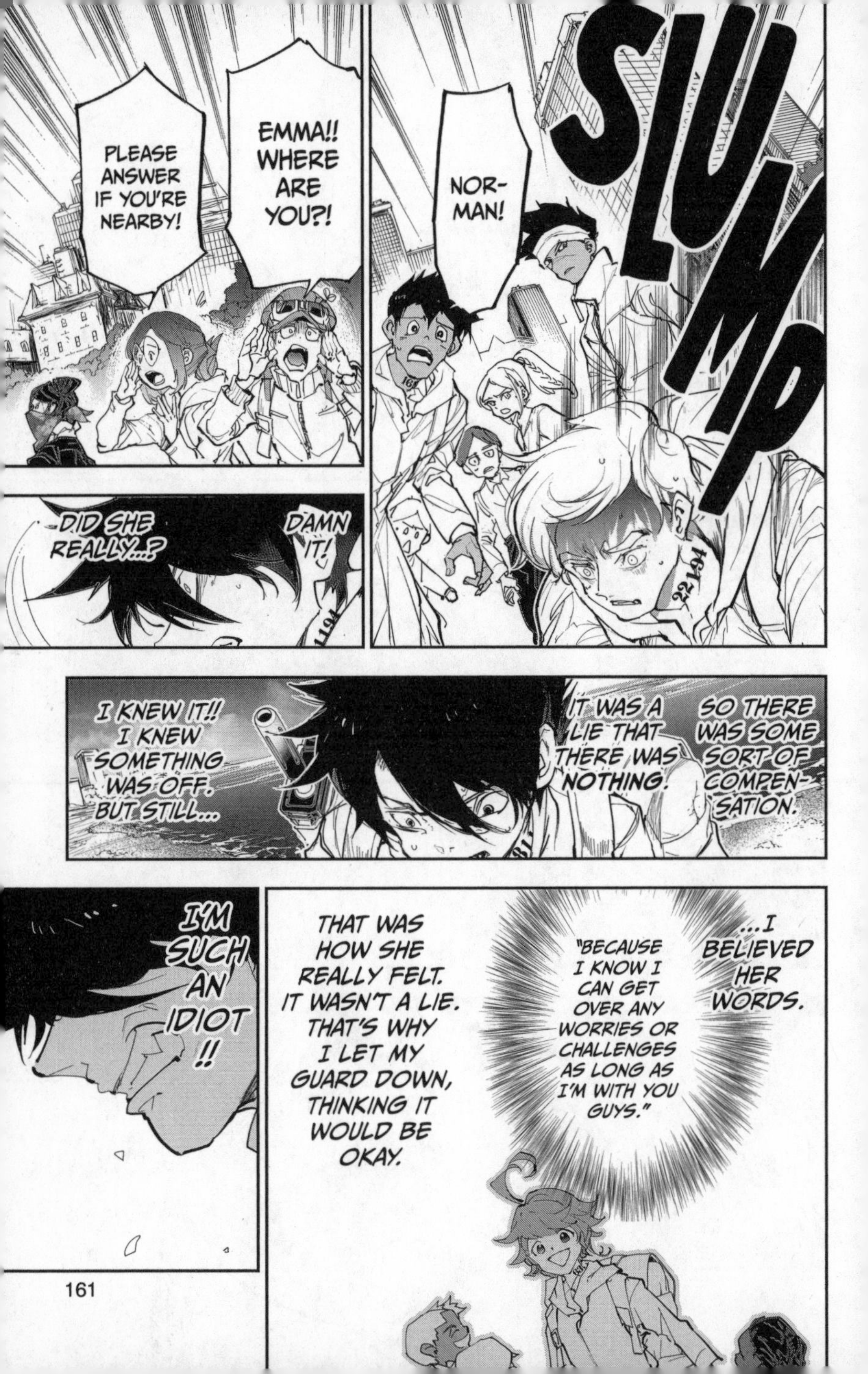
SLUMP
NOR-MAN!
EMMA!! WHERE ARE YOU?!
PLEASE ANSWER IF YOU'RE NEARBY!
DAMN IT!
DID SHE REALLY...?
SO THERE WAS SOME SORT OF COMPEN-SATION.
IT WAS A LIE THAT THERE WAS NOTHING.
I KNEW IT!! I KNEW SOMETHING WAS OFF. BUT STILL...
...I BELIEVED HER WORDS.
"BECAUSE I KNOW I CAN GET OVER ANY WORRIES OR CHALLENGES AS LONG AS I'M WITH YOU GUYS."
THAT WAS HOW SHE REALLY FELT. IT WASN'T A LIE. THAT'S WHY I LET MY GUARD DOWN, THINKING IT WOULD BE OKAY.
I'M SUCH AN IDIOT!!

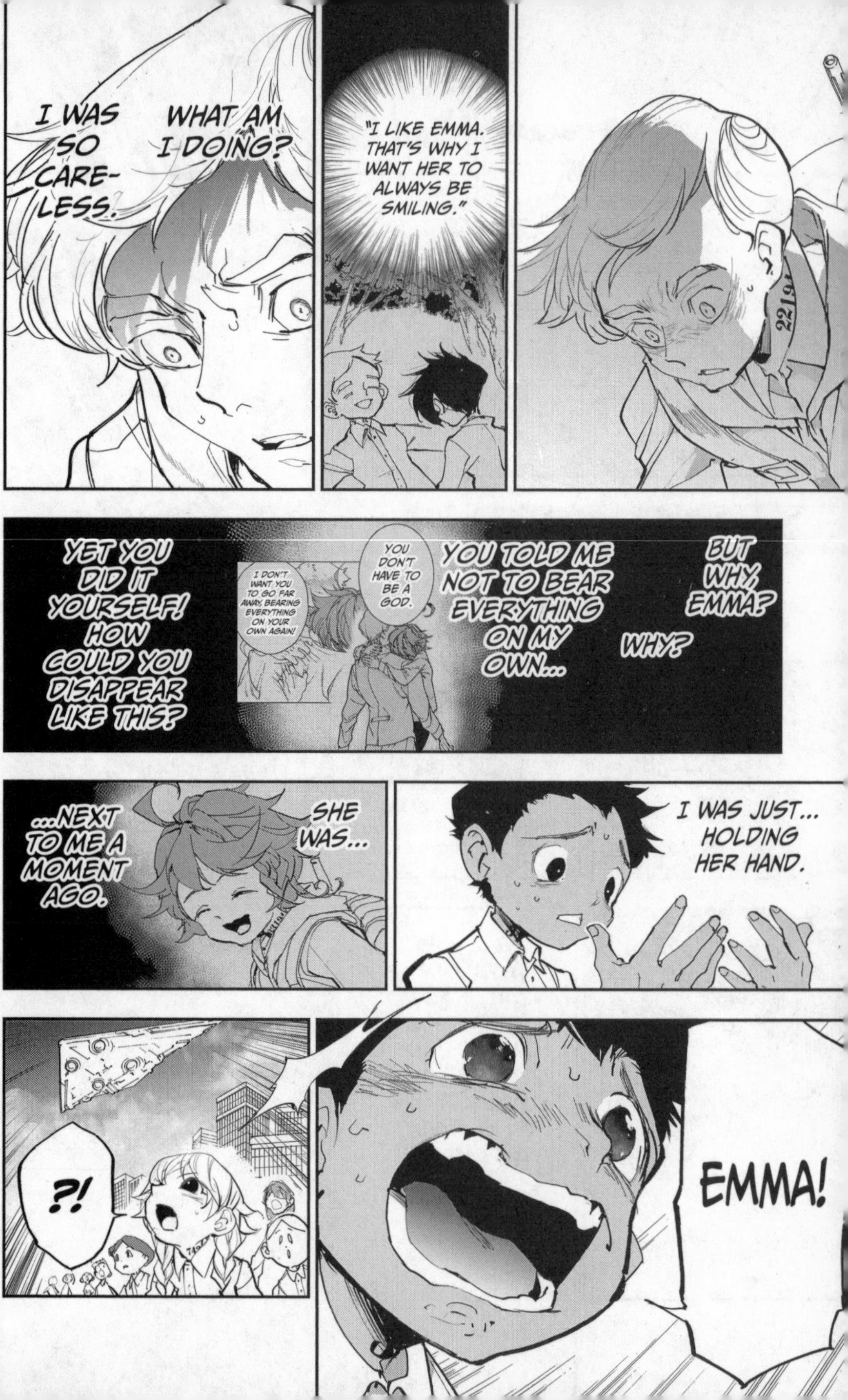
"I LIKE EMMA. THAT'S WHY I WANT HER TO ALWAYS BE SMILING."
WHAT AM I DOING?
I WAS SO CARE-LESS.
BUT WHY, EMMA?
WHY?
YOU TOLD ME NOT TO BEAR EVERYTHING ON MY OWN...
YOU DON'T HAVE TO BE A GOD.
I DON'T WANT YOU TO GO FAR AWAY, BEARING EVERYTHING ON YOUR OWN AGAIN!
YET YOU DID IT YOURSELF! HOW COULD YOU DISAPPEAR LIKE THIS?
I WAS JUST... HOLDING HER HAND.
SHE WAS...
...NEXT TO ME A MOMENT AGO.
EMMA!
?!

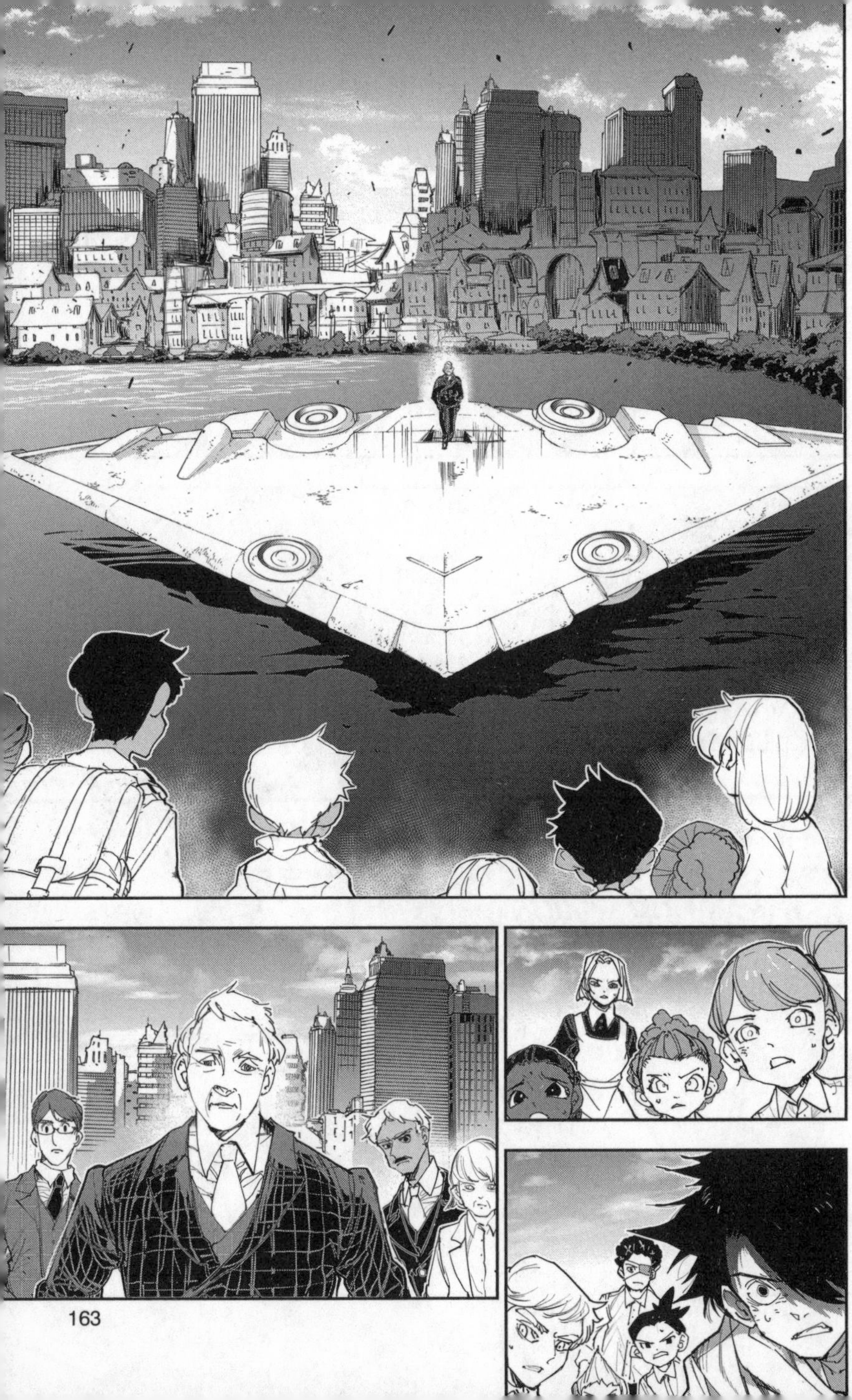

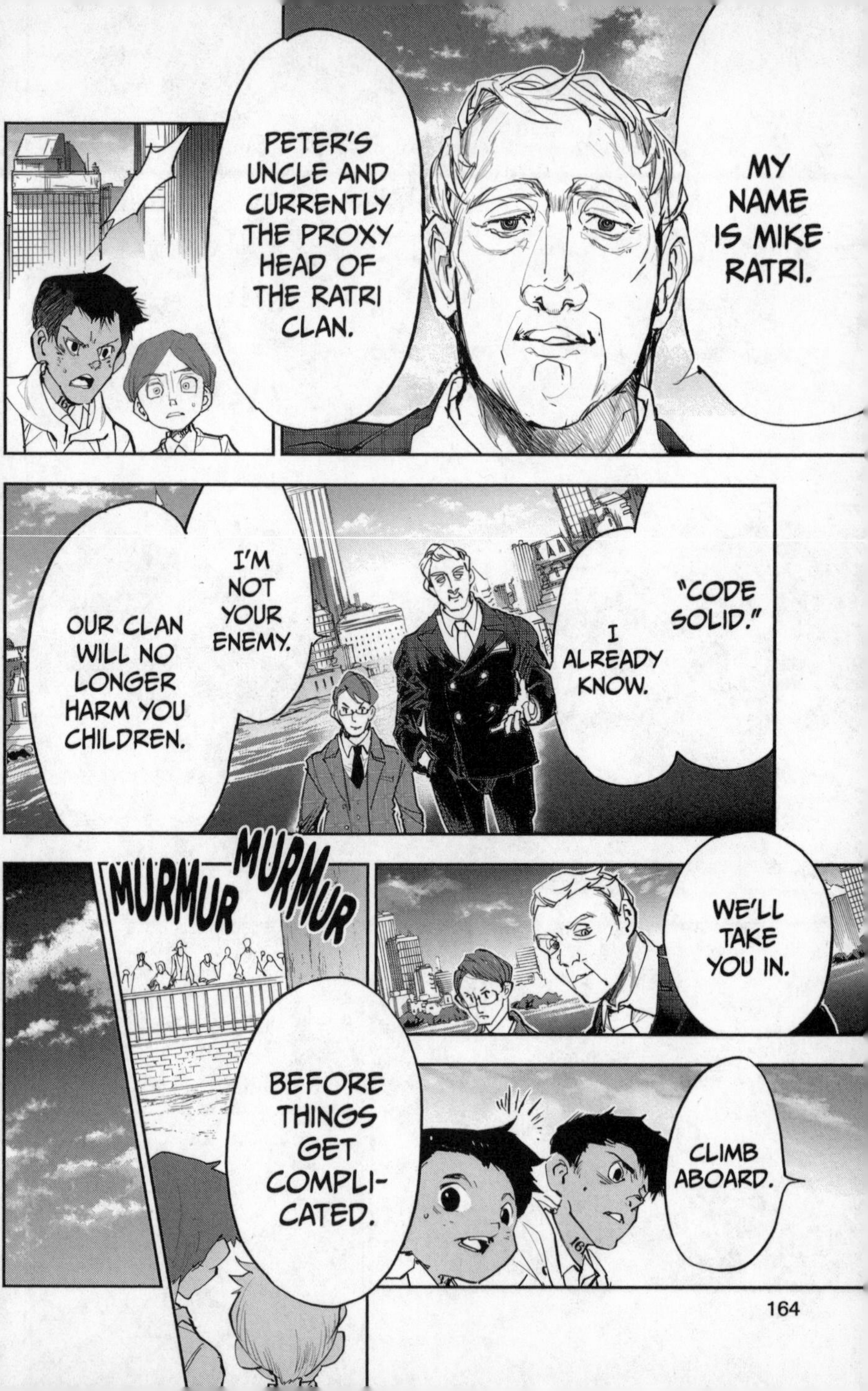
MY NAME IS MIKE RATRI.
PETER'S UNCLE AND CURRENTLY THE PROXY HEAD OF THE RATRI CLAN.
"CODE SOLID."
I ALREADY KNOW.
I'M NOT YOUR ENEMY.
OUR CLAN WILL NO LONGER HARM YOU CHILDREN.
WE'LL TAKE YOU IN.
MURMUR
MURMUR
CLIMB ABOARD.
BEFORE THINGS GET COMPLICATED.

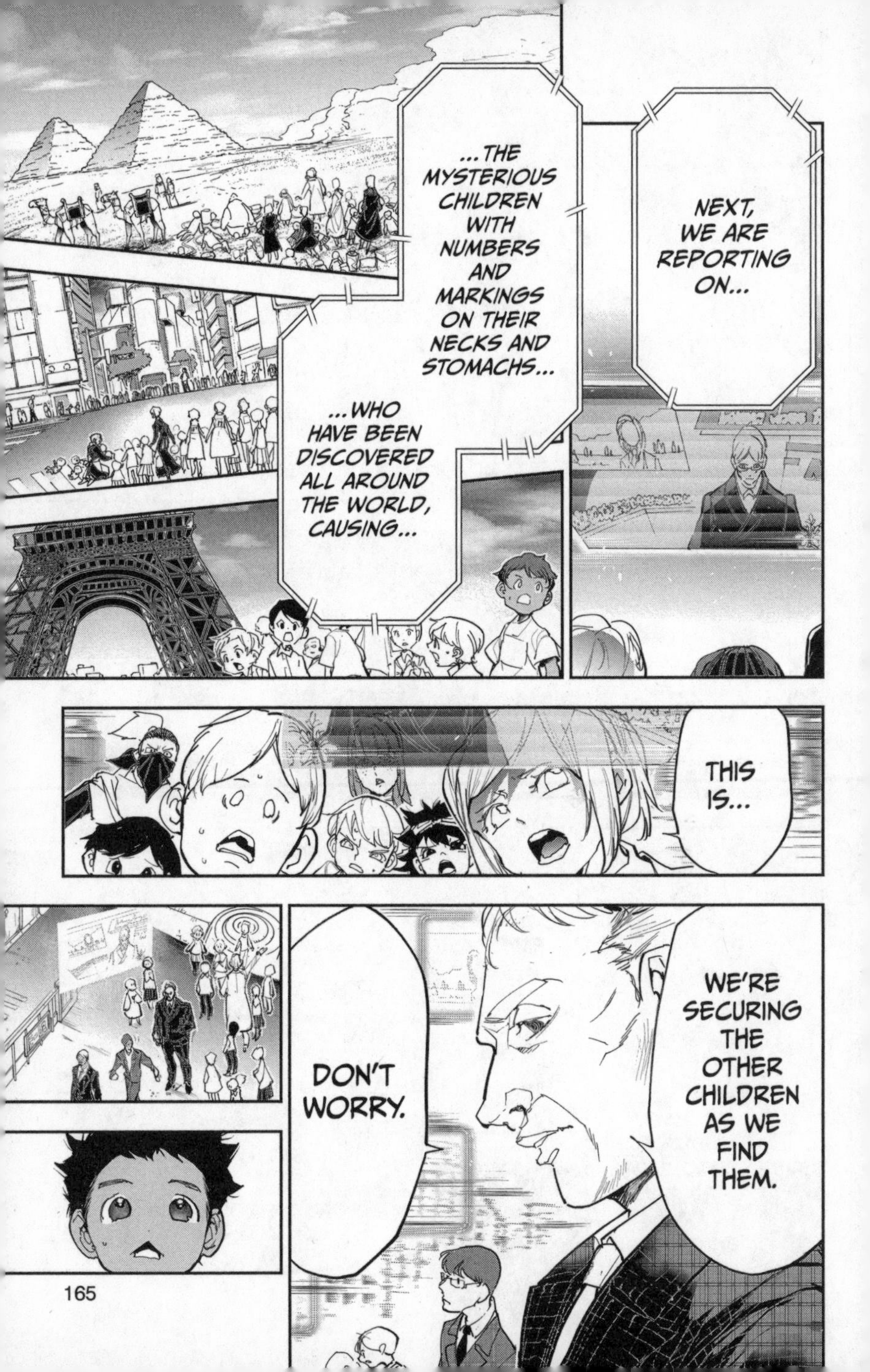
NEXT, WE ARE REPORTING ON...
...THE MYSTERIOUS CHILDREN WITH NUMBERS AND MARKINGS ON THEIR NECKS AND STOMACHS...
...WHO HAVE BEEN DISCOVERED ALL AROUND THE WORLD, CAUSING...
THIS IS...
WE'RE SECURING THE OTHER CHILDREN AS WE FIND THEM.
DON'T WORRY.

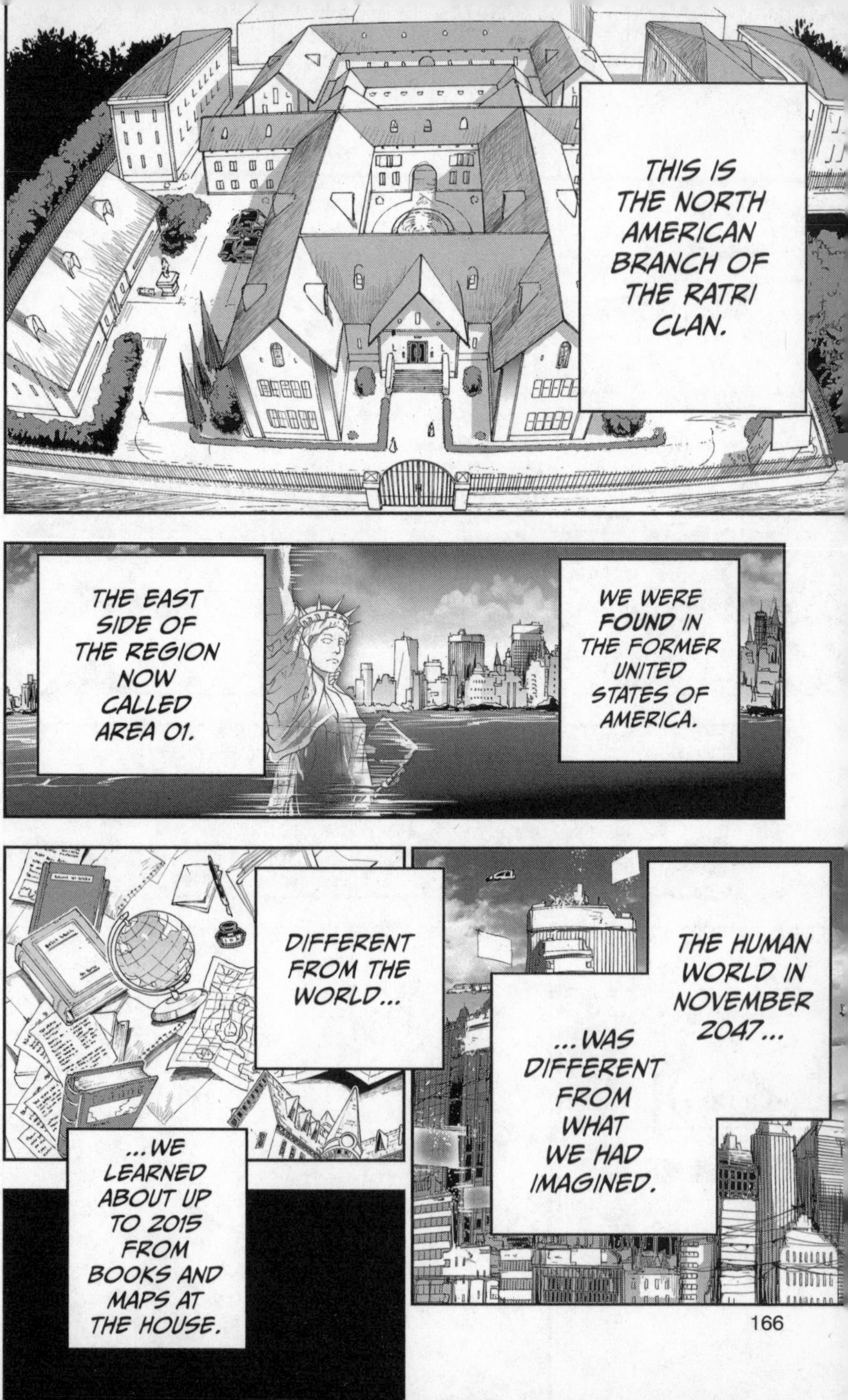
THIS IS THE NORTH AMERICAN BRANCH OF THE RATRI CLAN.
WE WERE FOUND IN THE FORMER UNITED STATES OF AMERICA.
THE EAST SIDE OF THE REGION NOW CALLED AREA 01.
THE HUMAN WORLD IN NOVEMBER 2047...
...WAS DIFFERENT FROM WHAT WE HAD IMAGINED.
DIFFERENT FROM THE WORLD...
...WE LEARNED ABOUT UP TO 2015 FROM BOOKS AND MAPS AT THE HOUSE.

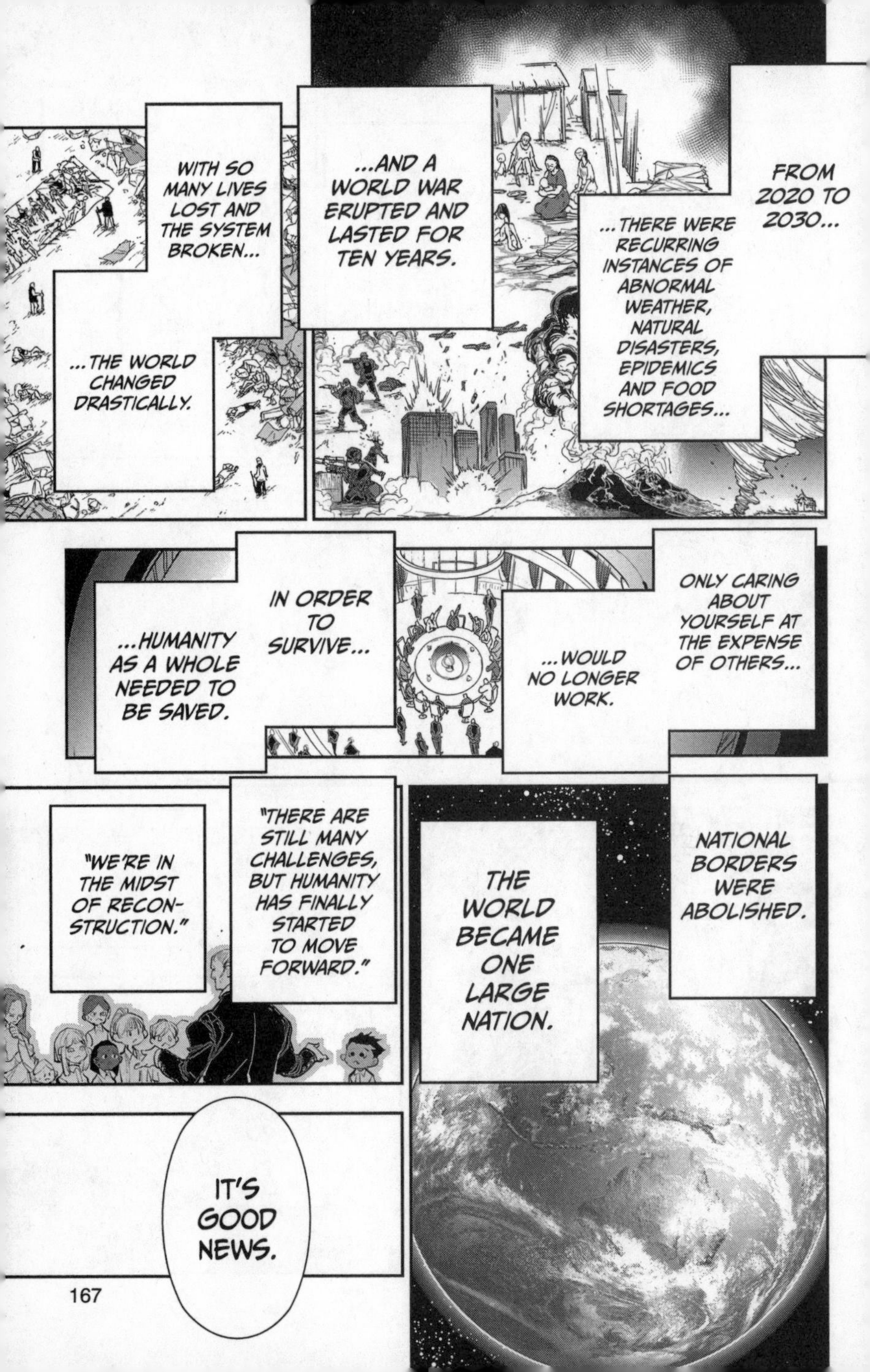
FROM 2020 TO 2030...
...THERE WERE RECURRING INSTANCES OF ABNORMAL WEATHER, NATURAL DISASTERS, EPIDEMICS AND FOOD SHORTAGES...
...AND A WORLD WAR ERUPTED AND LASTED FOR TEN YEARS.
WITH SO MANY LIVES LOST AND THE SYSTEM BROKEN...
...THE WORLD CHANGED DRASTICALLY.
ONLY CARING ABOUT YOURSELF AT THE EXPENSE OF OTHERS...
...WOULD NO LONGER WORK.
IN ORDER TO SURVIVE...
...HUMANITY AS A WHOLE NEEDED TO BE SAVED.
NATIONAL BORDERS WERE ABOLISHED.
THE WORLD BECAME ONE LARGE NATION.
"THERE ARE STILL MANY CHALLENGES, BUT HUMANITY HAS FINALLY STARTED TO MOVE FORWARD."
"WE'RE IN THE MIDST OF RECON-STRUCTION."
IT'S GOOD NEWS.

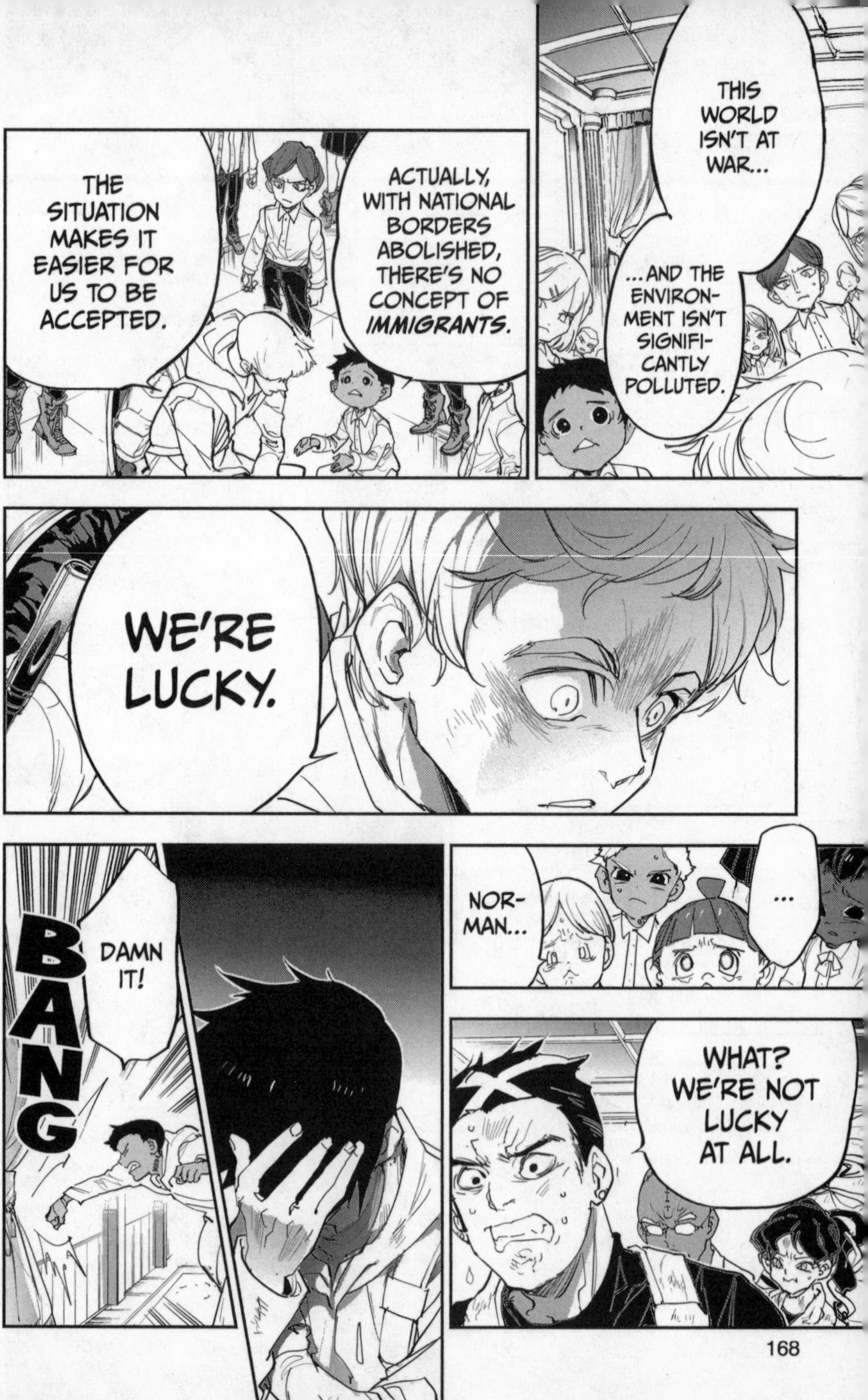
THIS WORLD ISN'T AT WAR...
...AND THE ENVIRONMENT ISN'T SIGNIFICANTLY POLLUTED.
ACTUALLY, WITH NATIONAL BORDERS ABOLISHED, THERE'S NO CONCEPT OF *IMMIGRANTS*.
THE SITUATION MAKES IT EASIER FOR US TO BE ACCEPTED.
WE'RE LUCKY.
...
NOR-MAN...
WHAT? WE'RE NOT LUCKY AT ALL.
DAMN IT!
BANG

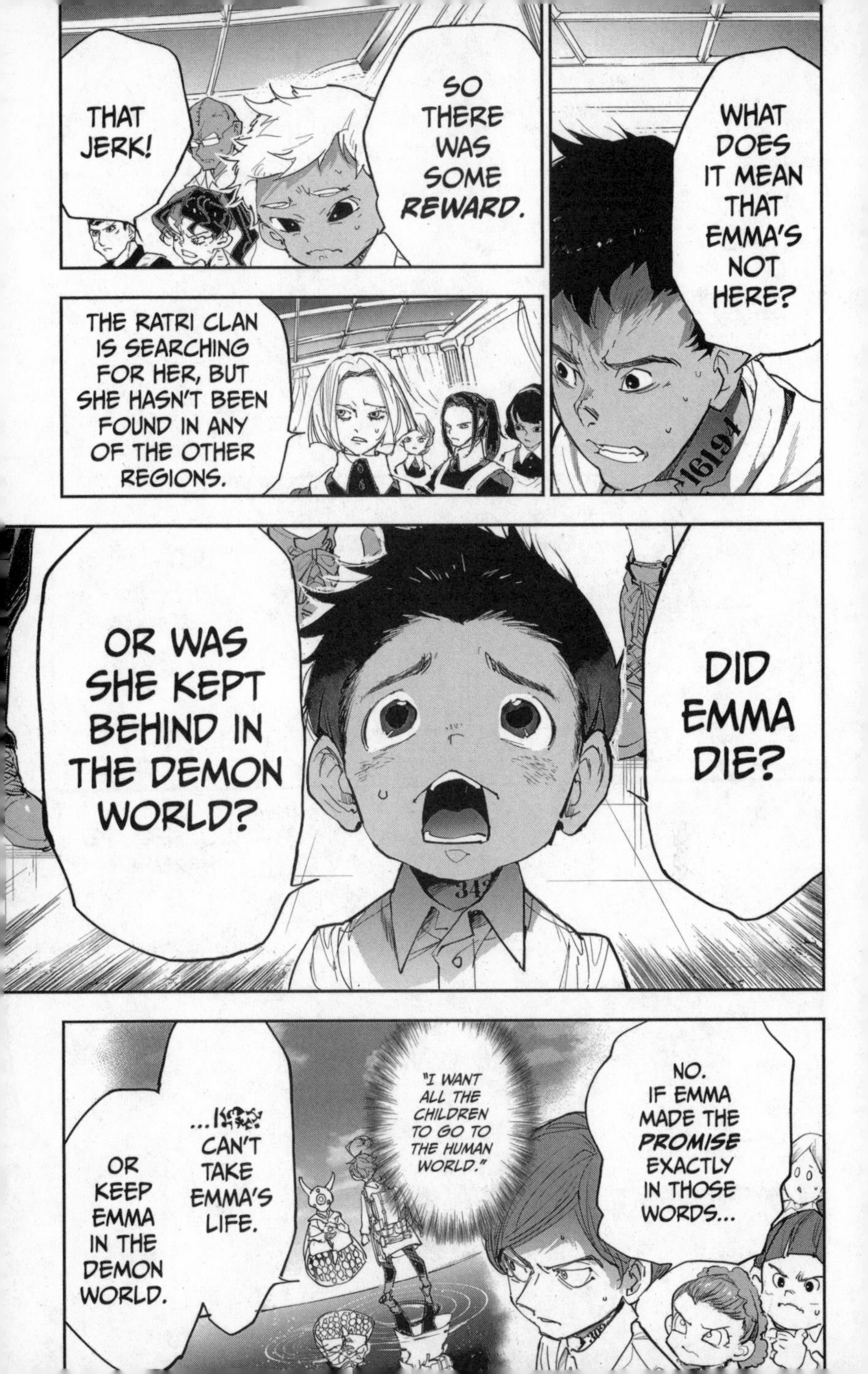
WHAT DOES IT MEAN THAT EMMA'S NOT HERE?
SO THERE WAS SOME REWARD.
THAT JERK!
THE RATRI CLAN IS SEARCHING FOR HER, BUT SHE HASN'T BEEN FOUND IN ANY OF THE OTHER REGIONS.
DID EMMA DIE?
OR WAS SHE KEPT BEHIND IN THE DEMON WORLD?
NO. IF EMMA MADE THE PROMISE EXACTLY IN THOSE WORDS...
"I WANT ALL THE CHILDREN TO GO TO THE HUMAN WORLD."
... CAN'T TAKE EMMA'S LIFE.
OR KEEP EMMA IN THE DEMON WORLD.

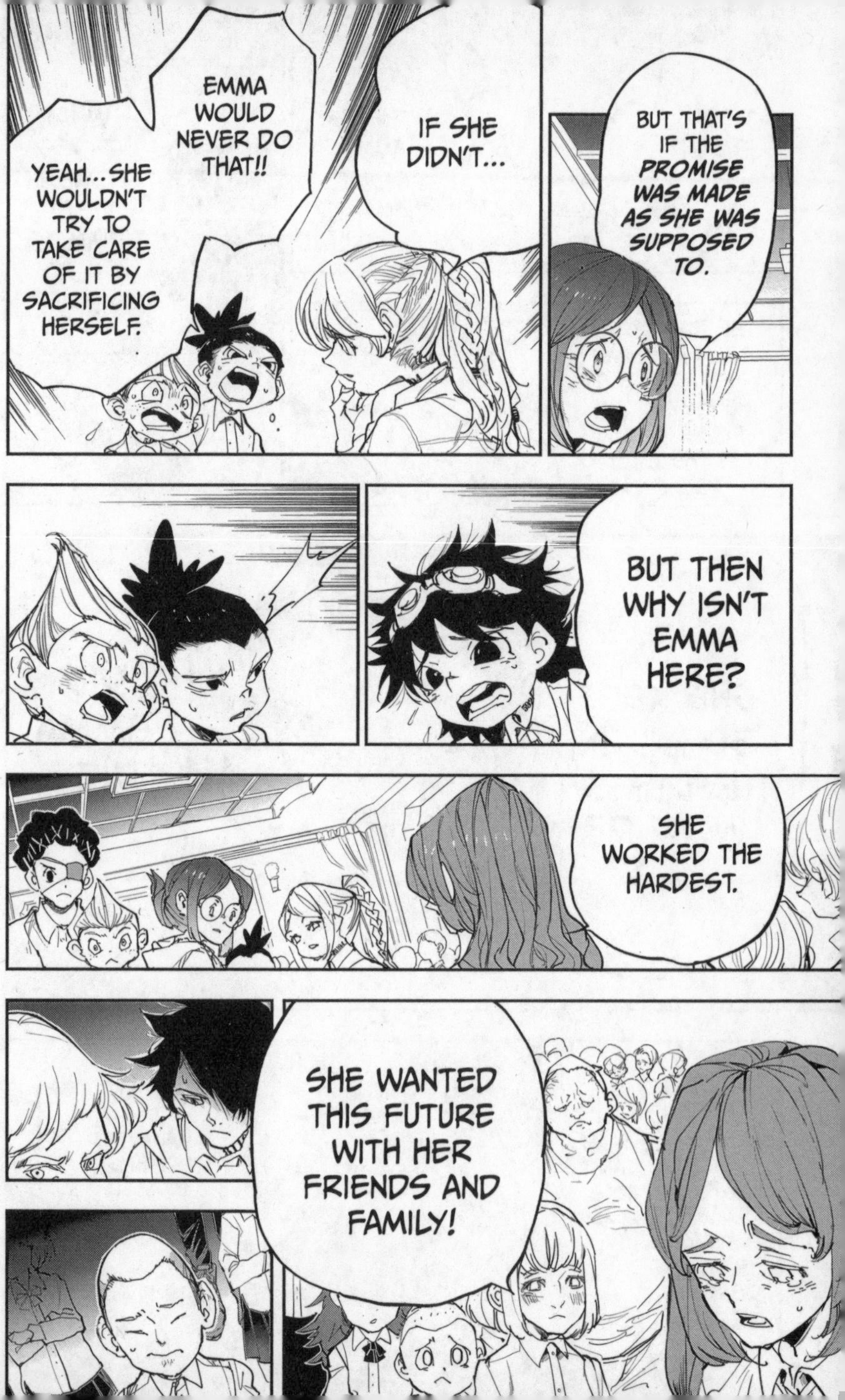
BUT THAT'S IF THE PROMISE WAS MADE AS SHE WAS SUPPOSED TO.
IF SHE DIDN'T...
EMMA WOULD NEVER DO THAT!!
YEAH...SHE WOULDN'T TRY TO TAKE CARE OF IT BY SACRIFICING HERSELF.
BUT THEN WHY ISN'T EMMA HERE?
SHE WORKED THE HARDEST.
SHE WANTED THIS FUTURE WITH HER FRIENDS AND FAMILY!

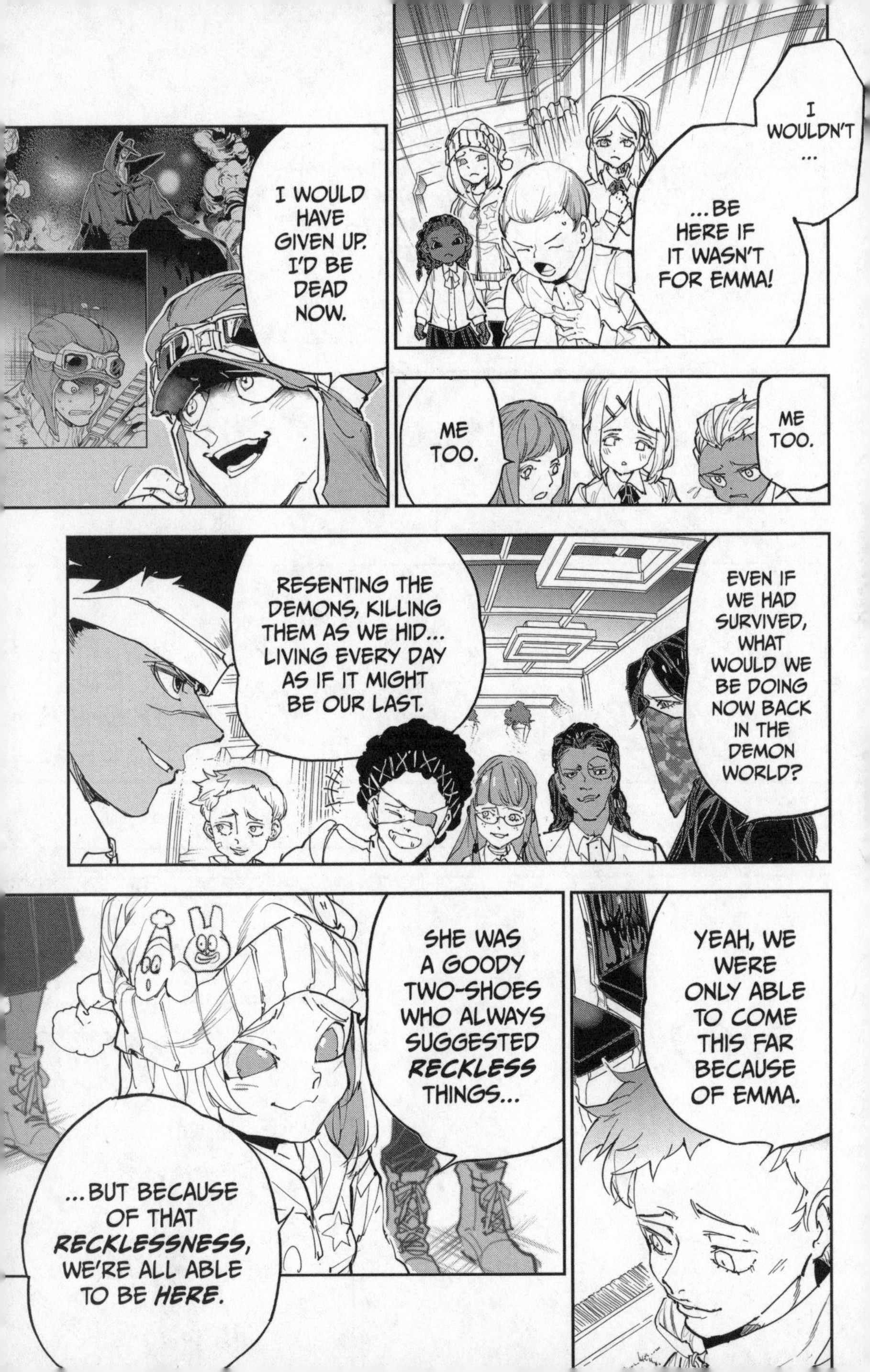
I WOULDN'T ...
...BE HERE IF IT WASN'T FOR EMMA!
ME TOO.
ME TOO.
I WOULD HAVE GIVEN UP. I'D BE DEAD NOW.
EVEN IF WE HAD SURVIVED, WHAT WOULD WE BE DOING NOW BACK IN THE DEMON WORLD?
RESENTING THE DEMONS, KILLING THEM AS WE HID... LIVING EVERY DAY AS IF IT MIGHT BE OUR LAST.
YEAH, WE WERE ONLY ABLE TO COME THIS FAR BECAUSE OF EMMA.
SHE WAS A GOODY TWO-SHOES WHO ALWAYS SUGGESTED *RECKLESS* THINGS...
...BUT BECAUSE OF THAT *RECKLESSNESS*, WE'RE ALL ABLE TO BE *HERE*.

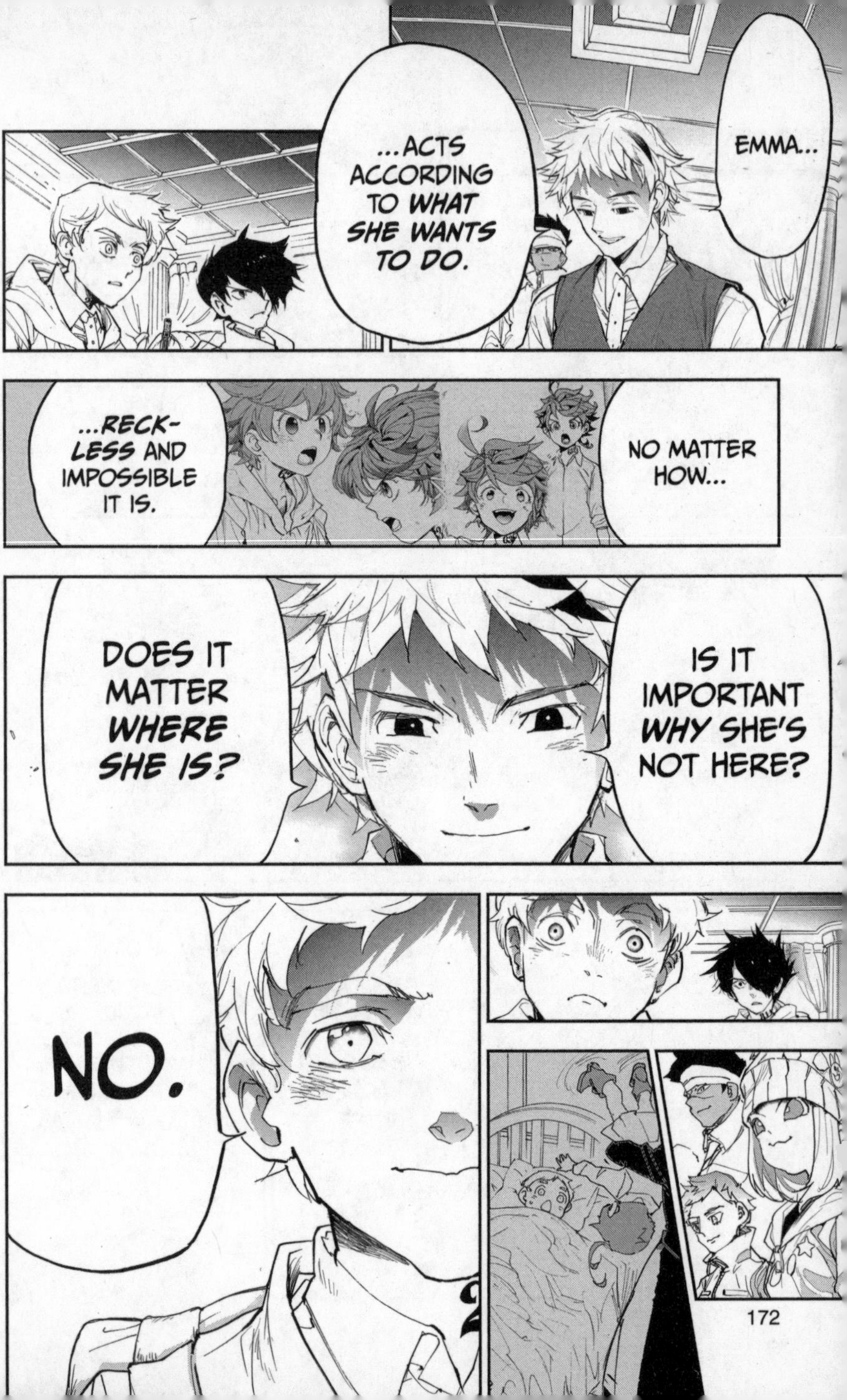
EMMA...
...ACTS ACCORDING TO WHAT SHE WANTS TO DO.
NO MATTER HOW...
...RECK-LESS AND IMPOSSIBLE IT IS.
IS IT IMPORTANT WHY SHE'S NOT HERE?
DOES IT MATTER WHERE SHE IS?
NO.

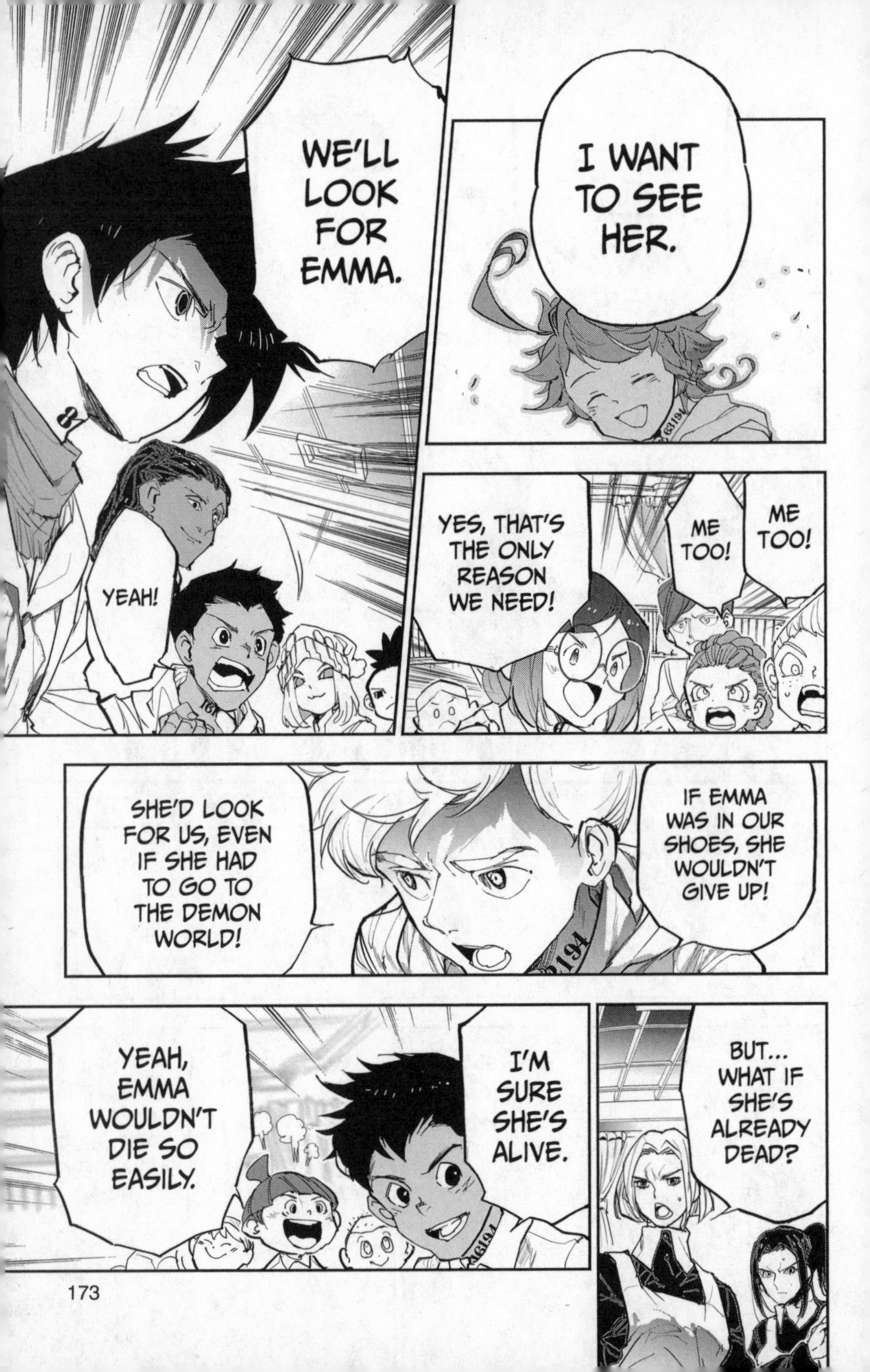
I WANT TO SEE HER.
ME TOO!
ME TOO!
YES, THAT'S THE ONLY REASON WE NEED!
WE'LL LOOK FOR EMMA.
YEAH!
IF EMMA WAS IN OUR SHOES, SHE WOULDN'T GIVE UP!
SHE'D LOOK FOR US, EVEN IF SHE HAD TO GO TO THE DEMON WORLD!
BUT... WHAT IF SHE'S ALREADY DEAD?
I'M SURE SHE'S ALIVE.
YEAH, EMMA WOULDN'T DIE SO EASILY.

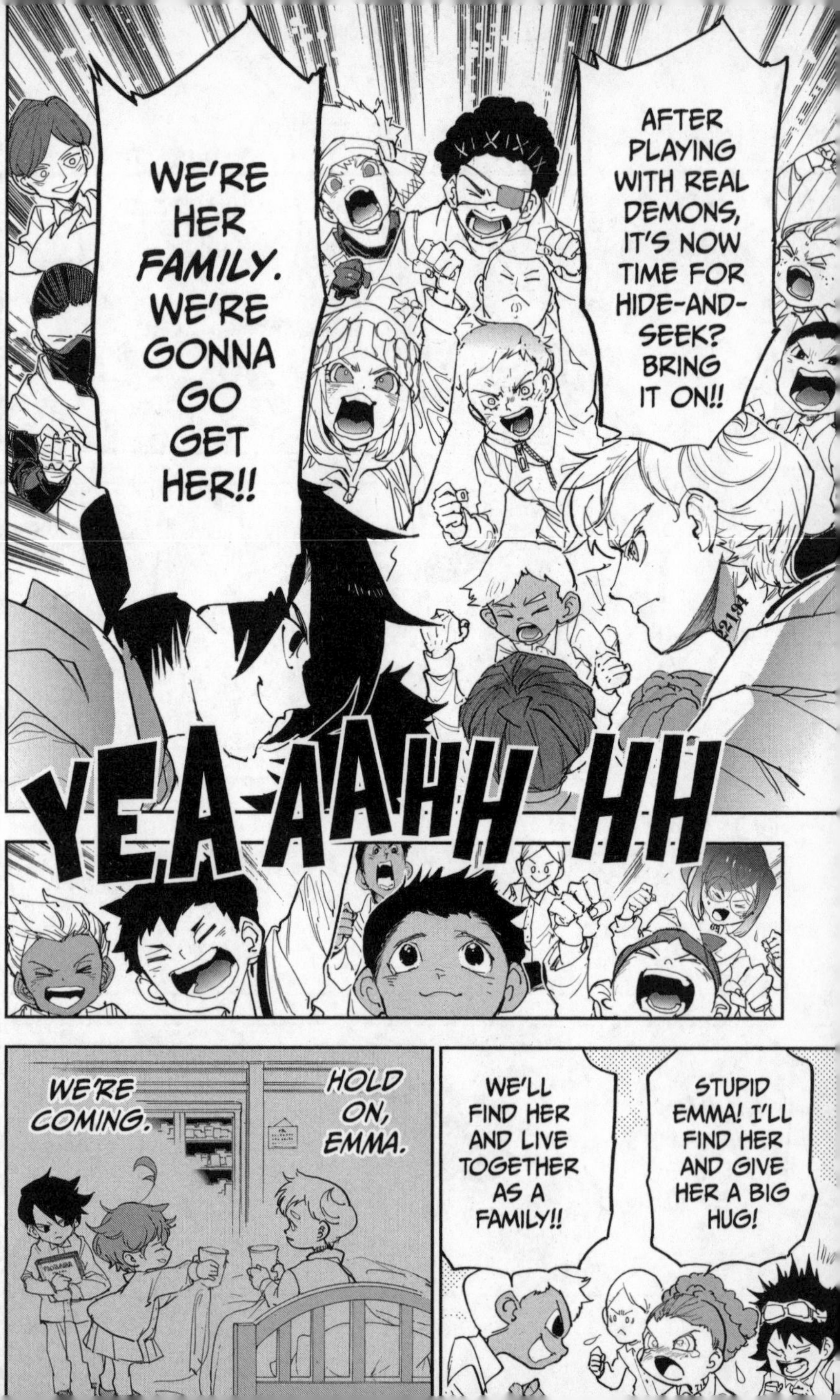
AFTER PLAYING WITH REAL DEMONS, IT'S NOW TIME FOR HIDE-AND-SEEK? BRING IT ON!!
WE'RE HER *FAMILY*. WE'RE GONNA GO GET HER!!
YEAAAHHHH
STUPID EMMA! I'LL FIND HER AND GIVE HER A BIG HUG!
WE'LL FIND HER AND LIVE TOGETHER AS A FAMILY!!
HOLD ON, EMMA.
WE'RE COMING.

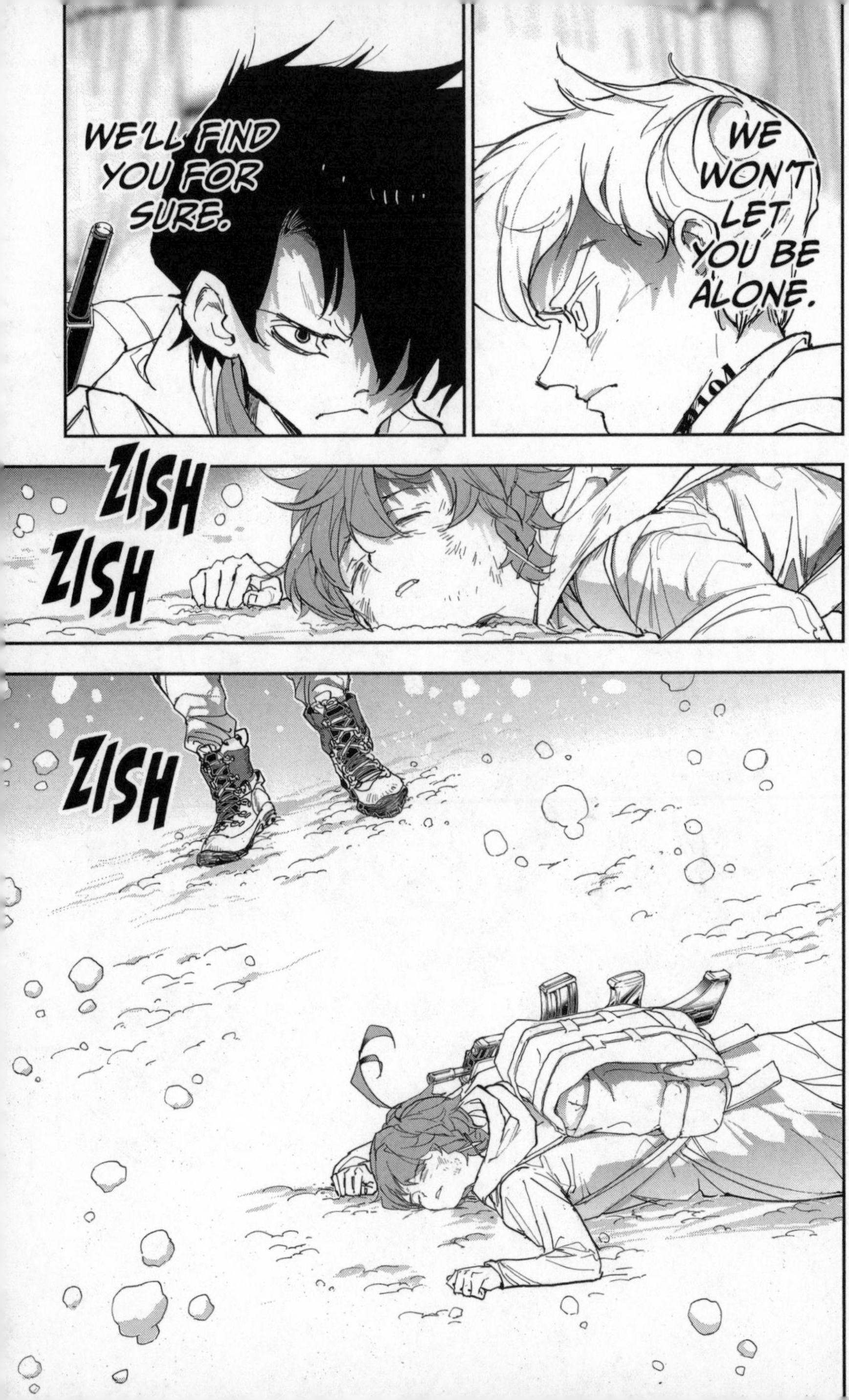
WE WON'T LET YOU BE ALONE.
WE'LL FIND YOU FOR SURE.
ZISH ZISH
ZISH

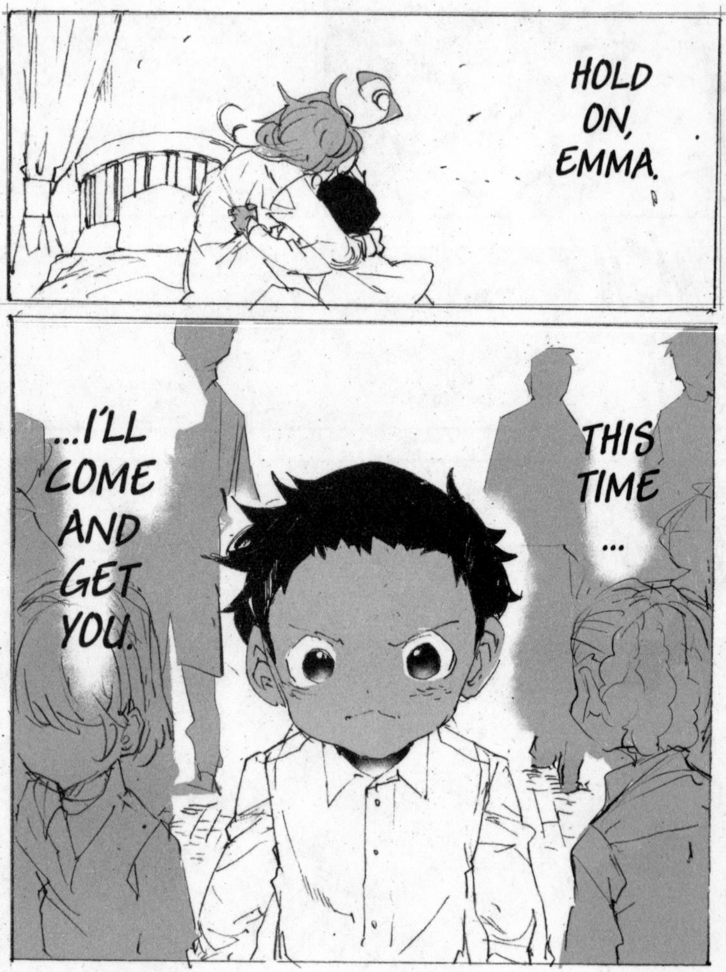
HOLD ON, EMMA.
THIS TIME...
...I'LL COME AND GET YOU.

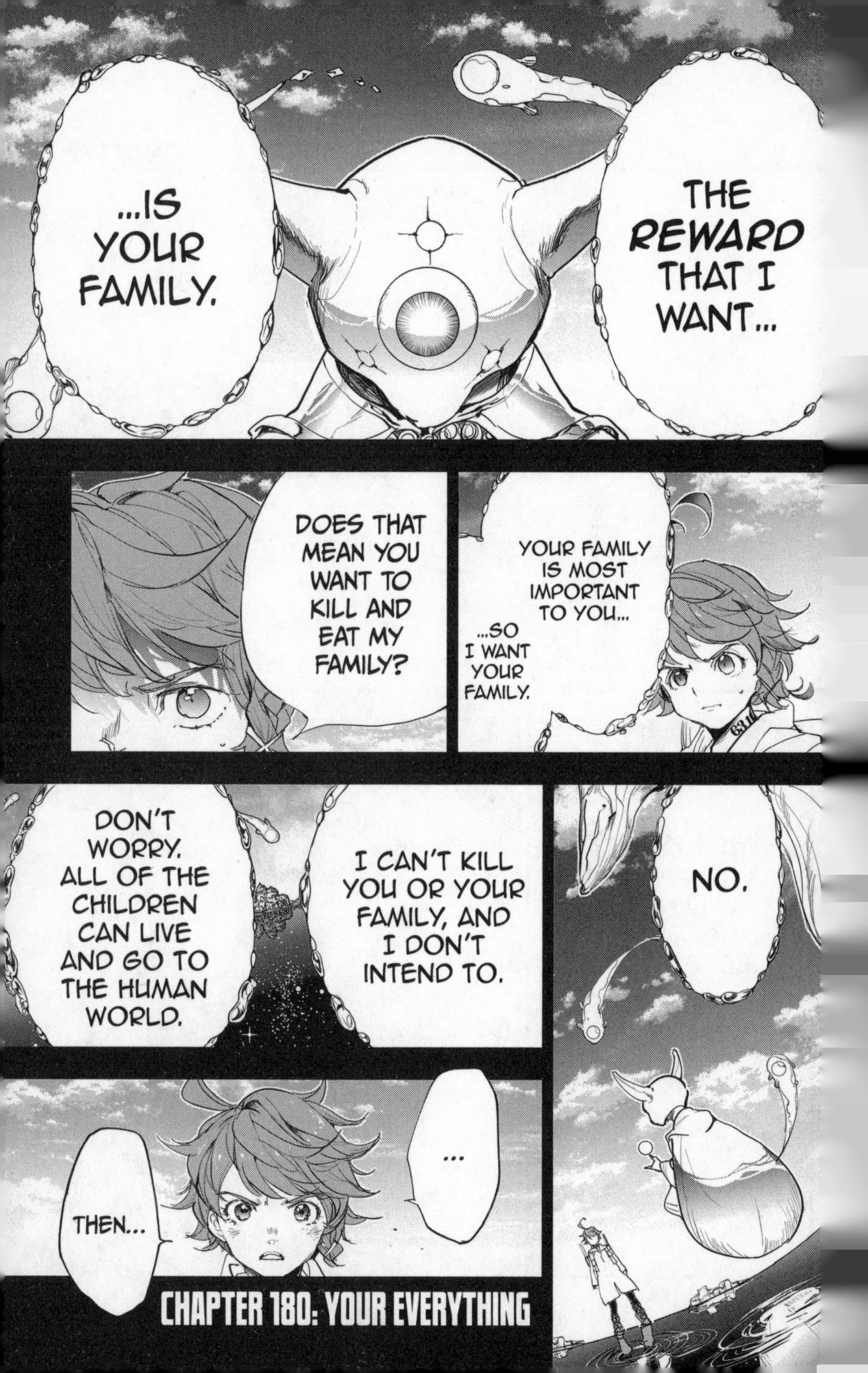
THE REWARD THAT I WANT...
...IS YOUR FAMILY.
YOUR FAMILY IS MOST IMPORTANT TO YOU...
...SO I WANT YOUR FAMILY.
DOES THAT MEAN YOU WANT TO KILL AND EAT MY FAMILY?
NO.
I CAN'T KILL YOU OR YOUR FAMILY, AND I DON'T INTEND TO.
DON'T WORRY. ALL OF THE CHILDREN CAN LIVE AND GO TO THE HUMAN WORLD.
...
THEN...
CHAPTER 180: YOUR EVERYTHING

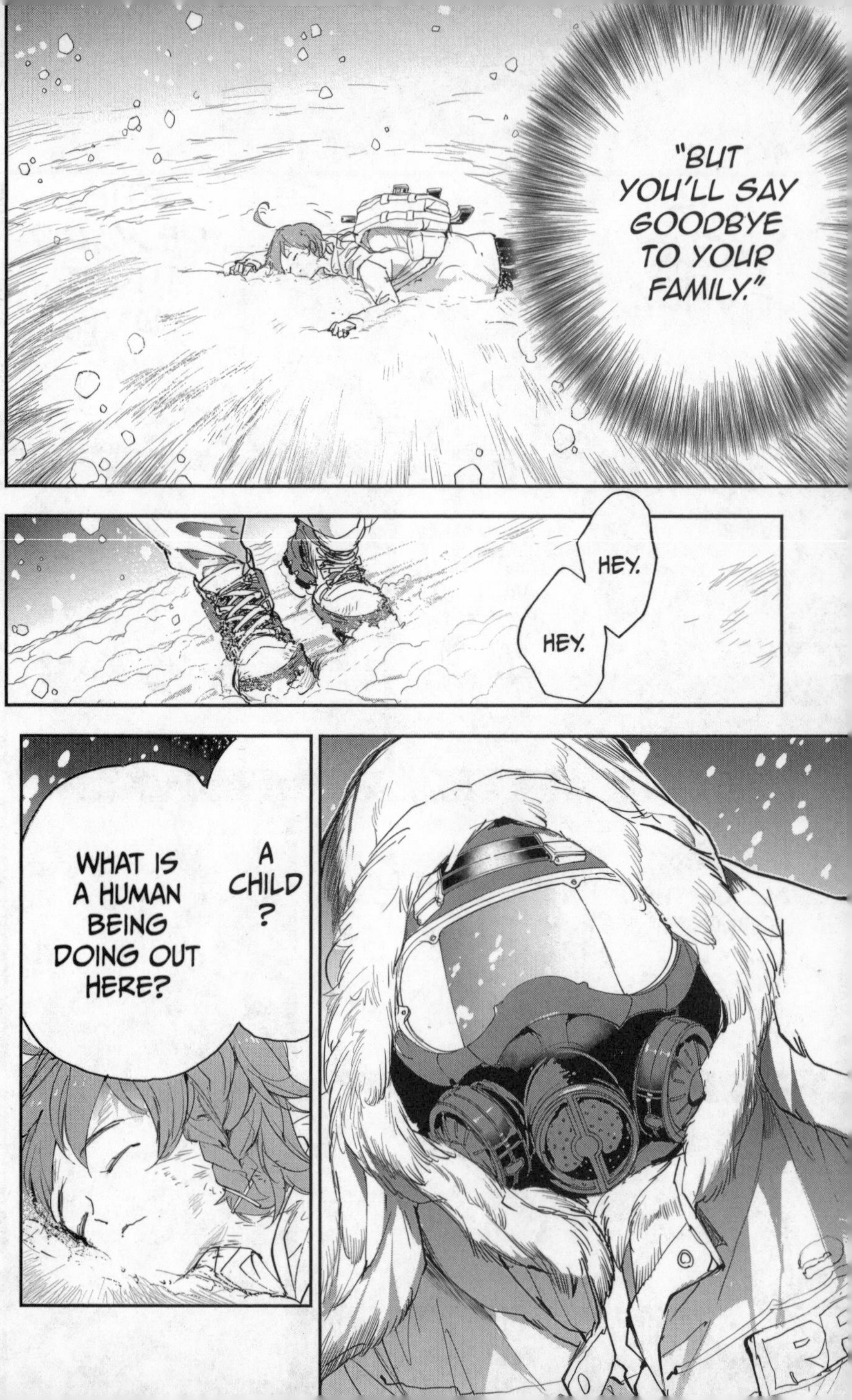
"BUT YOU'LL SAY GOODBYE TO YOUR FAMILY."
HEY.
HEY.
A CHILD?
WHAT IS A HUMAN BEING DOING OUT HERE?

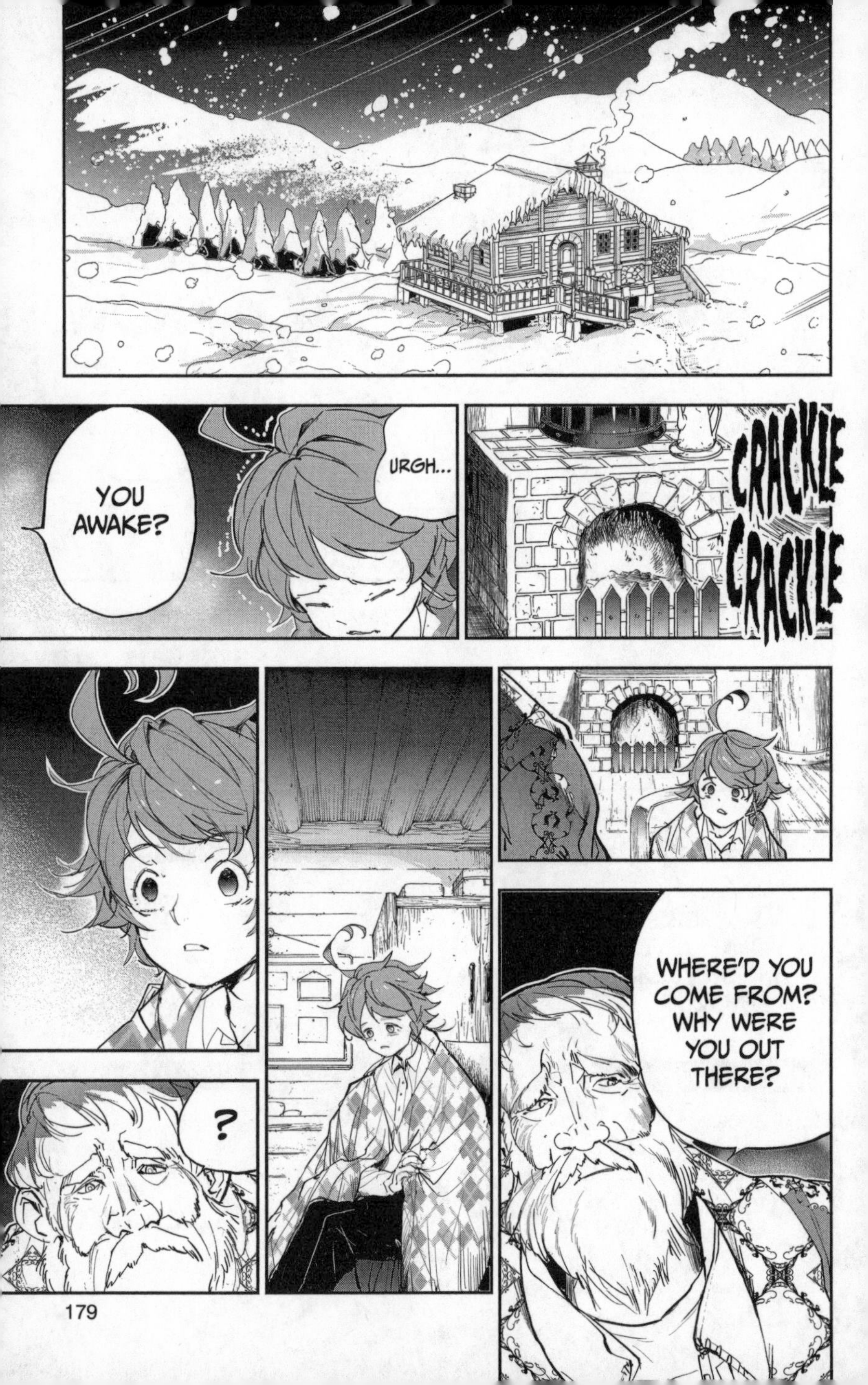
CRACKLE CRACKLE
URGH...
YOU AWAKE?
WHERE'D YOU COME FROM? WHY WERE YOU OUT THERE?
?

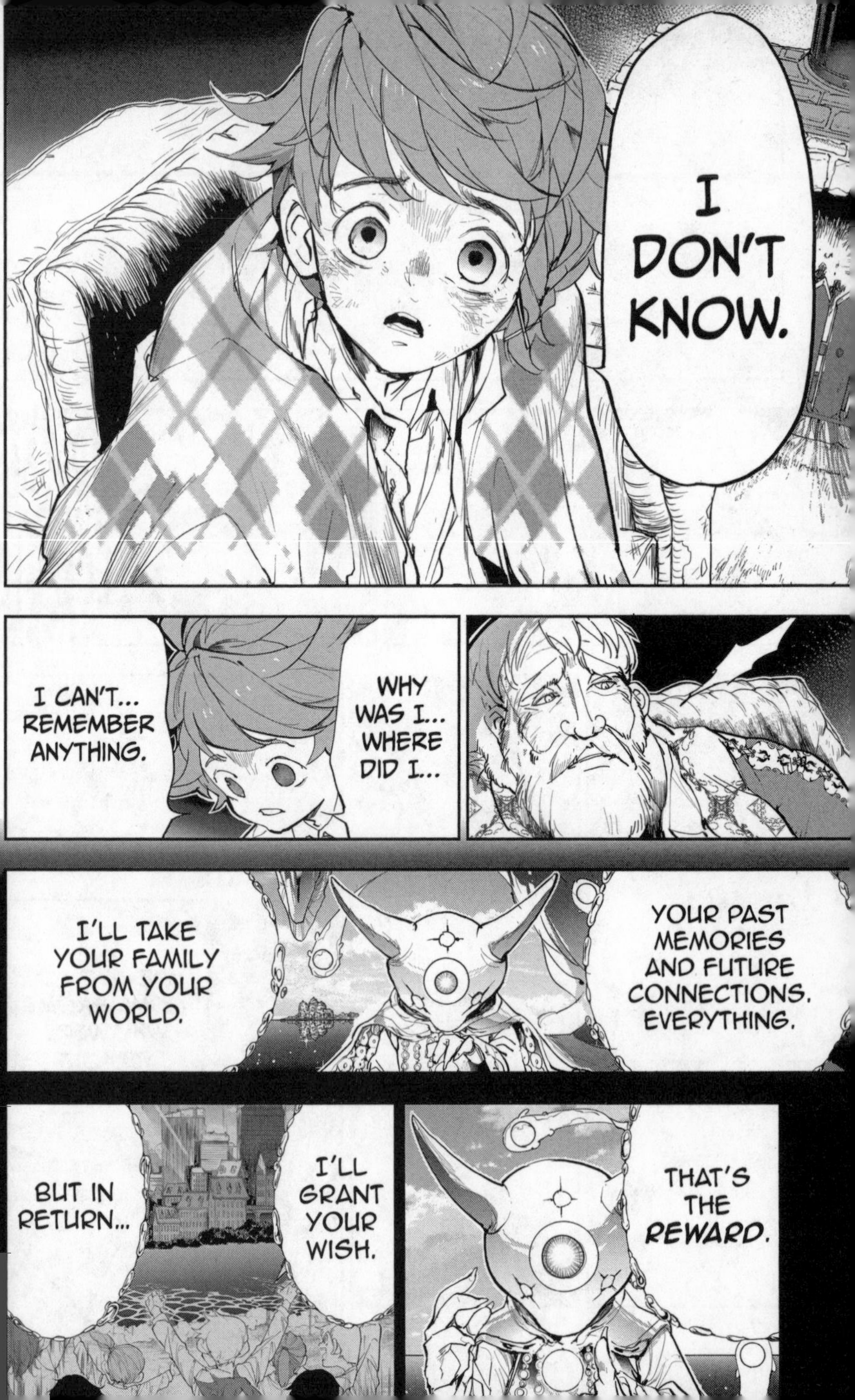
I DON'T KNOW.
WHY WAS I... WHERE DID I...
I CAN'T... REMEMBER ANYTHING.
YOUR PAST MEMORIES AND FUTURE CONNECTIONS. EVERYTHING.
I'LL TAKE YOUR FAMILY FROM YOUR WORLD.
THAT'S THE REWARD.
I'LL GRANT YOUR WISH.
BUT IN RETURN...

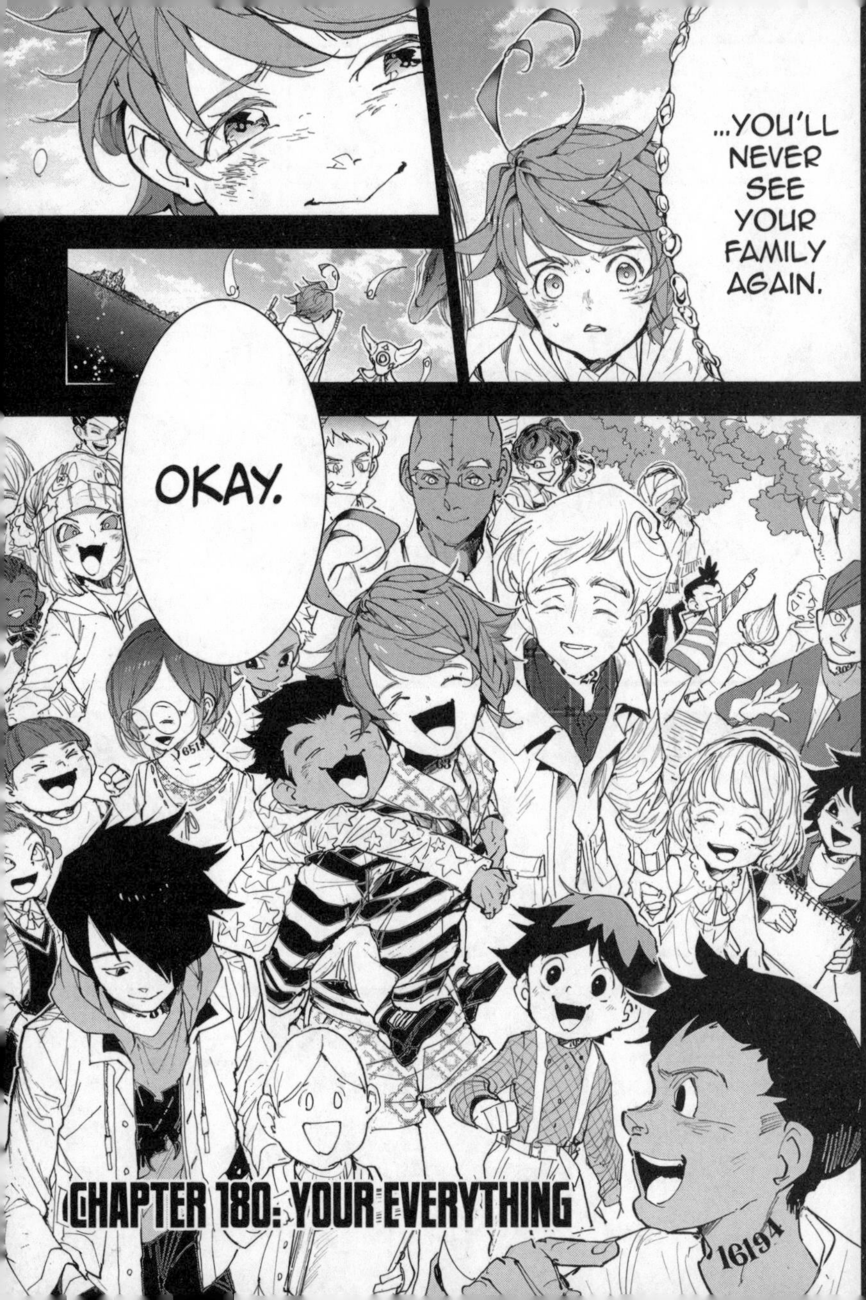
...YOU'LL NEVER SEE YOUR FAMILY AGAIN.
OKAY.
CHAPTER 180: YOUR EVERYTHING
16194

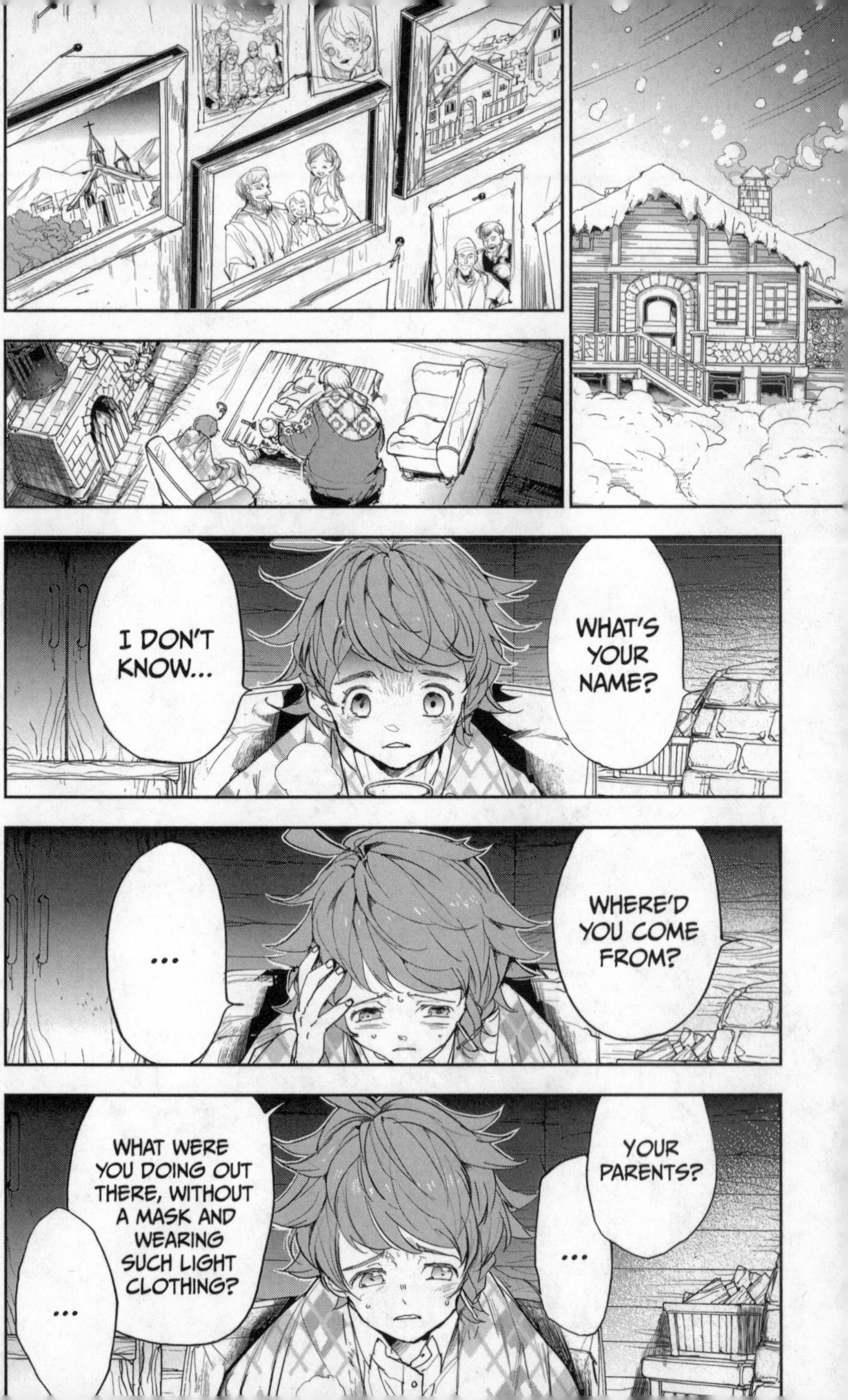
WHAT'S YOUR NAME?
I DON'T KNOW...
WHERE'D YOU COME FROM?
...
YOUR PARENTS?
...
WHAT WERE YOU DOING OUT THERE, WITHOUT A MASK AND WEARING SUCH LIGHT CLOTHING?
...

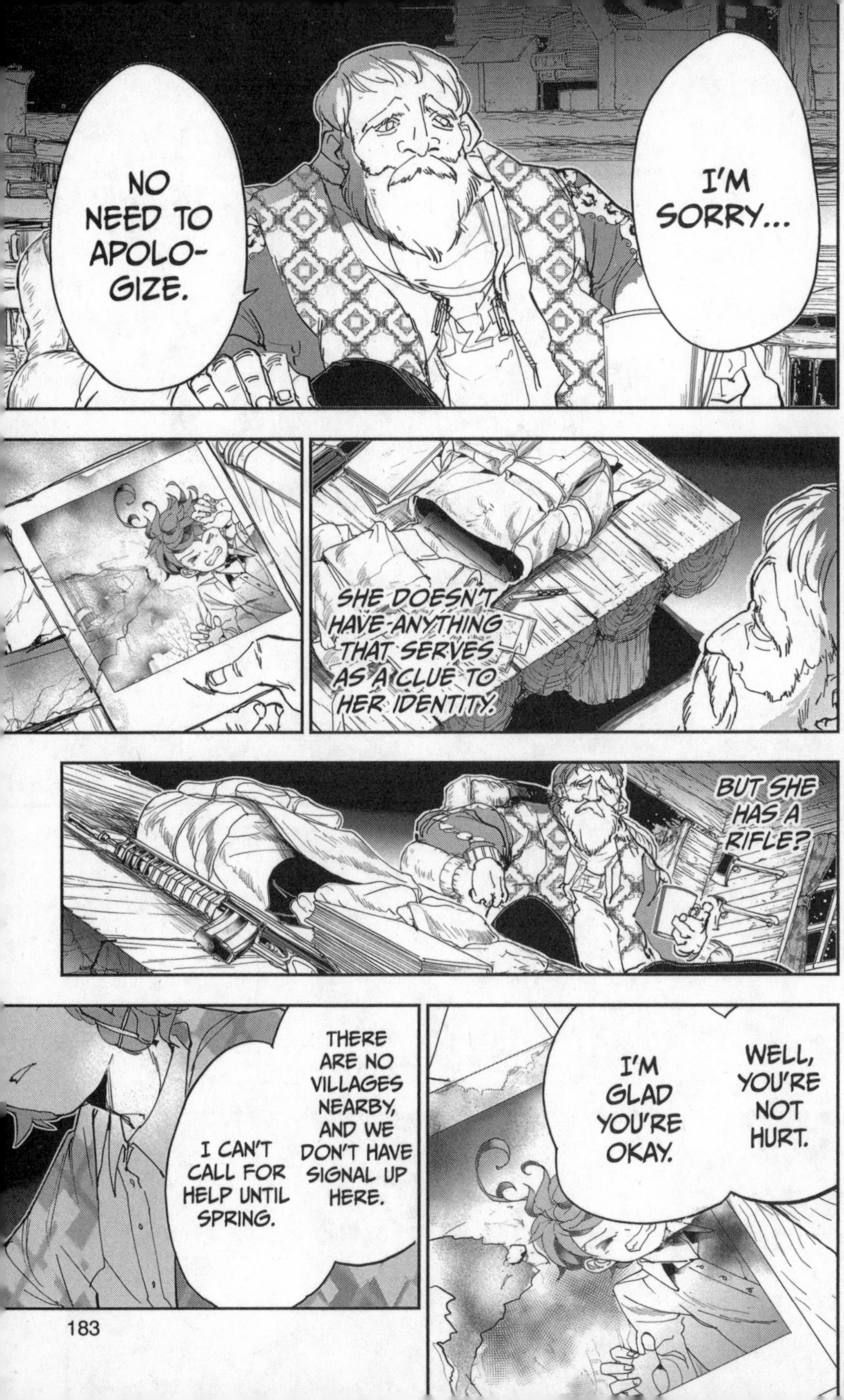
I'M SORRY...
NO NEED TO APOLOGIZE.
SHE DOESN'T HAVE ANYTHING THAT SERVES AS A CLUE TO HER IDENTITY.
BUT SHE HAS A RIFLE?
WELL, YOU'RE NOT HURT.
I'M GLAD YOU'RE OKAY.
THERE ARE NO VILLAGES NEARBY, AND WE DON'T HAVE SIGNAL UP HERE.
I CAN'T CALL FOR HELP UNTIL SPRING.

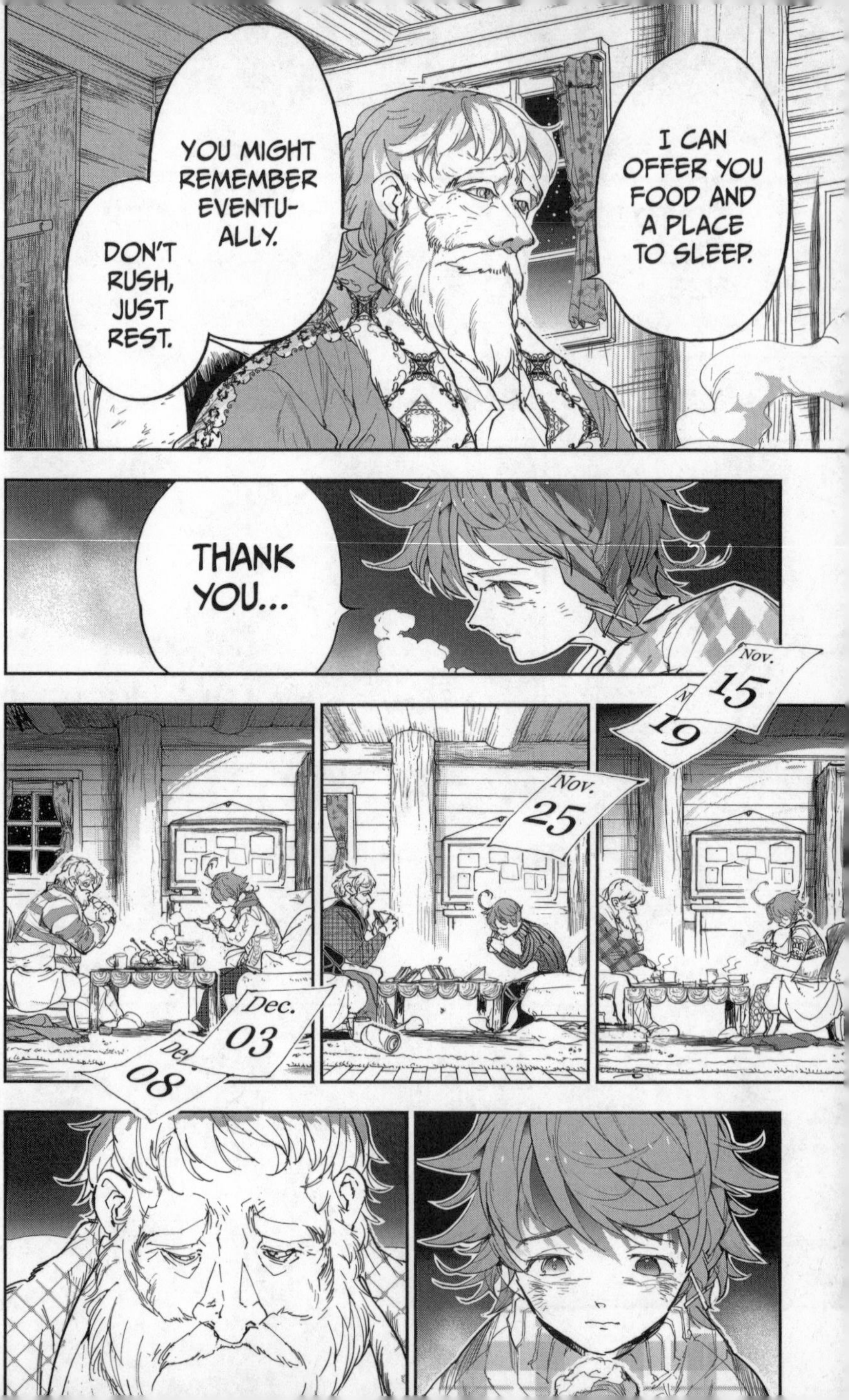
I CAN OFFER YOU FOOD AND A PLACE TO SLEEP.
YOU MIGHT REMEMBER EVENTU-ALLY.
DON'T RUSH, JUST REST.
THANK YOU...
Nov. 15
19
Nov. 25
Dec. 03
08

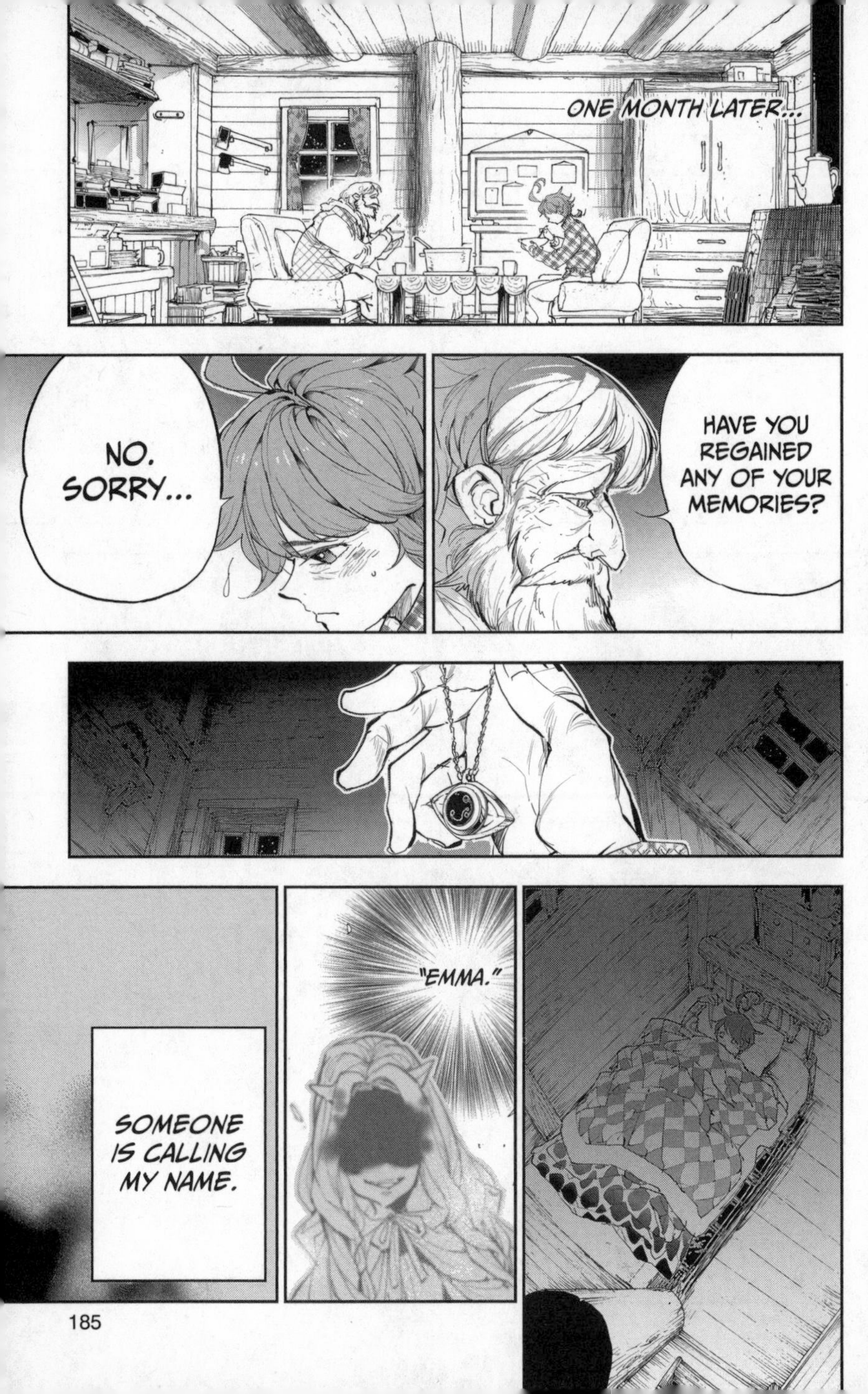
ONE MONTH LATER...
HAVE YOU REGAINED ANY OF YOUR MEMORIES?
NO. SORRY...
"EMMA."
SOMEONE IS CALLING MY NAME.

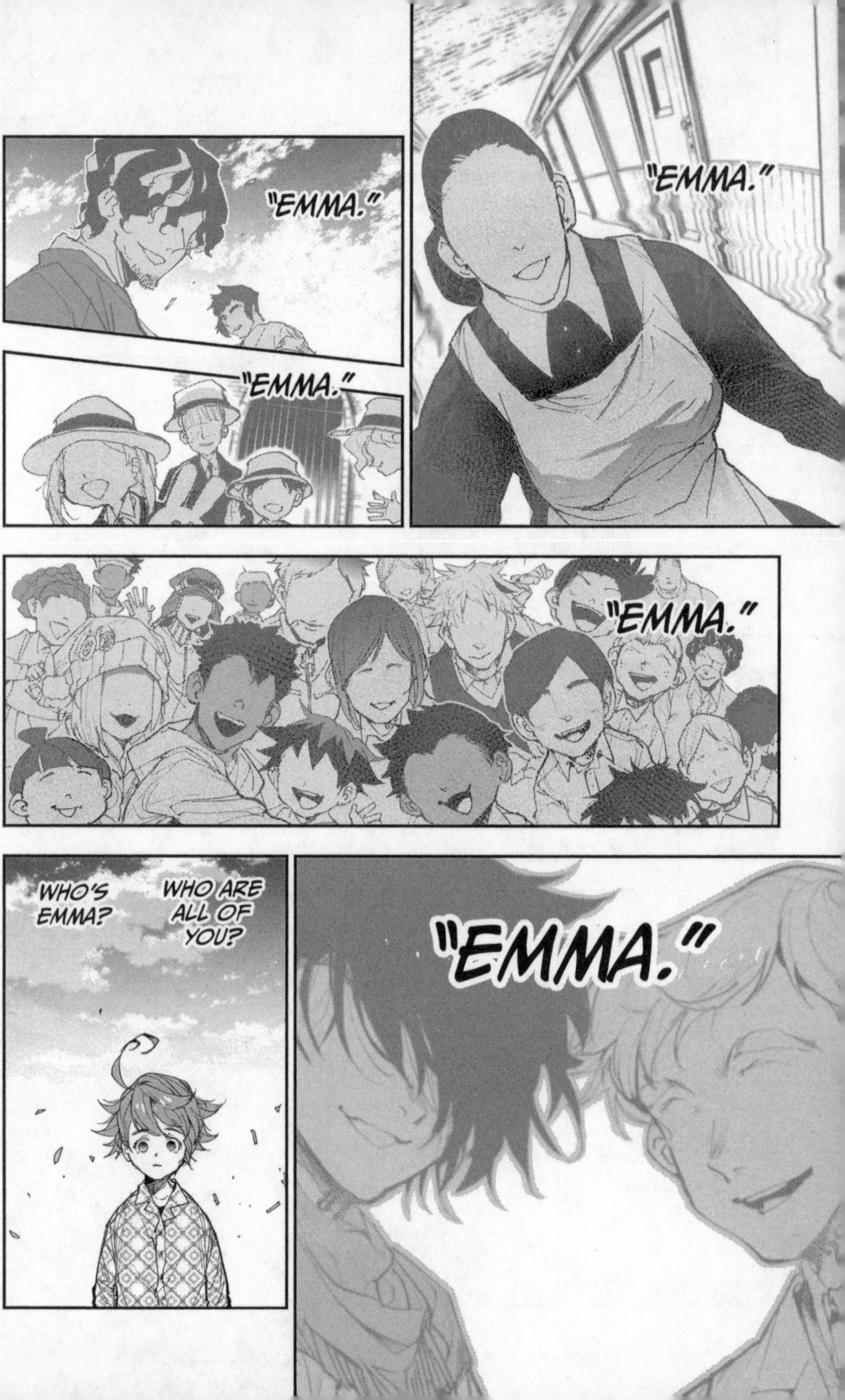
"EMMA."
"EMMA."
"EMMA."
"EMMA."
"EMMA."
WHO ARE ALL OF YOU?
WHO'S EMMA?

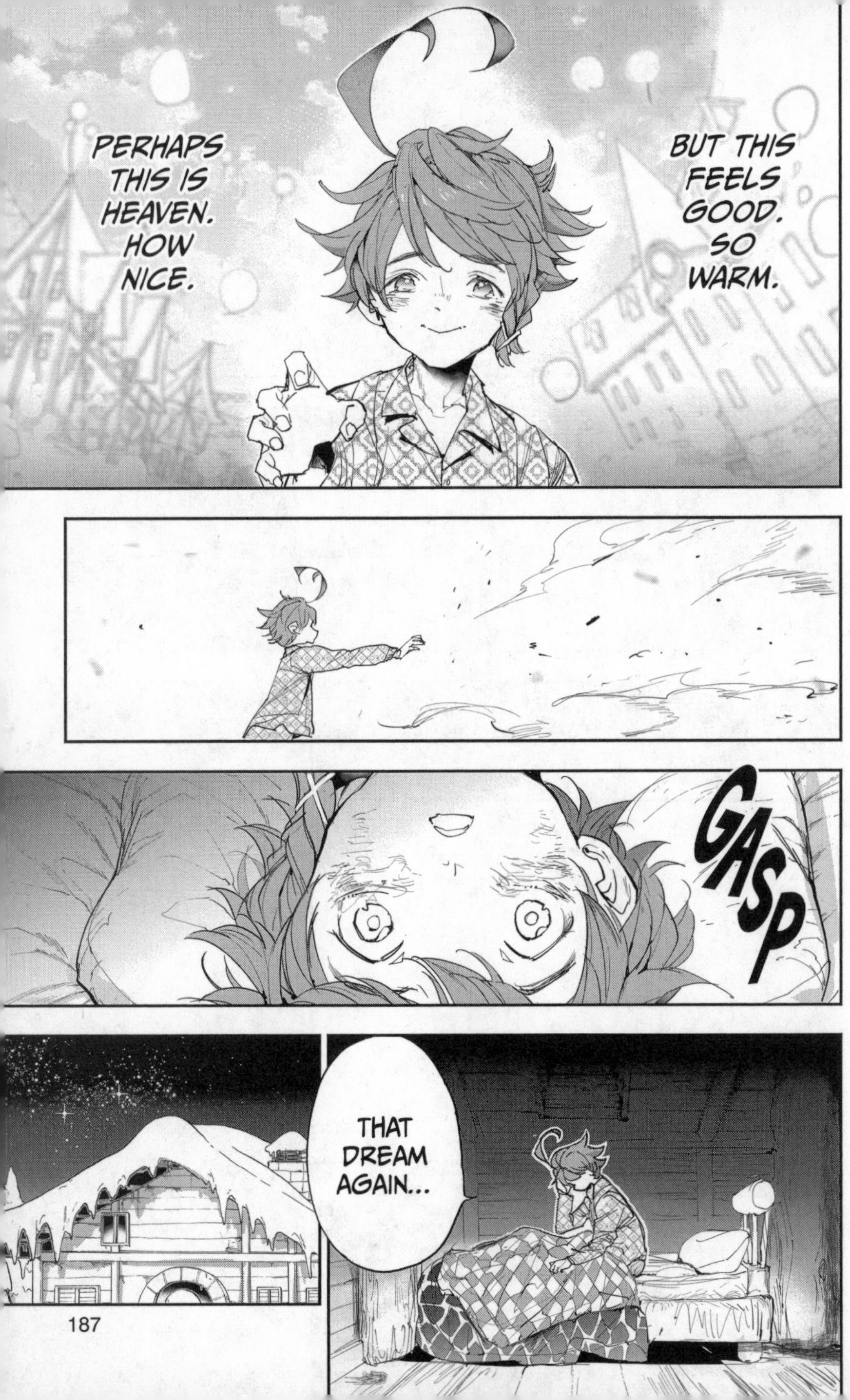
BUT THIS FEELS GOOD. SO WARM.
PERHAPS THIS IS HEAVEN. HOW NICE.
GASP
THAT DREAM AGAIN...

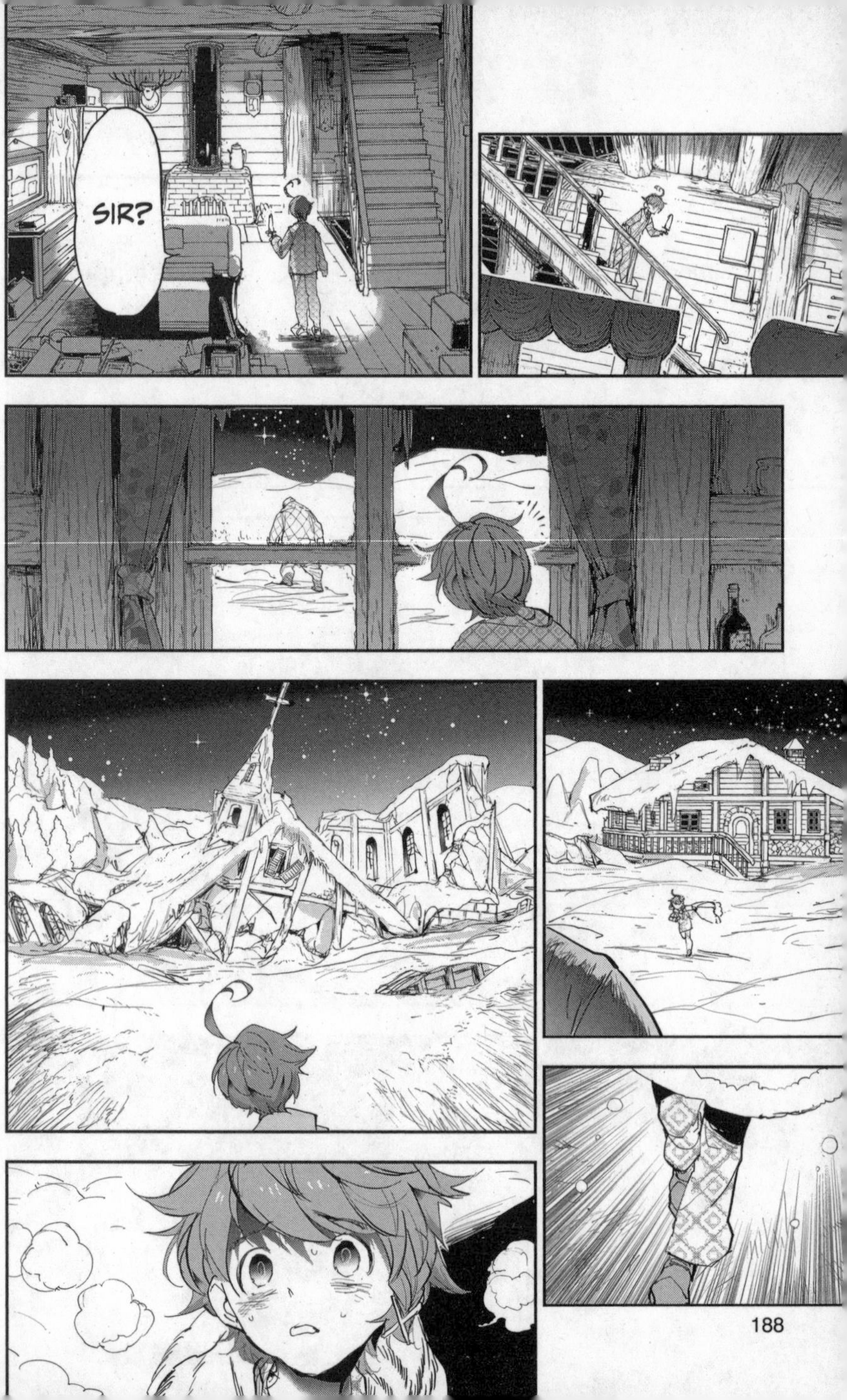
SIR?

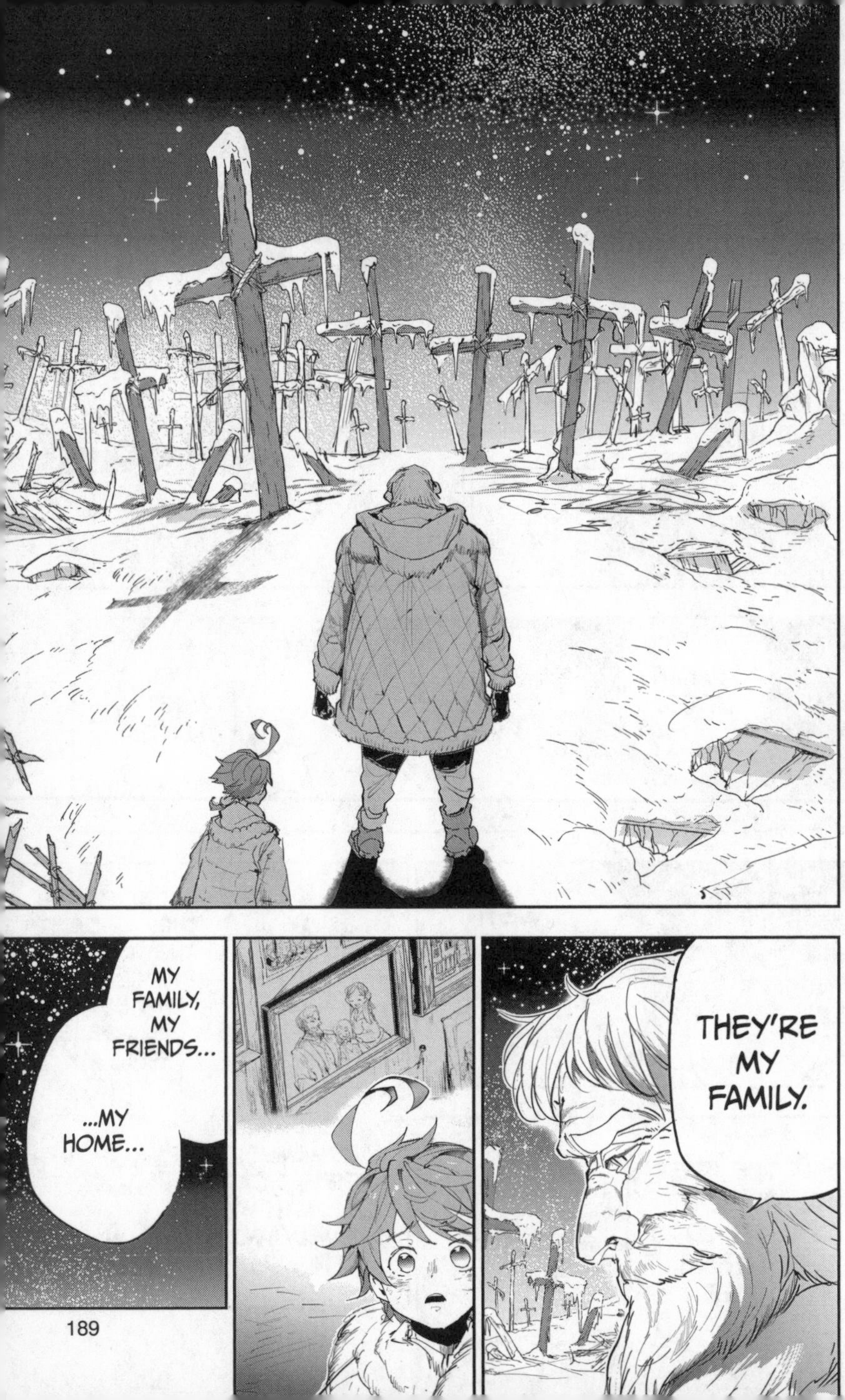
THEY'RE MY FAMILY.
MY FAMILY, MY FRIENDS...
...MY HOME...

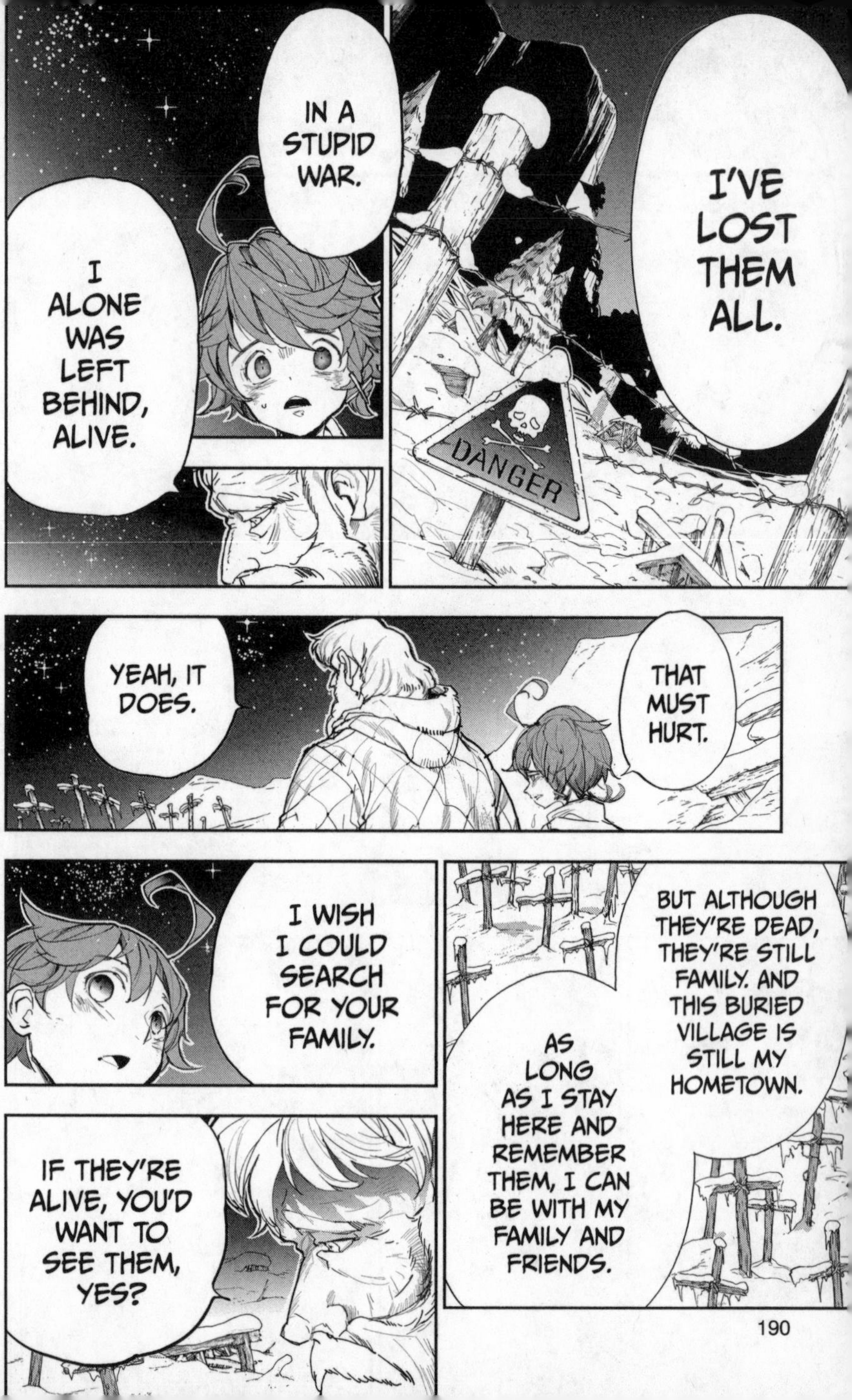
I'VE LOST THEM ALL.
IN A STUPID WAR.
DANGER
I ALONE WAS LEFT BEHIND, ALIVE.
THAT MUST HURT.
YEAH, IT DOES.
BUT ALTHOUGH THEY'RE DEAD, THEY'RE STILL FAMILY. AND THIS BURIED VILLAGE IS STILL MY HOMETOWN.
AS LONG AS I STAY HERE AND REMEMBER THEM, I CAN BE WITH MY FAMILY AND FRIENDS.
I WISH I COULD SEARCH FOR YOUR FAMILY.
IF THEY'RE ALIVE, YOU'D WANT TO SEE THEM, YES?

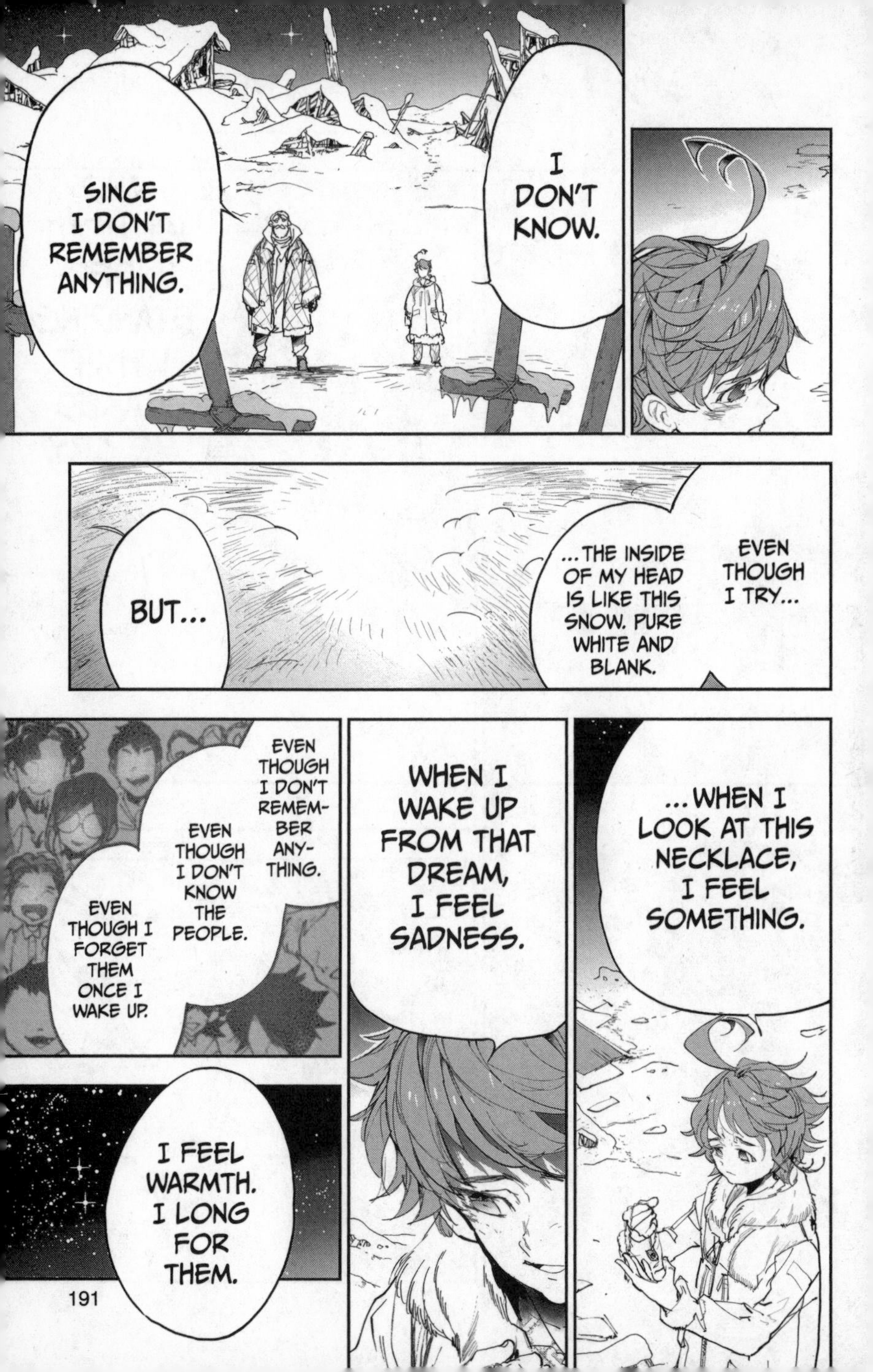
I DON'T KNOW.
SINCE I DON'T REMEMBER ANYTHING.
EVEN THOUGH I TRY...
...THE INSIDE OF MY HEAD IS LIKE THIS SNOW. PURE WHITE AND BLANK.
BUT...
...WHEN I LOOK AT THIS NECKLACE, I FEEL SOMETHING.
WHEN I WAKE UP FROM THAT DREAM, I FEEL SADNESS.
EVEN THOUGH I DON'T REMEMBER ANYTHING.
EVEN THOUGH I DON'T KNOW THE PEOPLE.
EVEN THOUGH I FORGET THEM ONCE I WAKE UP.
I FEEL WARMTH. I LONG FOR THEM.

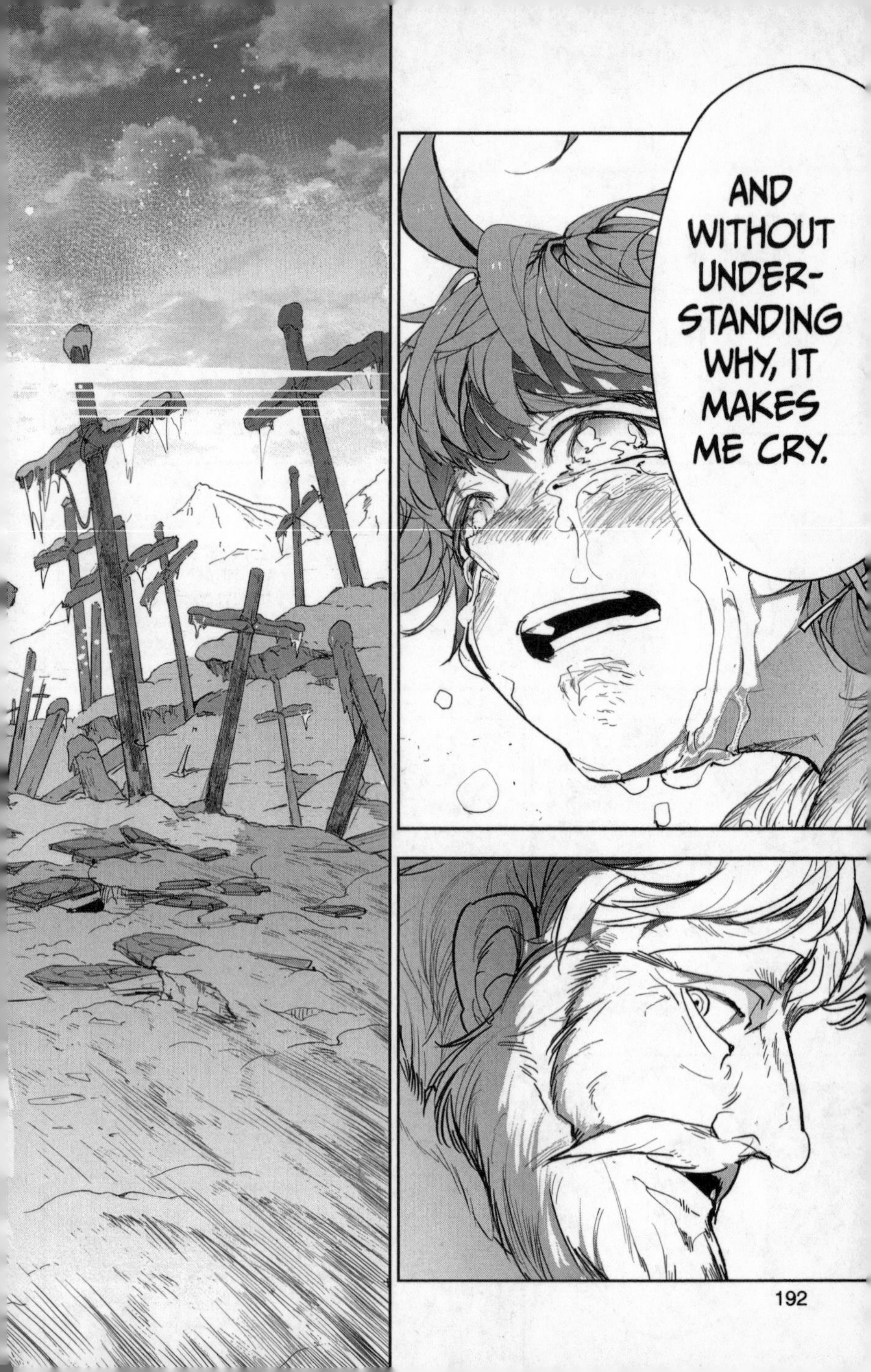
AND WITHOUT UNDER-STANDING WHY, IT MAKES ME CRY.

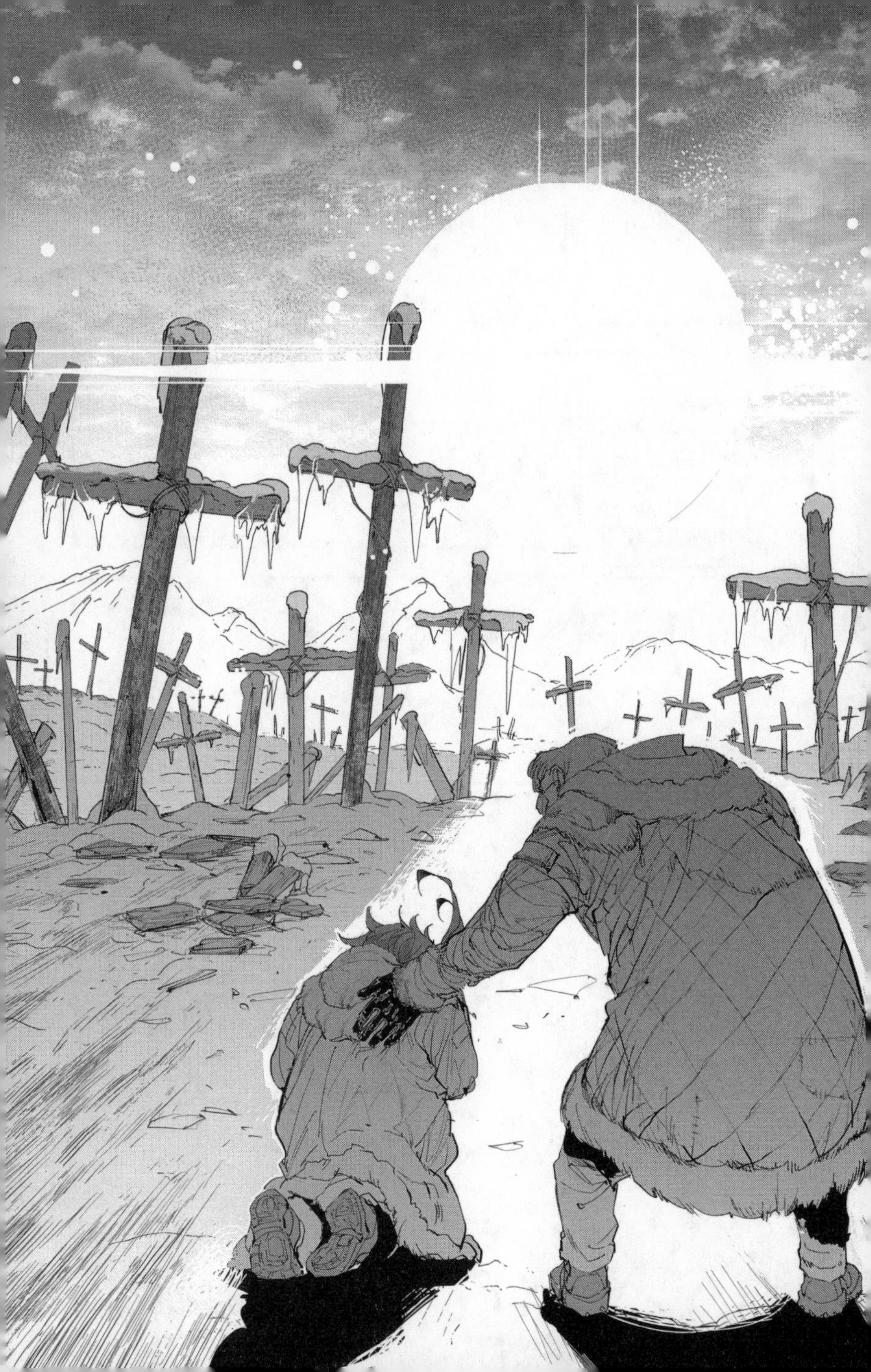

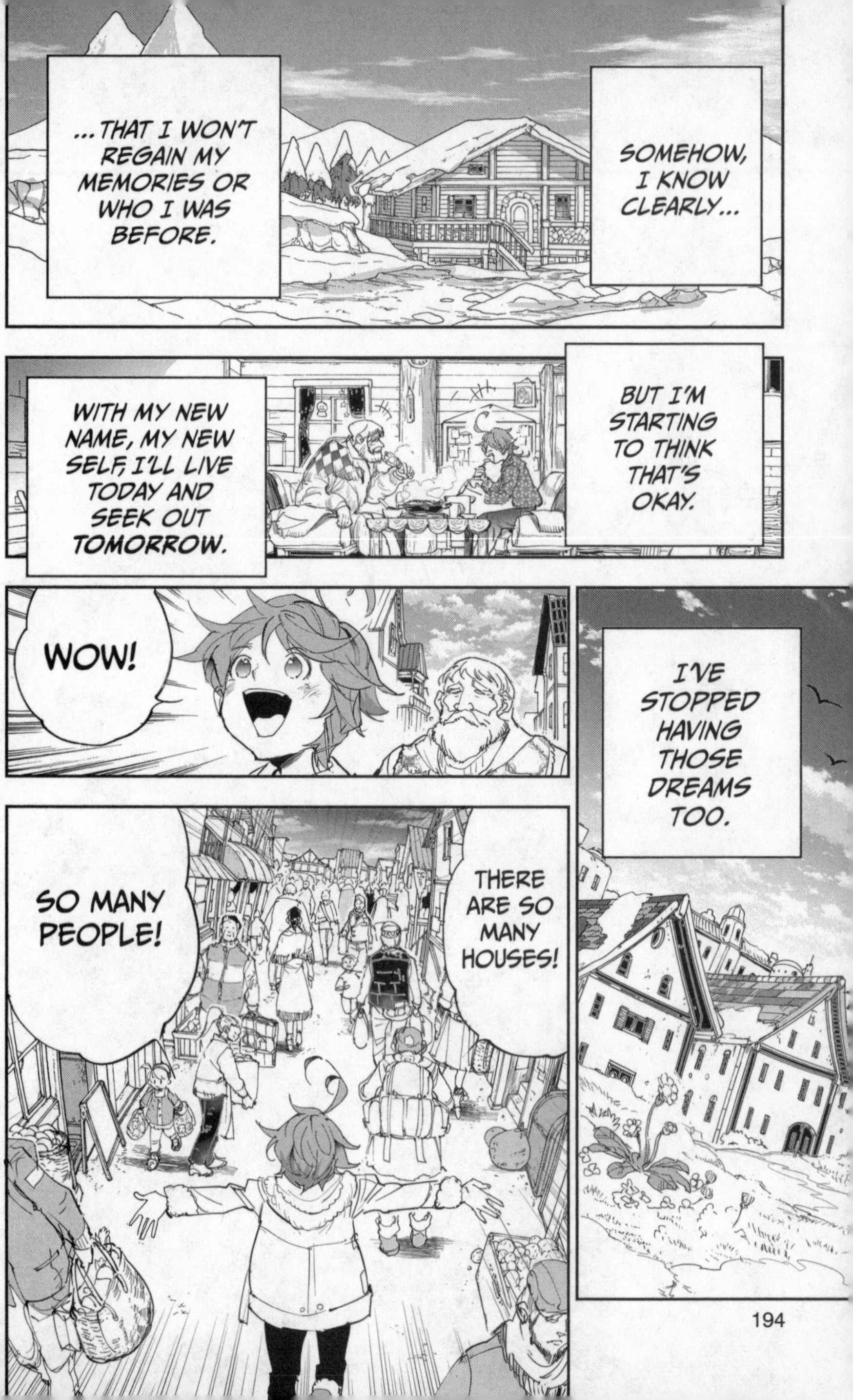
SOMEHOW, I KNOW CLEARLY...
...THAT I WON'T REGAIN MY MEMORIES OR WHO I WAS BEFORE.
BUT I'M STARTING TO THINK THAT'S OKAY.
WITH MY NEW NAME, MY NEW SELF, I'LL LIVE TODAY AND SEEK OUT TOMORROW.
I'VE STOPPED HAVING THOSE DREAMS TOO.
WOW!
THERE ARE SO MANY HOUSES!
SO MANY PEOPLE!

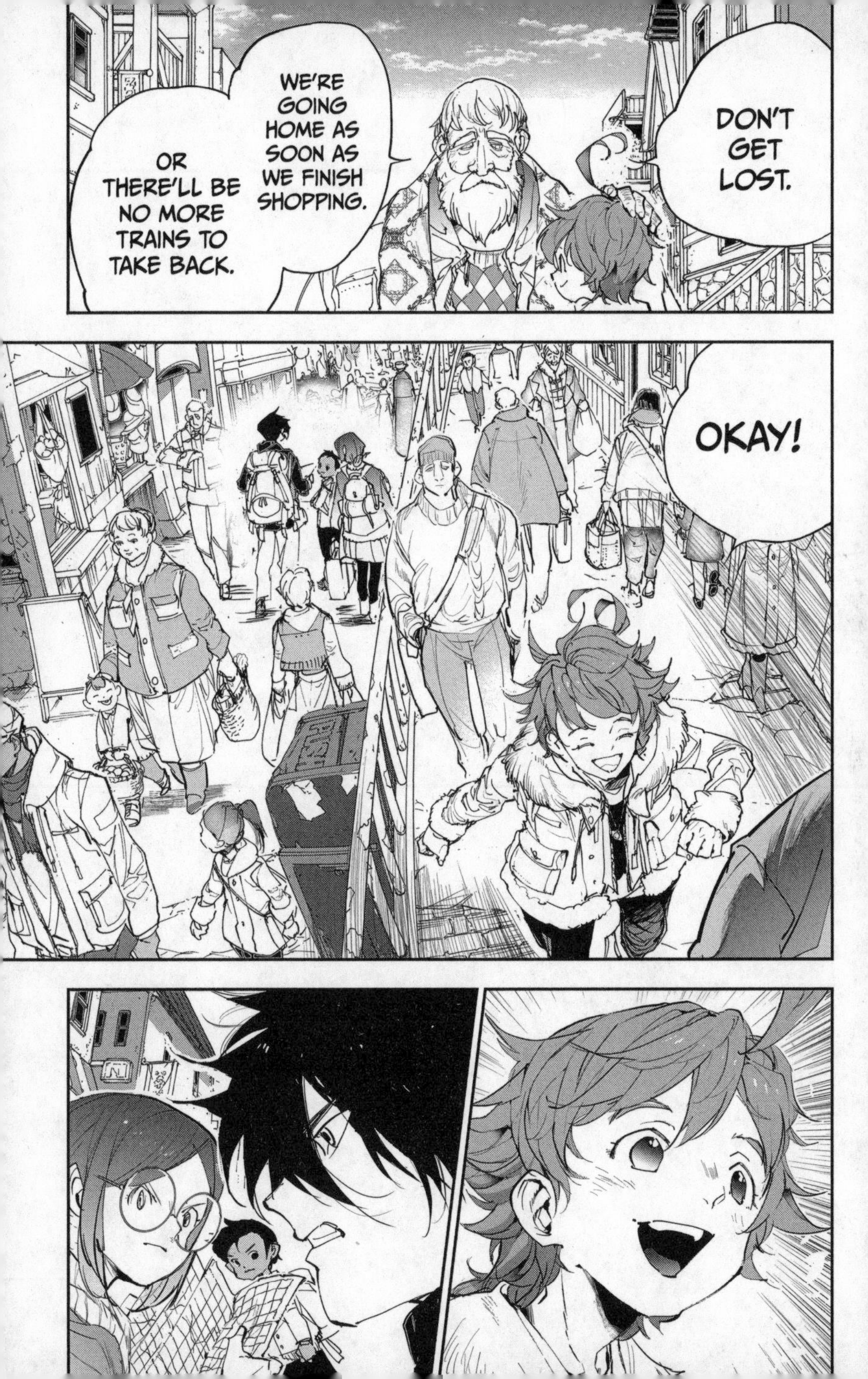
DON'T GET LOST.
WE'RE GOING HOME AS SOON AS WE FINISH SHOPPING.
OR THERE'LL BE NO MORE TRAINS TO TAKE BACK.
OKAY!

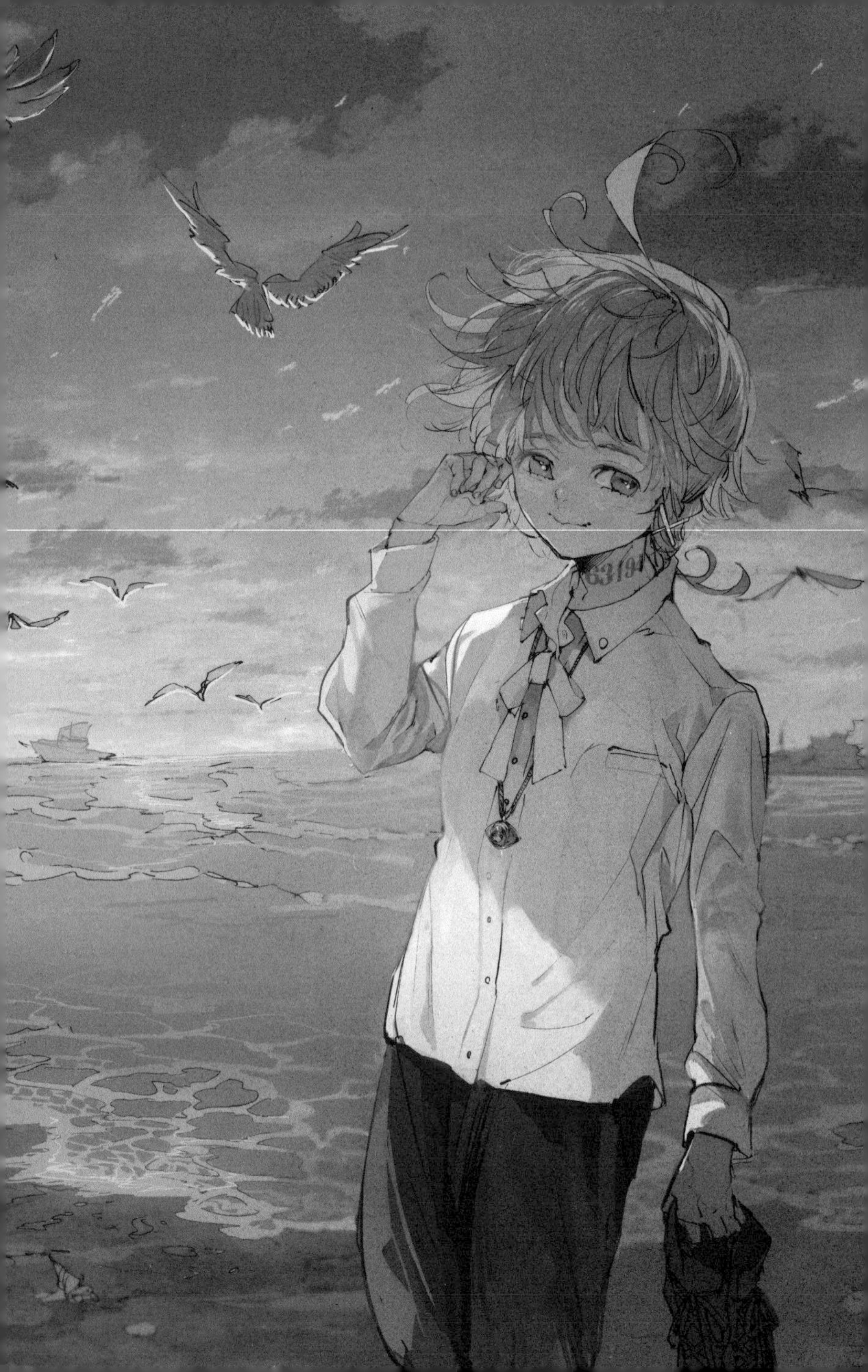

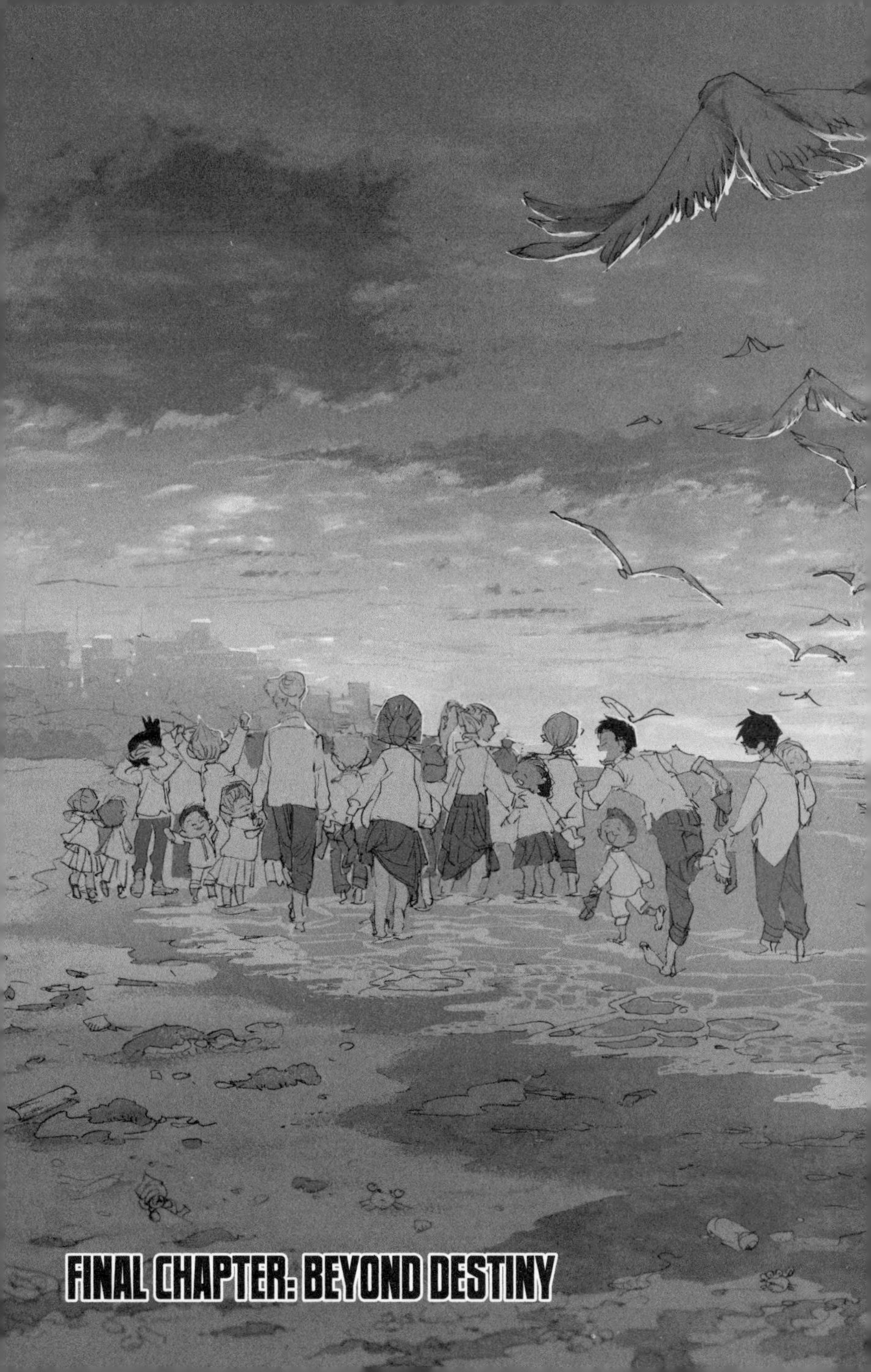
FINAL CHAPTER: BEYOND DESTINY

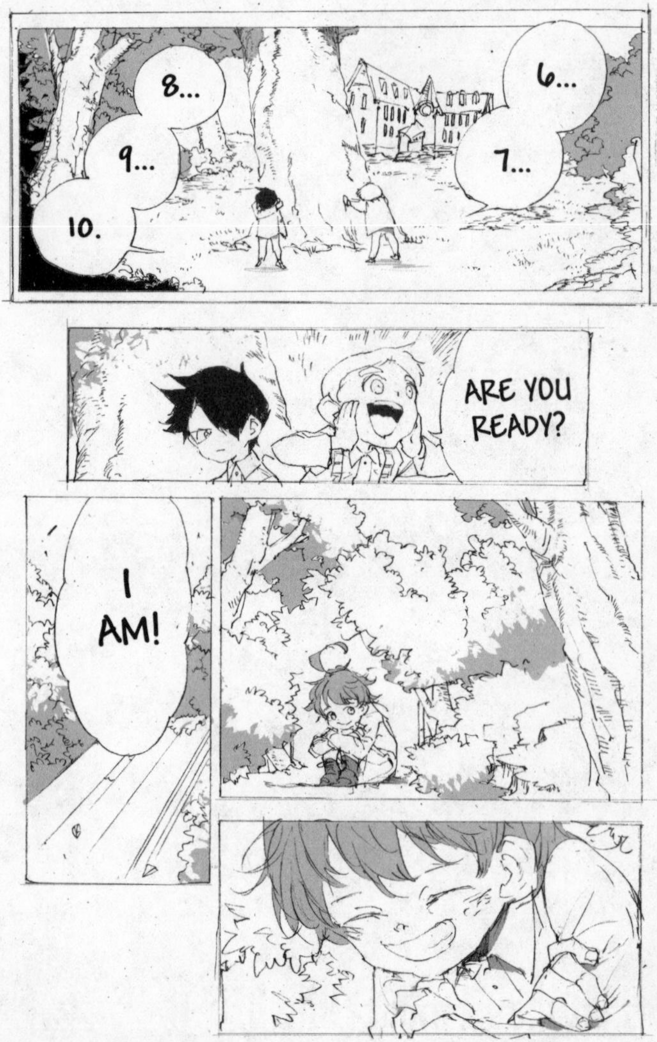
6...
7...
8...
9...
10.
ARE YOU READY?
I AM!

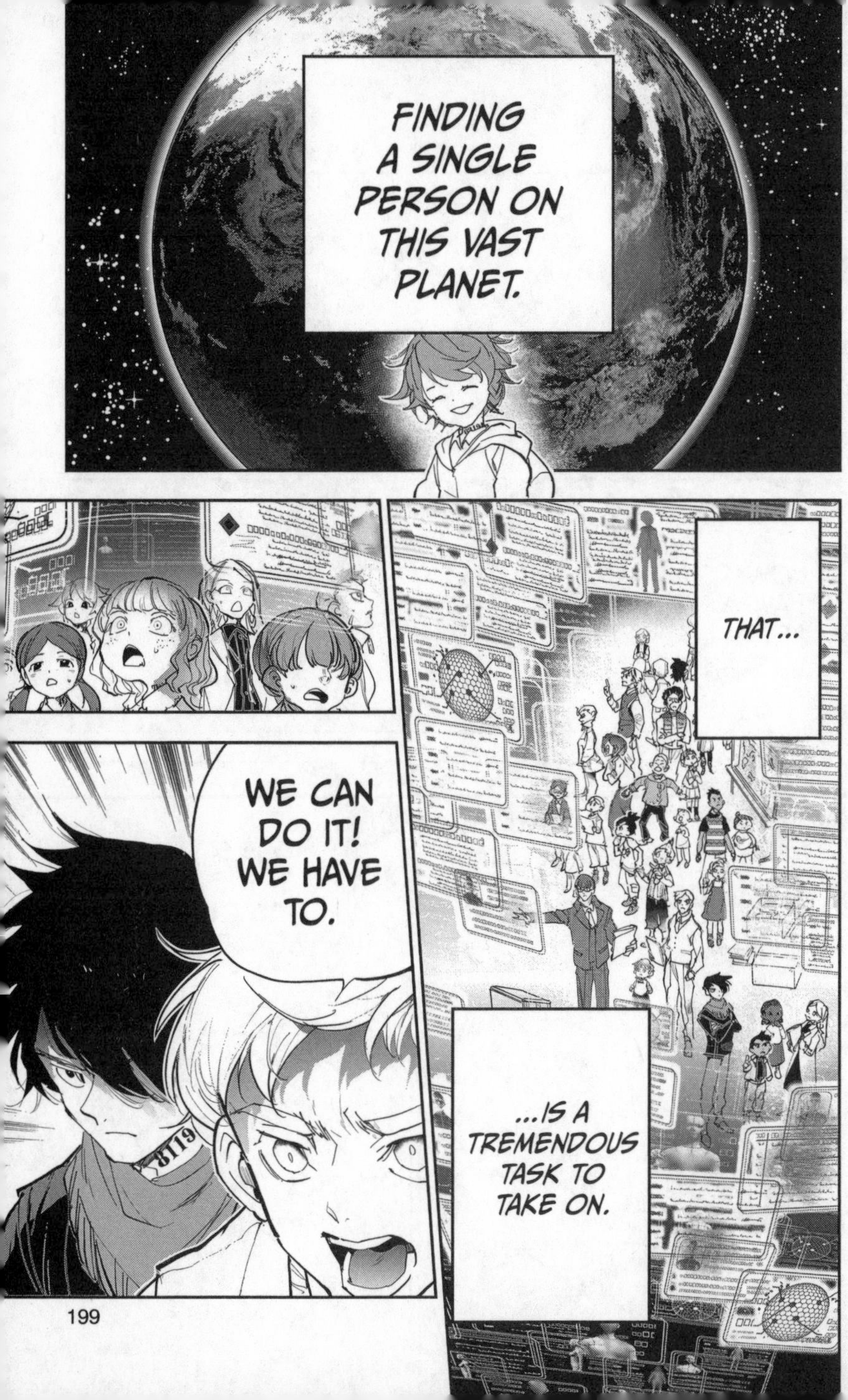
FINDING A SINGLE PERSON ON THIS VAST PLANET.
THAT...
...IS A TREMENDOUS TASK TO TAKE ON.
WE CAN DO IT! WE HAVE TO.

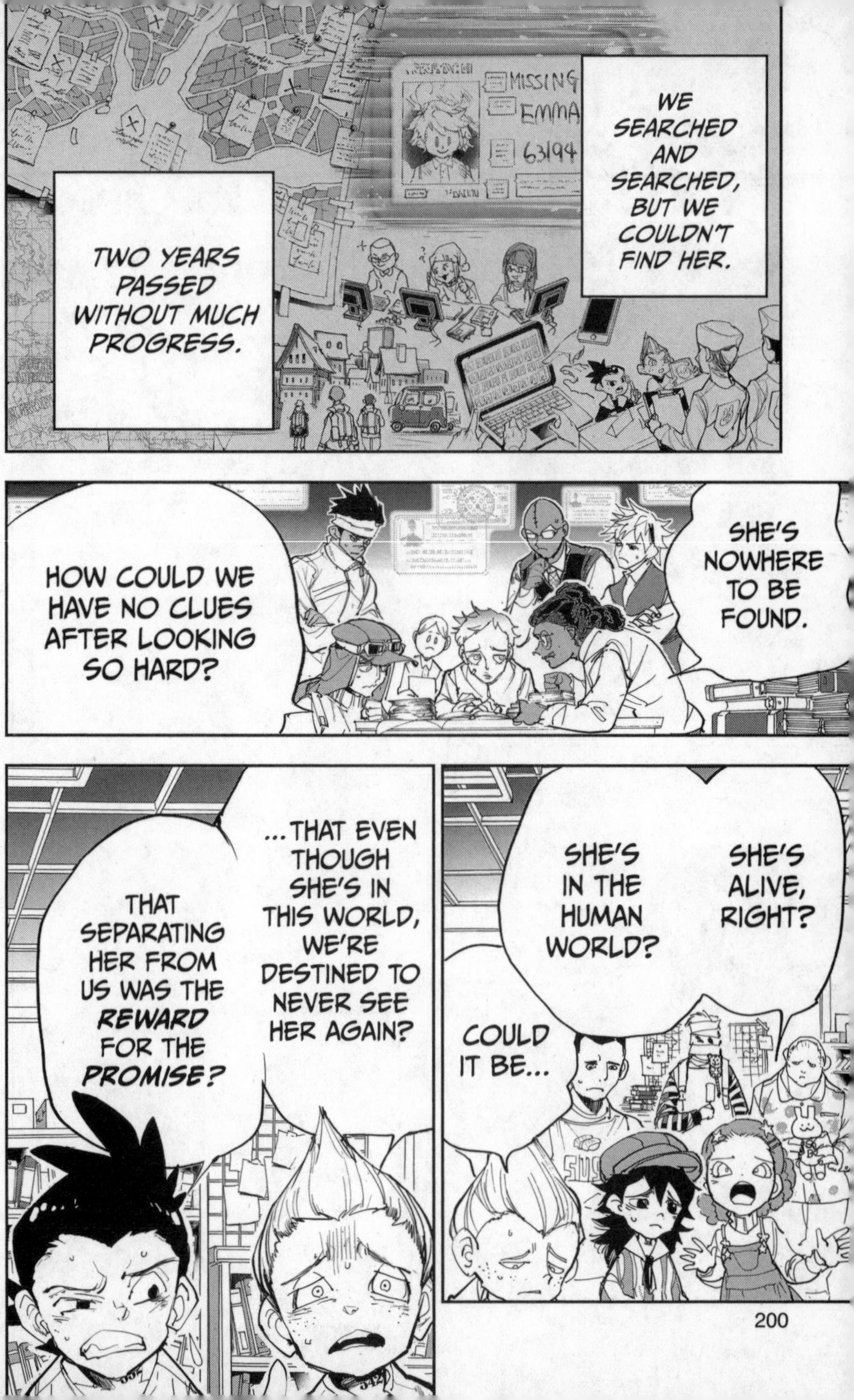
MISSING
EMMA
63194
WE SEARCHED AND SEARCHED, BUT WE COULDN'T FIND HER.
TWO YEARS PASSED WITHOUT MUCH PROGRESS.
SHE'S NOWHERE TO BE FOUND.
HOW COULD WE HAVE NO CLUES AFTER LOOKING SO HARD?
SHE'S ALIVE, RIGHT?
SHE'S IN THE HUMAN WORLD?
COULD IT BE...
...THAT EVEN THOUGH SHE'S IN THIS WORLD, WE'RE DESTINED TO NEVER SEE HER AGAIN?
THAT SEPARATING HER FROM US WAS THE *REWARD* FOR THE *PROMISE*?

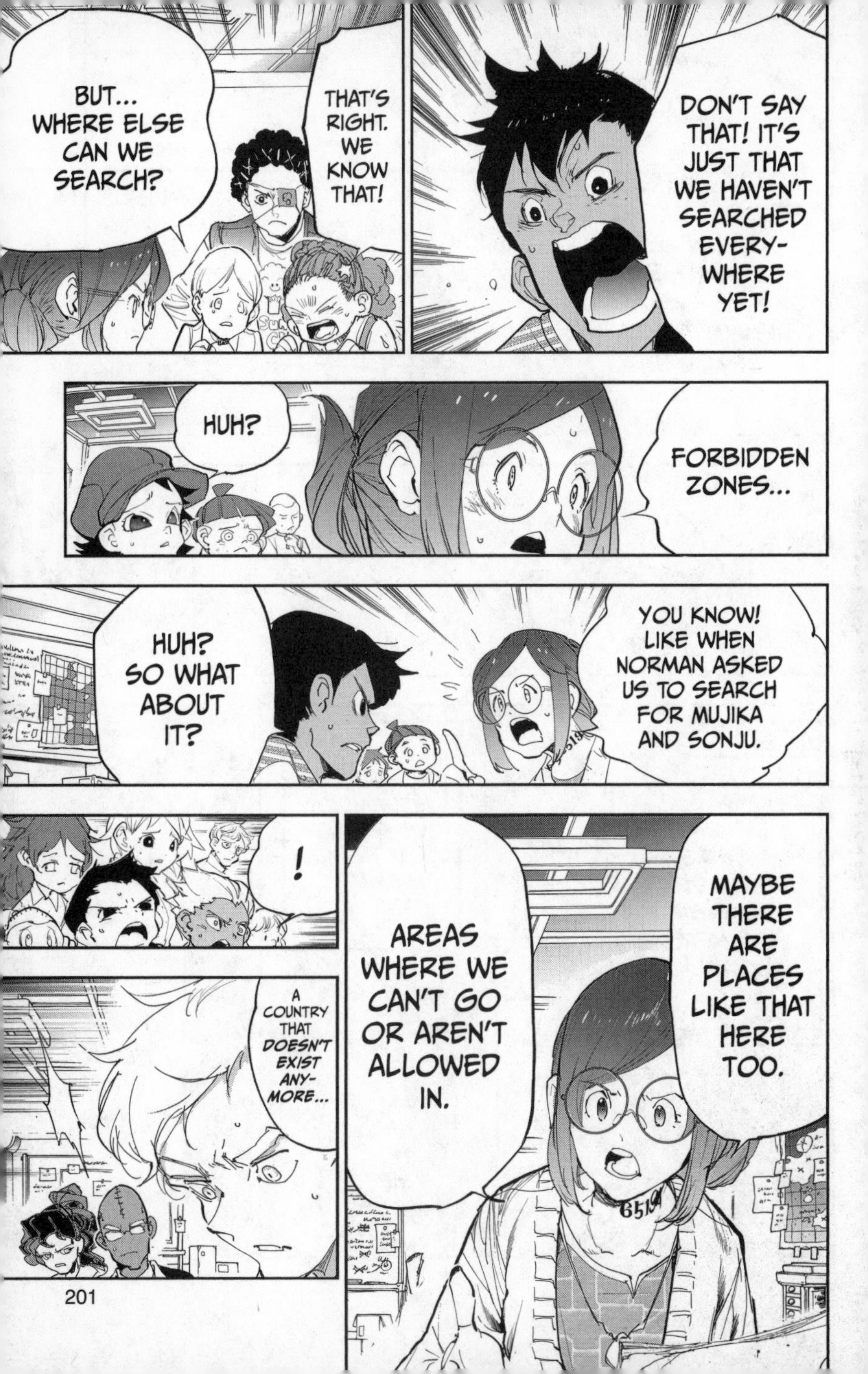
DON'T SAY THAT! IT'S JUST THAT WE HAVEN'T SEARCHED EVERY-WHERE YET!
THAT'S RIGHT. WE KNOW THAT!
BUT... WHERE ELSE CAN WE SEARCH?
FORBIDDEN ZONES...
HUH?
YOU KNOW! LIKE WHEN NORMAN ASKED US TO SEARCH FOR MUJIKA AND SONJU.
HUH? SO WHAT ABOUT IT?
MAYBE THERE ARE PLACES LIKE THAT HERE TOO.
AREAS WHERE WE CAN'T GO OR AREN'T ALLOWED IN.
!
A COUNTRY THAT *DOESN'T EXIST ANY-MORE*...

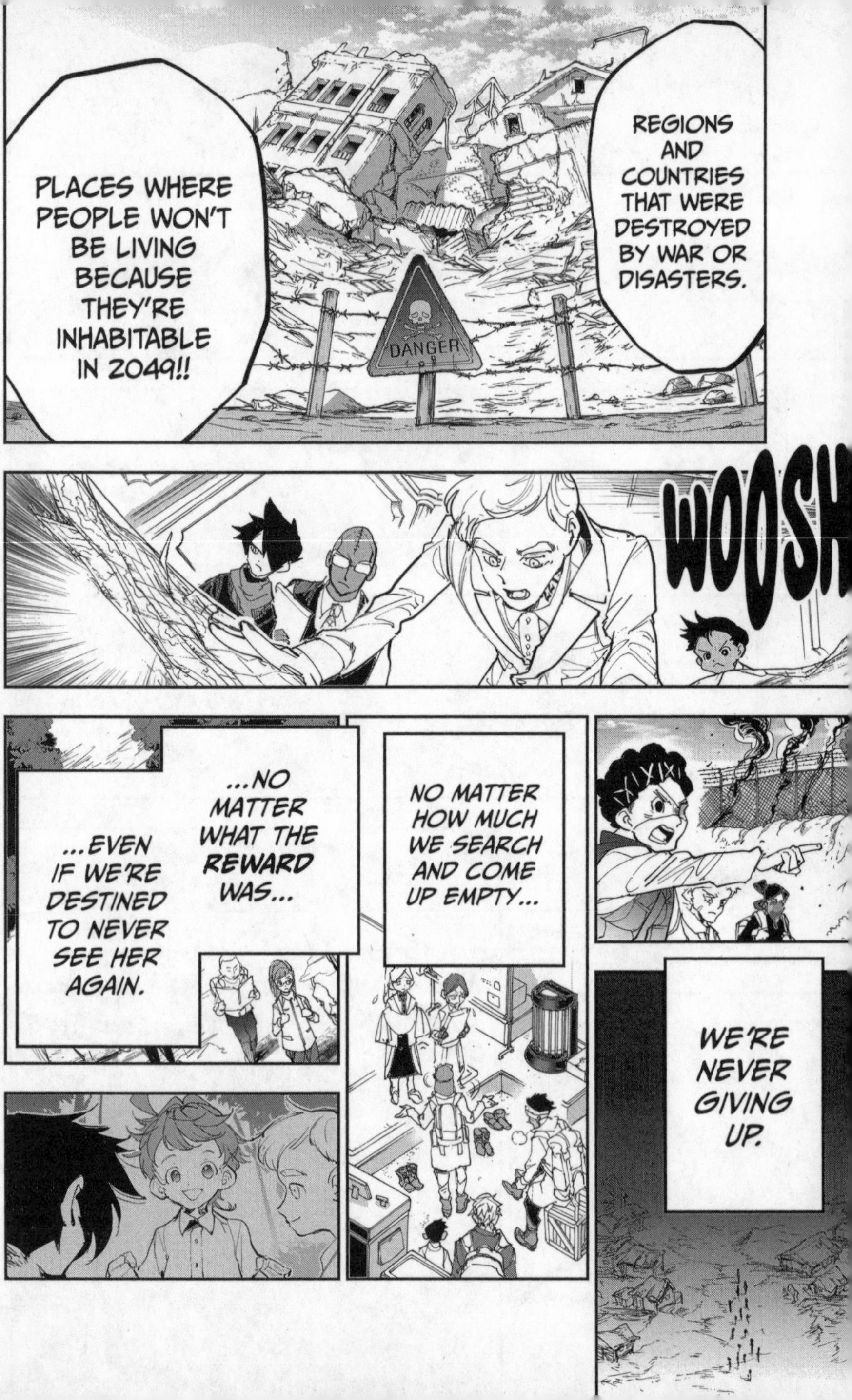
REGIONS AND COUNTRIES THAT WERE DESTROYED BY WAR OR DISASTERS.
DANGER
PLACES WHERE PEOPLE WON'T BE LIVING BECAUSE THEY'RE INHABITABLE IN 2049!!
WOOSH
WE'RE NEVER GIVING UP.
NO MATTER HOW MUCH WE SEARCH AND COME UP EMPTY...
...NO MATTER WHAT THE REWARD WAS...
...EVEN IF WE'RE DESTINED TO NEVER SEE HER AGAIN.

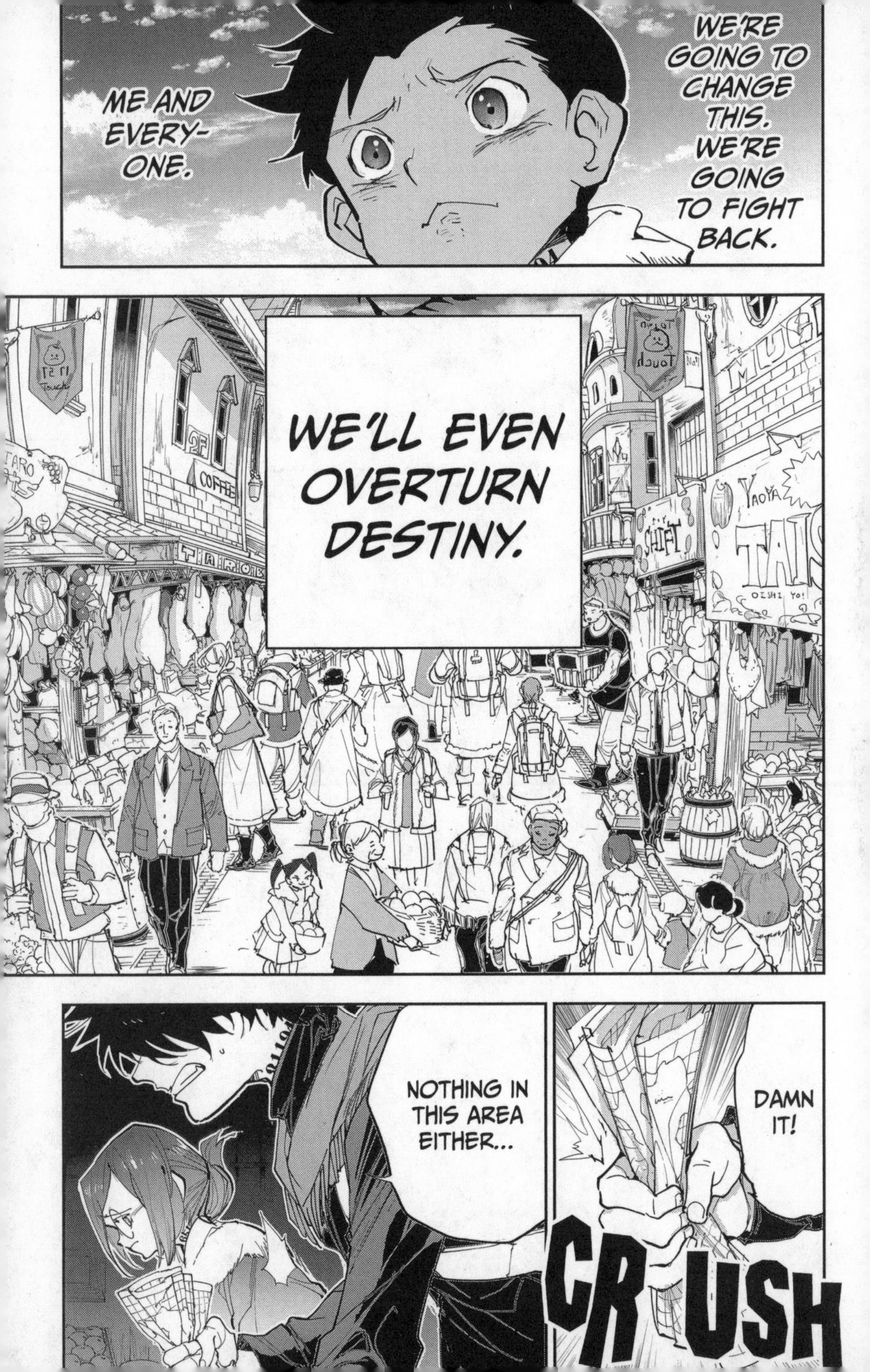
WE'RE GOING TO CHANGE THIS. WE'RE GOING TO FIGHT BACK.
ME AND EVERY-ONE.
WE'LL EVEN OVERTURN DESTINY.
YAOYA
OISHI YO!
SHIFT
Touch
COFFEE
DAMN IT!
CRUSH
NOTHING IN THIS AREA EITHER...

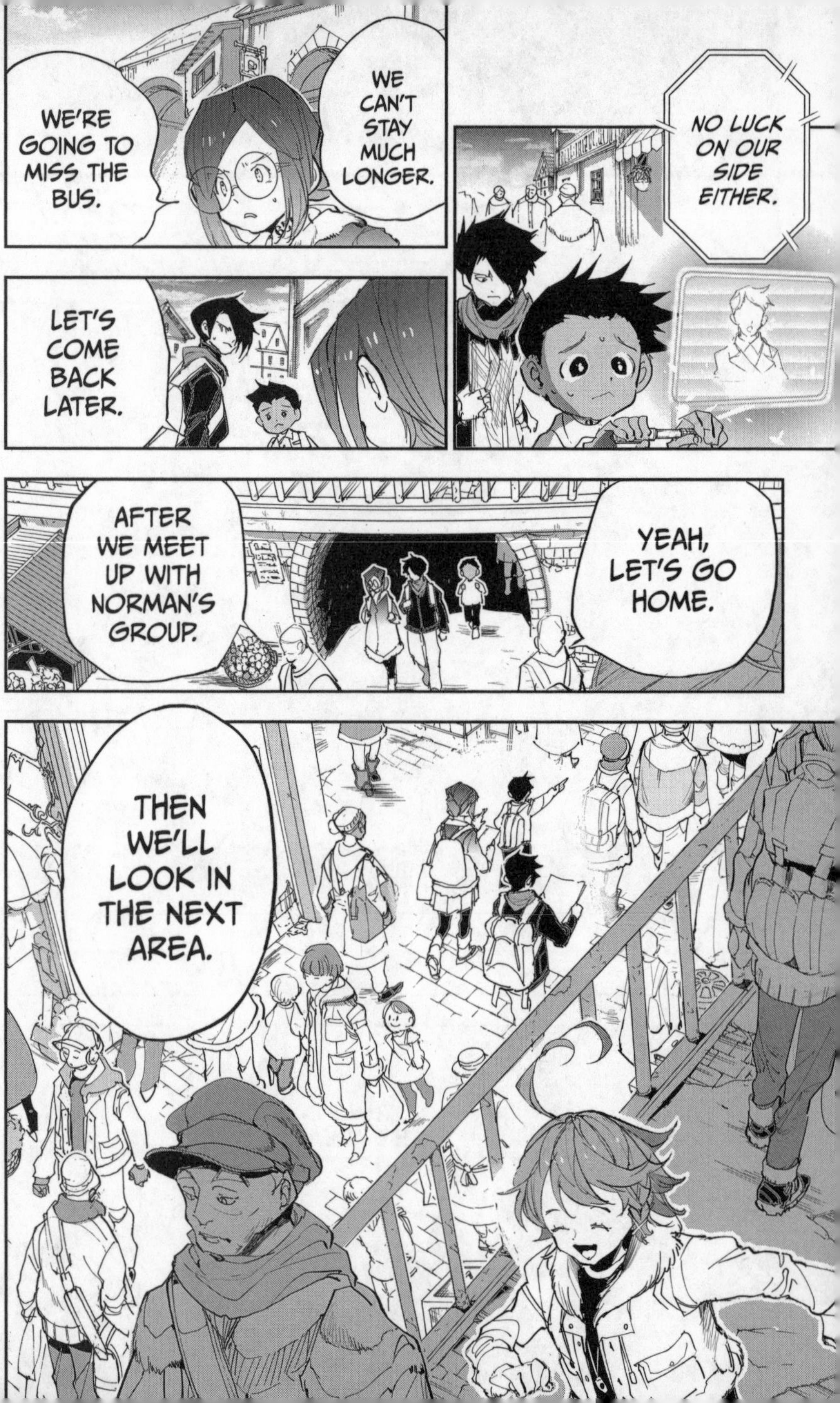

NO LUCK ON OUR SIDE EITHER.
WE CAN'T STAY MUCH LONGER.
WE'RE GOING TO MISS THE BUS.
LET'S COME BACK LATER.
YEAH, LET'S GO HOME.
AFTER WE MEET UP WITH NORMAN'S GROUP.
THEN WE'LL LOOK IN THE NEXT AREA.

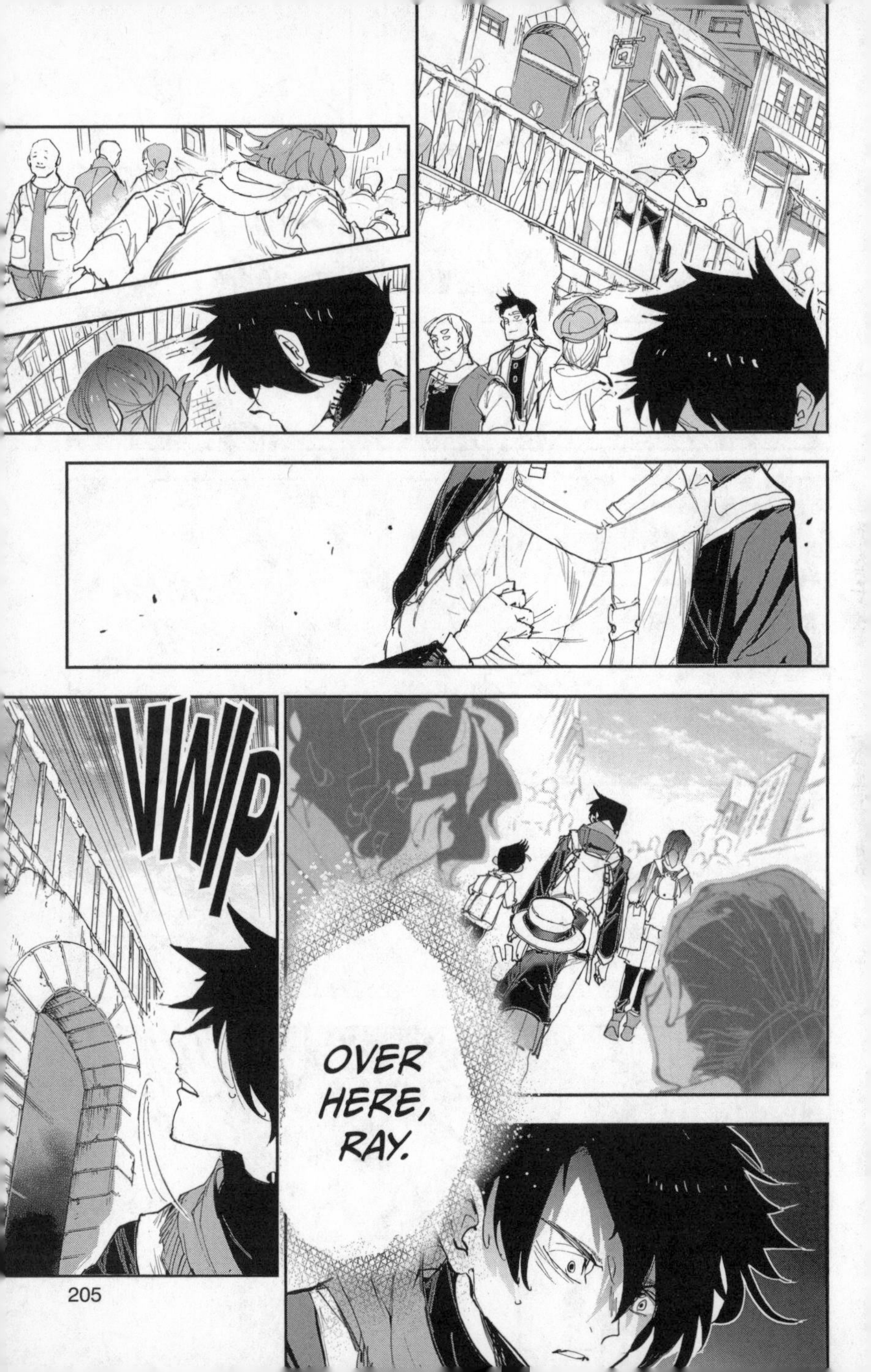
VWIP
OVER HERE, RAY.

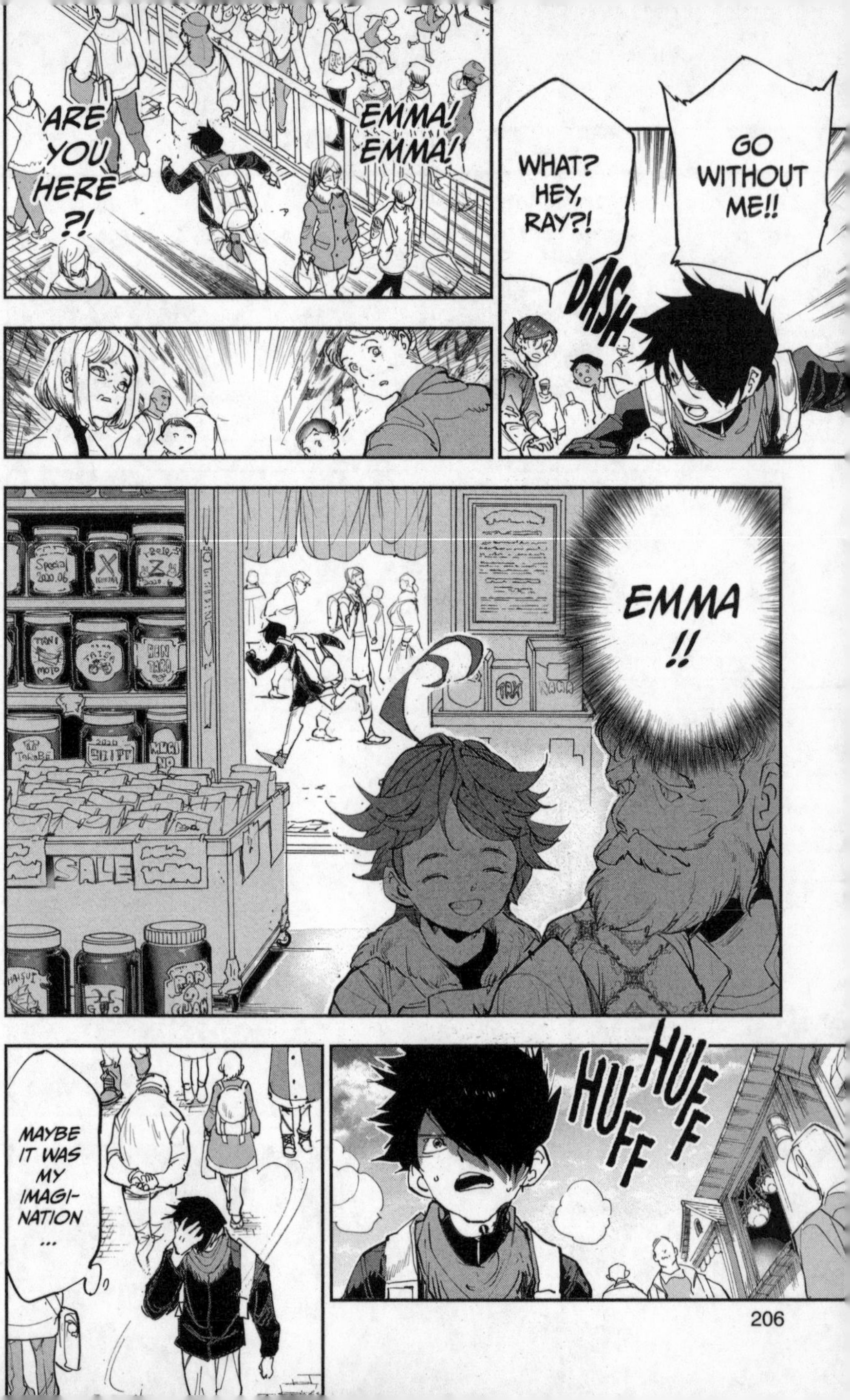
GO WITHOUT ME!!
WHAT? HEY, RAY?!
DASH
EMMA! EMMA!
ARE YOU HERE ?!
EMMA !!
HUFF HUFF
MAYBE IT WAS MY IMAGI- NATION ...

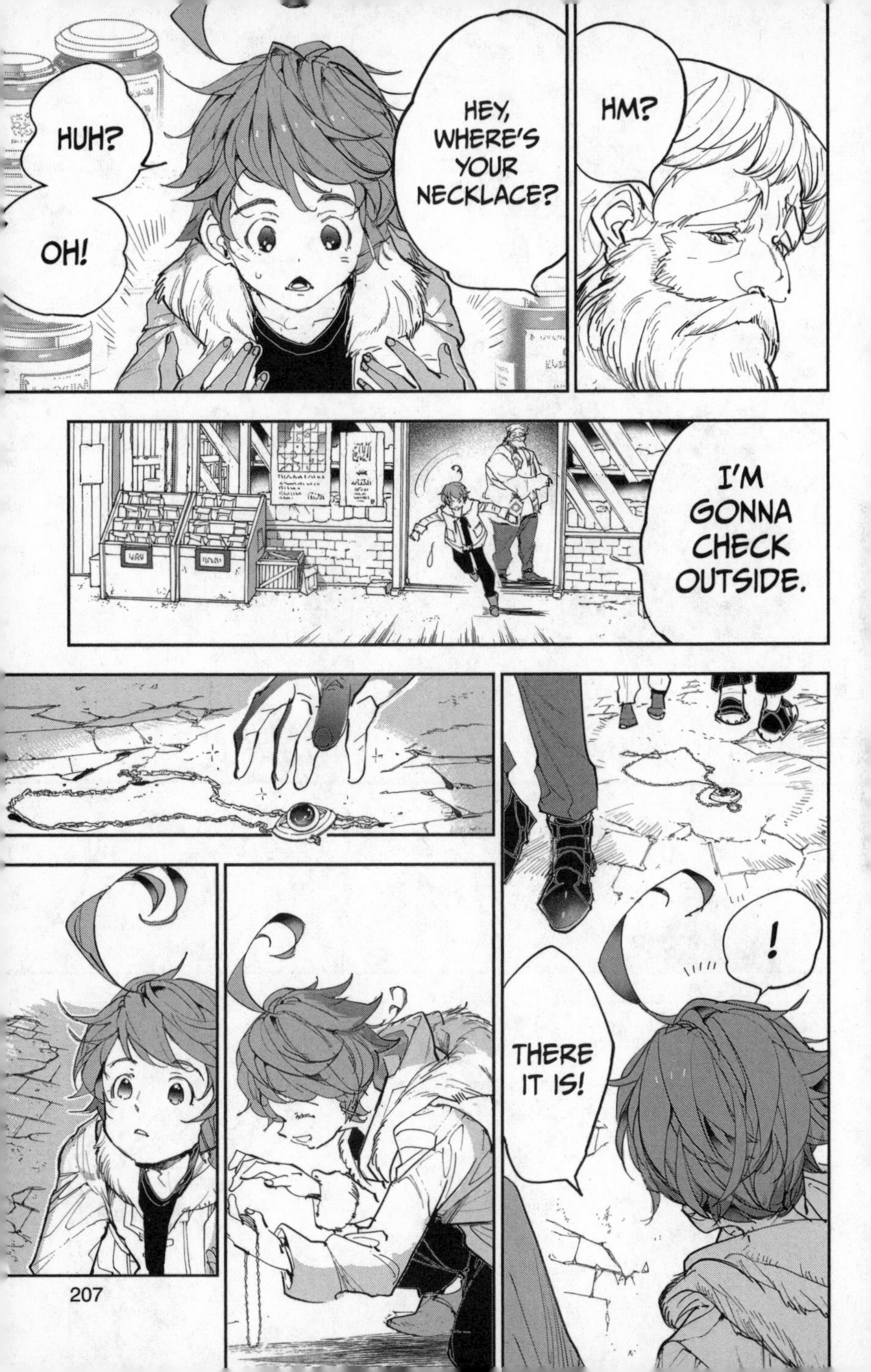
HM?
HEY, WHERE'S YOUR NECKLACE?
HUH?
OH!
I'M GONNA CHECK OUTSIDE.
!
THERE IT IS!

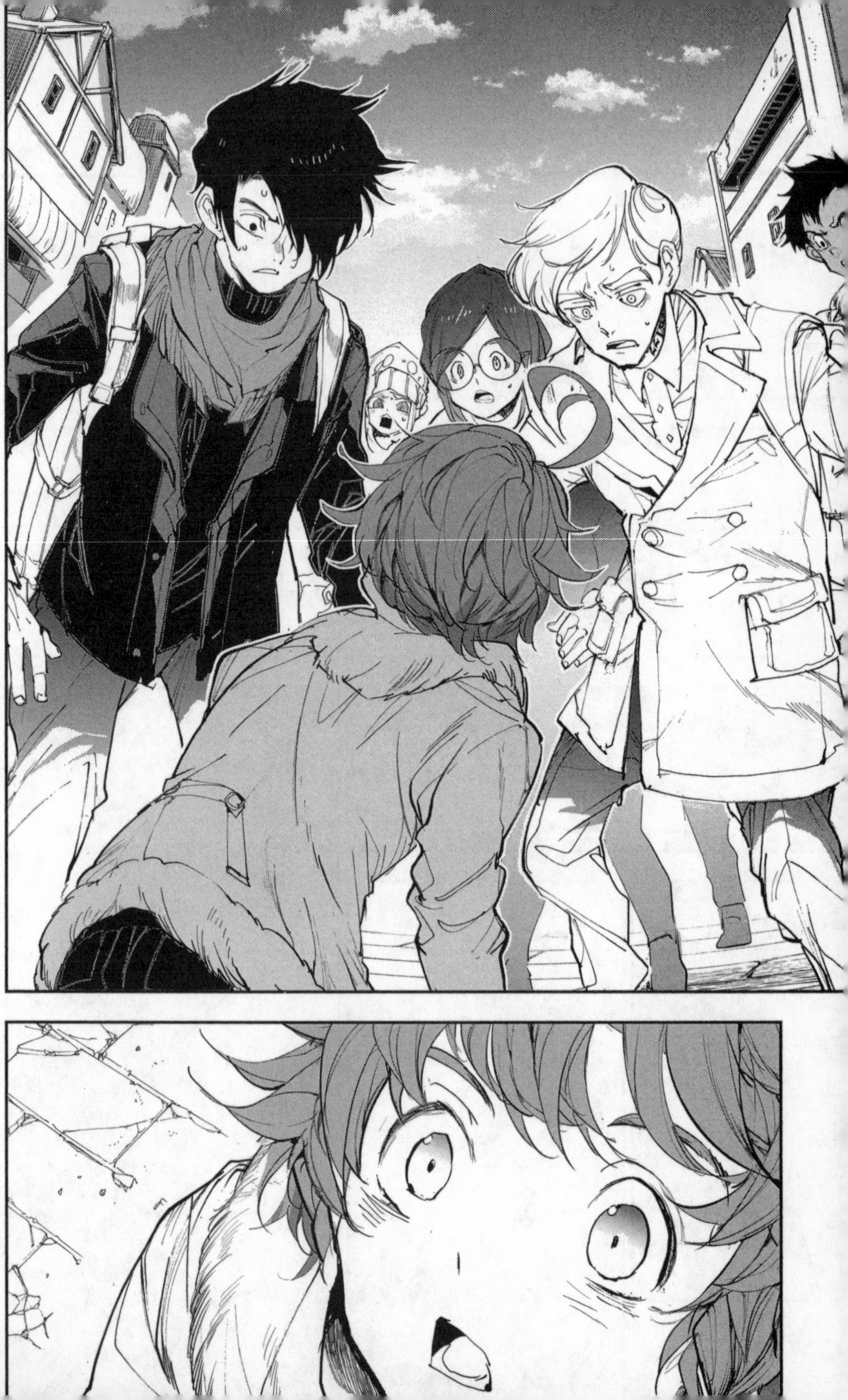

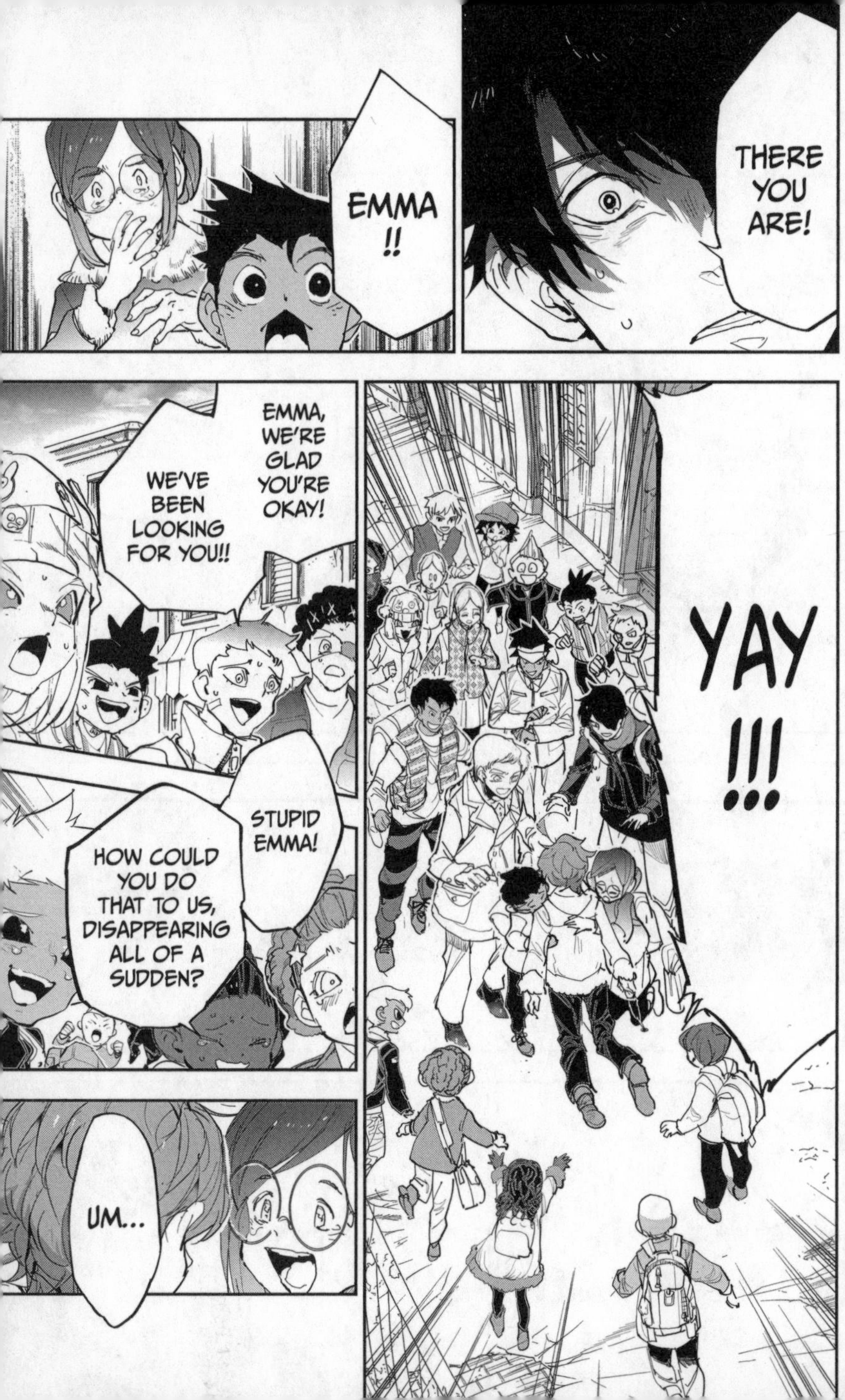
THERE YOU ARE!
EMMA!!
YAY!!!
EMMA, WE'RE GLAD YOU'RE OKAY!
WE'VE BEEN LOOKING FOR YOU!!
STUPID EMMA!
HOW COULD YOU DO THAT TO US, DISAPPEARING ALL OF A SUDDEN?
UM...

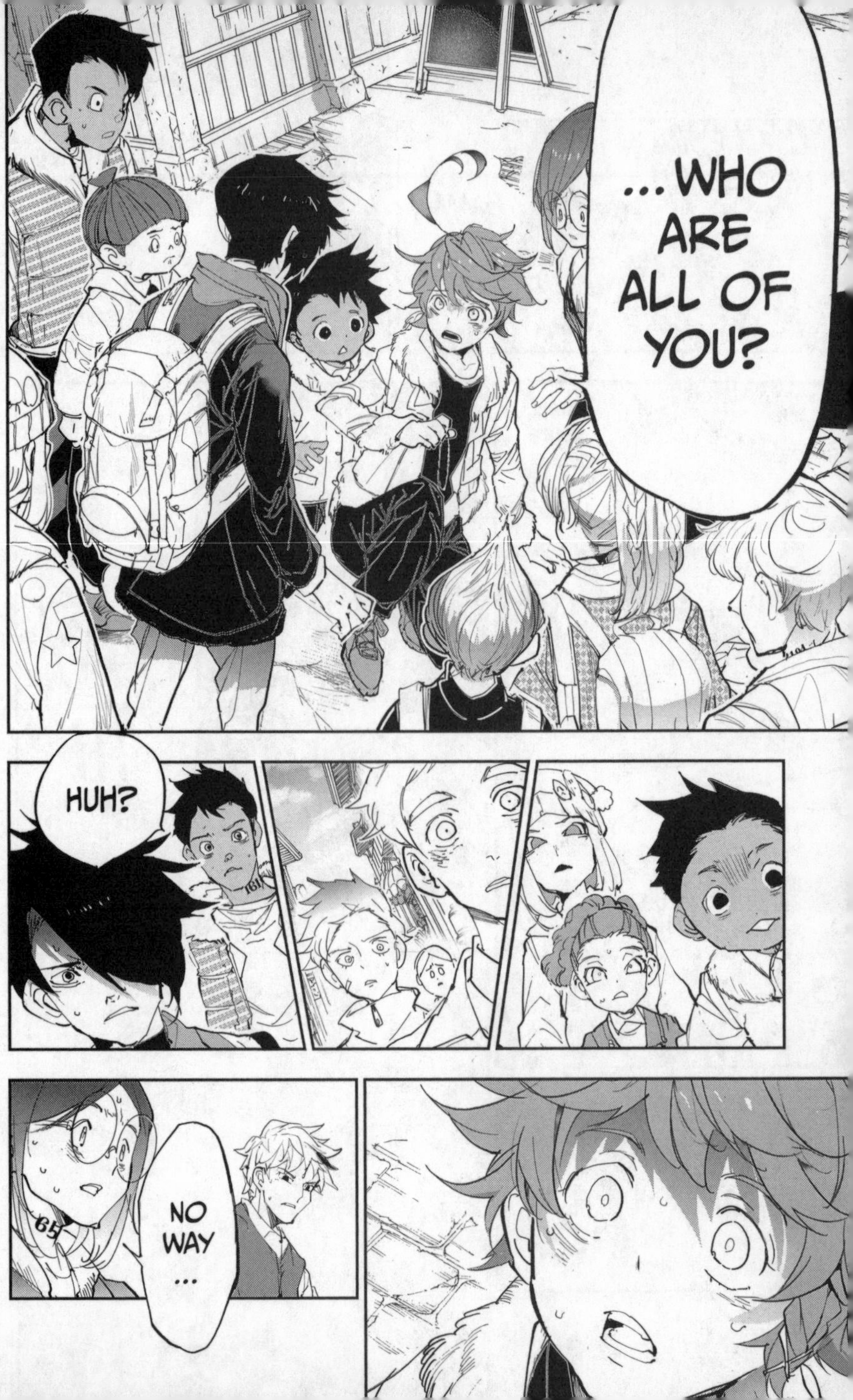
...WHO ARE ALL OF YOU?
HUH?
NO WAY ...

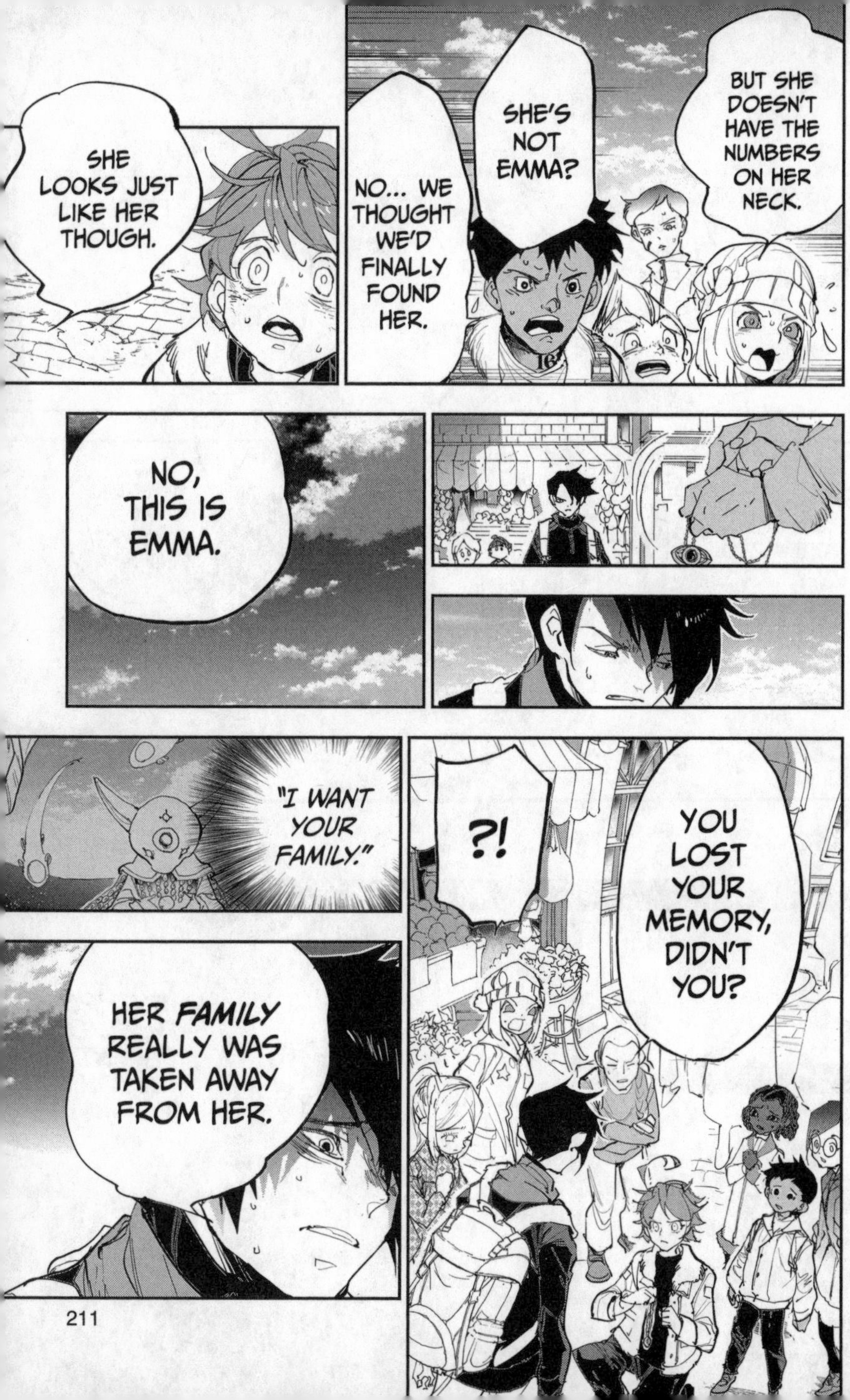
SHE'S NOT EMMA?
NO... WE THOUGHT WE'D FINALLY FOUND HER.
BUT SHE DOESN'T HAVE THE NUMBERS ON HER NECK.
SHE LOOKS JUST LIKE HER THOUGH.
NO, THIS IS EMMA.
YOU LOST YOUR MEMORY, DIDN'T YOU?
?!
"I WANT YOUR FAMILY."
HER *FAMILY* REALLY WAS TAKEN AWAY FROM HER.

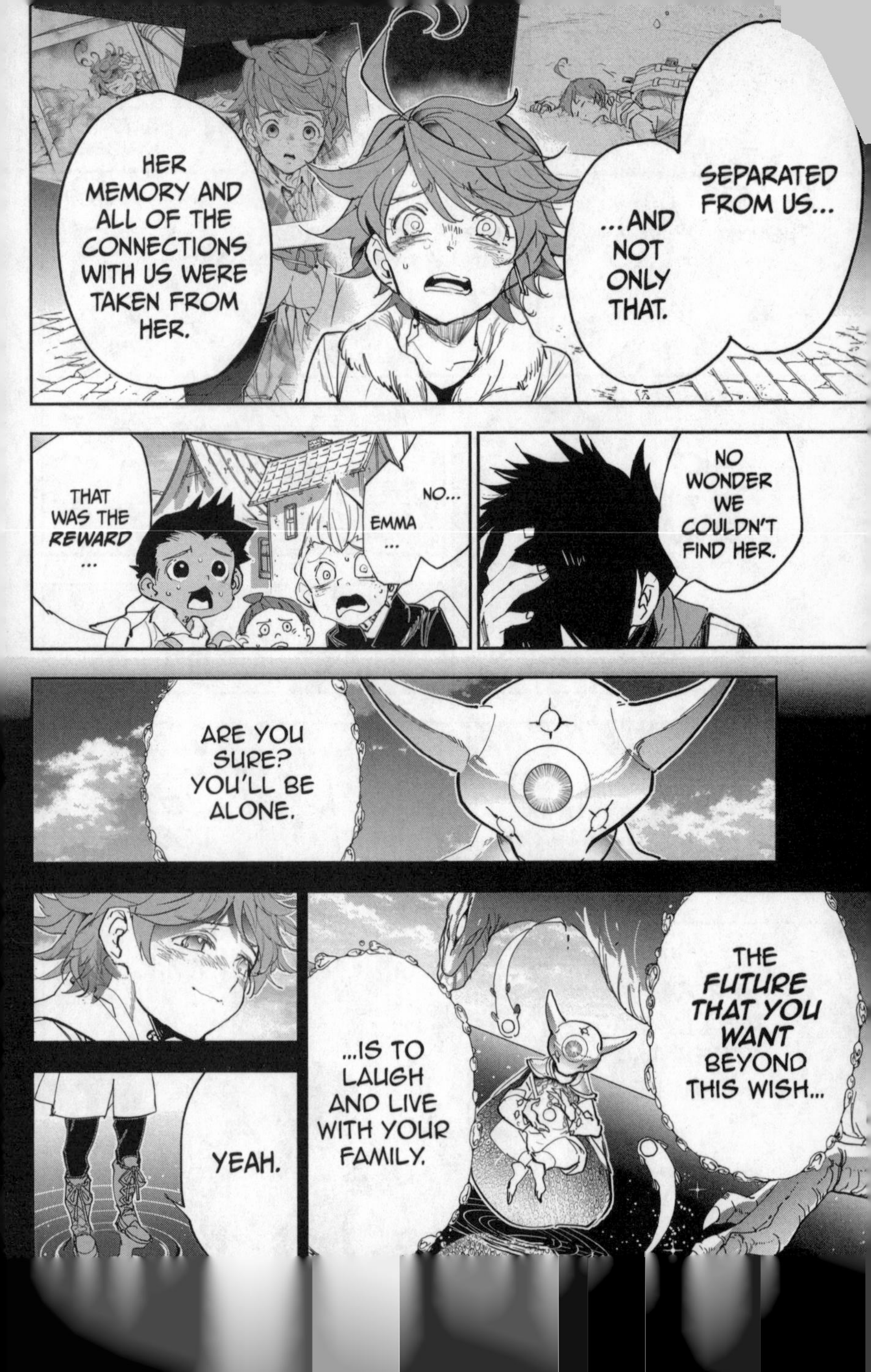
SEPARATED FROM US...
...AND NOT ONLY THAT.
HER MEMORY AND ALL OF THE CONNECTIONS WITH US WERE TAKEN FROM HER.
NO WONDER WE COULDN'T FIND HER.
NO...
EMMA ...
THAT WAS THE *REWARD* ...
ARE YOU SURE? YOU'LL BE ALONE.
THE *FUTURE THAT YOU WANT* BEYOND THIS WISH...
...IS TO LAUGH AND LIVE WITH YOUR FAMILY.
YEAH.

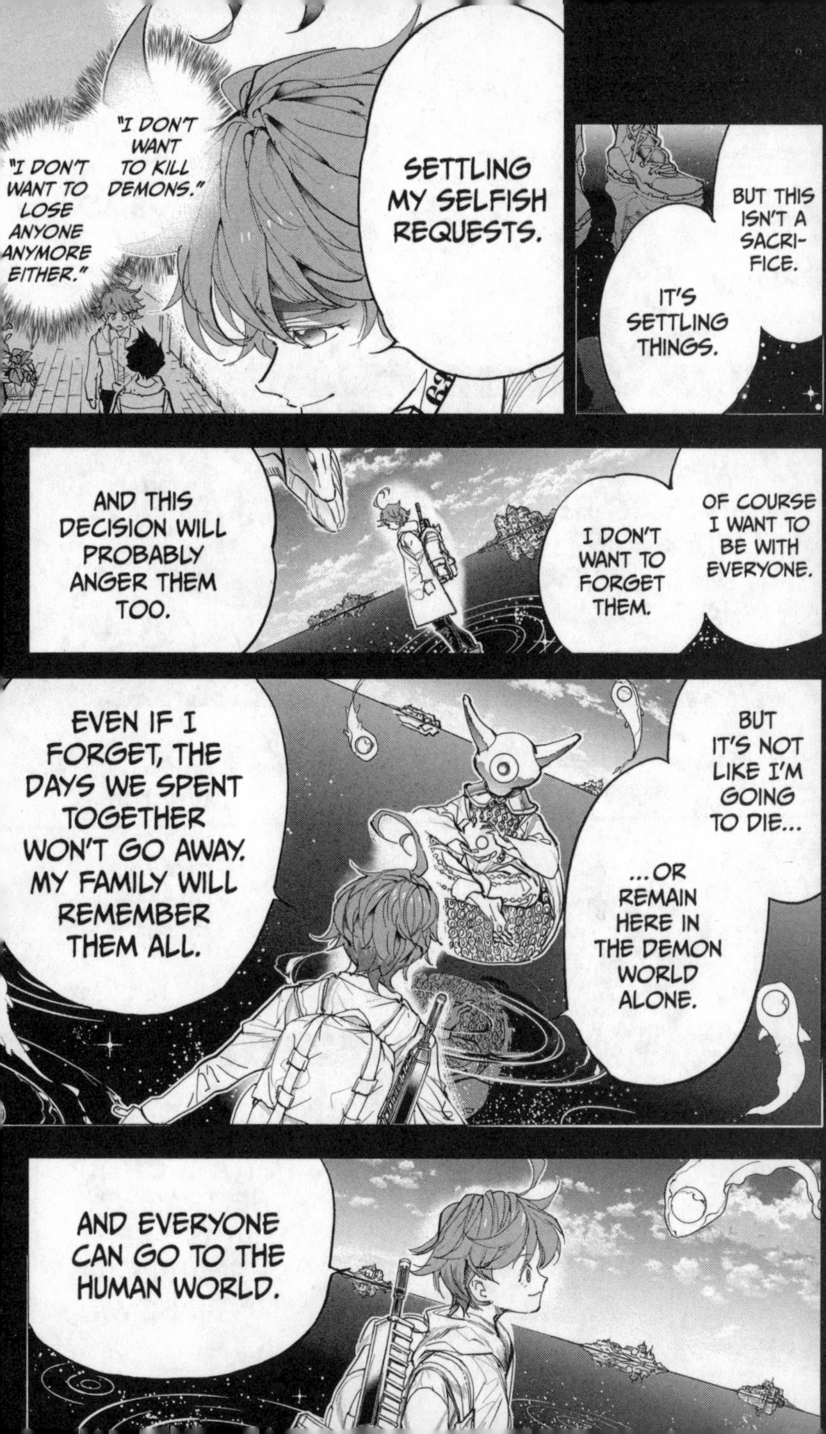
BUT THIS ISN'T A SACRIFICE.
IT'S SETTLING THINGS.
SETTLING MY SELFISH REQUESTS.
"I DON'T WANT TO KILL DEMONS."
"I DON'T WANT TO LOSE ANYONE ANYMORE EITHER."
OF COURSE I WANT TO BE WITH EVERYONE.
I DON'T WANT TO FORGET THEM.
AND THIS DECISION WILL PROBABLY ANGER THEM TOO.
BUT IT'S NOT LIKE I'M GOING TO DIE...
...OR REMAIN HERE IN THE DEMON WORLD ALONE.
EVEN IF I FORGET, THE DAYS WE SPENT TOGETHER WON'T GO AWAY. MY FAMILY WILL REMEMBER THEM ALL.
AND EVERYONE CAN GO TO THE HUMAN WORLD.

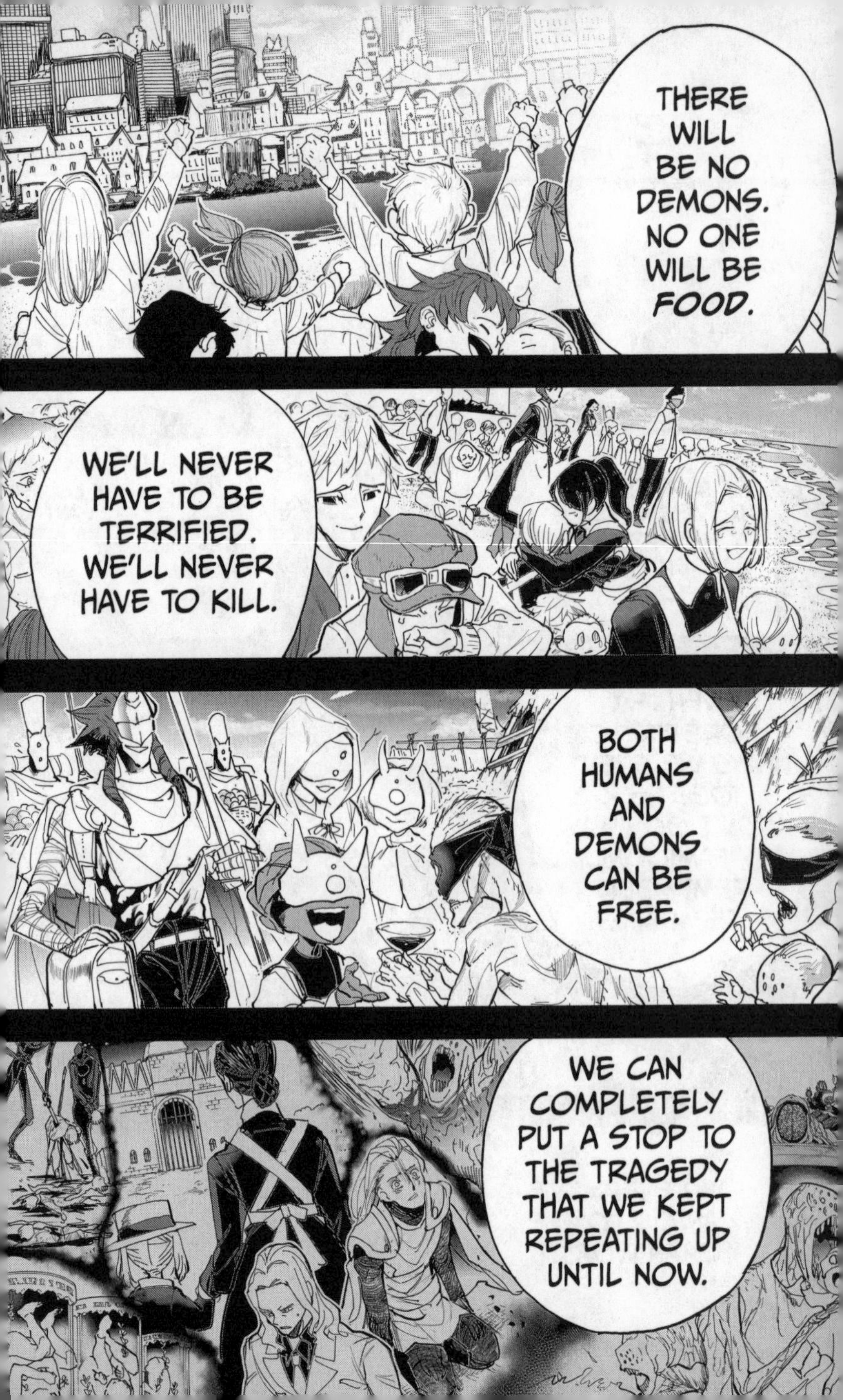
THERE WILL BE NO DEMONS. NO ONE WILL BE FOOD.
WE'LL NEVER HAVE TO BE TERRIFIED. WE'LL NEVER HAVE TO KILL.
BOTH HUMANS AND DEMONS CAN BE FREE.
WE CAN COMPLETELY PUT A STOP TO THE TRAGEDY THAT WE KEPT REPEATING UP UNTIL NOW.

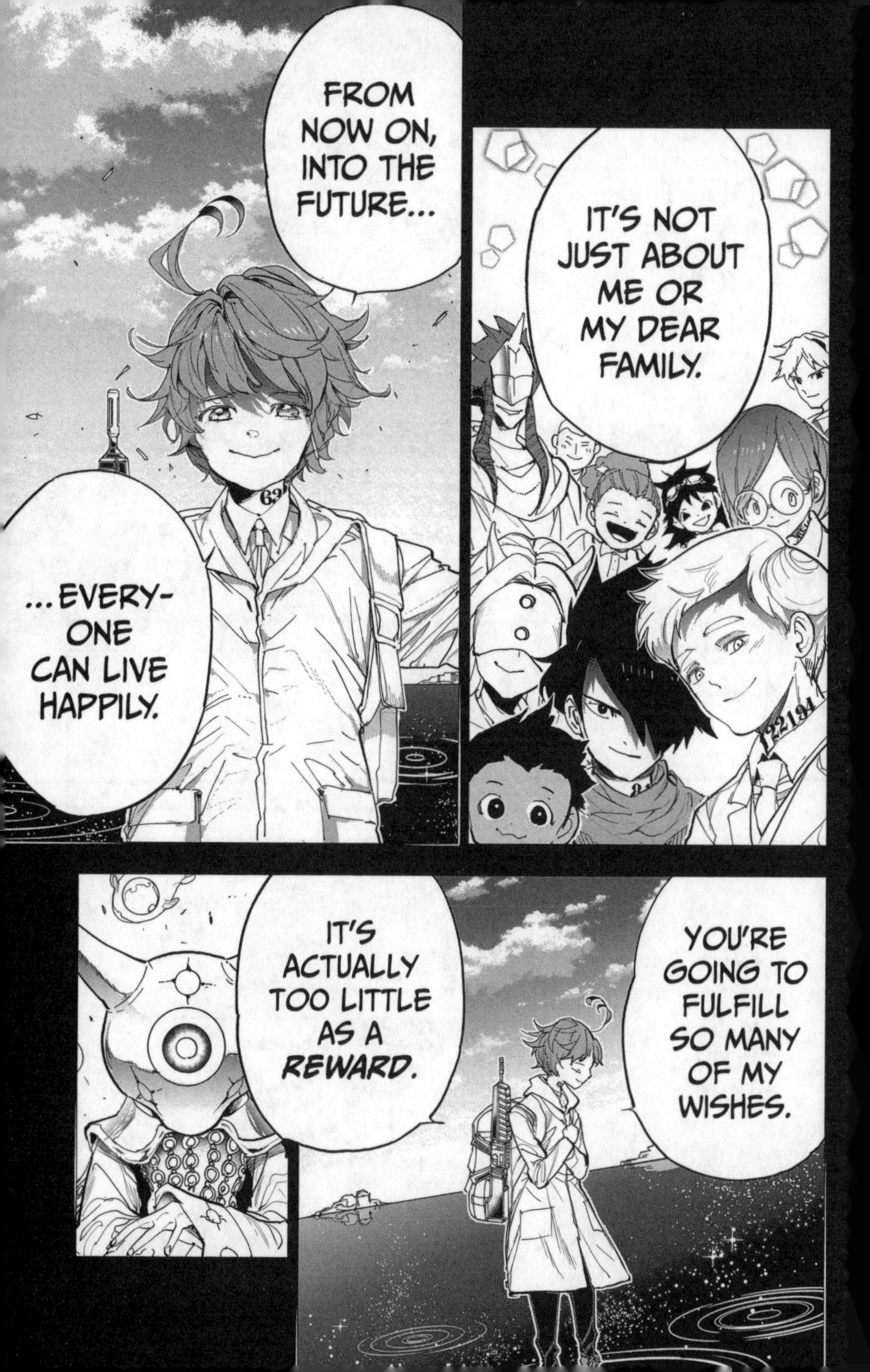
FROM NOW ON, INTO THE FUTURE...
IT'S NOT JUST ABOUT ME OR MY DEAR FAMILY.
...EVERYONE CAN LIVE HAPPILY.
YOU'RE GOING TO FULFILL SO MANY OF MY WISHES.
IT'S ACTUALLY TOO LITTLE AS A REWARD.

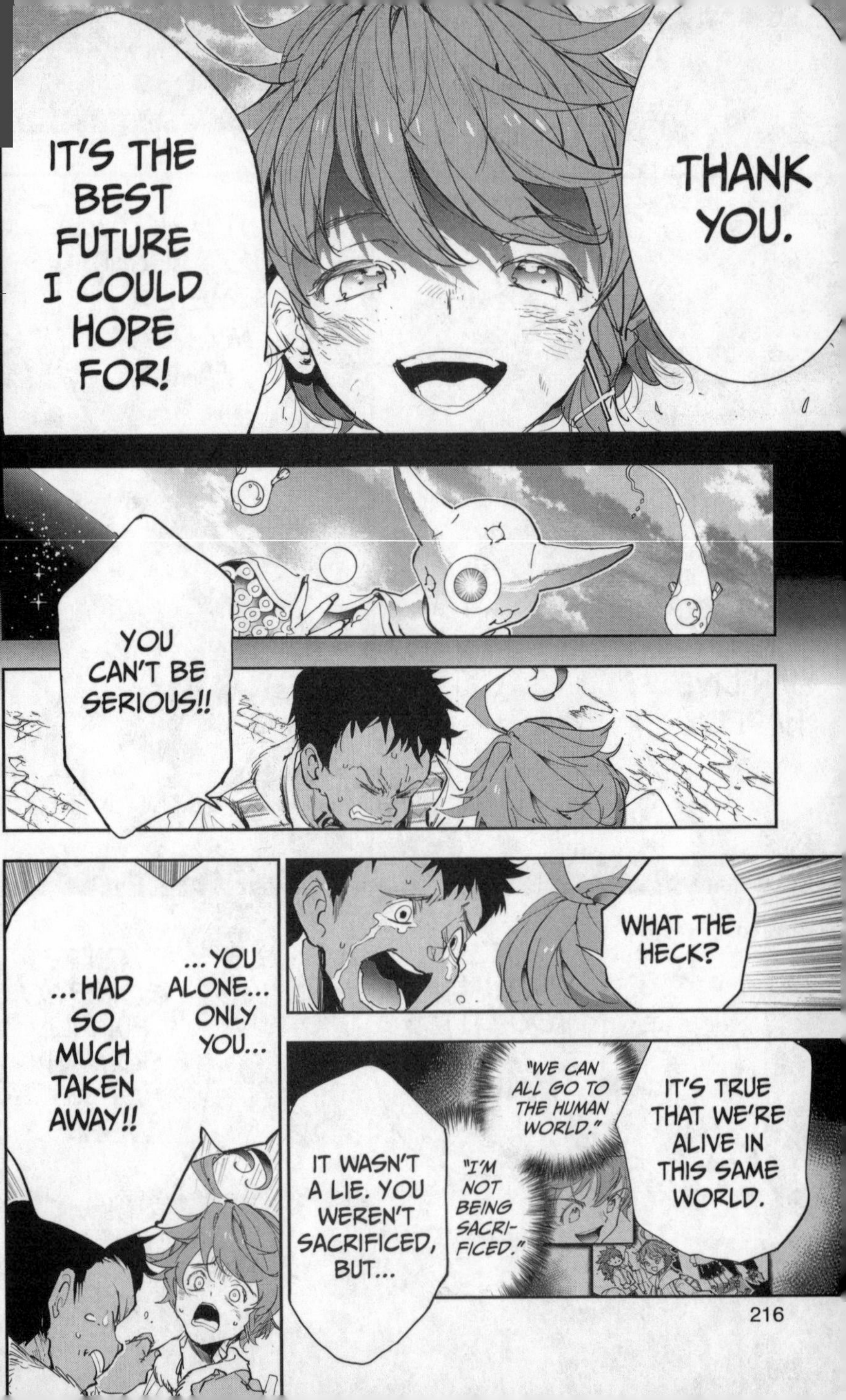
THANK YOU.
IT'S THE BEST FUTURE I COULD HOPE FOR!
YOU CAN'T BE SERIOUS!!
WHAT THE HECK?
IT'S TRUE THAT WE'RE ALIVE IN THIS SAME WORLD.
"WE CAN ALL GO TO THE HUMAN WORLD."
"I'M NOT BEING SACRIFICED."
IT WASN'T A LIE. YOU WEREN'T SACRIFICED, BUT...
...YOU ALONE... ONLY YOU...
...HAD SO MUCH TAKEN AWAY!!

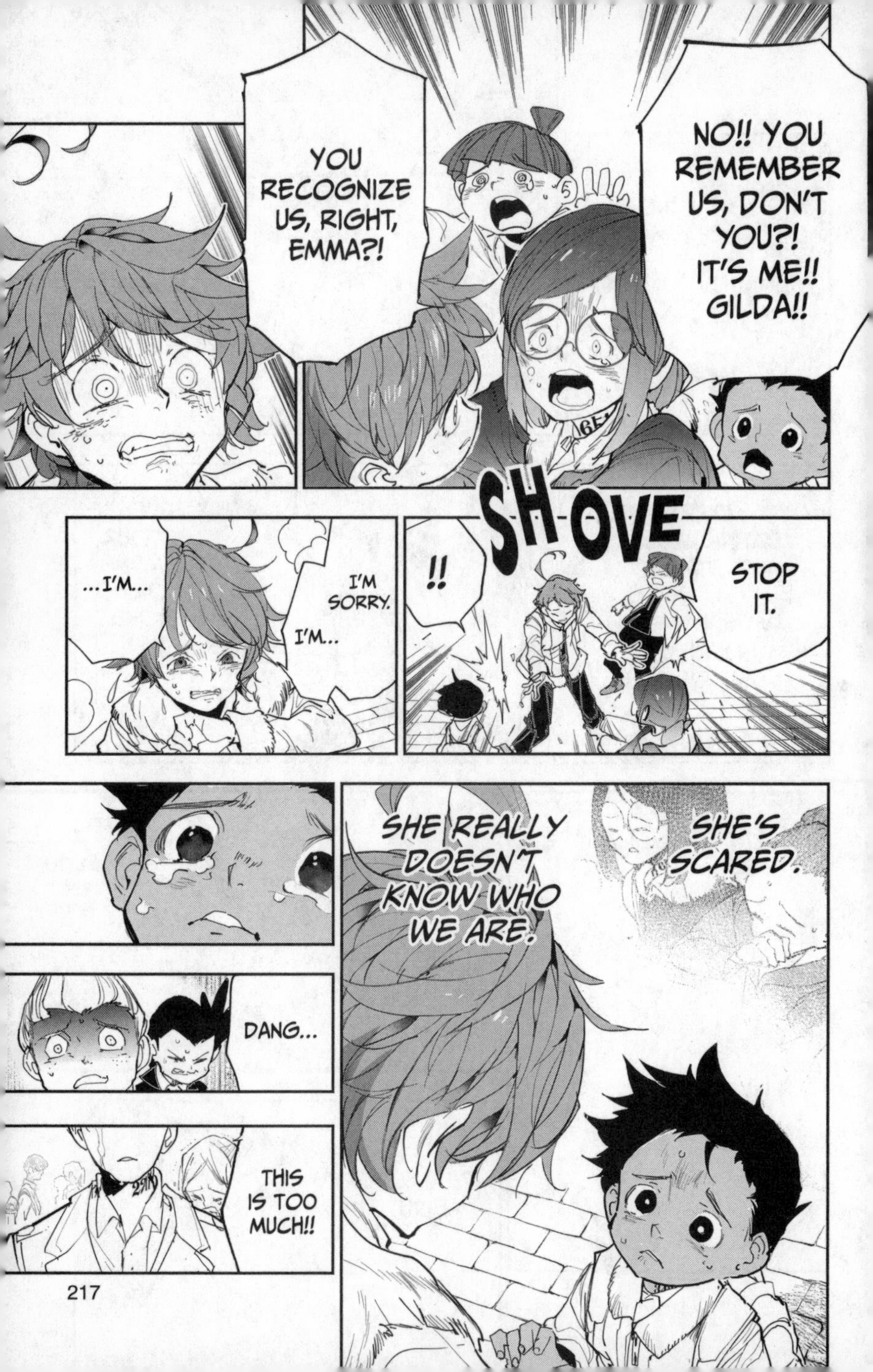
NO!! YOU REMEMBER US, DON'T YOU?! IT'S ME!! GILDA!!
YOU RECOGNIZE US, RIGHT, EMMA?!
STOP IT.
SHOVE
!!
I'M SORRY.
I'M...
...I'M...
SHE'S SCARED.
SHE REALLY DOESN'T KNOW WHO WE ARE.
DANG...
THIS IS TOO MUCH!!

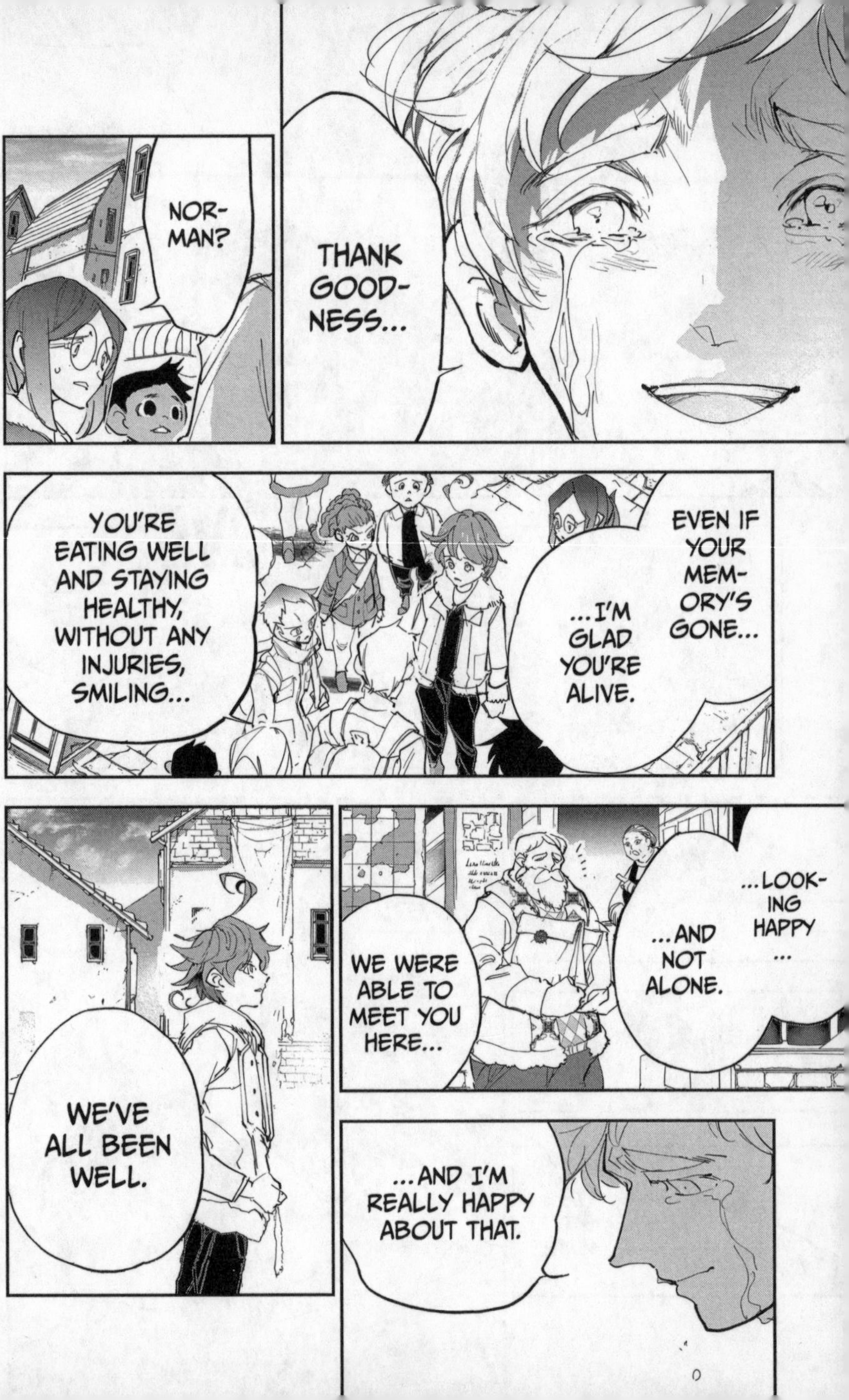
THANK GOODNESS...
NORMAN?
EVEN IF YOUR MEMORY'S GONE...
...I'M GLAD YOU'RE ALIVE.
YOU'RE EATING WELL AND STAYING HEALTHY, WITHOUT ANY INJURIES, SMILING...
...LOOKING HAPPY...
...AND NOT ALONE.
WE WERE ABLE TO MEET YOU HERE...
...AND I'M REALLY HAPPY ABOUT THAT.
WE'VE ALL BEEN WELL.

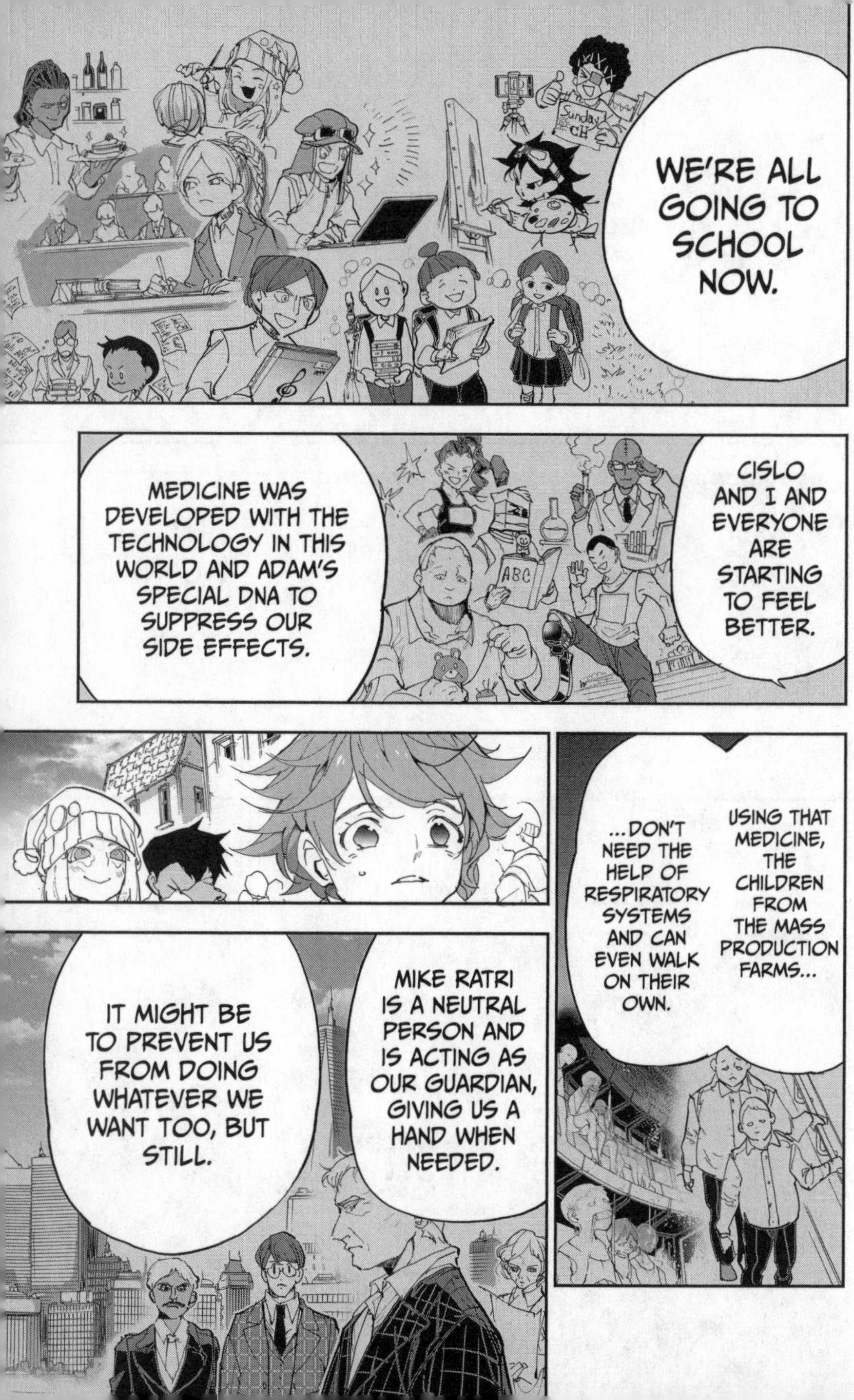
WE'RE ALL GOING TO SCHOOL NOW.
Sunday CH
CISLO AND I AND EVERYONE ARE STARTING TO FEEL BETTER.
MEDICINE WAS DEVELOPED WITH THE TECHNOLOGY IN THIS WORLD AND ADAM'S SPECIAL DNA TO SUPPRESS OUR SIDE EFFECTS.
ABC
USING THAT MEDICINE, THE CHILDREN FROM THE MASS PRODUCTION FARMS...
...DON'T NEED THE HELP OF RESPIRATORY SYSTEMS AND CAN EVEN WALK ON THEIR OWN.
MIKE RATRI IS A NEUTRAL PERSON AND IS ACTING AS OUR GUARDIAN, GIVING US A HAND WHEN NEEDED.
IT MIGHT BE TO PREVENT US FROM DOING WHATEVER WE WANT TOO, BUT STILL.

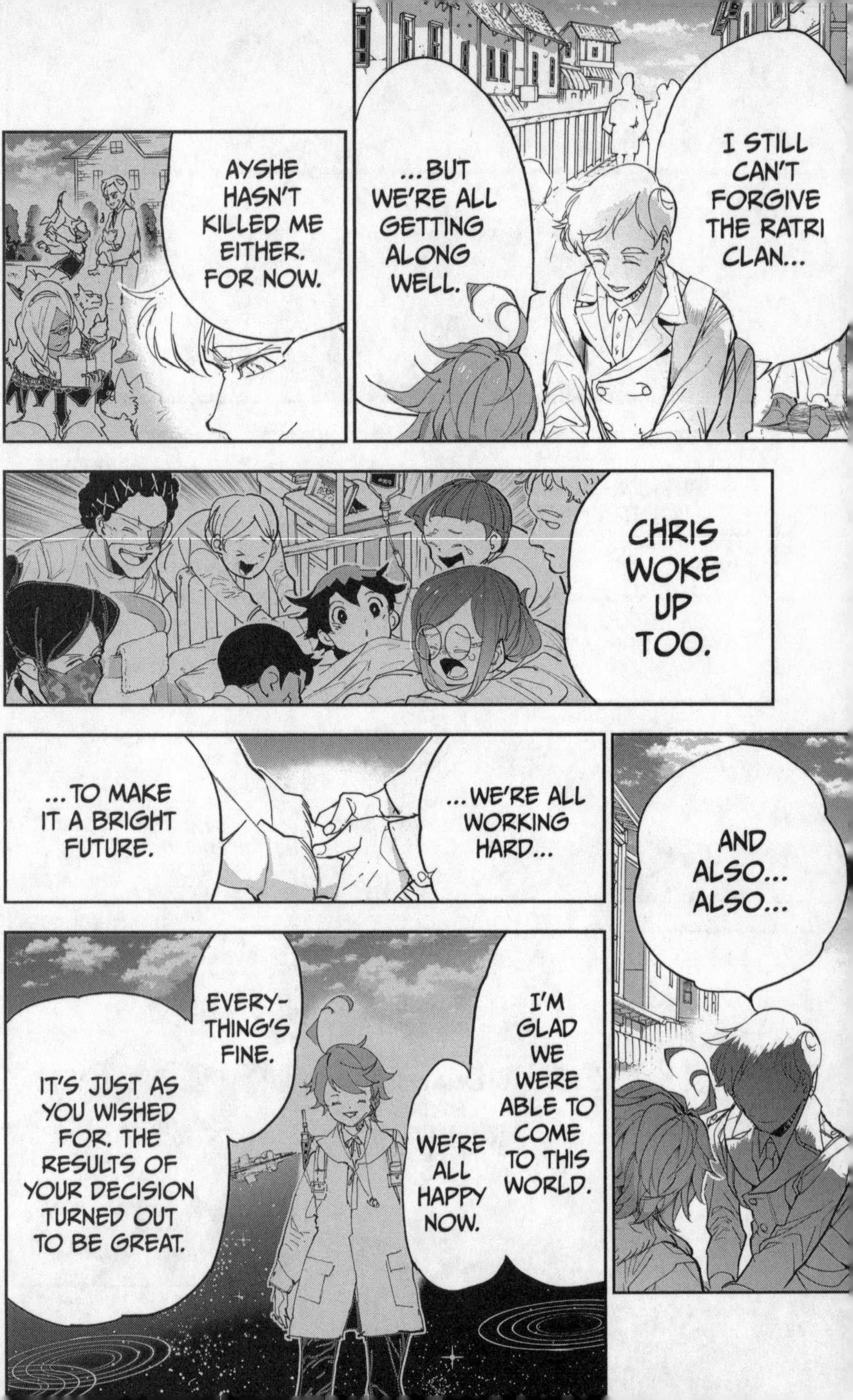
I STILL CAN'T FORGIVE THE RATRI CLAN...
...BUT WE'RE ALL GETTING ALONG WELL.
AYSHE HASN'T KILLED ME EITHER. FOR NOW.
CHRIS WOKE UP TOO.
AND ALSO... ALSO...
...WE'RE ALL WORKING HARD...
...TO MAKE IT A BRIGHT FUTURE.
I'M GLAD WE WERE ABLE TO COME TO THIS WORLD.
WE'RE ALL HAPPY NOW.
EVERY-THING'S FINE.
IT'S JUST AS YOU WISHED FOR. THE RESULTS OF YOUR DECISION TURNED OUT TO BE GREAT.

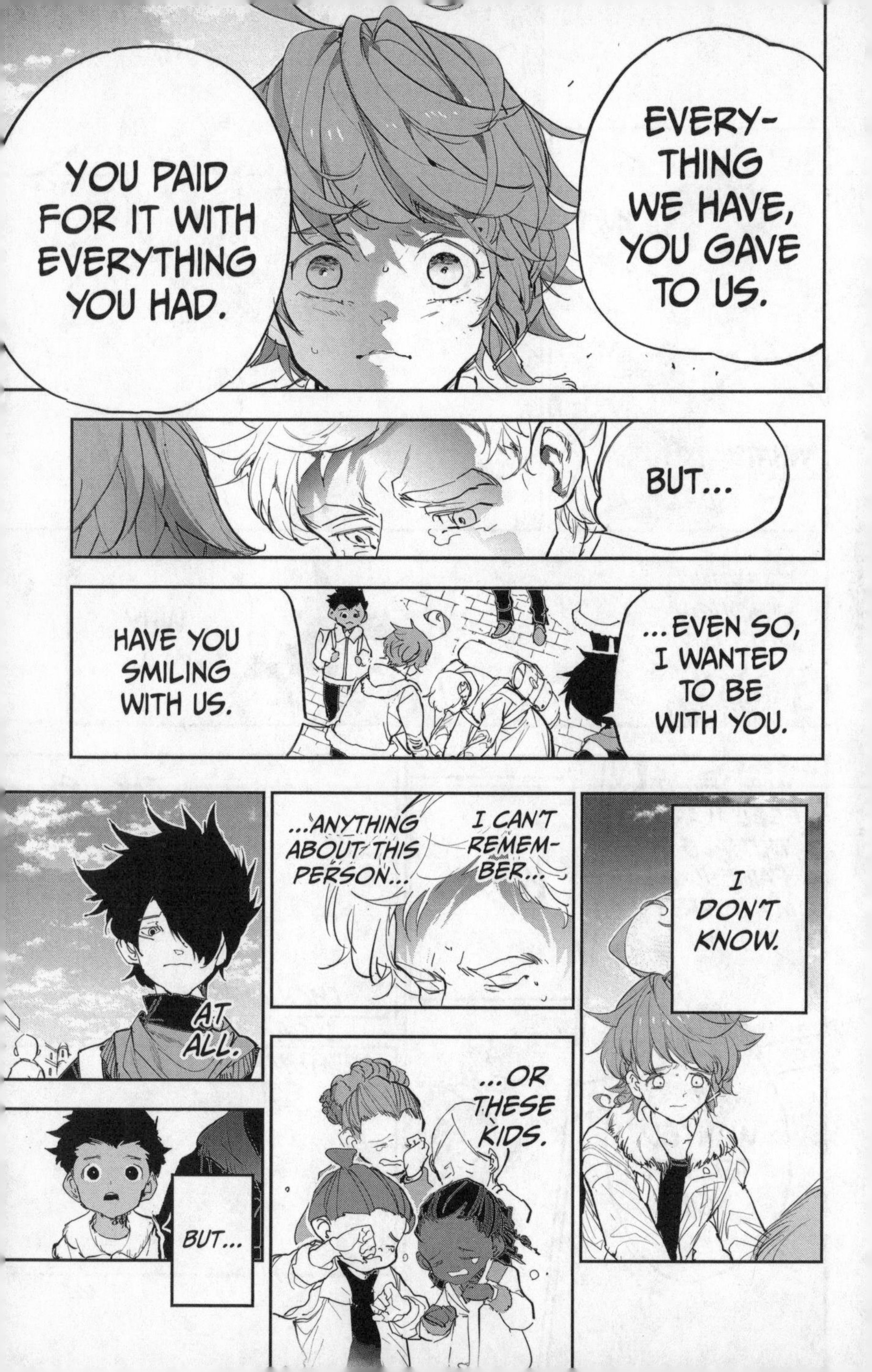
EVERY-THING WE HAVE, YOU GAVE TO US.
YOU PAID FOR IT WITH EVERYTHING YOU HAD.
BUT...
...EVEN SO, I WANTED TO BE WITH YOU.
HAVE YOU SMILING WITH US.
I DON'T KNOW.
I CAN'T REMEM-BER...
...ANYTHING ABOUT THIS PERSON...
AT ALL.
...OR THESE KIDS.
BUT...

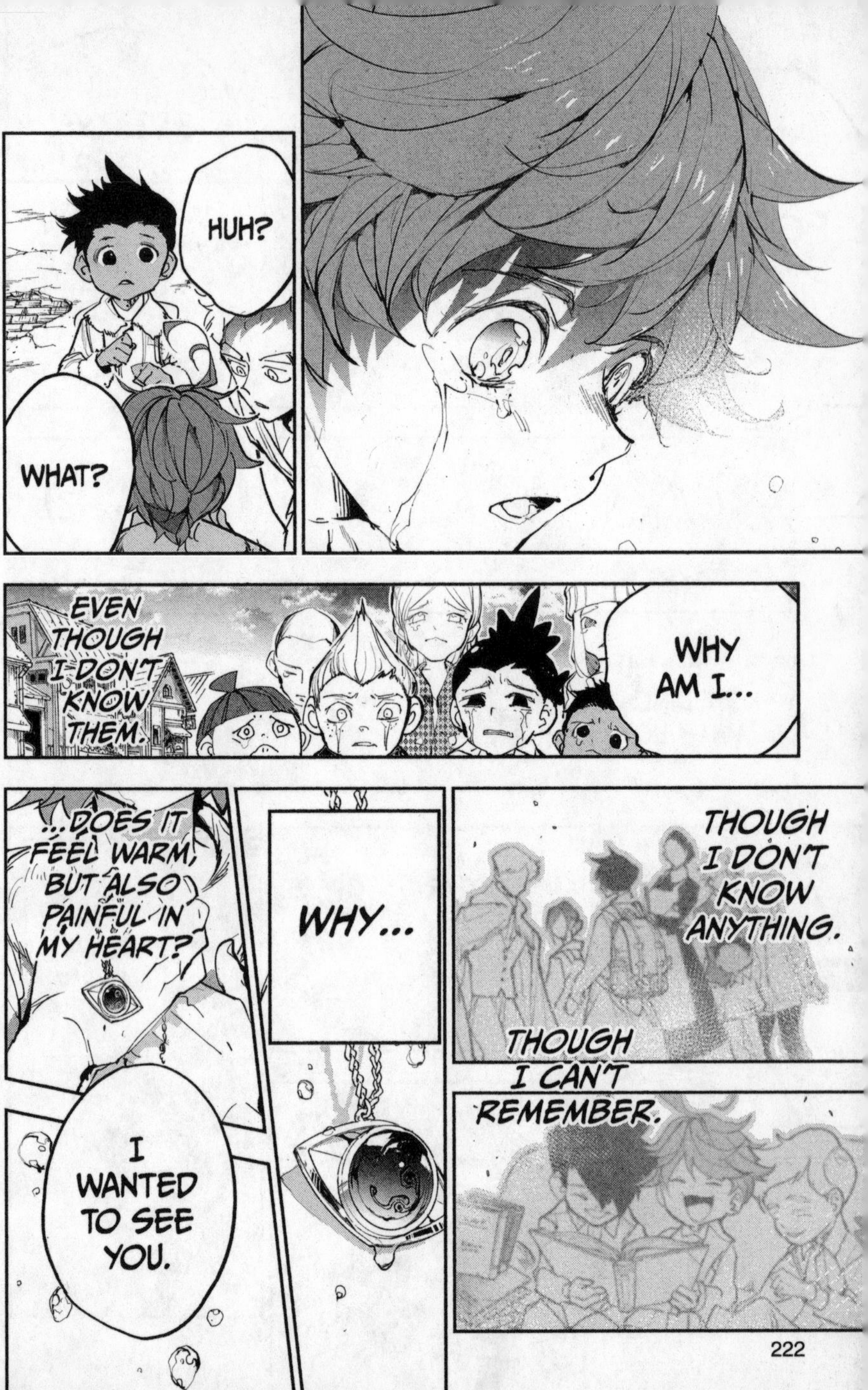
HUH?
WHAT?
WHY AM I...
EVEN THOUGH I DON'T KNOW THEM.
THOUGH I DON'T KNOW ANYTHING.
THOUGH I CAN'T REMEMBER.
WHY...
...DOES IT FEEL WARM, BUT ALSO PAINFUL IN MY HEART?
I WANTED TO SEE YOU.

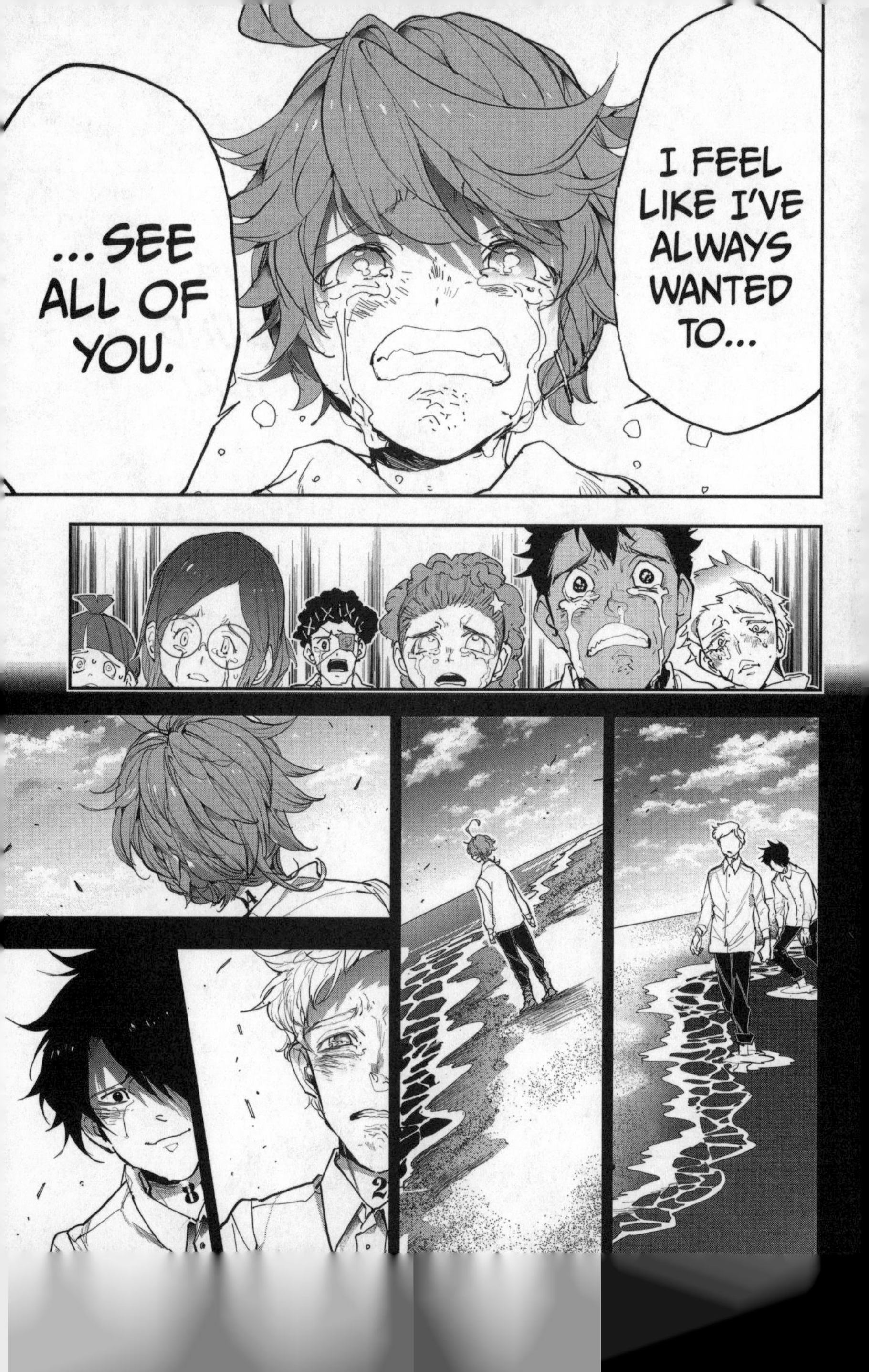
I FEEL LIKE I'VE ALWAYS WANTED TO...
...SEE ALL OF YOU.

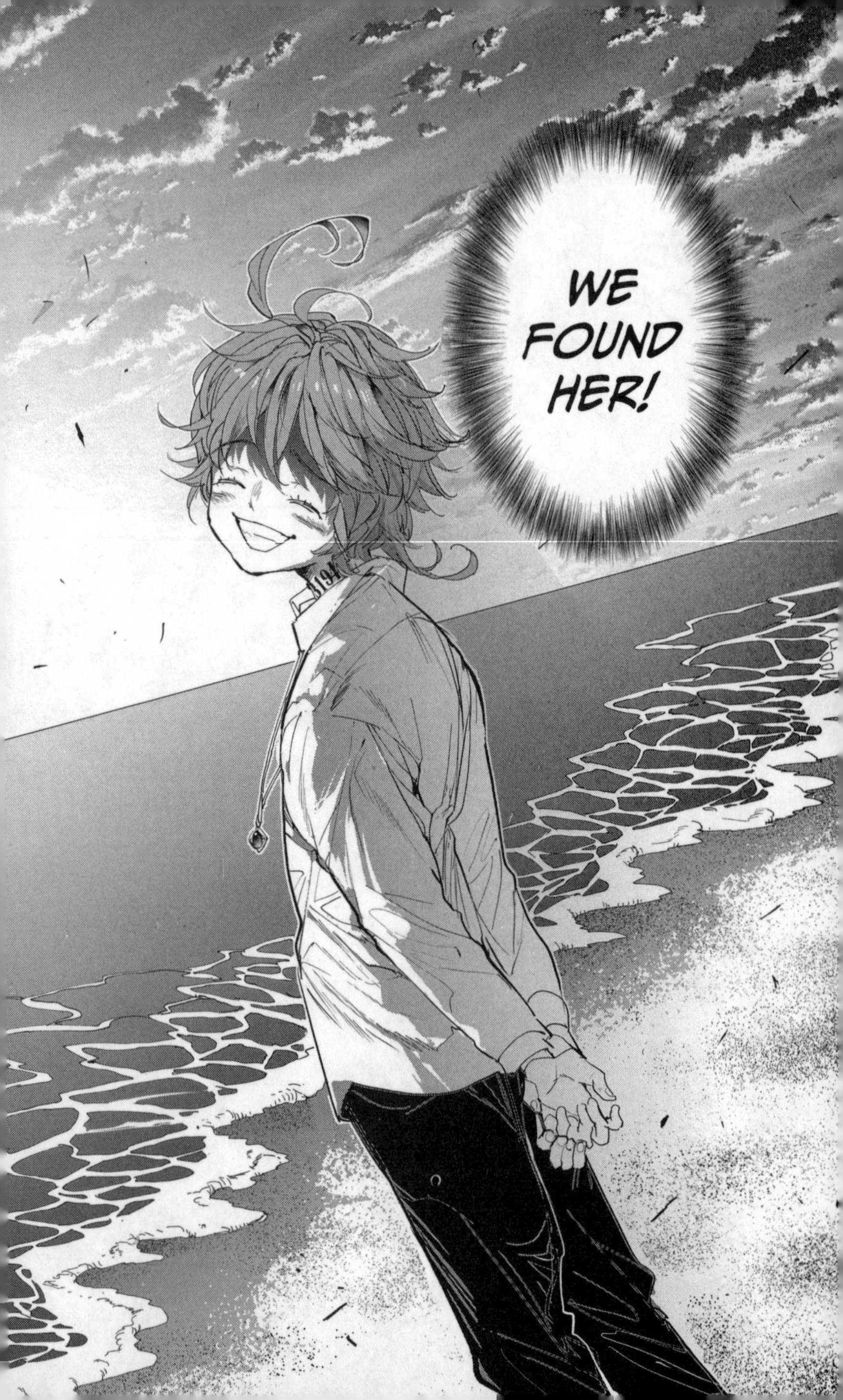
WE FOUND HER!

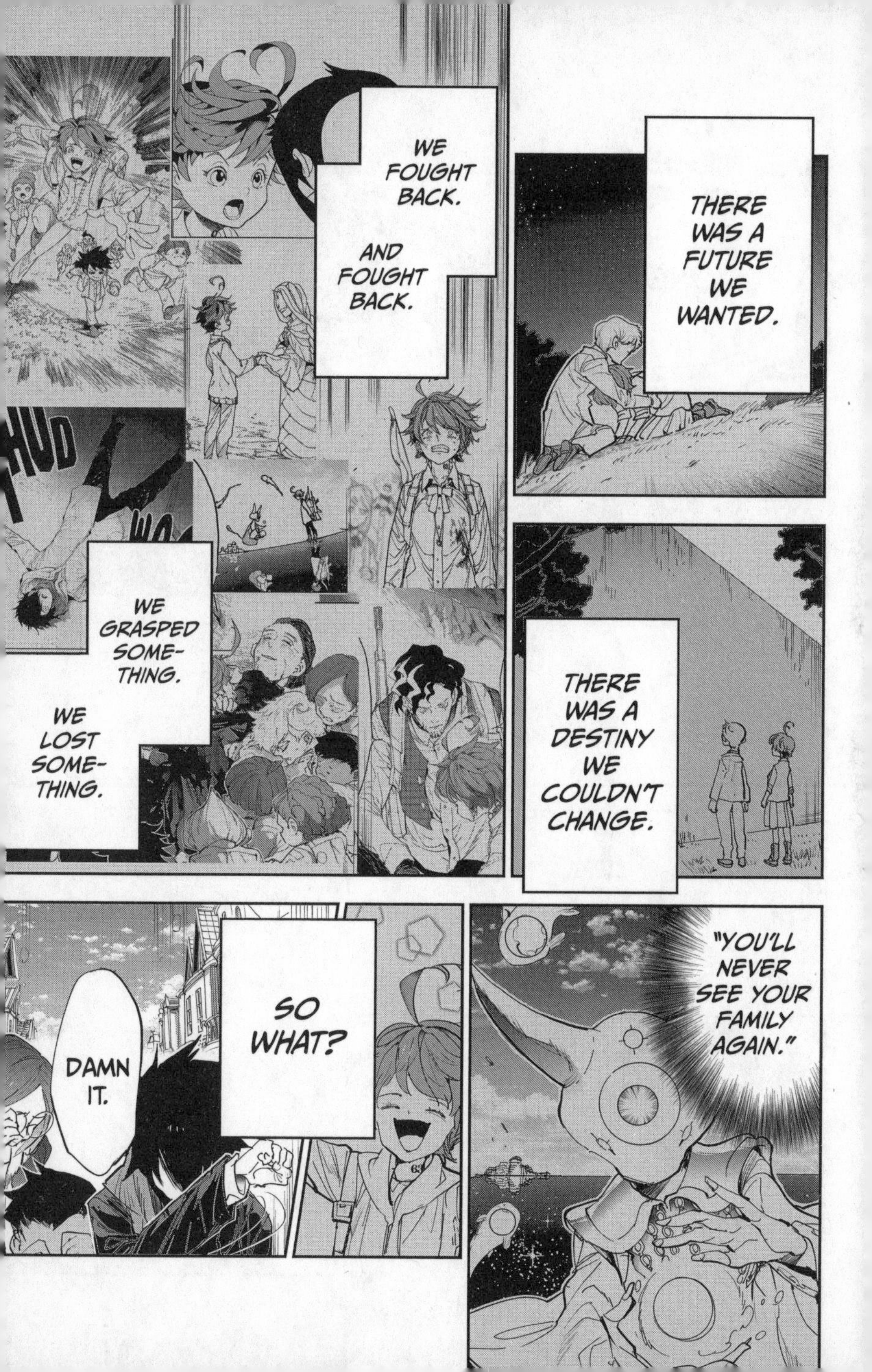
THERE WAS A FUTURE WE WANTED.
THERE WAS A DESTINY WE COULDN'T CHANGE.
WE FOUGHT BACK.
AND FOUGHT BACK.
WE GRASPED SOMETHING.
WE LOST SOMETHING.
"YOU'LL NEVER SEE YOUR FAMILY AGAIN."
SO WHAT?
DAMN IT.

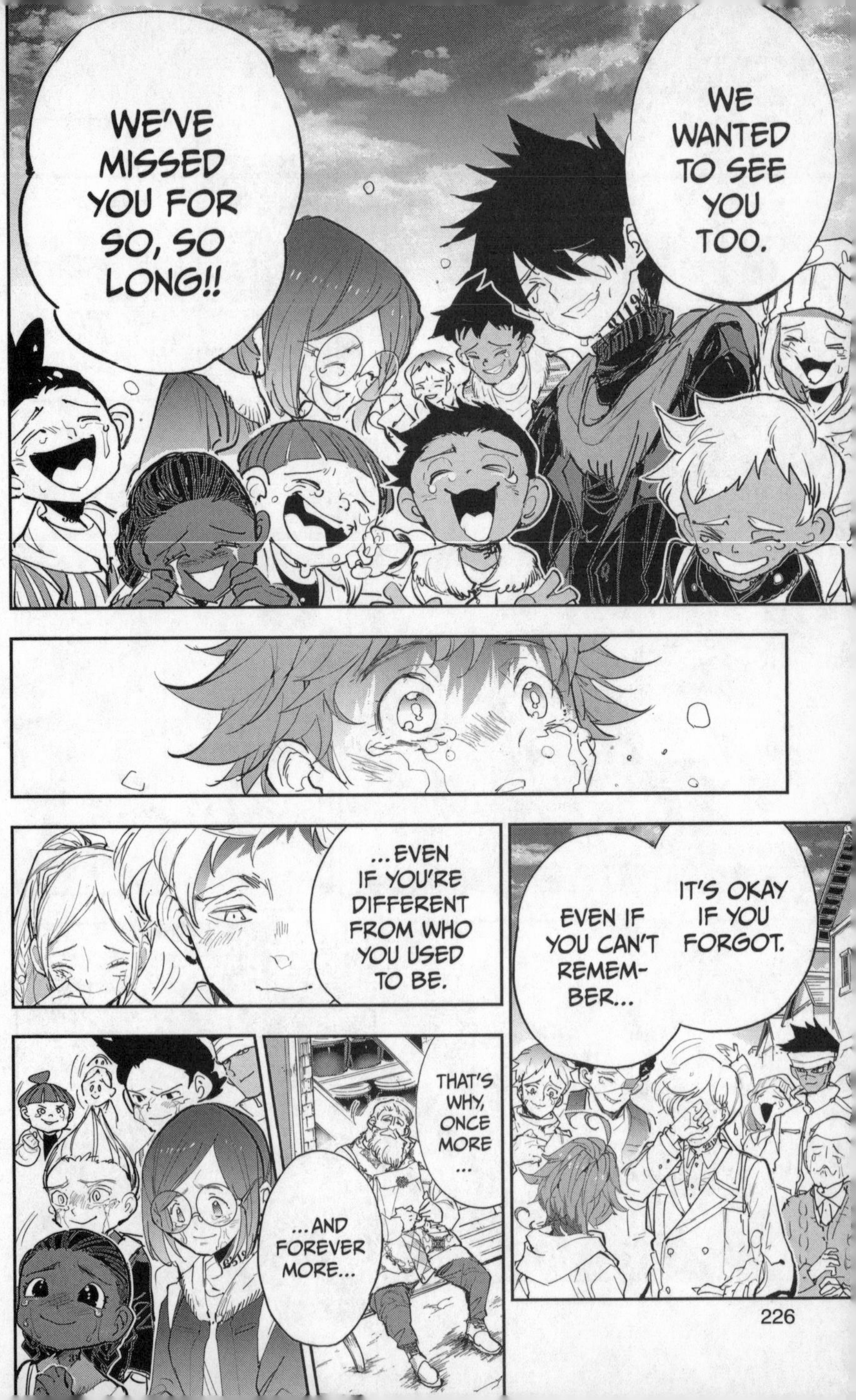
WE WANTED TO SEE YOU TOO.
WE'VE MISSED YOU FOR SO, SO LONG!!
IT'S OKAY IF YOU FORGOT.
EVEN IF YOU CAN'T REMEM-BER...
...EVEN IF YOU'RE DIFFERENT FROM WHO YOU USED TO BE.
THAT'S WHY, ONCE MORE ...
...AND FOREVER MORE...

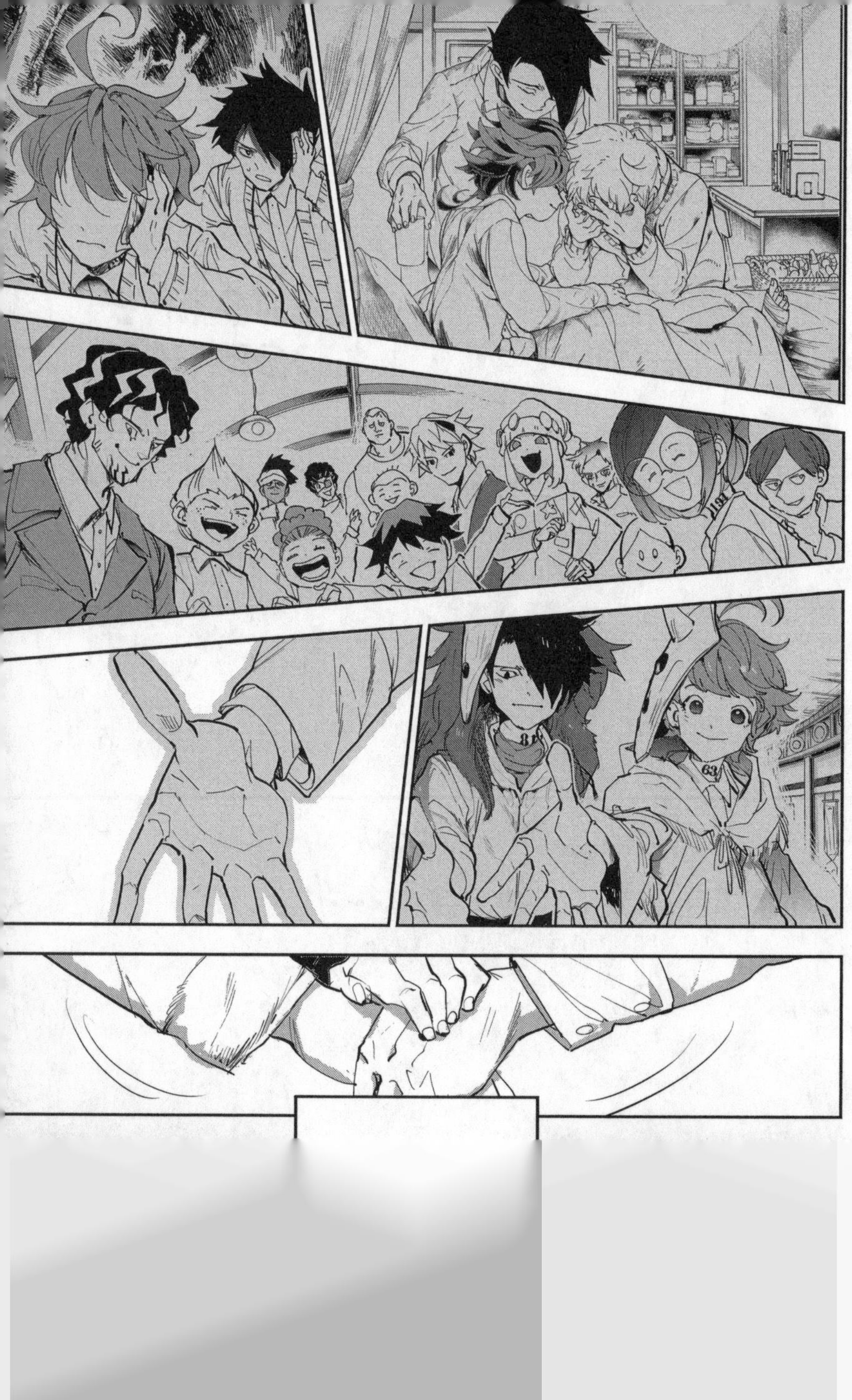

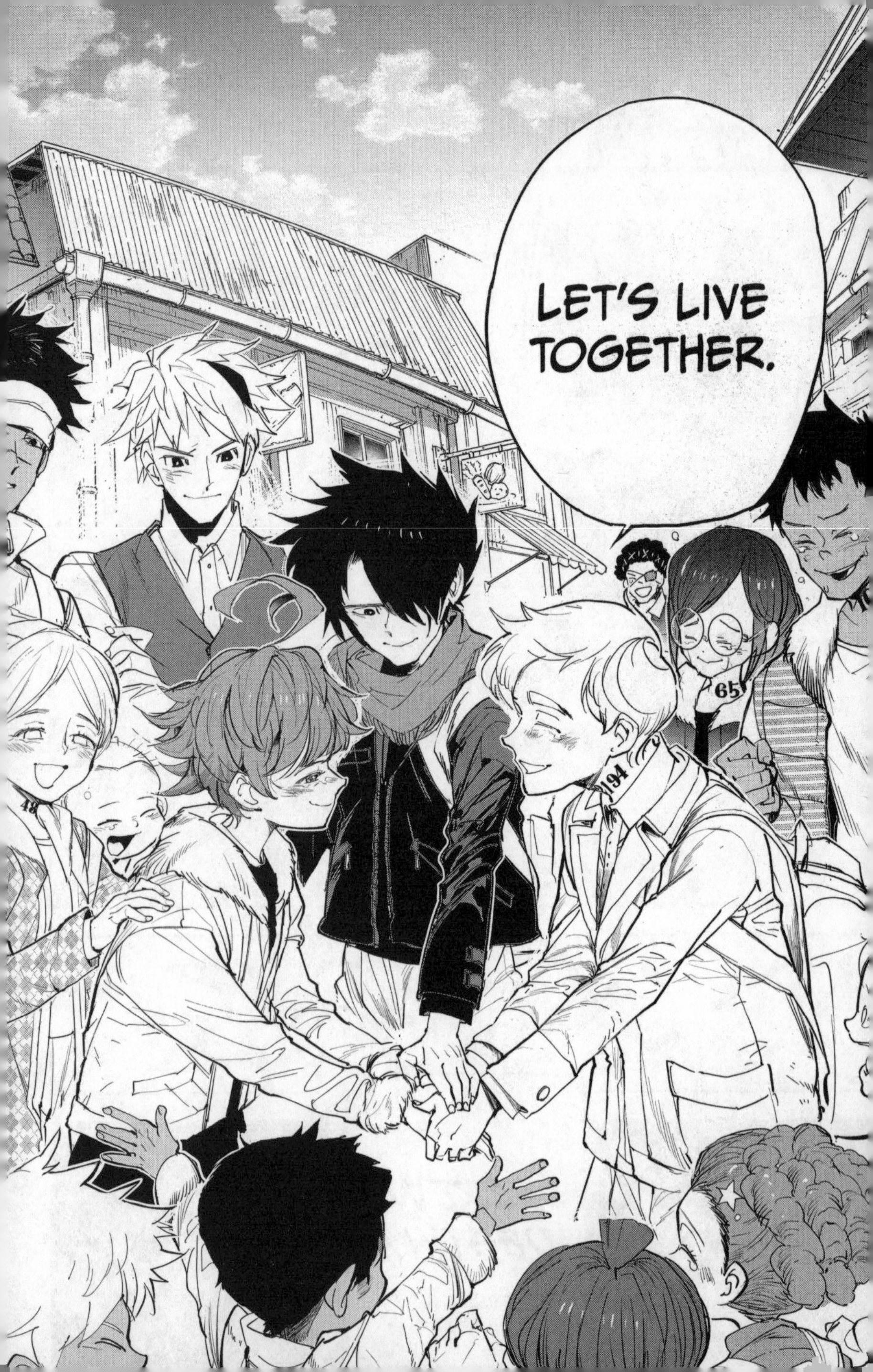
LET'S LIVE TOGETHER.

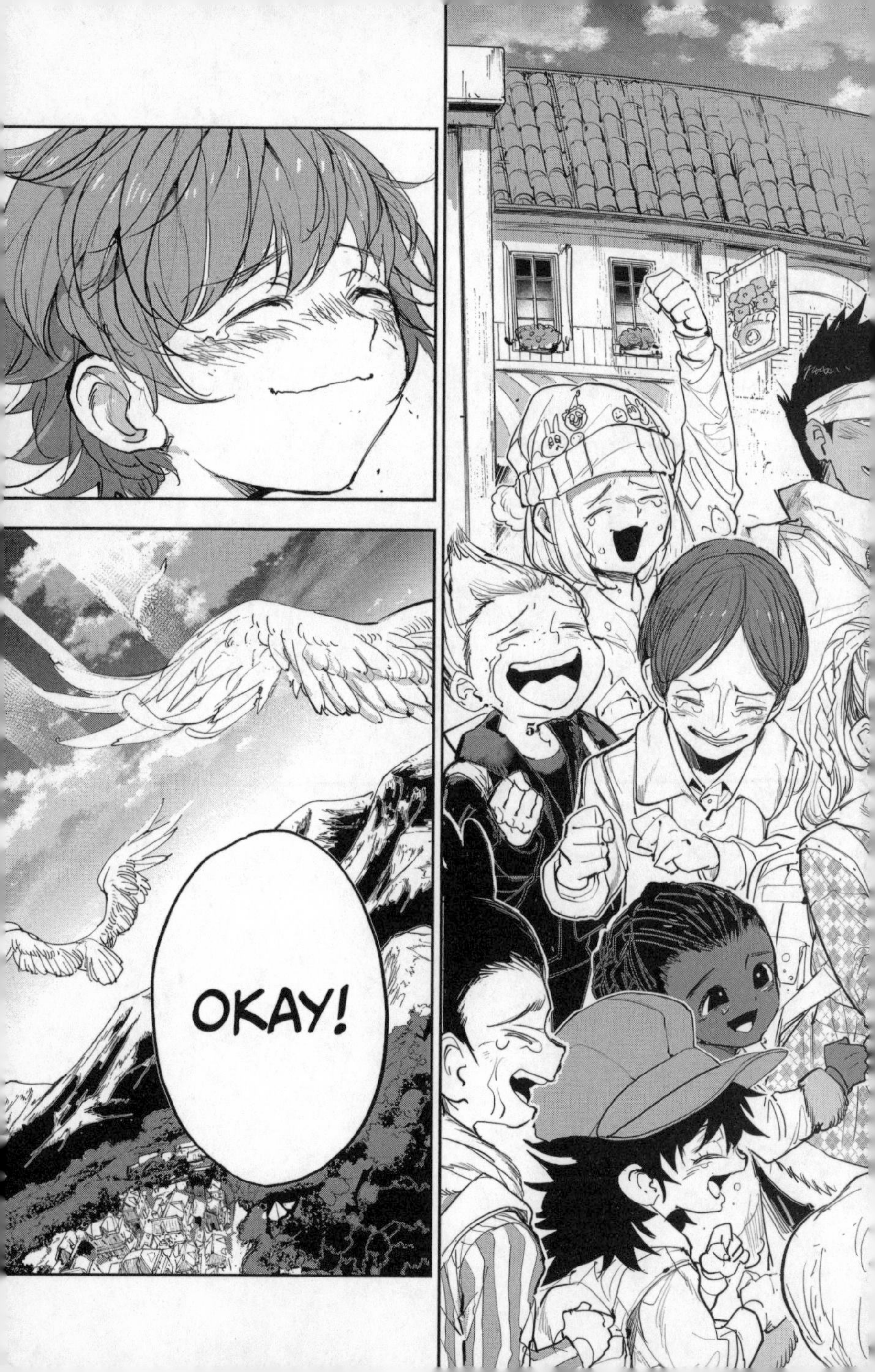
OKAY!

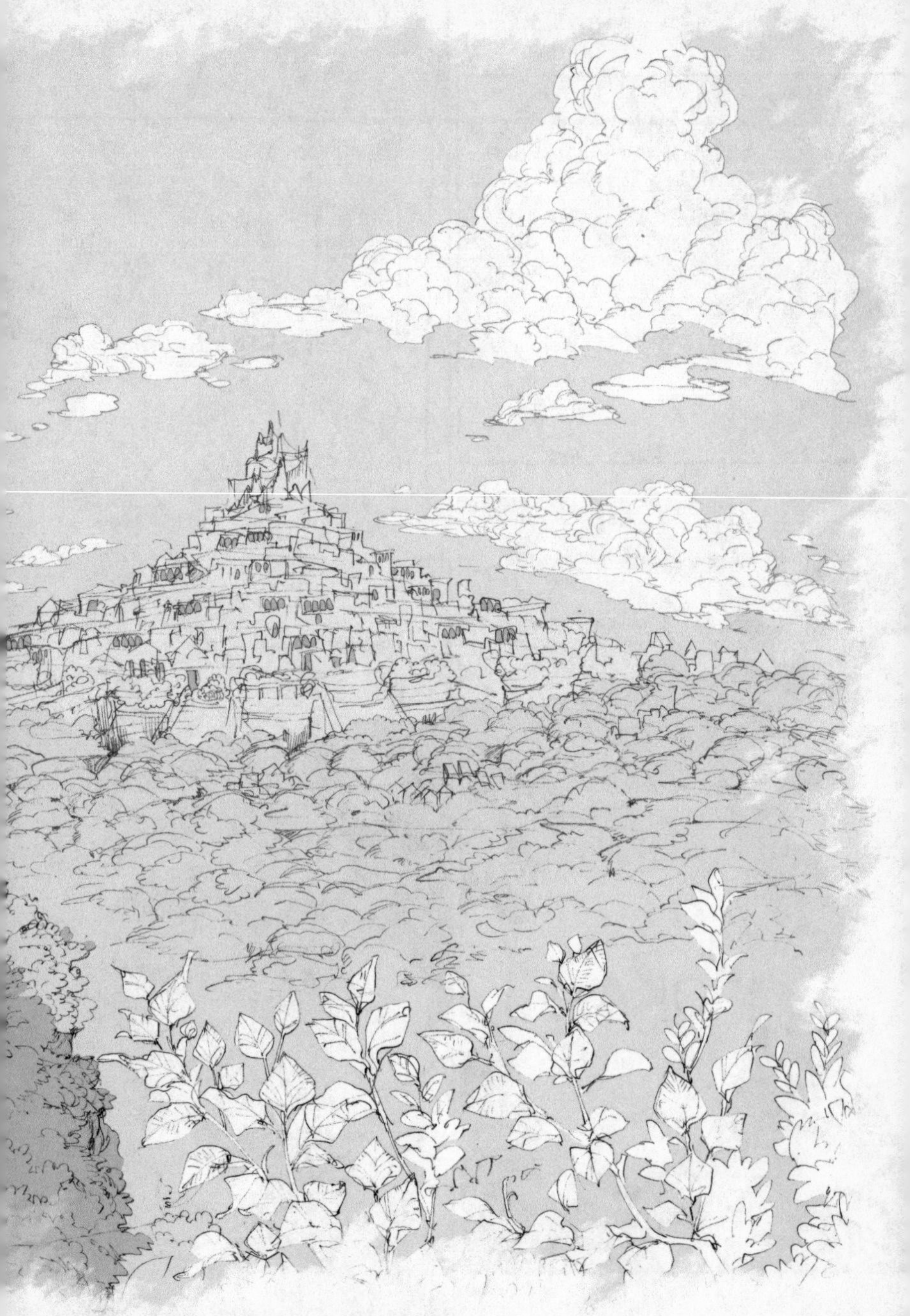

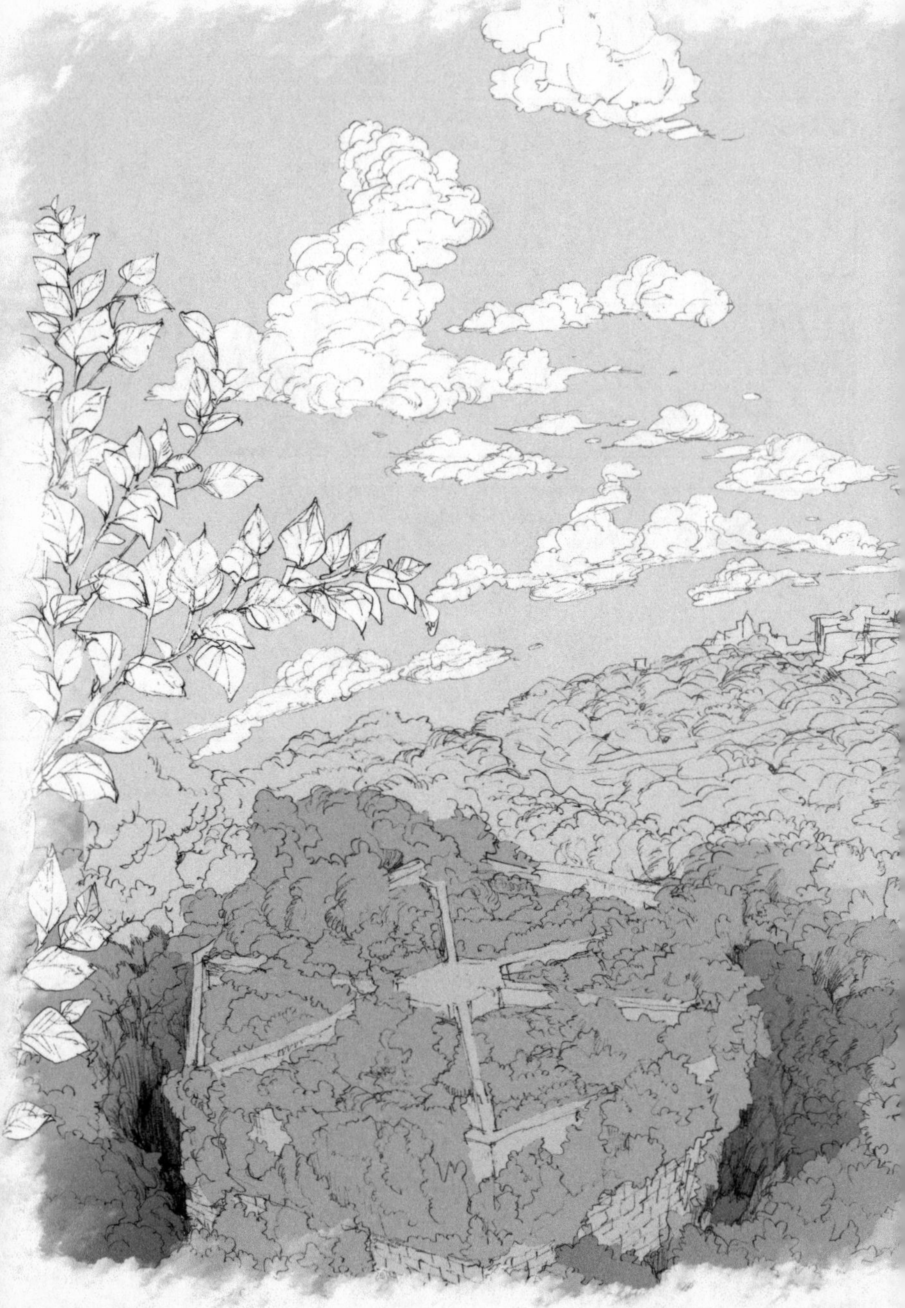

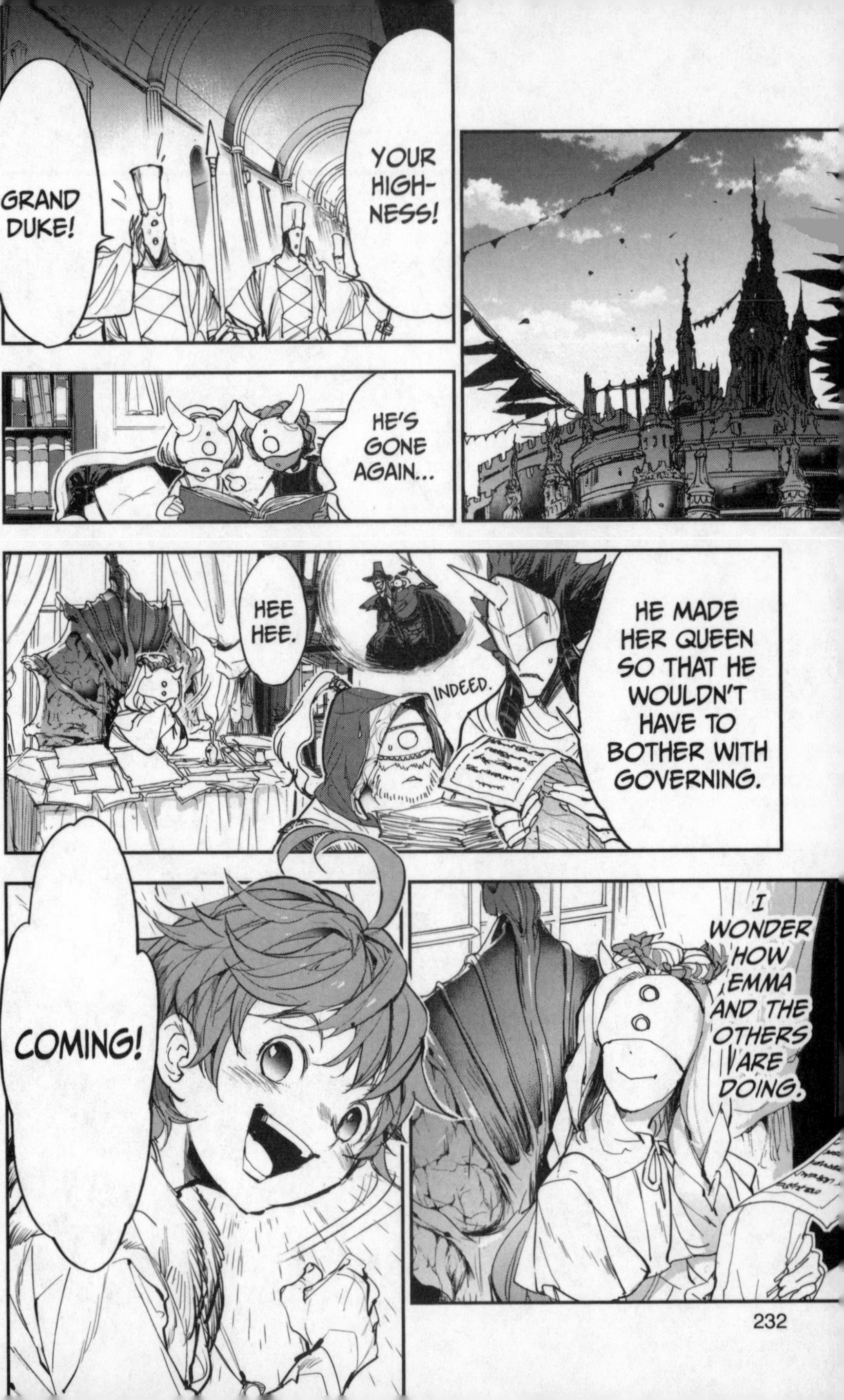
YOUR HIGH-NESS!
GRAND DUKE!
HE'S GONE AGAIN...
HE MADE HER QUEEN SO THAT HE WOULDN'T HAVE TO BOTHER WITH GOVERNING.
INDEED.
HEE HEE.
I WONDER HOW EMMA AND THE OTHERS ARE DOING.
COMING!

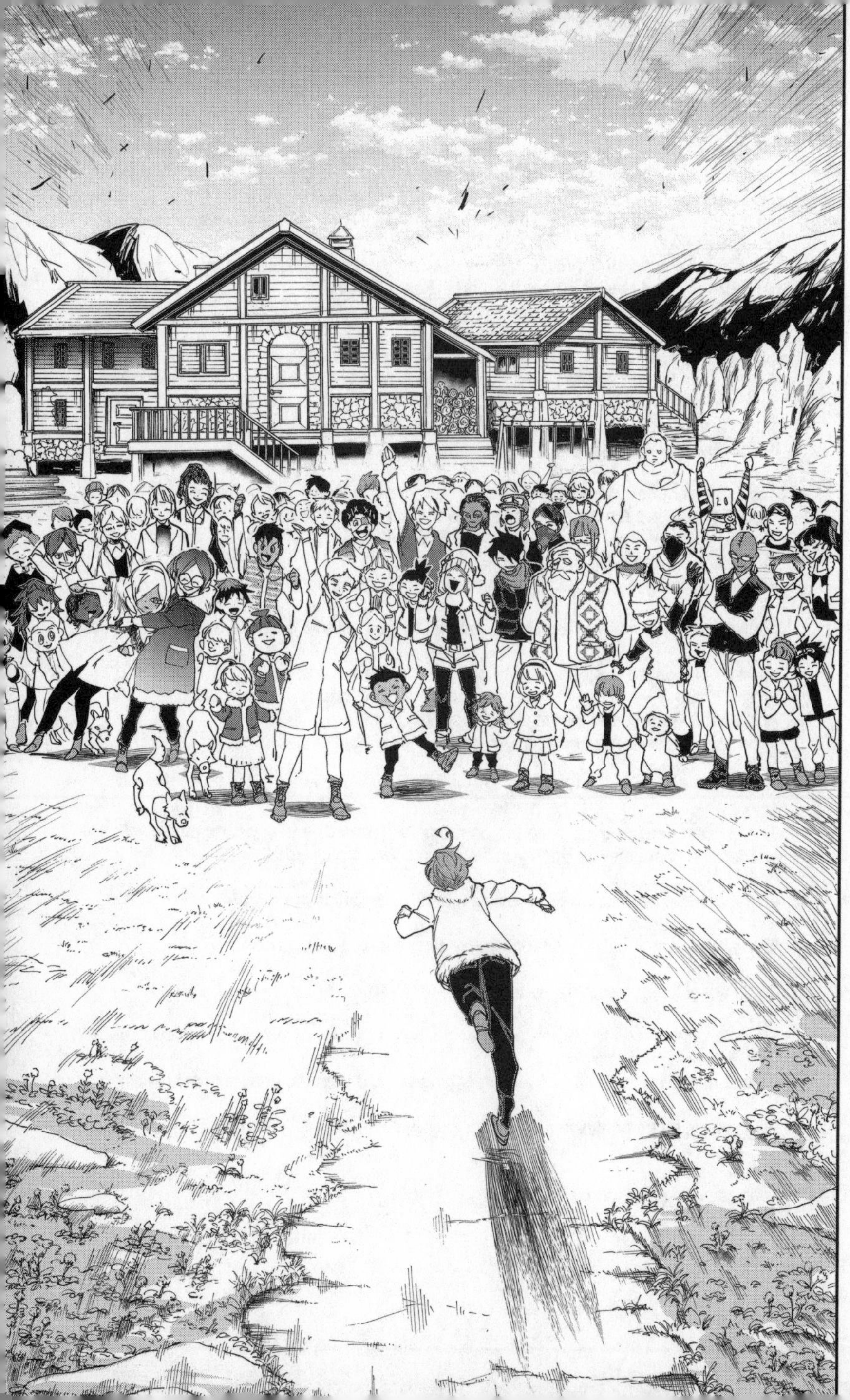
20

Around now, seven years ago…
I was drawing the prototype storyboards of *The Promised Neverland* that I would later submit to the *Shonen Jump* editorial department.
I was confident about my idea. But there were many elements of the story that didn't have the standard *Jump* traits. It had a female protagonist, and it was plot driven instead of character driven.
Even as I look back on it now, I strongly believe that depending on the editor, my submission could have been rejected on the spot.
But editor Sugita-san read these unconventional storyboards and said, "This is interesting!" Without hesitation, he gave me the chance. And then he helped me turn these poorly draw storyboards into a series by brainstorming with me and guiding me.
Even during the serialization, every single week, he never compromised in the search for a fun, concise and high-quality story. And even though he didn't have much time, he stuck with me until I was satisfied. I cannot put into words how much he's helped me from the day we met until now.

And Demizu Sensei. She jumped into this project with everything, willingly and fearlessly, even though I was a nobody who had never even won an award.
We had difficulty finding the artist, and at one point I thought this project was done. But then Demizu Sensei appeared before me like a god.
She overcame every difficult challenge with her amazing drawing skills.

I don't know how many times she saved me, helped me and gave me exciting moments.

What if I had called a minute later to bring in the storyboards?
What if I hadn't waited for the day to submit them and had given up instead?
And what if I hadn't met Sugita-san or Demizu Sensei?
I and *The Promised Neverland* might not be here in front of you today.

To Sugita-san and Demizu Sensei, who fought alongside me…

To my dear friend who first read the prototype storyboards and encouraged me with the words, "It's good, so why don't you just submit the storyboards?"

To the readers who supported me through the serialization and graphic novels…

To Demizu Sensei's staff, everyone in the *Jump* editorial department…

To designer Ishino-san, volume editor Takeuchi-san…

I was able to run this marathon because of you and everyone else who was involved with *The Promised Neverland*.
Thank you so much!! I appreciate everything you did from the bottom of my heart!!

By the way, those bottles in the final chapter were the credits. *(Laughs)*
Did you notice them?

I will see you again, somewhere!

October 2, 2020

白井カイウ 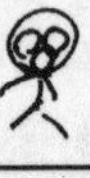

Kaiu Shirai

THANK YOU VERY MUCH!!

SHIRAI SENSEI, THANK YOU SO MUCH FOR GUIDING ME THIS FAR. YOU ARE THE BEST WRITER IN THE WORLD. AND TO OUR EDITOR, SUGITA-SAN FROM THE *JUMP* EDITORIAL DEPARTMENT, WE WERE ABLE TO ACHIEVE SO MUCH WITH *THE PROMISED NEVERLAND* BECAUSE OF YOU. I CANNOT EXPRESS MY APPRECIATION TO YOU ENOUGH. THANK YOU, AND I HOPE WE CAN KEEP WORKING TOGETHER.

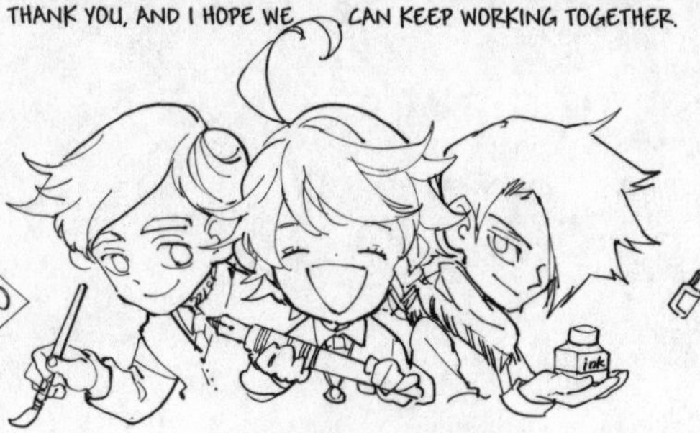
ink

ART PRODUCTION TEAM

Z

TETSUSABURO TAKANO

HIROSHI SENDODA

TATSUYA TANIMOTO

TSUBOKAWA

TAICHI MUGINO

KOTARO NAKAGAWA

MISUZU KONUMA

NEMI

I WAS ABLE TO COMPLETE THE MANGA DUE TO THE COOPERATION OF MANY PEOPLE. I THANK YOU ALL FROM THE BOTTOM OF MY HEART.

OCTOBER 2, 2020

POSUKA DEMIZU

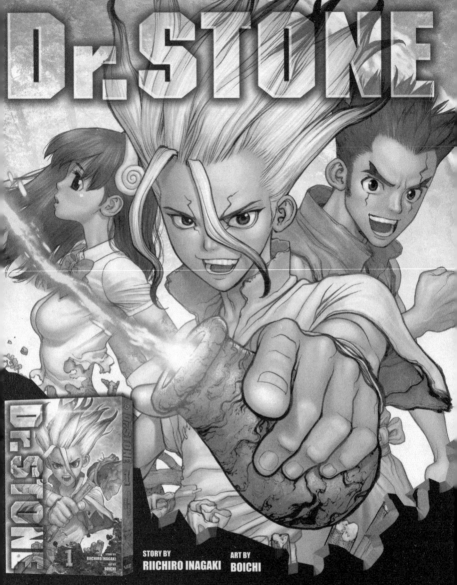

Dr.STONE

STORY BY
RIICHIRO INAGAKI

ART BY
BOICHI

One fateful day, all of humanity turned to stone. Many millennia later, Taiju frees himself from petrification and finds himself surrounded by statues. The situation looks grim—until he runs into his science-loving friend Senku! Together they plan to restart civilization with the power of science!

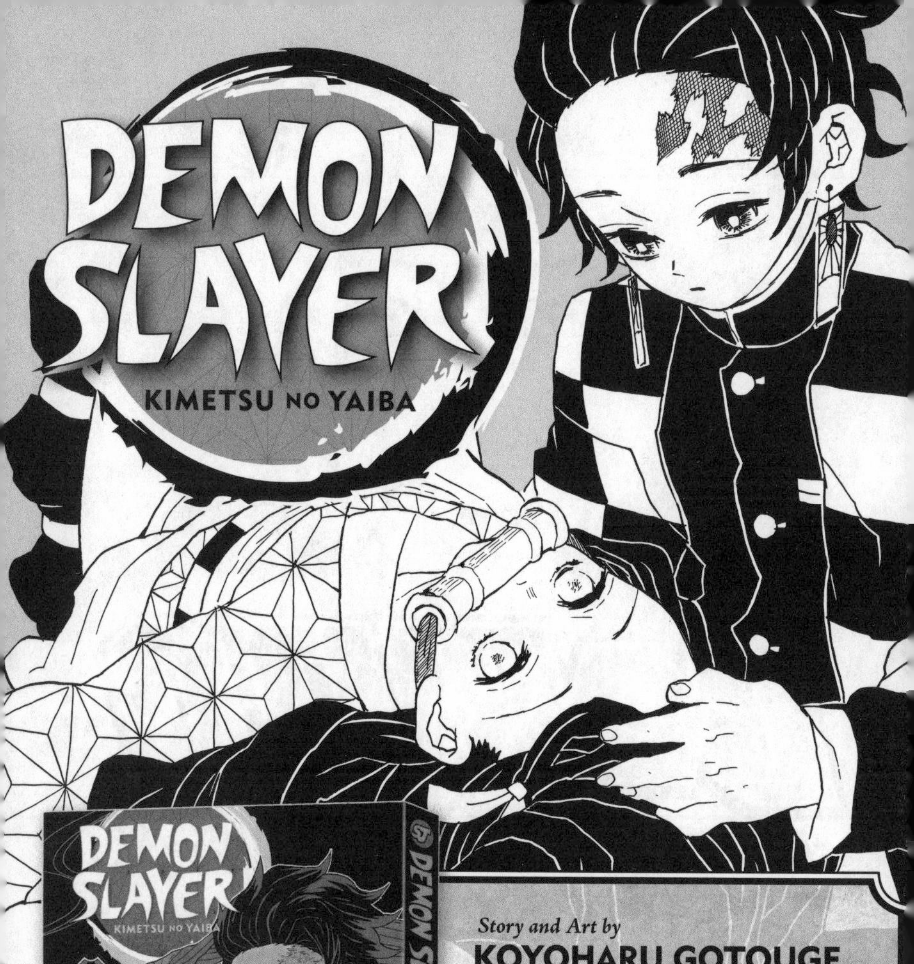

DEMON SLAYER
KIMETSU NO YAIBA

Story and Art by
KOYOHARU GOTOUGE

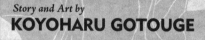

In Taisho-era Japan, kindhearted Tanjiro Kamado makes a living selling charcoal. But his peaceful life is shattered when a demon slaughters his entire family. His little sister Nezuko is the only survivor, but she has been transformed into a demon herself! Tanjiro sets out on a dangerous journey to find a way to return his sister to normal and destroy the demon who ruined his life.

YOU'RE READING THE **WRONG WAY!**

The Promised Neverland reads from right to left, starting in the upper-right corner. Japanese is read from right to left, meaning that action, sound effects and word-balloon order are completely reversed from English order.

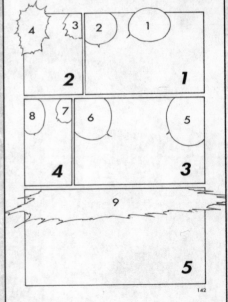